LIBERATION STORIES

LIBERATION STORIES

Building Narrative Power for 21st-Century Social Movements

Shanelle Matthews,
Marzena Zukowska, and the
Radical Communicators Network

THE
NEW
PRESS

NEW YORK
LONDON

*The New Press gratefully acknowledges the support of
the California Endowment for the publication of this book.*

Cover art by Matt Worthington (@prettycoolstrangers)
Cover art includes derivative images of a press photo of Shireen Abu Akleh and Emory Douglas's
Paper Boy (1969). The Paper Boy copyright was provided by Emory Douglas / Artists Rights Society
(ARS), New York © 2024. The press photo of Shireen Abu Akleh was provided by Al Jazeera Media
Network used under CC BY-SA 4.0.

Illustrations throughout the book by Milli.

Published in the United States by The New Press, New York, 2025
Distributed by Two Rivers Distribution

ISBN 978-1-62097-930-3 (hc)
ISBN 978-1-62097-942-6 (ebook)
CIP data is available

The New Press publishes books that promote and enrich public discussion and understanding of
the issues vital to our democracy and to a more equitable world. These books are made possible
by the enthusiasm of our readers; the support of a committed group of donors, large and small; the
collaboration of our many partners in the independent media and the not-for-profit sector; booksellers,
who often hand-sell New Press books; librarians; and above all by our authors.

www.thenewpress.com

Book design by Bookbright Media
Composition by Bookbright Media
This book was set in Janson Text and Gill Sans

Printed in the United States of America

2 4 6 8 10 9 7 5 3 1

Contents

Gender Justice and Violence Prevention

Immigrant Justice

Health and Dignity

Economic Equality and Workers' Rights

Democracy for All

Visuals and Tactics

LIBERATION STORIES

Foreword

Left Narrative Power: An Antidote to Authoritarianism

By Malkia Devich-Cyril and Jen Soriano

We are living in a polarized time, a time of deliberate and profound collective amnesia, a time calling out for a new insurgent consciousness coupled with visionary action to fuel new ways of being, leading, and loving.

These new ways of being, leading, and loving need orators, griots, and futurists to breathe life into them, so that people can see these ways not as fantasy but as possibility. This is the work of the radical communicator. To accomplish our work we first need to understand the obstacles and the opportunities ahead.

Liberal communicators might attempt to bypass polarization by wringing their hands and asking "why can't we all get along?" But radical communicators recognize polarization as a consequence of widening social and economic inequalities—inequalities only made worse by intensifying climate change. Radical communicators recognize that we are at an urgent crossroads where these inequalities can only be addressed through two means: we will either build power to shift conditions toward equality and transformative democracy, or surrender to policies and practices that shift conditions toward authoritarianism.

This crossroads not only presents a challenge, but also an opportunity. As corporate autocracy attempts to deepen inequalities along nuanced lines of race, class, religion, gender, and sexual orientation, we must be equally nuanced with bringing both targeted communities and unlikely allies into the fold. While engaging strange bedfellows has historically been tough for the left, we face the urgent opportunity to do something different, to build larger coalitions of noncooperation toward better conditions for all. Movements for justice can be guided through this crossroads by the words of freedom fighter Amilcar Cabral: "Always bear in mind that the people are not fighting for ideas, for the things in anyone's head. They are fighting to win material benefits, to live better and in peace, to see their lives go forward, to guarantee the future of their children. National liberation, the struggle against colonialism, the construction of peace, progress and independence are hollow words devoid of any significance unless they can be translated into a real improvement of living conditions."

But aren't we fighting for ideas, you might ask? We are communicators. We are narrative strategists and storytellers. The raw material and the end product of our labor are one: new ideas. And we know the adage made popular by conservative economist Milton Friedman, who said that, in response to crisis, the actions taken depend on the *ideas* lying around.

And yet, to counter Friedman with veteran narrative strategist, author, and organizer Makani Themba, there are very few new ideas when it comes to the most fundamental aspects of narrative change. In fact, many of the ideas we are fighting to popularize are actually values that are old as dirt: justice, humanity, equality, interdependence. These are values we seek to reframe and reclaim through story as we prioritize the long arc of struggle over the proximal battle, as Working Families Party Director Maurice Mitchell reminds us to do. The endgame and the prefigurative praxis of this long arc are the same: the cultural shifts—of which narrative is a part—that allow us to improve all of our material living conditions toward justice and peace.

It will take the long arc to popularize our values because for decades, the forces that have devolved into the MAGA movement have succeeded in manufacturing a "common sense" of Orwellian values, including dismantling government in the guise of efficiency and mass surveillance as a norm. But that doesn't mean we can't make significant gains in the short term. The work of the radical communicator in this time is to grow our ranks, expose "who gets paid and who gets played,"[1] and engage people through vision and hope. At the same time, our work is not just in the realm of narrative; it is on all fronts of meaning-making, including supporting a revival of mass organizing, and building widespread skills in power analysis, community facilitation, and political education. This is the foundation of grassroots power-building, and it's what we need to develop a movement-wide strategy to shift common sense narratives—and therefore material conditions—toward core left values. We can accomplish this in part by doing more and more of the good work documented in this anthology.

As radical communicators we stand on the shoulders of a global lineage of narrative thinkers, organizers, and institutions, including but not limited to Paolo Freire, Frantz Fanon, Bayard Rustin, Aimé Cesaire, Antonio Gramsci, Stuart Hall, James Scott, Makani Themba, Grace Lee Boggs, Charlotte Ryan, Lori Dorfman, Hunter Cutting, Kim Deterline, Linda Stout, Carolyn Cushing, Shanelle Matthews, Marzena Zukowska, Mervyn Marcano, Joseph Phelan, Chelsea Fuller, Rashad Robinson, Marshall Ganz, Doyle Canning, Patrick Reinsborough, Annie Neimand, Trevor Smith, Rachel Weidinger, We Interrupt This Message, Media Justice, Color of Change, the Center for Story-Based Strategy, ReFrame, the Praxis Project, the Berkeley Media Studies Project, the Media Research and Action Project, the Progressive Communicators Network, the Movement for Black Lives, the Radical Communicators Network, and more.

As we grow our ranks, it's also important to counter ahistoricism and remember that we come from somewhere, and we are going somewhere. We emerge from the civil rights and Black power and global liberation movements of the recent past, and we are moving forward as part of the rising multiracial U.S. left. We are already a larger "we" than some of us might know.

Facing the Political Terrain

The rising U.S. left is emerging. We are still evolving from the New Left of the 1950s and 1970s, which grew from the decolonial global struggles and labor movements of the early twentieth century. These struggles in turn shaped migration and the borders of engagement for decades to come. As descendants of these earlier movements, we are inspired by their profound daring, their willingness to engage in principled debate, their prolific ideas popularized in music, speeches, manifestos, and images broadcast the world over. Where they erred—and they most certainly did—we have a duty to learn.

We stand on higher ground because of their work. Over the past two decades, we advanced a vision of abolition and undermined the legitimacy of the police state. We made gains in minimum and living wage standards, protections for exploited workers, and family medical leave policies. We popularized a care economy and guaranteed income. We grew a larger movement to support migrant and refugee rights while challenging imperialism and U.S.-backed genocide. We created new cross-sector alliances and new political parties, and elected progressive and left leaders in local, state and national races, while advancing demands for more participatory and representative democracy.

At the same time, infrastructure and resources for base-building in community organizations have dwindled. Consistent spaces for political education have dwindled too. While philanthropy has "discovered" narrative and has made investments in the field, such investments continue to be timid compared to the bold resourcing we need to counter the galvanized right-wing. The resulting in-field competition for resources forces many to prioritize institution building over movement building and funder priorities over movement priorities. All of this narrows movement-level narrative strategy to organizational and issue-based strategy at best, and to tactical deliverables at worst.

The New Right has been playing a longer and more strategic game, resourced by unrestricted funding, fueled by reaction to civil rights movements, and rooted in a fantasy of American Exceptionalism. Today's New Right is bolstered by the spread of right-wing authoritarianism across the globe, while it also pushes for a transactionalist, technofeudal, and patriarchal nationalism undergirded by theories of "great replacement" and a dangerous ethos of white male fragility and violence.

In the New Right's way forward, a methodical army of conservative fundamentalists have begun dismantling the neoliberal administrative state, replacing it with a corporate-authoritarian regime of MAGA loyalists across the fifty states and Puerto Rico. These MAGA loyalists rally around abortion bans, immigration bans, education bans, book bans, mass deportations, mass incarceration, a partisan right-wing legal system, and a growing military, police, and corporate state led by a messianic figure.

MAGA communicators package these horrific policies in a simple narrative of "might makes right." In their narrative, our nation's anxieties will be banished by the might of scapegoating and patriarchal control. Unwavering certainty over good vs. bad is cast as safety in uncertain times, while democracy and minorities are cast as the threat. In their way forward, democracy is chaotic; it allows minorities—cast as unequal and undeserving criminals of a certain color, "sexual deviants" and people from "shithole countries"—to compromise our nation. In a classic move from the fascist playbook, MAGA communicators appeal to a mythic "going back" as the only way forward. They leverage their powerful propaganda machine to "arouse and mobilize" what psychologist Erich Fromm calls "the diabolical forces in man,"[2] and cast the growing authoritarian state as the solution to the very structural problems they have created and seek to cement.

And yet, another future *is* possible. This is our shared future—a necessary future where left power building moves us meaningfully forward. To reach this shared future we stay grounded in radical values while projecting bold solutions that help our people reach the sky. We keep our communities out of the weeds of proximal battles and stay focused on the long arc where we envision and practice new ways ofcbeing, leading, and loving, and yes, new ways of growing and distributing power.

What is the rising left's way forward toward this future? This is a question that radical communicators can help answer. Over the next generation, as the New Right's policies fail our people, we must be ready with a web of power-based storytelling, organizing and narrative infrastructure, and community-led solutions that can be brought to scale to catch us all. As Cabral reminds us: "National liberation, the struggle against colonialism, the construction of peace, progress and independence are hollow" unless we focus our work on tangible improvements to living conditions for people the New Right would at best leave behind.

Narrative Strategies of the Rising Left

Narratives are a cornerstone of culture. They are a keystone in the superstructure of meaning-making. Narratives are developed not through messaging guides alone, but through a historical process of becoming, a dialectical relationship between systems, structures, and the individual and collective self.

As radical communicators, we sometimes narrowly think of narrative strategy as tactical communications absent history and organizing to shift conditions. But, to move new narratives requires more than the right message or one-off content designed to go viral. It requires new leadership skilled in historical and power analysis, transitional infrastructure, long-term power-building strategies, and the resources to sustain this work beyond single campaigns.

Narrative strategy is part and parcel of a broader strategy for building power. Building power from our current lack of power is necessary to achieve lasting shifts in social relations and to see our values embodied through structural change. To achieve this requires more than strategic communications. Strategic communications focuses on short-term policy or public relations gains. It prioritizes the proximal struggle and is just one component of a longer-term strategy. Narrative strategy elevates values to advance the long arc of change. Both are useful to our movements, but we have been investing more in strategic communications than in the massive infrastructure and alignment project necessary to developing movement-level narrative strategy that sticks.

For narrative strategy to stick and become common sense, it must operate on three levels. It must be: (a) embedded in organizing and movement strategy—repeated, integrated, organized, (b) embodied in core civil and cultural infrastructure like schools, popular culture, and institutions of faith, and (c) evoked in individuals' psyches, where people feel generative emotion that leads them—in the rising left's goals—to actions that promote connection, fairness, and peace.

Modern freedom movements have been better at evoking and provoking for the proximal battle than at embodying and embedding for the long arc struggle. Much like evolution happens through extended periods of incremental change, but also through punctuated leaps of extraordinary transformation, stories can leap from being told to becoming narratives that are understood through key moments of disruption and opportunity. But these narratives don't stick without repetition through ongoing organizing and integration. Unfortunately, the moments of disruption and opportunity we have been able to create on the left (mostly through mobilizations) have been largely episodic and static rather than cumulative and grounded in long-term strategy. From the modern antiwar movements of the early 2000s to Occupy Wall Street and the recent uprisings for Black lives, public protest movements have largely operated independent of power-building organizations, shaping narratives without rooting them. Radical communicators have our work cut out for us.

National and multinational networks like Movement for Black Lives, National Domestic Workers Alliance, and Women's March, initially raised against the growing politic of hyperbolic pessimism, blossomed into narrative fronts for new visions of democracy, economy, and society, teaching a new generation of activists that the big and little stories we tell can be the difference between winning and losing. The next task is to root narrative in long-term power-building strategies across organizations, sectors, and issues. This requires long-term investment in infrastructure and experimentation. Some formations are already doing this, including many who are connecting Palestinian liberation with fights against right-wing fascism and antisemitism, and with fights for demilitarization linked to climate justice, land stewardship, and decolonization. We can use the guidance in this anthology to further this work.

Narrative's Structural Problem

Just as the values we seek to popularize are old as dirt, the narrative frames we hope to root are variations on recurring themes of multiracial democracy, a fair and care-based economy, and civil and human rights for all. We will nuance these frames to meet current conditions—for example, we will have to continuously pull back the curtain on Orwell and Oz, exposing the detailed ways that MAGA is both dismantling government and leveraging it for repression, and naming who exactly the targets are. But as we do, we must have a clear power analysis of the existing infrastructure through which we're waging our narrative battles.

Radical communicators have a mandate to build the infrastructure necessary to move narratives from marginal to mass line, which means contending with corporate power in a digital age. The corporations who control the infrastructure of culture are increasingly consolidated, biased toward disinformation, and aligned with authoritarian objectives of deregulation and mass surveillance.

Six corporations control 90 percent of U.S. media: AT&T, CBS, Comcast, Disney, News Corp and Viacom. Since 2004, more than 1 in 5 local newspapers in the United States have shuttered. Eight media giants control 818 broadcast TV stations, resulting in local news that all looks and sounds the same. Of newsroom staff, 83 percent are white, 7 percent are Black; BIPOC individuals make up less than 17 percent of newsroom staff at print and online publications, and only 13 percent of newspaper leadership. For example, the newsrooms of *The New York Times* and *The Wall Street Journal* are both 81 percent white, while *The Washington Post* is 70 percent white. BIPOC individuals make up 72 percent of the population of Los Angeles, but only 33 percent of the *Los Angeles Times*. White journalists make up about half (53 percent) of those who report on social issues and policy, but they make up large majorities of the other ten beats studied, including 84 percent of those who cover environment and energy. Despite the existence of some amazing Black journalists, journalism as the portal for official stories remains largely the dominion of white people.

Today, the pace, scale, and anonymity of communication has transformed meaning-making, increasing the quantity and effectiveness of propaganda and disinformation, while also expanding access to production and distribution. The internet and social media have democratized content development—yet the companies who provide these platforms also mine our data and censor us when our content threatens the powers that be. Meanwhile AI is advancing with little regulation in the United States, and for the profit of companies who have never had the best interests of the marginalized at heart. Under these conditions, our mandate can never simply be to produce, though many of us find comfort in that objective. Instead, we must contend with this infrastructure of culture by holding corporations accountable to democratic practice and governmental regulation, by preserving open access to these platforms, and by investing in our own forms of autonomous media infrastructure. We can also integrate "three degrees of influence" social network theory[3] into our infrastructure design—which is just a scaled way to apply the age-old practice of organizing through word of mouth.

Comprehensive narrative infrastructure design is the work of radical communicators. We knew then what we know now: meaning is made through structures and how they interact through history, and in context with physical geography, current conditions, and human lives. This is how meaning is made. Our narrative strategies, the ways in which we build power, must be structural in order to be cultural. Culture is created through these interactions between an individual and institution, between self and structure. Our strategies must also do this.

If we want our narratives to have the power to shape worldviews we must invest in the infrastructure to grow them and root them, so they can embed, embody, and evoke liberation for generations to come.

The Mandate of the Radical Communicator

As we find new ways of being, leading, and loving for tomorrow, first we must honor the past. Honor the dead, whose stories are in your hands now, whose fallen bodies have become both legacy and fodder for the narrative gunslinging in our cultural environment—a war not of words but of meaning.

Honor the living, those Black and Brown bodies, those female, queer, and trans bodies, those disabled and sick bodies, those poor bodies that experience the violence of visibility. Honor the living, those Asian and Indigenous bodies, those bodies behind the bars and across the borders, and all those who suffer the violence of invisibility.

Honor the living by remembering that narrative strategy is, at its best, about listening to people more than it is about changing them. Listening so that we can understand where the pain and the possibility live. Listening so that we may embody the truth that building narrative power requires building people power, and that building people power requires building trust. Honor the living by fighting like hell to organize our communities. By starting with our own affinity groups, then expanding our circles of trust.

Honor the living, whose grief has become the context in which we now work. Like our society, our grief is also at a crossroads. Honor the living by choosing grief that is insurgent rather than individualist, radical rather than reactionary. Honor the living by building ideological power for the next generation, power that not only defends our lives and our freedoms, but determines what freedom means.

We believe in you. You are the meaning makers who can remember freedom. You are the meaning makers who can help heal the ungrieved losses of global pandemic. You are the meaning makers who will promote agency, protagonism, and connection in a time of manufactured isolation and fear. We believe in you because we have faced similar crossroads in the past. In 2002, post 9/11 and just before the war on Iraq, a dozen people, including chapter co-author Malkia Devich-Cyril, got together at the Highlander Center in Tennessee and coined the term "media justice." We coined the term because we were at the edge of a digital and telecommunications explosion that would transform the platforms through which our messages pass, thereby changing how meaning is made. At the same time, those of us at the Youth Media Council (later renamed MediaJustice), including chapter co-author Jen Soriano, were at the edge of a new era where we believed criminalized communities could build the power to speak for ourselves. We learned to engage in this expanding media terrain as subjects, not objects; producers, not consumers; in other words, as protagonists of our own stories, and of the narratives that govern our world.

We are facing tough times. But journalist Maria Ressa, author of *How to Stand Up to a Dictator*, reminds us where to start:

> When I wake up and look out the window, I am energized. I have hope. I see the possibilities—how, despite the darkness, this is also a time when we can rebuild our societies, starting with what's right in front of us: our areas of influence.

We can also start by adapting Daniel Hunter's framework of resistance to the battle front of meaning-making.

Here is a spell for our beginning:

May we tell stories about collective protection and mutual aid, may we uplift every attempt to disrupt and disobey the authoritarian state, may we defend the civic institutions corporate autocracy seeks to dismantle, may we vision and build alternatives from the community to local to state and transnational levels. May we remember that authoritarianism relies on fear and the narrowing of minds. so that we tell stories that apply love toward the expansion of minds. And may we include everyone in our vision for the future, and we mean everyone—full stop. May we build our paradise on abundance, and not, as Kai Cheng Thom suggests, on the rubble of anyone else's bones.

*   *   *

We leave you with a quote from Subcomandante Galeano, a Zapatista rebel reflecting on the forty-three disappeared Ayotzinapa students who said, "Your struggle is a crack in the wall of the system. Don't allow it to close up. Your children breathe through that crack, but so do the thousands of others who have disappeared across the world. So that the crack does not close up, so that the crack can deepen and expand, you will have in us Zapatistas a common struggle: one that transforms pain into rage, rage into rebellion, and rebellion into tomorrow."

Toward common struggle, rooted change, and more cracks in the system to let in the light of our joy. Today and tomorrow. And for those who have come before. Adelante, isulong, àṣẹ.

Introduction

By Shanelle Matthews and Marzena Zukowska

History is not the past. It is the stories we tell about the past. How we tell these stories—triumphantly or self-critically, metaphysically or dialectically—has a lot to do with whether we cut short or advance our evolution as human beings.

—*Grace Lee Boggs,* The Next American Revolution: Sustainable Activism for the Twenty-First Century[1]

Eight Minutes and Forty-Six Seconds

Darnella Frazier was born in St. Paul, Minnesota, a historic Midwestern city situated between the Mississippi and Minnesota rivers, with roots stretching back to nine years before the Civil War. Outside of being a student at Roosevelt High School, Frazier spent her days working at the mall, enjoying time with her boyfriend, and honing her skills in the kitchen, where she lovingly cooked for her mother—whom she affectionately and reverently called her "queen."

Just before 8:00 p.m. on May 25, 2020, seventeen-year-old Frazier, with her brown skin and high cheekbones, agreed to walk her nine-year-old cousin to the corner store to buy snacks. This seemingly ordinary walk would forever change the trajectory of her life and the world.

That Monday evening, on the corner of Chicago Avenue and East 38th Street in South Minneapolis, Frazier watched as the Minneapolis Police Department wrestled a tall, handcuffed Black man to the ground. The man, who had allegedly used counterfeit money to buy cigarettes, cried out in agony, "I can't breathe," and called for his mother as one officer knelt on his neck, choking him in front of dozens of onlookers. Instinctively, Frazier pulled out her cell phone and began recording, allowing millions more to witness the horrific scene.

One minute.

Two minutes.

Three minutes.

Four minutes.

Five minutes.

Six minutes.

Seven minutes.

Eight minutes and forty-six seconds later—roughly the time it takes to walk eight city blocks—the man whom the world would come to know as forty-six-year-old George Floyd was unconscious and unresponsive. He was soon pronounced dead from a traumatic, irreversible brain injury caused by low oxygen; the police officer, Derek Chauvin, had suffocated him to death.

Frazier's viral video, which shows police taking a series of actions that violated the policies of the Minneapolis Police Department, would go on to spark a global uprising against police violence and become a defining force in a long-standing narrative battle between the police state and Black communities in the United States.[2]

Floyd's murder was one of a succession of extrajudicial murders of Black people at the hands of the police in the twin cities of Minneapolis and St. Paul, where Black people make up only about 10 percent of the population. The area's Black population grew significantly at the turn of the twentieth century, during the Great Migration, when six million Black families fled states like Texas, Arkansas, Louisiana, and Mississippi to escape segregation and Jim Crow laws in search of more welcoming regions of the states.

Much like the states below the Mason-Dixon Line, Minnesota has proven deadly for Black people when it comes to violence inflicted by state forces. Despite the profound social, cultural, and economic contributions of Black communities throughout the Twin Cities—not to mention their inherent worth and dignity as humans—police brutality has claimed numerous lives. In 2015, twenty-four-year-old Jamar Clark was killed by police; in 2016, thirty-two-year-old Philando Castile was murdered during a routine traffic stop; and in 2022, twenty-two-year-old Amir Locke was fatally shot during a no-knock raid in a downtown Minneapolis apartment. These are just a few of the many victims, while countless others remain unknown, their stories untold, as they continue to endure the terror of unchecked police violence.

A year after Floyd's death, Frazier reflected on her role in an Instagram post: "Even though this was a traumatic life-changing experience for me, I'm proud of myself. If it weren't for my video, the world wouldn't have known the truth."[3]

Access to technology and social media enables marginalized communities to tell their stories from their perspective without coercion or critique from those who would benefit from their silence.[4] The accounts of those whose experiences have been made invisible or erased are an antidote to the status quo, challenging the hegemonic and often harmful narratives imposed by mainstream media. However complicated or co-opted by corporations, these platforms provide people in the twenty-first century a booth to share their stories and experiences in the digital public square, countering one-sided angles that historically dominate news media and mainstream discourse.

How stories are told determines whose lives are valued and whose are not. In its seminal report *Media 2070: An Invitation to Dream Up Media Reparations*, the *Free Press* illustrates how "since the colonial era, media outlets have used their platforms to inflict harm on Black people through weaponized narratives that promote Black inferiority and portray Black people as threats to society."[5] Mainstream media are not just complicit in promoting anti-Black narratives; they serve as a central channel for the white-supremacist propaganda apparatus. This apparatus has long collaborated with state forces to craft and disseminate stories designed to foster deep-seated hatred toward Black people, ultimately justifying economic, structural, and physical violence against them.

From the era of chattel slavery to the ongoing terror of unchecked state violence, these institutions reinforce stereotypes depicting Black communities as criminal and inferior. These media portrayals influence public perceptions and can legitimize both police and vigilante violence.[6] This creates a feedback loop whereby stereotypes are perpetuated, and violence against Black people is normalized.

Frazier was right; if it hadn't been for her quick, strategic thinking, people would not have known the truth. The headline of a statement released by the

Minneapolis Police Department two hours after Floyd's death read, "Man Dies After Medical Incident During Police Interaction."[7] Mainstream-media narratives of Black people's encounters with the police cannot be trusted.

Although often given little to no attention by mainstream media and seldom the inspiration for mass mobilizations, Black women are victims of state violence and deadly police terror, too. A month before Floyd was murdered, Louisville, Kentucky, police killed twenty-six-year-old Breonna Taylor. Officers shot thirty-six rounds of ammunition into her home in a bungled raid serving a "no-knock" warrant, realizing later that the suspect they were looking for was already in custody. For Black women, excessive force by police isn't the exception when it comes to deadly encounters; it's the norm. Yet the grievous violence Black women suffer at the hands of police continues to attract little to no media attention.

Taylor's and Floyd's deaths sparked nationwide and global uprisings, with more than 26 million people taking to the streets against police violence and for racial justice in the United States. The uprisings prompted vigorous debates about the police's role in public safety. Coalitions like the Movement for Black Lives (M4BL) and organizations like Black Visions brought global attention to abolitionist arguments that the only way to prevent deaths such as Floyd's and Taylor's is to defund the police and reinvest those resources into alternative public-safety measures.

Narrative as Resistance:
Shaping a New Social Order

The role of the narrative-movement practitioner in combating oppressive forces is to advance counterhegemonic values, frameworks, and practices across the domains of power that structure the organization of society and influence the experiences of individuals within it. *Counterhegemony*, as defined by political prisoner and Marxist theorist Antonio Gramsci, refers to the process and efforts to challenge and overturn the dominant social, cultural, and political consensus (hegemony) that perpetuates the interests of the ruling class. Gramsci argued that the ruling class maintains control not just through coercive means (such as police and military force) but also through ideological means—by establishing a cultural and social "common sense" that upholds their interests as universal and beneficial to all.[8]

At the core of every dominant power structure is a narrative foundation. White supremacy, for example, is built on a narrative of inherent racial inferiority, insisting on a racial hierarchy as both a natural and essential order. Colonialism champions narratives of boundless expansion, justifying resource exploitation, Indigenous subjugation, and genocide as manifest destiny. Meanwhile, neoliberal capitalism infiltrates every corner of our existence, from health care commercialization to the enforcement of borders and prisons, propelled by the narratives that prioritize profit over people and individual success over communal well-being. These narratives are not mere backdrops but the very mechanisms through which power is exercised and maintained, shaping what we see as "normal," "right," and "justifiable."

Society's narrative hierarchy, underpinned by institutional forces—government, economy, religion—and mediated through culture and digital spaces, assigns credibility in a way that often silences marginalized voices. This hierarchy dictates who gets to speak and whose stories are deemed legitimate. Narrative oppression and the dominance of specific stories precondition our perceptions of worthiness, identity, and entitlement, perpetuating old debates about humanization and deservedness. These dominant narratives—rooted in imperialism, capitalism, and other power structures—frame our collective consciousness and societal values.

Counterhegemony involves creating and popularizing counternarratives, values, and beliefs that question and resist this so-called common sense. It seeks to build a new cultural and ideological consensus representing oppressed groups' interests and perspectives. By unraveling these stories, we confront the foundational myths that uphold systemic inequalities and challenge ourselves to envision a radically different world. In these pages, communications workers from the most impactful social movements of the twenty-first century—from the fight for immigrant rights and the work of organizations like M4BL to the #MeToo uprising and the struggle for labor justice—explore how narrative organizing and power are used to dismantle and rewrite the stories that shape the material conditions of our lives.

Narrative power refers to the ability to shape and control the stories told within a society, including which ones are told, who tells them, and how they are interpreted. It's about the capacity to influence perceptions, beliefs, and behaviors through storytelling, using frameworks grounded in social-movement traditions.

A narrative-power framework is a way of seeing and acting to use symbolic resources, stories, messages, and narratives to resist oppression and build power for a liberatory society for all. At the Radical Communicators Network (RadComms), we believe a narrative-power framework can be understood as a function of six interconnected elements:

1. **Narrative power analysis**, which examines how stories influence perceptions, behaviors, and social outcomes.
2. **Principles**, which are values-based and provide guardrails for communicating about people, places, and ideas in inclusive and humanizing ways.
3. **Traditions**, which provide a foundation for movement activities, fostering collective identity and continuity while connecting movements to historical roots.
4. **Narrative possibilities**, which refer to the potential within the political system to influence beliefs and behaviors through storytelling and assessing what is desirable and achievable in the current context.
5. **Narrative opportunities**, which are specific situations that allow effective influence on public policy or social change, arising from accessible political channels, changes in government, the presence of allies, times of crisis, and shifts in public opinion.
6. **Narrative interventions**, which are strategic actions to reshape or introduce new narratives, including reframing narratives, introducing new ones, and using counternarratives while focusing on both potential and specific moments for achieving goals.

Not all frameworks within social-justice and nonprofit communications work to subvert oppressive systems—indeed, many reinforce them. This leads to the implementation of reformist reforms, which are changes or adjustments within existing systems (particularly those related to social, political, or economic structures) that aim to improve conditions or address specific issues without fundamentally altering the system's underlying power dynamics or structures.[9]

The essence of building narrative power lies in its potential to aid oppressed communities in envisioning a world beyond their immediate circumstances.

A **narrative power framework** is a way of seeing and acting to use symbolic resources, stories, messages, and narratives to resist oppression and build power for a liberatory society for all. **At RadComms, we believe a narrative power framework can be understood as a function of five interconnected elements:**

NARRATIVE POWER ANALYSIS, which examines how stories influence perceptions, behaviors, and social outcomes;

PRINCIPLES, which are values-based and provide guardrails for communicating about people, places, and ideas in inclusive and humanizing ways.

TRADITIONS, which provide a foundation for movement activities, fostering collective identity and continuity while connecting movements to historical roots;

NARRATIVE POSSIBILITIES, which refer to the potential within the political system to influence beliefs and behaviors through storytelling, assessing what is desirable and achievable in the current context;

NARRATIVE OPPORTUNITIES, which are specific situations that allow effective influence on public policy or social change, arising from accessible political channels, changes in government, the presence of allies, times of crisis, and shifts in public opinion;

NARRATIVE INTERVENTIONS, which are strategic actions to reshape or introduce new narratives. These include reframing narratives, introducing new ones, and using counternarratives, focusing on both theoretical potential and specific moments for achieving goals.

Stories are the lifeblood of social cohesion, acting as the adhesive that binds the framework of societal norms and expectations. Within this framework, narratives spark the imagination, creating the blueprint for emerging cultures and social paradigms.

The transformative power of narrative means that the stories of the oppressed can forge new paths of resistance and redefine power dynamics. Counternarratives don't just challenge the status quo; they are acts of dissent that manifest the change we envision. But for stories to truly resonate and catalyze change, they must be woven into the fabric of everyday life and become part of our lived experience. In this way, narrative power shapes, and is shaped by, the interplay of power and resistance, laying the groundwork for a reimagined future.

As political challengers, we must stay grounded in our work's long-term nature. Brown University professor of political science and author of *The Politics of Common Sense: How Social Movements Use Discourse to Change Politics*, Deva Woodly, reminds us that:

> There is more to being a successful social movement than winning immediate or direct favorable outcomes in either the legislative or judicial arenas. Social movements have their most lasting and permanent effect not through particular policy victories but instead by changing politics, redefining what is at stake and what can and ought to be done about a politicized problem.[10]

Ideas that appear impossible or extreme may not be immediately implemented. Still, history shows that people who face a crisis will look for new and novel solutions and be eager for something different. You put out ideas with a long-term vision for change. You prime people, and then something will happen that can make a fringe idea seem newly possible.[11]

As narrative organizers, our task is to carve a path in the galaxy of ideas that will mold our future. We must build the public and political will of a society that measures success in terms of happiness instead of stakeholder profits. We must make relationships—not transactions—with an axis on which our togetherness turns. We are political challengers, not politicians or passive political observers. Our job is to disrupt the status quo of power and privilege;

to contest against dominant, oppressive, well-resourced forces; to influence public opinion, policies, and social norms; and to win political acceptance.

A Year of Unrest: Pandemic, Protest, and the Fight for a New World

As the uprisings swelled, so did the number of people in the United States testing positive for COVID-19—overwhelming a fragile and exploited health care system; shuttering schools, retail, and factory floors; and putting millions of people out of work. By June 2020, 40,000 people a day became infected, and the most vulnerable—those with disabilities, the chronically ill, the disabled, and the elderly—began dying. As families depleted their savings, they lined up at food banks and churches, and sought mutual aid, eager to supplement their resources with donations. The concept and language of frontline and essential workers took on new meaning as the poorest people, least likely to have health care, and health care workers themselves faced dire conditions while interfacing with the deadly virus every day and returning home to their families. Disability-justice organizers fiercely confronted and dismantled ableist and eugenicist ideologies that sought to dehumanize vulnerable populations. Their strategic efforts not only exposed the inherent dangers of these oppressive beliefs but also effectively discredited antivaccination propaganda, ultimately saving countless lives.

Building on the momentum generated by drawing explicit parallels between historic and contemporary state violence, organizers and policy makers successfully propelled reparations into the mainstream discourse of the summer. Progressive candidates—from New York to Colorado to Texas—publicly championed reparations as a critical policy issue. Meanwhile, cities and states initiated bold experiments to confront and begin repairing the lasting harms inflicted on Black Americans. Notably, California led the way by establishing the nation's first state task force dedicated to studying historic and systemic racism, and developing actionable recommendations to address these enduring injustices.[11]

Beyond the United States, 2020 saw a wave of protests that reverberated across the globe, with everyday people rising against authoritarian regimes and defending democracy. In Brazil, the oppressed and disenfranchised fought back against the tyrannical rule of Jair Bolsonaro, paving the way for the 2022 election of leftist leader Luiz Inácio Lula da Silva and the emergence of influential Black social-movement leaders like Douglas Belchior and Vilma Reis. In Belarus, there was the Slipper Revolution, a series of prodemocracy protests that boldly challenged the electoral fraud upholding Alexander Lukashenko's decades-long dictatorship. In Venezuela, citizens continued to protest against President Nicolás Maduro as families struggled to secure basic necessities. In Nigeria, young people led a powerful uprising against police brutality, explicitly targeting the notorious Special Anti-Robbery Squad (SARS), known for its rampant torture and killings. The convergence of public health and political dissent was stark, with antilockdown protests erupting in at least twenty-six countries, highlighting the global intersection of health crises and civil unrest. In the United States, this tension was palpable as armed demonstrators stormed the Michigan State Capitol to oppose pandemic stay-at-home orders.[12]

At the same time, in 2020, social movement workers, activists, and advocates catalyzed significant sociopolitical shifts, and the narrative power behind these changes was evident. Long-standing beliefs in unchecked capitalism were challenged by frontline workers—nurses, teachers, and nonunion employees—who led mass strikes, igniting a national conversation about labor rights. As climate change continued to warm the Earth, 2020 became the second-warmest year in the 141-year history of record keeping. A broadtent progressive coalition advanced the Green New Deal, a policy platform to transform the economy by addressing the urgent issue of climate change while promoting social justice. In February 2020, twenty Sunrise Movement activists, including six underage students who demanded lawmakers back the policy, were arrested in a protest at the Capitol. Meanwhile, the coalition that successfully mobilized to unseat Donald Trump reinforced a narrative of democratic resilience and the importance of collective action. These events reshaped public consciousness and demonstrated the power of narrative in driving political change.

Narrative shifts are influenced by various factors, including the political context and conditions under which these shifts can occur. The discussion around and organizing of narrative power spans both academic research and popular discourse. Books like *Re:Imagining Change*, by Patrick Reinsborough and Doyle Canning; *The Politics of Common Sense*, by Deva Woodly; and *Rising Up: The Power of Narrative in Pursuing Racial Justice*, by Sonali Kolhatkar; and institutions and organizations like the Opportunity Agenda, ReFrame, the Center for Story-Based Strategy, Media Justice, the Center for Public Interest Communication, Race Forward, BLIS (Black Liberation-Indigenous Sovereignty) Collective, and the Narrative Initiative all contribute to a rich coalition and collaboration of nonprofit and movement forces committed to transforming society through the power of story.

Narrative Organizing for a New Era

To add to the toolbox for building progressive and leftist narrative power, this book delves into the policy making, base building, and narrative organizing—which Rachel Weidinger defines as the act of building, creating, and using narrative to shift power toward justice, equity, and democracy[13]— that have shaped the early twenty-first century. This anthology serves multiple purposes: First, it provides social-movement workers with a capstone text that deconstructs how organizers, activists, and advocates have harnessed narrative power and communication strategies to advance the vision of a multiracial, multinational, radical democracy across diverse movements, geographies, and regimes. Second, it offers everyday people, parents, scholars, and those invested in a more just future an insider's perspective on how narratives are used to wield immense power. The anthology also aims to equip readers with the tools to collectively develop counterhegemonic strategies and a proactive vision for a society that benefits the many rather than a privileged few.

Liberation Stories is intended for a broad and diverse audience of individuals actively engaged in social-justice movements and those who want to center liberatory values in their professional and personal lives. These include parents, teachers, communicators, organizers, cultural workers, academics, advocates, policy makers, artists, and others for whom narrative and storytelling play a vital role in their daily lives and work. The book is designed to cater to both newcomers and seasoned practitioners.

While people have long engaged in community and media relations, political persuasion, and narrative organizing, they are rarely recognized as leaders in social movements. Despite their work's fundamental role across every discipline in the social-movement ecosystem, these efforts often remain unseen. Social-movement and nonprofit workers who carry forward the tradition of using storytelling to deconstruct and communicate about complex systems—employing rhetoric, signs, symbols, messaging, literary and rhetorical devices, music, and even our bodies, to advance a more liberatory society—possess unique strategic insights and guidance that are invaluable to everyday people, social movements, philanthropic institutions, scholars, and students. This book, written and edited by RadComms, puts the thinking and action of communicators front and center.

A Decentralized Network for Narrative Power

After the 2016 election of Donald Trump, U.S. social and political tensions sharply escalated. His administration's brutal border family-separation policy and the resurgence of white nationalism, fueled by fascist and white-supremacist ideologies, ignited movements like Abolish ICE and brought racist voter suppression to the forefront of national consciousness.

RadComms was born out of the urgent need to unify the social-movement left, with a focus on harnessing narrative power to confront fascism, systemic oppression, and entrenched injustice. RadComms is more than a community; it's a radical space for movement and communications workers to engage in transformative dialogue and build the narrative power needed for a just and liberatory future.

RadComms addresses three unique challenges facing social-justice communications: the isolation of practitioners focused on narrative power, top-down models reinforcing privilege, and communications frameworks maintaining the status quo. By amplifying grassroots expertise and fostering a global network, RadComms radically politicizes social-change communications, cultivating narratives that empower marginalized communities and dismantle hegemonic ideologies.

In this era of deepening crisis, reshaping narratives and achieving radical transformation requires sustained solidarity and collective action. RadComms embodies this revolutionary spirit, proving that we can challenge dominant stories and forge a new, emancipatory vision for society by building narrative power together.

Chapter Overview: A New Millennium and a New Age of Activism

The dawn of the twenty-first century marked a pivotal shift in the sociopolitical and economic landscape of the United States and the trajectory of social movements. The 1990s closed with the end of Bill Clinton's two-term presidency, during which his neoliberal policies steered the Democratic Party further to the right on critical issues such as welfare, mass incarceration, policing, and free trade.[14] This period was characterized by the narrative of *superpredators*,[15] a term infamously used by Hillary Clinton to demonize and criminalize Black children, and by Bill Clinton's pledge to "end welfare as we know it"[16]—a policy shift that led to millions of poor people, including a disproportionate number of children, being denied food, housing, and other life-affirming resources.

In response to these regressive policies, the decade also witnessed some of the largest mobilizations in U.S. history. The 1993 March on Washington for Lesbian, Gay, and Bi Equal Rights and Liberation attracted nearly one million participants, including people from well-known movement groups like ACT UP and PFLAG.[17] The following year, nearly 70,000 people mobilized in California against Proposition 187, an anti-immigrant ballot initiative prohibiting undocumented people from accessing critical social services.[18] Most notably, the 1999 antiglobalization protests aimed at disrupting the World Trade Organization conference in Seattle became the largest of its kind in the United States against any world meeting.[19] These protests signaled the growing resistance to neoliberalism and set the stage for the social movements of the new century.

Clinton's Third Way politics—a centrist approach that sought to blend traditional liberalism with elements of conservative ideology—was widely regarded as a successful electoral strategy.[20] However, the contentious 2000 presidential election saw the White House return to Republican control. George W. Bush's presidency, which followed, was soon defined by a seismic event that reshaped global and domestic politics: the September 11, 2001, terrorist attacks. Al-Qaeda's coordinated assault on the United States resulted in nearly 3,000 deaths and more than 25,000 injuries. In response, Bush declared a "War on Terror," vowing that it would start with al-Qaeda but would not end "until every terrorist group of global reach has been found, stopped, and defeated," setting the stage for a new era characterized by mass surveillance, extreme Islamophobia, and an expansion of the carceral state.[21]

Two decades later, the impact of Bush's prophetic language and War on Terror rhetoric remains profound and far-reaching, shaping both the political trajectory of the United States and the activist response to it. Domestically, the War on Terror expanded the U.S. security, military, and surveillance apparatus, disproportionately targeting Black, Brown, Muslim, and immigrant communities. Internationally, the pursuit of defeating the "global terror network" has been used to justify military interventions in Iraq, Afghanistan, Syria, Pakistan, Somalia, and Yemen, legitimizing a widespread use of force and violence—justified by anti-Arab and Islamophobic propaganda. This shift also catalyzed a new era of activism, as organizers mobilized to challenge U.S. imperialism at home and abroad.[22]

This is where our story—and the stories of this book's contributors—begins: at the outset of the twenty-first century. From the War on Terror in 2001 to the mobilizations of the Palestine Liberation Movement in 2023 and 2024, through essays, case studies, visual examples, and interviews, we deconstruct how social movements in the United States and beyond have challenged dominant narratives, built power, and shifted public discourse to change material conditions. While each chapter offers an intersectional analysis across various issues, the book is organized into nine emerging themes, drawing connections between social movements.

We begin with *Anti-Imperialism*, where contributors delve into how Islamophobia and anti-Muslim hate have been weaponized to legitimize state violence from the 1948 Nakba to 9/11. They examine the narrative foundations of the War on Terror, rooted in colonial legacies that continue to perpetuate violence both domestically and internationally (Hilal and Petersen-Smith). The same racist discourse underpinning U.S. empire and settler colonialism has also been used to justify the colonization, occupation, and genocide of the Palestinian people (interview with Keilani and Erakat). Both analyses highlight the narrative power built by movement actors, from the Palestine Liberation Movement to efforts to close Guantánamo Bay.

In *Black Liberation and Indigenous Resistance*, we delve into the narrative underpinnings of the U.S. empire and the fight against white supremacy and police militarization. Contributors examine how the Movement for Black Lives dismantled narratives of Black pathology, shifting blame onto the state (Matthews and Noor), and how the 2020 uprisings for racial justice and police abolition became a convergence point for the environmental-justice movement (Chavis and Oglesby). Others analyze the successes and challenges in building narrative power for reparations (Smith, Torres, and Brutus) and offer insights into movements for Indigenous sovereignty, particularly through the lens of Standing Rock (interview with Black Elk and Wise).

In *Gender Justice and Violence Prevention*, contributors explore the intersections of gender, sexuality, and race in amplifying violence. They analyze the #MeToo movement's role in building narrative power for survivor justice (Fuller and Beek) and trace the gun violence–prevention movement from its radical origins in Chicago to March for Our Lives (Jacoby and Bosley). The section concludes with a case study on the fight for trans liberation, focusing on the 2016 battle against North Carolina's "bathroom bill" (cortés and St. Louis).

In *Immigrant Justice*, we examine the intersection of immigration status with other marginalized identities, particularly within Black LGBTQIA+ communities in the United States and globally (interview with Black LGBTQIA+ Migrant Project). Contributors delve into campaigns that successfully challenged harmful media narratives about undocumented individuals (Sen and Lovato) and highlight the grassroots efforts to provide relief for migrant communities during the peak of the COVID-19 pandemic (Pérez and Feng).

Health and Dignity delves into how narratives have historically been used to control, pathologize, and marginalize vulnerable communities. Contributors trace the lineage of health movements from the HIV/AIDS epidemic to long COVID, exploring who is deemed worthy of care (Davids and Avril) and analyzing narrative shifts in the conversation around access to abortion (Bracey Sherman and Mahone). We examine city- and state-level policy campaigns that challenge the neoliberal health care model and reaffirm human dignity, from health care as a human right (Palmquist and Rudiger) to fat rights as civil rights (Osborn, Cooper, and Mejia).

Economic Equality and Workers' Rights explores how marginalized communities have been at the forefront of economic-justice battles in the United

States. Contributors examine key workers' rights struggles, from Occupy Wall Street and Fight for $15 (Warren and Ollenburger), which offered and expanded alternatives to neoliberalism, to the Toys 'R' Us workers who exposed Wall Street's greed (Sabharwal and DuMonthier). The section concludes with a critical look at philanthropic institutions, their ties to racial capitalism and colonialism, and how movement workers can envision a world where philanthropy is rendered obsolete (Mohammed and Van Deven).

Democracy for All addresses the erosion of trust in democratic institutions and strategies to counteract it. Contributors investigate the role of policy in setting grassroots agendas (Pandit and Bayetti Flores), strategies for combating racialized misinformation and disinformation that threaten social cohesion (Mason and Longoria), and the use of surveys and data to build and sustain social-movement infrastructure (Cohen, Ramanathan, and Nelsen).

In *Visuals and Tactics*, we explore movements' specific strategies for operationalizing their goals. Contributors examine the power of visual media and photography to create mass counternarratives (Fayne Wood and Gichobi), the role of aesthetics in fostering belonging (Steez), and the power of narrative in direct-action campaigns on the left (Tutashinda and Faison). Looking forward, we reflect on the evolving significance of social-media influencers in shaping movements (Blocker and Jewell).

We conclude with *Global Perspectives*, highlighting the necessity for progressive and leftist movements to organize across borders. Contributors examine Black liberation struggles in Nigeria, focusing on the #EndSARS movement against police brutality (Adegbola, Abdulateef Elega, and Ayinke Taiwo), and in Brazil, where effeminate young Black gay men are using digital content to disseminate antiracist and anti-cis-heteronormative narratives (Cotta and Saavedra). The section ends with a call to build narratives of solidarity against the global rise of far-right and fascist ideologies, with case studies from the United Kingdom and Poland (Zukowska and Lunt).

Looking Ahead

As we conclude the editing of *Liberation Stories* in September 2024, we find ourselves just two months away from a U.S. presidential election that starkly represents a choice between fascism and neoliberalism, placing social movements both in the United States and globally at a critical crossroads. The far right is using narrative organizing to advance a white-supremacist agenda bolstered by the MAGA propaganda apparatus, corporate interests, and undemocratic access to information. The Rising Majority, a leftist social-movement formation, aptly describes this period as "a uniquely dangerous moment for our people and planet," where the future remains precariously undetermined.[23]

In their 2050 strategy, they reflect on the changing poles of power. Globally, China is on the brink of overtaking the United States as the world's largest economy and, alongside other BRICS nations (the acronym stands for Brazil, Russia, India, China, and South Africa—grouped initially together to describe foreign investment strategies), is increasingly asserting its independence in global political arenas. This signals the emergence of a multipolar world, with the United States and its European allies forming one pole and China and Russia leading another. The Russian invasion of Ukraine in 2022 has accelerated this shift, potentially offering nations in the Global South more space to pursue economic and political agendas free from U.S. imperialism.[24] Far-right authoritarian groups, driven by ideologies of hate, exclusion, and fascism, have gained significant political and social influence. These campaigns deepen global narratives of racism, xenophobia, and misogyny, with long-term consequences for marginalized communities.

Across the globe, activists, organizers, and communications workers are challenging authoritarian and liberal democratic governments, fighting for power, and communicating values and demands to win lasting change. In a time of rising global right-wing populism, Black activists are bolstering democracy in Colombia and Brazil by supporting the elections of Francia Márquez and Luiz Inácio Lula da Silva. In Iran, hundreds of thousands have taken to the streets, rejecting patriarchal norms and demanding an end to the Islamic Republic. In Gaza, Palestinians resist a generations-long siege and genocide. In Ukraine, people fight against Russian aggression and the ideologies of manifest destiny and supremacy.

What can the narrative insights from the first quarter of the twenty-first century offer future generations of movement workers at the height of this future largely undetermined?

We know that narratives wield transformative power. Echoing the insights of revolutionary thinker Grace Lee Boggs, the narratives we champion through storytelling play a critical role in determining whose lives are valued and marginalized in our society. The pervasive tale of Black women as "welfare queens" has not only stereotyped but also systematically influenced everything from educational access to judicial fairness. The glorified narrative of a "labor of love" has been used to exploit and confine women to certain types of work, dictating the value and compensation of their labor. The "lazy" versus "hardworking" immigrant narratives have drawn a harsh line, determining that only the most resilient and self-denying individuals are worthy of rights and dignity.

Liberation Stories, however, was never meant to be about individual stories, myths, and tropes, which, while important, on their own are small parts contributing to much larger wholes, like a drop in the ocean or a tile in a mosaic. This book is about *narrative power*—the ability to shape and control the stories told within a society, including who tells them, what stories are told, and how they are interpreted. It's about the capacity to influence perceptions, beliefs, and behaviors. The Black welfare queen, the woman laboring out of love, and the hardworking immigrant are all cut from the same narrative cloth—one that has been woven over centuries and shaped the realities within which these perceptions are formed. This narrative fabric maintains existing power structures, reinforcing societal norms that privilege some while marginalizing others.

To transform society, our narrative organizing must dismantle these oppressive narratives, challenging and rewriting the stories that devalue lives and justify oppression. By examining these collective stories, we can unravel the threads of systemic inequality and highlight the mechanisms through which narratives shape our understanding of worth, labor, and belonging.

This is precisely the exploration that *Liberation Stories* offers. The chapters in this book dive into the unseen currents that guide our society and uphold the status quo—narratives far more pervasive and entrenched than any single story could convey. These narratives lack a clear structure or defined endpoints, yet they are the architects of our relationships, beliefs, societal norms, and power dynamics, silently dictating the rhythms of our daily lives. Only through this deep exploration into how narratives have been constructed and perpetuated can we ultimately transform our futures toward dignity, self-determination, and a radical democracy.

Reflecting on Darnella Frazier's intuitive decision to record George Floyd's murder: It was not just an act of courage, it was a radical confrontation of the oppressive systems that perpetuate state-sanctioned violence against Black people. In a moment, she shattered the carefully constructed narratives that have long been used to dehumanize Black communities and justify police brutality. Frazier's instinct to document the truth ripped the veil off a system designed to protect the powerful at the expense of the vulnerable, igniting a global uprising that demanded not just reform but a complete dismantling of the racist structures upholding the status quo.

Her actions underscore the radical potential of narrative power: how unfiltered stories, bolstered by narrative organizing and movement building, can disrupt the lies that maintain systemic oppression and inspire mass resistance. *Liberation Stories* builds on that legacy, urging readers to recognize the revolutionary power of narrative and storytelling as a weapon against the forces of white supremacy, capitalism, and state violence. It challenges us not only to expose the brutality of these systems but to actively participate in tearing them down, rewriting the narratives that have kept us oppressed, and forging new paths toward collective liberation. Darnella's defiance shows us that, in the face of tyranny, the truth is a powerful tool of insurgency. We can spark society's radical transformation through the relentless telling of our stories.

ANTI-IMPERIALISM

Weaponizing Rhetoric: Legitimations of State Violence in the War on Terror

By Dr. Maha Hilal and Khury Petersen-Smith

As for the Afghans, we and our partners have airlifted 100,000 of them. No country in history has done more to airlift out the residents of another country than we have done.[1]

—President Joe Biden (August 31, 2021)

In 2021, the United States chaotically withdrew from Afghanistan after two decades of a long and brutal war, which failed to achieve any of Washington's stated objectives. The resulting withdrawal led to nearly 200 Afghans and 13 U.S. service members being killed, and left the majority of Afghans behind to face uncertain violence and a country in shambles. Quickly after the United States withdrew, the Taliban regained leadership and has continued to govern the country ever since.

In this light, the above remarks from President Joe Biden are striking: Rather than acknowledging the reason for needing to airlift Afghans out of Afghanistan, the statement reframed the catastrophic withdrawal of the United States into a celebration of its generosity. Biden's narrative is representative of the United States' long-standing stories of its war on Afghanistan post–9/11—a war that was characterized as necessary, legitimate, humane, and generous. This framing was designed to absolve the United States of responsibility for the political and social destruction of Afghanistan since 2001, and preemptively, far into the future, to allow the United States to plausibly deny its role in the country's trajectory.

The narratives that Biden deployed, however, were not unique or novel. They were put in place before him by the Bush administration, which built, sustained, and perpetuated the discursive foundation of the War on Terror. After more than two decades of the War on Terror, the narratives constructed to legitimize the war have effectively convinced the public of the necessity of the government's chosen interventions. Moreover, they have continued to position Muslims as a threat to the global world order—an idea that has been adopted, adapted, and weaponized by countries around the world, including China, India, and Israel.

This chapter lays out the narrative beginnings of the War on Terror and the foundation on which state violence was and continues to be justified. Underscoring the durability of this narrative, we will examine specific constructions of the United States as a blameless victim and Muslims as an omnipresent terrorist threat. Rather than viewing War on Terror narratives as abstract, we analyze the ways they have been wielded to support U.S. state violence, including wars in Muslim-majority countries, indiscriminate surveillance, and detention. Understanding that U.S. wars never really end, we also highlight the country's colonial history and how the War on Terror is built on its legacy. Finally, we consider the creation and deployment of counternarratives and end with a call for transformative change: what it will take to build narratives that center the humanity and dignity of Muslims and other communities that have been viciously targeted in the War on Terror.

The Narrative Beginnings of the War on Terror

Whether we bring our enemies to justice, or bring justice to our enemies, justice will be done.[2]

Our war on terror begins with al Qaeda, but it does not end there. It will not end until every terrorist group of global reach has been found, stopped, and defeated.[3]

On September 20, 2001, nine days after the 9/11 attacks, President George W. Bush delivered a speech to a joint session of Congress, marking his first use of the term *War on Terror*. In addition to employing an abstract term to excuse what would become the war's excesses, the use of "our war on terror," as Otago University professor Richard Jackson argues, was "a very carefully and deliberately constructed public discourse . . . specifically designed to make the war seem reasonable, responsible, and inherently 'good.'"[4]

Framed as responsive to Americans' concerns and fears after the 9/11 attacks, Bush's speech was structured around a set of questions sprinkled throughout that he claimed "Americans were asking," and to which he and the American government had answers. These questions included:

- Who attacked our country?
- Why do they hate us?
- How will we fight and win this war?
- What is expected of us?

Whether or not Americans had actually made these inquiries, providing this set of questions and answers was essential to the story that the Bush administration was trying to tell. The story, which has remained cemented in the official narrative, was promoted as an ahistorical account of the perpetrators' motivations for attacking the United States; the United States' unique and blameless victimhood; and what interventions—including mass atrocities and violence—would be framed as necessary, principled, legal, and legitimate.

At the same time, to buttress the idea of violence as necessary, War on Terror rhetoric has been and continues to be framed around "justice"—an assertion that justice is whatever the United States defines it to be. This discursive use of the term not only has allowed the United States to operate with impunity; it has served to separate and make irrelevant any objective definition and assessment of whether said violence complies with domestic and international law.

The "War on Terror"

Bush's answer to the question of "who attacked us" was "al-Qaeda," and to the question of why they hate "us," he made the claim that it was because they despised "our freedoms" and democracy—which the United States epitomized to perfection. To the question of how the war would be fought and won, Bush asserted that the United States would direct "every resource at our command"; there would not be a "swift conclusion"; and "Americans should not expect one battle, but a lengthy campaign, unlike any other we have ever seen."[5] Referred to pejoratively as the Forever Wars, the violence unleashed through military campaigns under the guise of the War on Terror has been far lengthier than what most people imagined.

Psychiatrist Jay Lifton writes that the U.S. government capitalized on Americans' raw responses and emotions to the 9/11 attack and seized the opportunity of the public's vulnerability to make meaning: "Emotions were experienced by political leaders, who were able to channel them into an official survivor mission of a 'war on terrorism'—a series of far-flung military and paramilitary actions, sometimes considered a crusade against evil, without clear limits in time or place."[6] Conflating the needs of survivors with the launch of a massive war apparatus would continue to pay off in the U.S. government's perpetuation of the War on Terror.

It is no surprise, then, that the Bush administration chose to define and construct the response to the 9/11 attacks using a metaphor: the War on Terror. As philosophy scholar Rebecca Gordon notes, defining the war through metaphor does not change the actual impacts of war. Instead, she argues, "When we declare war on phenomena like crime, drugs, or terror, instantly militarizing such problems, we severely limit our means for understanding and dealing with them."[7] If the War on Terror narrative has accomplished anything, it has been to convince the public that the government's chosen interventions are not only necessary but legitimate.

This metaphor has had violent consequences at home and abroad, and required a legal infrastructure with loopholes outside the bounds of international and U.S. law to support it. These included measures beyond U.S. borders, such as the creation of CIA Black Sites as detention and torture facilities, and of the legal designation of the *enemy combatant*, which described people whom U.S. forces could detain but handle without the rights and obligations that are afforded to prisoners of war. The beginning of the War on Terror also involved the rewriting of the U.S. domestic rules for governance. This included the passage of legislation like the USA PATRIOT Act (an acronym that has become shorthand for the Uniting and Strengthening America by Providing Appropriate Tools Required to Intercept and Obstruct Terrorism Act), which severely undermined civil liberties by expanding surveillance powers of police agencies and providing new powers for detention of migrants suspected of "terrorism."[8]

The "Blameless Victim"

Positioning the United States as a blameless victim was part of Bush's strategy to justify the War on Terror and all it would entail. In this vein, he stated:

> Americans have known the casualties of war—but not at the center of a great city on a peaceful morning. Americans have known surprise attacks—but never before on thousands of civilians. All of this was brought upon us in a single day—and night fell on a different world, where freedom itself is under attack.[9]

Adopting a hegemonic posture of victimhood, which rendered the suffering of Americans unique and exceptional, has been a strategy to minimize the United States' disproportionate and catastrophic state violence and garner public support for it. Moreover, by dwelling on American victimhood, despite other countries experiencing far greater atrocities, this narrative has made it possible for the United States to displace moral responsibility for its violence onto the attackers—even to this day, after millions of Muslims and others have been killed.[10]

The durability of the narrative of the United States as blameless, and the undisputed and sole victim, has persisted. Upon announcing the assassination of Ayman al-Zawahiri, Osama Bin Laden's successor to al-Qaeda, in August 2022, President Biden said:

> The United States did not seek this war against terror. It came to us, we answered with the same principles and resolve that have shaped us for generation upon generation to protect the innocent, defend liberty, and we keep the light of freedom burning—a beacon for the rest of the entire world.[11]

The travesty of this statement was not only that the United States was absolving itself of its past violence, but that the violence was being characterized as principled—despite the war's entire infrastructure being built on new legal frameworks meant to allow and excuse the worst abuses.

The "Terrorist" and "Terrorism"

War on Terror narratives have been so compelling and recycled so many times over that the trillions of dollars spent, mounting death tolls, and the perpetuation of a war with no conceivable end have largely gone uncontested by mainstream American society. Cementing the United States' victimhood required the American public to assume that there was an omnipresent terrorist threat. Central to this frame was the development of a villain in the American mind. Whereas previous wars involved formal, uniformed military opponents, this war has targeted a shadowy adversary in faraway places like Afghanistan and Yemen, but also lurking within American communities.

The cultivation of the "terrorist" character has leaned heavily on Islamophobic tropes, including the notion that irrational, fanatical, and foreign beliefs and behaviors are endemic to Islam. In this characterization, Muslim societies are portrayed as uniquely misogynistic, with extraordinarily aggressive men and exceptionally helpless women. The "terrorist" enemy does not play by the rules, unlike the United States and its allies, who make up the constituents of the "international community." Instead, the terrorist takes advantage of Western generosity and then attacks.

The actual history and reality of the War on Terror indict the very conceptual framework of "terrorism" and, by extension, "counterterrorism," except as tools to dehumanize a foreign "other" and enable state violence. More than two decades after 9/11, the U.S. government has used the word *terrorism* to describe and condemn acts ranging from car bombings in Mogadishu by al-Shabab, to attacks on U.S. forces occupying Iraq by Iraqi fighters, to direct action by climate activists against the Dakota Access Pipeline.[12] In Afghanistan, the portrayal of Afghan victims of violence as merely a "terror problem" has allowed the United States to justify incredible state violence and war crimes, such as the bombing of Tora Bora[13] and the Dasht-i-Leili Massacre,[14] where U.S. forces and allies suffocated prisoners of war to death. The U.S. government, legal system, and military pushed the boundaries of rules of war, justifying torture and cloaking it in the euphemism *enhanced interrogation.*

From Bush to Obama: Continuity and Change in the War on Terror Narrative

In the earliest days of the War on Terror, narrative was critical to legitimation, which academics Ronald R. Krebs and Stacie E. Goddard define as the way that

> political actors publicly justify their policy stances before con-
> crete audiences, seeking to secure these audiences' assent that
> their positions are indeed legitimate and thus potentially to garner
> their approval and support.[15]

While the term *War on Terror* was largely abandoned when Barack Obama became president, the change in discourse did not signal a shift in the war. In fact, under Obama, the war escalated, demonstrating that the rhetorical shift was not about curbing violence but, instead, obfuscating it.

In his analysis of counterterrorism policies across multiple administrations, academic Marc Barnett writes that Obama expanded military operations and increased U.S. troop presence in fifteen countries beyond Bush, rendering the abandonment of the term *War on Terror* as "mainly cosmetic as other rhetorical flourishes and policy remained untouched."[16] Gabriel Rubin, associate professor of justice studies at Montclair University, notes that, while Obama spoke far less about the threat of terrorism in general, this was because "Bush had already done the policy selling for him,"[17] not because he was less willing to execute the violent policies of the War on Terror.

There was, however, something more insidious in Obama's rhetoric and the state violence that would be unleashed under his command—namely, the use of the narrative of legality meant to persuade Americans of the war's legitimacy. Obama's war making would be governed by the law instead of sidestepping it.

In the first year of his presidency, Obama, giving a speech on national security, asserted:

> We are indeed at war with al-Qaeda and its affiliates. We do need
> to update our institutions to deal with this threat. But we must do

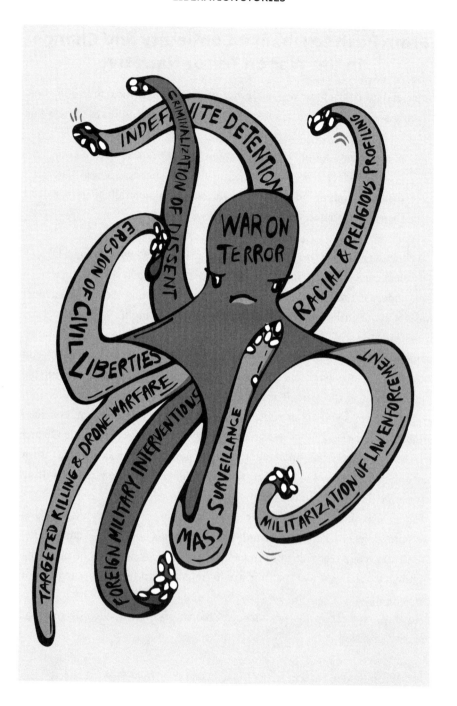

so with an abiding confidence in the rule of law and due process, in checks and balances and accountability.[18]

Obama used the cover of legality to expand and intensify the war, including by dramatically escalating the U.S. drone-warfare program far beyond its use during the Bush administration. This illustrated the notion that legality was flexible, and the use of specific narratives ensured this flexibility aligned with the U.S. government's justification for particular state-sanctioned violence.

This language was also used to downplay and soften the perception of the violence waged in the War on Terror, particularly against Muslim communities in the United States. In August 2011, the Obama administration released a National Strategy guide titled *Empowering Local Partners to Prevent Violent Extremism in the United States*, which included a specific focus on targeting Muslim Americans, who "are part of our American family."[19] By portraying Muslim Americans as victims who needed protection from extremism, in addition to being necessary allies in the fight against violent extremist ideologies, the government fostered divisions within Muslim communities by urging Muslim American communities to monitor and surveil each other. This led to the creation of the Countering Violent Extremism (CVE) program, framed as community partnerships that encouraged interventions from within targeted communities—most notably, Muslims.

The Tentacles of the War on Terror: From Colonialism to Military Tactics at Home

The narrative infrastructure of the War on Terror has proved to be remarkably durable. As University of Minnesota professor Ronald R. Krebs writes in his book *Narrative and the Making of U.S. National Security*, "the War on Terror was more than a slogan"; it defined the "common-sense givens" for the public post–9/11.[20] What made it commonsense is the existing narrative infrastructure of colonization, white supremacy, and systemic oppression, which has construed communities of color, particularly Black and Indigenous, as a threat for centuries.

Thus, the tactics and strategies of the War on Terror are a continuation of this long-standing history. For example, the centuries-old wars waged by the United States against Indigenous peoples of North America reveal patterns of behavior that include land dispossession, cultural genocide, and systematic violence—mimicking tactics used in the War on Terror. For example, the U.S. war on Iraq was launched and fought on the basis of the lie that the country and its president, Saddam Hussein, had weapons of mass destruction. However, it was truly motivated by the theft of resource extraction and, in particular, oil. As a result of the imperialist war, hundreds of thousands of Iraqi civilians have been killed[21] with no accountability. As University of Toronto PhD student Isra Saymour notes, "Operation Iraqi Freedom was a resource war that targeted not only natural but also cultural resources, leading to the parallel extraction and displacement of oil and heritage."[22]

Similarly, the War on Terror has disproportionately targeted Muslim communities, many of whom are Black, both within the United States and globally. This targeting cannot be separated from the broader context of anti-Blackness that pervades U.S. institutional structures, influencing policy and public perception. War on Terror narratives draw heavily from racialized concepts of criminality that have historically been applied against Black people within the U.S. domestic sphere. For example, when officials publicly discussed the Guantánamo Bay prison camp, they justified its existence as a necessary measure to detain the "worst of the worst" detainees. This language mirrors the rhetoric used in the United States during the rise of mass incarceration, specifically in the justification of "supermax" prisons designed to house "superpredators," who were disproportionately Black.[23]

The War on Terror has not only shaped narratives to justify U.S. violence abroad, but it has also facilitated the racist deployment of similar state violence and surveillance domestically. In the aftermath of the 9/11 attacks, the NYPD and other police departments were celebrated as heroic, using this credibility as a mandate to pursue far-reaching spying operations, detentions, repression, and other forms of violence.

The 1033 Program, for instance, enabled the extensive transfer of military weapons and equipment from foreign battlefields to local police departments in the United States. This equipment was justified under the premise that domestic security issues should be handled as terrorist threats, thus necessitating military-grade weapons and vehicles.[24] The very concept of *homeland security*, introduced during the War on Terror, marked a new era of increased border militarization and stringent migration controls based on explicit demarcations around who belonged in the United States. This pattern of behavior is reminiscent of the mass internment of Japanese Americans during World War II, another period when domestic policies of confinement and surveillance paralleled military actions abroad.[25]

In recent years, the Movement for Black Lives (M4BL) has presented the most significant domestic challenge to the legitimacy of U.S. policing since the beginning of the War on Terror. With a series of uprisings—from Ferguson, Missouri, in 2014, to the global uprisings of 2020 in response to the murders of George Floyd and Breonna Taylor—M4BL asserted a national conversation about American policing as rooted in the history of slavery and ongoing institutional racism.

In response to the 2020 uprisings, the U.S federal government, in a flagrant abuse of power and at the express direction of disgraced former president Donald Trump and former attorney general William Barr, deliberately targeted supporters of the movement in order to disrupt and discourage participation. This persecution resulted in hundreds of organizers and activists facing years in federal prison with no chance of parole.[26]

This context is fertile ground for an internationalist, antimilitarist critique that incorporates an analysis of the relationship between U.S. violence abroad and domestic policing, and the significance of Islamophobia in contemporary political struggles, such as the Palestinian liberation movement. Social movements aiming to counteract War on Terror narratives must highlight how these modern policies and actions are directly linked to a history of colonization and racism. By doing so, they can illuminate the cyclical nature of oppression and challenge its social acceptance as isolated or necessary measures. Alternative frameworks for understanding security, community, and international relations should prioritize reparative justice, respect sovereignty, and dismantle systems of oppression, to challenge the very assumptions that underpin the War on Terror.

Counternarratives

The rhetoric of the War on Terror has often been difficult to shift, especially when considering the impact of language on policy and vice versa. Two examples that illustrate these challenges are the efforts to close the Guantánamo

Bay prison, established by George W. Bush in 2002 to hold "illegal enemy combatants" at the start of the War on Terror, and efforts to resist Donald Trump's Muslim Ban, an executive order issued in 2017 that was marred by several lawsuits for its unconstitutionality.

Guantánamo Bay Prison

Since the prison opened in 2002, 779 Muslim men and boys have been held at Guantánamo Bay—nearly all of them without being charged or convicted.[27] Today, 30 men remain in detention, many of them survivors of rendition and torture at the hands of the U.S. government.[28]

At a site that has come to epitomize national security and keeping the "terrorists" at bay, the men who have been detained at Guantánamo Bay have maintained the stigma of being labeled the "worst of the worst," thanks to remarks by former vice president Dick Cheney.[29] Despite hundreds of men having been released without charge or conviction, this narrative of vilification and demonization, rooted in racism and Islamophobia, has not only remained but has been perpetuated. In fact, it has been so entrenched that merely mentioning the humanity of the men incarcerated is seen as a roadblock in efforts to close the prison.

For example, Senator Dick Durbin, who has been lauded as an advocate for closing Guantánamo, gave a speech in June 2023 saying, "The United States is a nation of laws. When we indefinitely detain people who have never been charged with a crime and who have been deemed safe to release, we are betraying our own basic constitutional values."[30] Thus, in his mention of the incarcerated men, Durbin is not acknowledging their humanity and deserved justice, but is instead focused on prioritizing the rehabilitation of the U.S. image. This narrative and others that have been similarly deployed do nothing to challenge the Islamophobic perceptions post–9/11 and, in fact, do the opposite, which is to allow for the continued implication that Muslims are guilty until proven innocent. Moreover, by emphasizing that these men are "safe to release," despite stating that those who should be transferred had never been charged with a crime, Durbin's words effectively signaled that Muslims can never actually be innocent, much less vindicated. They also suggest that the violence they experienced, including torture, doesn't require acknowledgment in any meaningful sense.

Outside the halls of Congress, even human-rights organizations campaigning for the prison's closure have relied on these tired narratives. In a 2022 op-ed titled "The High Cost of Guantánamo's 'Forever Prisoners,'" author Leah Hebron, former Human Rights Watch associate, writes that the prison should be closed because of its exorbitant cost, the fact that it serves as a tool for terrorist recruitment, and how it denies justice to victims of 9/11 and their families. The only nod to the humanity of those incarcerated is in stating that the military commissions have violated their rights.[31]

None of these narratives that are propagated address or challenge the reason people were detained in the first place. For example, the vast majority of those in Guantánamo were captured as a result of enormous bounties that were provided by the United States. According to the UK human-rights organization Reprieve:

> The U.S. flew planes over parts of Afghanistan and Pakistan offering $5,000 for any "suspicious" person. This amounted to approximately seven years' average salary for most people in the area, encouraging them to turn over innocent men in exchange for a life-changing amount of money.[32]

Since then, those held have been treated as guilty until proven innocent, with little focus on justice.

Moreover, the oft-repeated idea that Guantánamo serves as a terrorist recruitment tool ignores why that is or may be the case. The prison is a clear example of how far the United States will go and has gone to target Muslims. Rather than acknowledging the root of the problem—U.S. empire and persisting legacies of colonialism—this narrative continues to promote an already-enduring trope about Muslims being fundamentally irrational, inherently rageful, and prone to violence. Meanwhile, the United States remains a blameless victim.

Contending with these dehumanizing narratives, urgency to close down the prison remains. This not only requires dismantling the Islamophobia that led to its creation in the first place, but also asserting the humanity and dignity of those who have been held there. This is especially true as we recognize the long-term impacts of these narratives and how they continue to subject those released to the stigma and violence associated with the label *terrorist*. In order to powerfully intervene in these narratives, the men's stories should continue to be told, and their claims for justice must be asserted as inherent, not only in relation to the purported values of "constitutionality" and the "rule of law" the United States holds.

Muslim Ban

While narratives demonizing Muslims have long justified Guantánamo's atrocities, they have also continued to fuel Islamophobic laws and policies in the United States, such as the Muslim Ban. A 2015 campaign statement preempted Donald Trump's execution of the ban, stating the implementation of "a total and complete shutdown of Muslims entering the United States until our country's representatives can figure out what is going on."[33] The Muslim Ban, first issued in 2017 to prevent people from majority-Muslim countries from entering the United States, was rescinded by President Joe Biden in 2021 after years of mass protests, yet continues to reverberate through immigration policies and practices.[34]

At the heart of the Muslim Ban is the notion of collective responsibility—that a group as a whole could and should be held accountable for the actions of individuals. While this logic has been used to fuel racist narratives about Muslims, it has also been deployed in challenges and criticism of the Muslim Ban. Ironically, an argument that was frequently repeated to push back on the ban was that none of the terrorist attacks carried out in the last two decades in the United States were by individuals from the banned countries. This narrative did not challenge the notion of collective responsibility and, in fact, left a window open to the ban's legitimacy—at least rhetorically, if someone from these countries were to commit an act of violence thereafter.

In a *Vox* article titled "There Is No Rational Justification for Trump's Travel Ban,"[35] author Zack Beauchamp leverages this critique of the ban, while also referring to research conducted by University of North Carolina–Chapel Hill sociologist Charles Kurzman on the rates of Muslim American involvement in violent extremism. Although his point is to demonstrate that Muslim Americans don't pose a real or relative threat, Beauchamp seems to ignore the fact that, even with these findings, singling out the community for study communicates a particular narrative—one rooted in Muslims' so-called propensity for violence.

The narrative underpinnings that have criminalized Muslims, whether in the case of Guantánamo or the Muslim Ban, have led to the creation of important discursive interventions. In the case of the Muslim Ban, personal stories from the community have served as effective tools to illustrate its harms. However, the Muslim Ban differs in this sense from Guantánamo, because those who have been incarcerated at the prison have had far fewer opportunities to share their stories, while also facing a much higher threshold to overcome the degree of criminalization ascribed to them. In either case, centering and asserting narratives rooted in Muslim life as inherently valuable and dignified remains imperative—and not only as a means to prove or rehabilitate the image of the United States as a democratic country that adheres to the rule of law and welcomes immigrants.

A Call for Transformative Change

So this will not be a "Muslims are like us" poem
I refuse to be respectable
Instead
Love us when we're lazy
Love us when we're poor
Love us in our back-to-backs, council estates, depressed, unwashed
* and weeping*
Love us high as kites, unemployed, joy-riding, time-wasting, failing
* at school*

Love us silent, unapologizing, shopping in Poundland
skiving off school, homeless, unsure, sometimes violent
Love us when we aren't athletes, when we don't bake cakes
when we don't offer our homes, or free taxi rides after the event
when we're wretched, suicidal, naked and contributing nothing

Love us then

Because if you need me to prove my humanity
I'm not the one that's not human[36]

In a powerful piece and performance, "This Is Not a Humanising Poem," British artist Suhaiymah Manzoor-Khan addresses and rejects the demand for Muslims to prove their humanity. Rather, she shifts the narrative focus and blame onto those doing the dehumanizing.[37]

Manzoor-Khan's poem contrasts sharply with the War on Terror, which demonstrates a profound misuse of narrative—rooted in U.S. historical practices of racial and colonial domination—to legitimize extensive state violence, both domestically and internationally. The framing of the United States as a blameless victim in a perpetual war against a nebulous enemy has facilitated not only the acceptance of overseas military interventions, but also the militarization of domestic police forces and the erosion of civil liberties under the guise of national security.

The narratives crafted to sustain the War on Terror have obscured the real costs of war—measured in human lives and global stability—and reinforced the hegemonic role of the United States as a so-called global arbitrator of justice. Despite shifts in rhetoric, the fundamental strategies of American warfare have remained consistent, showcasing a patterned continuity across different regimes.

As we reflect on more than two decades of the War on Terror, it is crucial to recognize the emerging counternarratives that challenge the foundations of this endless conflict. These counternarratives, often spearheaded by grass-roots movements and critical thinkers, not only question the legitimacy of the war but also seek to redefine concepts of security and justice in a more equitable form. They call for an honest engagement with the imperialist past and present of the United States, advocating for policies that prioritize human dignity over geopolitical dominance.

Our future challenge lies in amplifying these voices of dissent and trans-forming public discourse to finally end the cycles of violence perpetuated in the War on Terror. It is only through such transformative efforts that we can hope to address the deep-seated issues of racism, colonialism, and militarism that this prolonged conflict has highlighted. As we continue to witness the repercussions of the War on Terror on global and domestic stages, the need for a comprehensive reevaluation of our approach to international relations and homeland security becomes even more urgent.

Echoes of the Nakba: The Battle for Narrative Power in the Palestinian Liberation Struggle

Interview with Tanya Keilani and Noura Erakat

By Shanelle Matthews and Marzena Zukowska

Tanya Keilani and Noura Erakat originally wrote a chapter on narrative power in 2021, in the aftermath of the Unity Intifada. By publication, the chapter had become outdated and is now replaced by this interview.

Tanya Keilani is a Palestinian communications strategist living in New York City. She is the communications director at an organization that supports journalists at mainstream news outlets by providing access to sources and analysis, and producing digital content that centers Palestinian stories. She received her MA in anthropology at Columbia University, where she surveyed Israeli policies impacting Palestinian familial life and used digital media to tell each family story.

Noura Erakat is a human-rights attorney and professor at Rutgers University, New Brunswick, New Jersey, in the Department of Africana Studies and the Program in Criminal Justice. Noura is an editorial committee member of the Journal for Palestine Studies *and a co-founding editor of* Jadaliyya, *an electronic magazine on the Middle East that combines scholarly expertise and local knowledge. She recently completed a Non-Resident Visiting Fellowship in the Religion, Conflict, and Peace Initiative at the Religious Literacy Project at Harvard Divinity School. She was a 2022 Mahmoud Darwish Visiting Fellow in Palestinian Studies at Brown University. She is the author of* Justice for Some: Law and the Question of Palestine *(Stanford University Press, 2019).*

Shanelle and Marzena: You wrote the original chapter for this book in 2021, four years before the book was published. Between then and now, the Israeli regime, backed by the West, exacted genocide upon the Palestinian people, killing tens of thousands—while millions worldwide resisted. Why was it essential to revise this chapter?

Noura: Reflecting on this chapter, I remember the tone of celebration when we wrote it. I often used the phrase *we broke the dam* because, at that time, there was an unprecedented shift in how mainstream media engaged with the question of Palestine. I experienced this personally as someone who has been involved in media intervention for over a decade and a half. For the first time, I wasn't invited to debate or to be corrected. Instead, I was invited to speak, teach, and share my expertise.

I noticed a broader change in the media, as well. Israeli talking points were not parroted as the starting point for discussions. While it still happened, it was far less frequent. Sheikh Jarrah, as a microcosm of Israeli settler colonialism, provided a lens through which the broader struggle for Palestine could be understood. This allowed the conversation to move beyond isolated events and instead provide context. We were experiencing a media moment that was shaped by context—something that is often stripped away to further racialize oppressed populations, making them appear as the source of their own harm or the cause of the problem altogether.

However, by 2023, it was painfully clear that whatever gains we had made seemed to have disappeared. After October 7, there was zero context in the media, and no more invites. Palestinians who were invited to speak were not treated as experts but, rather, as punching bags or targets in a morality litmus test. Every interview began with describing Palestinians as barbaric, followed by questioning whether they condemned Hamas. According to them, history started on October 7, with Gaza being completely removed from its context— not just from Palestine and the broader Palestinian struggle, but from the entire region.

It's been devastating to witness, even now, nearly eleven months later. The media continues not only this harmful practice but has also become outright complicit in what has become a full-blown genocide.

Tanya: For me, and I think for many Palestinians, this moment has been both illuminating and incredibly heartbreaking. We're not only witnessing the genocide of our people, but we're also experiencing a complex mix of love and hate from others. The deep-seated racism, rooted in decades of supremacy and propaganda, truly revealed itself after October. This racism drove many of the narratives that enabled the genocide, making it clear just how disposable our lives were perceived to be.

Israeli government statements, even those without evidence, were widely circulated and accepted because it was convenient and made it easier to justify the killing of Palestinians. We saw how quickly power mobilized to support this—from mainstream media to the White House, especially with [President] Biden's comments.

Broadly speaking, in the aftermath of October 7, the mainstream media readily manufactured consent, and many of the tenets of journalism were cast aside. As Noura noted, reporting often omitted key context, such as Israel's decades-long oppression of Palestinians and suffocating siege on Gaza, and how Israel responded with violence to peaceful protests during Gaza's Great March of Return in 2018 and 2019. In addition to the lack of context, we saw mind-bending use of passive voice, continued victim blaming, and just how much humanizing reporting [was] dedicated to Israeli lives versus Palestinian lives.

Palestine liberation protests, 2023–2024. Photo by Shadia Fayne Wood

In this moment, we're realizing just how much effort it takes to undo decades of propaganda and racism. While we made progress as a movement in 2021, and the relationships and organizing efforts from that time were crucial to the protests we're seeing today, it feels like we've lost significant ground in media and narrative. The pervasive racism and bigotry against Palestinians have served a greater purpose: making it easier for Israel to oppress us, kill us, and continue stealing more of our land.

Shanelle and Marzena: The narrative ecosystem of Palestinian liberation and oppression is vast and ever-changing, and has been made more visible to billions of people for nearly a year. In your assessment, what hegemonic and counterhegemonic narratives have emerged as most dominant in their salience and permanence?

Tanya: First, it's essential to understand how we got here. As Noura mentioned, October didn't just happen out of nowhere, yet many treat it as though the timeline starts there. There's a real lack of understanding about the history leading up to this point. Palestinians have tried every possible path to freedom—art, civil disobedience, boycotts—everything you can imagine. When you don't have freedom, you'll do whatever you can to achieve it, right? It's something that occupies your thoughts daily because every aspect of Palestinian life is shaped by this lack of freedom, whether it's getting to work or school, accessing medical care, or simply existing under Israel's military rule. Palestinians have tried every form of protest and resistance, and in each case, Israel has responded by imprisoning or killing those who protest. Every form of resistance has been suppressed, and that critical context is often missing. Instead, the narrative portrays Palestinians as if this situation emerged out of thin air, disconnected from the long history of oppression.

Another central point is the misunderstanding of the root cause. Many people want to blame Netanyahu as if he's the sole problem, but that's a complete falsehood. Palestinians have been oppressed by every Israeli leader; this oppression is fundamental to the Israeli state. From the very beginning, Israel's goal has been to push Palestinians out and suppress them to achieve that aim. This is a critical lack of understanding and a deliberate effort to push a particular narrative.

Lastly, there's the dehumanization of Palestinians. Even in cases where there's sympathy, Palestinians are often seen merely as victims, destined to suffer in the thousands as if that's normal. But we're real people—full human beings capable of building, inspiring, and leading. We know the life we could have and the world we could build if we were free, just as we know the life we had before Israel was built on top of our land. Yet it's clear that not everyone sees us as full human beings. These are some of the narratives that come to mind, and the groups pushing these narratives are the same ones that have been trying to suppress Palestinian freedom for decades—organizations like AIPAC [American Israel Public Affairs Committee] and Israeli government leaders.

Noura: I would add that none of this would be possible without the infrastructure created by the discourse of the War on Terror. Much of what is being thrown at Palestinians fits within that framework—one that has racialized Muslims as latent threats, as outsiders who can't integrate into Western society but are instead planning to impose "creeping Sharia." The narrative paints them as inherently violent, as if modernity has passed them by. It also suggests that they are a threat not only to others but to themselves—perpetuating stereotypes about Brown men being dangerous to their own women, among other harmful ideas.

This deeply ingrained racist discourse isn't unique to Palestinians, but in the United States, it has been used to justify the construction of antiterrorism laws. As Daryl Li's work on the Anti-Terrorism Act shows, from its inception, this legislation has been used to target Palestinian resistance, and it has since been expanded to cast suspicion on Palestinians, Arabs, and Muslims, more broadly. This framework has been incredibly debilitating and difficult to dismantle. How do you even begin to take apart something so patently false yet so deeply embedded in a narrative that perpetuates American empire?

This discourse isn't just in service of Zionism; it also serves the broader interests of U.S. empire, which continues to undermine the possibility of democracy across the Middle East by propping up authoritarian regimes. These regimes are not accountable to their own populations but are, instead, beholden to the United States for external security in exchange for promises of American protection against perceived threats. In return, the United States gains access to oil and other geopolitical resources that sustain its empire.

This reality is often lost on the average American, who, whether consciously or not, benefits significantly from this structure—even as racialized minorities living within the heart of the empire. To get to the point where we can ask people to examine these issues critically, we first have to work against a narrative that has already framed us as the problem simply for existing.

Shanelle and Marzena: From your perspective, what forces and formations of the Palestinian Liberation Movement have been most effective in building narrative power during this time, and why?

Noura: I am continually amazed by the resilience and ingenuity of Palestinians, especially in this moment. As a people existing in diaspora, often [as] racialized and targeted minorities, with no substantial infrastructure—certainly nothing comparable to a national liberation movement—we face immense challenges. Our own government acts as a subcontractor for the United States and Israel. Yet, despite these overwhelming odds, Palestinians have managed to craft and sustain a powerful counternarrative. This is achieved with minimal funding and coordination, especially compared to our adversaries. Yet we continue to produce coherent and unified narratives about our struggle for freedom on a global scale.

One of the most remarkable aspects of this counternarrative is the emphasis on the Nakba—the shared tragedy that unites Palestinians as a people. We understand that the Palestinian struggle cannot be fully grasped without acknowledging the Nakba, an event whose erasure has been systematically attempted to normalize our dispossession. This is why figures like Edward Said have lamented that understanding the Palestinian struggle is impossible without recognizing that we have a homeland worth fighting for. The Nakba serves as a point of national unity, grounding us in our collective demand for the right to return, the end of all forms of occupation from the river to the sea, and our right to self-determination.

Despite our legal and geographic fragmentation, which separates us not only within the global diaspora but even within Palestine itself—where we are increasingly confined to Bantustans and refugee camps across the region—we have consistently maintained this counterhegemonic narrative. This has been achieved through the work of academics, activists, and media professionals.

For instance, the *Journal of Palestine Studies* is a crucial platform where Palestinian academics produce knowledge that allows us to speak for ourselves. However, even more significant is the role of activists in shaping this narrative, driven by the movement itself and its global connections. Media workers, too, have played a critical role, even though this is a relatively young field compared to the others. Though relatively new, organizations like the Institute of Middle East Understanding (IMEU) have become significant sources of this counternarrative, particularly in the media.

In short, despite our myriad differences and the severe challenges we face, Palestinians have consistently and effectively produced a counterhegemonic narrative that continues to challenge and resist dominant discourses.

Tanya: I want to add a thought about mainstream media. Noura and I have both shared a deep disappointment—though that's an understatement—in how the media has mobilized to support propaganda. However, I would also say that this moment has pushed Palestinian stories to the forefront, especially through social media. We've seen incredible journalists on the ground—like Motaz Azaiza, Bisan Owda, or Plestia Alaqad—and even young kids, doctors, and parents in Gaza telling their stories. Some of these stories make it into mainstream media, while others remain on social media, but they are being seen.

Despite where the White House and the halls of power stand, something is shifting among everyday Americans. We're witnessing changes in understanding and a greater ability to connect with Palestinians as human beings, challenging the mainstream narrative that has been forced on people for so long. This gives me some hope.

Additionally, there's a growing connection between the situation in Palestine and broader value systems here in the United States. Americans, who are struggling to make ends meet and drowning in medical debt, are beginning to question why billions of dollars are being sent to Israel—a country with free health care—while those funds are used to bomb Palestinian children and families. This values-based narrative is resonating with people as they reflect on the kind of world we want to build. I believe this narrative is inspiring many.

Shanelle and Marzena: Where have these counternarratives diverged?

Noura: There's been a remarkable consistency in narratives of liberation. Where I've seen divergence, it's more around the scope of resistance and strategy. In the past, there was a clearer divide between those who believed in a two-state solution, with a Palestinian state in the West Bank and Gaza, and those who supported a one-state solution. But now, we're seeing a shift toward thinking beyond the state altogether, which has been a growing trend.

The narrative of a Palestinian state has largely been maintained in diplomatic circles, where it's used as a liberal veneer to enable Israel's ongoing settler-colonial expansion and consolidation of its territorial gains. The real divergence now centers on questions about the future—what kind of future we're envisioning and with whom. This part is murky because there are so many unknowns.

Even within the framework of the one-state solution, there has been debate. Some advocate for juridical equality—one person, one vote—while others, like myself, argue that full decolonization is necessary. A juridical solution alone isn't enough because it doesn't address the supremacist ideology that underpins these conditions. It's like dismantling Jim Crow laws without addressing white supremacy and the reparations needed to make the change meaningful. That's why we continue to face these challenges in the United States and South Africa, where juridical solutions haven't been sufficient.

This debate is also about whom we live with in this decolonial future. Israelis, who have forfeited the right to be sovereign on this land due to their supremacist ideology and genocidal actions, pose a critical question: Can we coexist? This is a sensitive and often-unspoken topic, but it's crucial. It's not the right time to ask Palestinians to consider living with people who see our death as a sovereign right and who justify killing our children in the name of self-defense.

This leads to another debate about legitimate targets: who can be targeted and how resistance is regulated, especially if one believes in armed resistance. However, these topics haven't been discussed openly among Palestinians. We're still struggling to find the space to mourn, to justify our right to live, and to convince others, particularly the Democratic establishment, that we're not evil for wanting to stop a genocide. These are delicate issues. While we haven't had the space to address them fully, they represent the core of the current debates within our community.

Tanya: I want to emphasize that we haven't had the space to have these conversations. Movements are inherently messy, and envisioning the future is especially challenging when everything works against you. When you're not allowed to build, breathe, or mourn because every day brings a new crisis, it's difficult to think beyond the immediate struggles.

However, I also believe that we're in a moment of unprecedented unity. In my own experience and in recent history, I don't think we've seen this level of collective mobilization before, especially in the U.S. context. While there have been many debates over strategy in the past, it feels like we're now in a place where more people are coming together. I'm seeing individuals who once felt unable to speak out about Palestine now finding the courage to do so, despite the risks, because they know it's a matter of life or death. This collective courage and solidarity are significant and beautiful.

Shanelle and Marzena: How does the Israeli propaganda apparatus operate? What drives it? Do you believe it has been successful in achieving its goals?

Noura: Tanya is the expert on this, so I'll defer to her. The coordination among these groups is the one thing I'd like to highlight. These efforts are highly organized, aiming to control media narratives and political, social, and academic discourses. I've been following the work of Yousef Munnayyer, who traces this network back to the establishment of the Ministry of Strategic Affairs in 2015. In response to the growing success of the BDS [Boycott, Divestment, Sanctions] movement, the Israeli government decided that the only way to counter a global network was to build one of their own.

They funded this ministry with $25 million and created a global network of organizations divided into categories that included social-media and advocacy organizations. This network comprises several hundred individuals and organizations, all coordinated by the Israeli government. This isn't just civil society—it's a government-coordinated effort funded by the state, and it's engaging in harassment, intimidation, and pushing a redefinition of anti-Zionism as antisemitism. They're targeting funders of Palestinian NGOs, using legal avenues to harass and imprison Palestinians, and even going after their bank accounts.

This is a significant apparatus directly connected to a foreign government. Under other circumstances, this would fall under the Foreign Agent Registration Act [an act requiring individuals and agencies to register with the Department of Justice if they represent foreign interests], yet it operates largely undercover. The impact is profound; many people who are morally opposed to the genocide remain silent—not because they don't care, but because they're afraid. The cost of speaking out is high, and one or two individuals are often targeted severely to set an example for the rest.

Tanya: I agree. It's clear that at every level—government, campus, and media—there are coordinated efforts linked to the Israeli government to push specific agendas and make it increasingly difficult for Palestinians and their allies to organize. On the media front, having been in this space for a long time, I've worked with journalists who have privately expressed to me just how challenging it is to do their jobs. Reporting basic facts without facing attacks has become incredibly difficult. Organizations like the Committee for Accuracy in Middle East Reporting in America (CAMERA) target any positive mention of Palestinians or any factual reporting on Israel's military occupation. We've even heard of Israeli government officials calling U.S. news outlets to complain about coverage. Then there are the threats from donors to these media outlets, further complicating the landscape for journalists simply trying to do their jobs.

This situation threatens not just the truth, but also journalism as a whole. It undermines the ability to tell honest stories about what's happening. This is precisely what makes propaganda possible—when the truth is suppressed, and certain narratives are pushed because those in power want them to dominate the conversation.

Shanelle and Marzena: The Israeli Defense Forces' social-media accounts have ramped up pinkwashing efforts, attempting to mobilize LGBTQ+ communities against Palestinians by using divide-and-conquer tactics. Beyond the blatant mis- and disinformation, are there specific narrative threads that the propaganda apparatus targets?

Noura: It's frustrating how simple and obvious this tactic is, yet how effective it remains. The idea that Israel cares about queer life is clearly a talking point, especially when their bombs don't discriminate based on sexual orientation, nor do home demolitions spare the homes of nonqueer individuals, allies or not. This narrative is a classic colonial trope, framing the native population as backward and out of step with modernity, particularly in terms of LGBTQ+ rights and women's rights. These are the same kinds of justifications used historically to legitimize colonial violence against so-called "savages."

This rhetoric is built on the infrastructure of the War on Terror. We saw it in the U.S. invasion of Afghanistan, which was framed as a mission to save women—by bombing them, tearing apart families, and creating instability that only empowered the Taliban. Yet liberals bought into it because figures like First Lady Laura Bush called it a fight against tyranny, and Oprah staged dramatic moments on her show, like unveiling a woman from a burqa. These narratives aren't just xenophobic; they're deeply entrenched colonial tropes that have been around for a long time.

It's disheartening that these outdated, transparently racist narratives still hold credibility, which circles back to what Tanya mentioned earlier: It shows us the insidious power of racism and the work it continues to do.

Shanelle and Marzena: Narrative power shapes how people perceive and engage with the world, while structural power shapes the realities within which these perceptions are formed. What does the success of the Israeli propaganda machine say about the relationship between narrative and structural power as Israel continues to ramp up its genocidal and colonial ambitions?

Tanya: I want to emphasize that Israeli propaganda has had mixed success. On one hand, there are clear signs that it's not working on everyone. We see this in the polls and in the streets, where Palestinians are receiving significant support from young people, people of color, and women in the United States. People are mobilizing for Palestine in ways I've never seen before. This shows that the propaganda isn't universally effective.

However, narrative power needs to shift further before we can see structural change. While we're making progress, there's still a long way to go. We haven't reached all young people or all people of color, and we never will—but we don't need to. The goal is to reach a tipping point where enough people see our struggle as their own and understand that this fight is about a broader value system where human lives are valued and oppression is universally opposed.

We're making strides, but there's much more work to be done on the narrative front before we can achieve the structural change we aim for. We're up against a powerful system, and I don't fully know what it will take to enact radical, significant change. But I know it will require enough of us to keep fighting and pushing for justice until the status quo becomes unsustainable.

Noura: I agree with Tanya and just want to add that it's incredibly disheartening to witness the most diverse Democratic National Committee (DNC) in history mock and malign Palestinians, including those who are supposed to be part of their own party. It's equally troubling to see that same Democratic establishment collaborate to sabotage efforts for a cease-fire—a cease-fire that could end this suffering.

Despite this, the one thing that keeps me from despair is the belief that we are ultimately on the right side of history. Morally, Israel's actions have been exposed for what they are, and Zionism as an ideology no longer has broad moral sway, as it once did among Americans. The only way Israel has been able to maintain its position is through coercive force, punishment, harassment, and threats—by silencing those who speak out against it. There's no longer a robust, widespread support for the idea of Jewish liberation as manifested by the Israeli state. Those who do support it are a minority, relying on state violence to suppress opposition.

This realization brings me some solace. I think of the countless ancestors of many peoples who have faced similar apocalyptic moments and knew that, despite the overwhelming pain, they were on the path to victory. That's where I stand right now.

Shanelle and Marzena: Has this movement moment expanded the possibilities for the decolonial project? Has it shifted how people perceive decolonization—not as a distant, theoretical idea, but as a tangible, daily practice within reach?[1]

Tanya: If we're talking about the American public—which is where my perspective comes from, working within U.S. narrative and media—I don't think we're there yet. I don't think the average person, or enough of the general public, fully understands colonialism as a concept. There's still a lot of work to be done on this front. That being said, I do think more people are starting to recognize that Israel has been oppressing Palestinians for decades and that this didn't just begin in October. Awareness of root causes is growing, but more work must be done. The more we can help people understand those root causes, the more precise the general understanding of colonialism and, therefore, decolonization will become.

Noura: I don't think we're any closer, unfortunately. In fact, what's coming down the line is likely more oppression. We're already seeing increased punishment for those of us who have participated. Universities are starting to create new rules; for example, the University of California system has just banned encampments and face masks. Here at Rutgers, we see measures that essentially reduce protests to mere performance theater—allowing you to speak but not challenge or impact power.

At the same time, I believe this generation, who have directly experienced or participated in protests and encampments, is going through a formative period. There's a deep generational divide, with young people getting their information from social media while their elders rely on cable networks. This divide has become particularly pronounced among those whose bodies have been on the front lines, bearing the brunt of police violence. For instance, my nephew, who was maced and jailed during a protest on his college campus, couldn't understand why his university was punishing him for standing up to protect children and babies. This kind of experience profoundly shapes young people, who will eventually come to power in one way or another.

So, while I think we're headed for more repression in the short term, there's also hope. This generation's understanding of colonization, state violence, and the weaponization of terms like *terrorism* is no longer just theoretical—it's rooted in their lived experiences. And that will shape who they become and how they move forward, even if we don't see the full impact immediately.

Tanya: Thank you, Noura, for that bit of hope, which can feel so hard to find these days. I remind myself that sometimes things have to get worse before they get better. Especially with this, because we're challenging the very foundation of the state of Israel—its oppressive, colonial nature—and that's no small feat. It will take everything we have, knowing this is a marathon, not a sprint.

In many ways, this is just the beginning, despite the decades of work behind us and the efforts of our elders before us. This moment is different, and while the road ahead is long, we are also witnessing the awakening of a generation that won't return to the status quo. As Noura said, people have been awakened, and there's no going back.

Shanelle and Marzena: It has been seventy-six years since the 1948 Nakba, when Palestinians were massacred and expelled from their homes. Since then, the Palestinian people have been under decades of occupation, oppression, and genocide, as well as organizing a powerful and ongoing resistance. Considering this revolutionary lineage, what is your vision for the Palestinian people in 2048, a century after the Nakba? What is extinct because of this work? What exists?

Noura: I envision a Palestinian future where children are mostly concerned with learning how to share toys, not with how to find their friends under rubble. It's tragic that such a simple, basic future is what we have to imagine—just the ability to dream without limitations. For me, any Palestinian future isn't about returning to the time before Israeli colonization; it's about the future we create together. I hope we can find the space to build that future together—to experience self-determination as a people, as a collective, with a shared past and a common future that we can forge together.

Tanya: That's so beautiful, Noura. You captured everything I'm thinking—and what so many Palestinians are thinking. A question we often ask ourselves as Palestinians: What would you be doing with your life if you weren't fighting for liberation? It's a beautiful thought. Fighting for our freedom is a duty, and we'll always do it, as long as it's necessary. Still, I look forward to a world where we can just be human beings with full lives, hobbies, desires, and the chance to know ourselves and our community outside of this struggle. A world where the fight for freedom is part of our history but not something that defines our daily lives, and we can simply live and exist.

BLACK LIBERATION AND INDIGENOUS RESISTANCE

The Movement for Black Lives, Narrative Power, and the Black Radical Tradition

By Shanelle Matthews and Miski Noor

We Gon' Be Alright: A New Era of Black Liberation

It was a hot July day on the campus of Cleveland State University, where thousands of people buzzed between buildings on the final day of an inaugural convening hosted by the Movement for Black Lives. This newly formed coalition, born from the resistance to the killings of Trayvon Martin and Michael Brown and the Ferguson uprisings of 2014 and 2015 that followed, had brought together 2,000 people and organizations from across the United States, the Dominican Republic, and several African countries. United by common experiences of police and state violence, participants spent two and a half days deliberating on how to nurture a mass movement for Black safety, power, and self-determination. Many had never before been part of formal organizing collectives. Still, they were driven by a collective outrage and a deep-seated passion to continue the tradition of Black organizing for a self-determined future.

As the convening wrapped up and people began boarding buses and packing up cars, a situation unfolded in the street. A young boy, around fourteen years old, was being interrogated by police for allegedly drinking in public. Despite the boy being a minor with no parent or guardian present, the police intended to detain and arrest him. Quickly, a congregation of participants, some trained in de-escalation tactics, formed a protective circle around the boy and the police, locking arms in solidarity. The security team and legal observers from the convening were deployed. Rukia Lumumba, a Jackson,

Mississippi, attorney and activist, intervened by contacting the boy's mother, whom the police had not allowed him to call.

Despite the police's antagonism, the crowd's persistence prevented the boy from being taken into custody. Many participants, more concerned with the boy's safety than their travel plans, stayed to ensure his release. When his mother arrived, the boy was released into her custody, and a Breathalyzer test revealed that he had not been drinking. As they left, the congregation formed a celebratory soul train line, chanting, "We love you! We, we love you!" This act of "de-arresting" the boy exemplified the abolitionist values of the coalition, which is committed to reducing the size, scope, and power of the carceral state—a system designed to control and criminalize marginalized communities.

Policing in the United States has long been an apparatus for organizing and controlling the lives of Black people, with a history rooted in anti-Black oppression. To justify this oppression, the ruling class has employed various narrative strategies over the centuries, each aimed at dehumanizing Black people and legitimizing their subjugation. From the "Curse of Ham" and the "civilizing mission," to pseudoscientific racism and the portrayal of Black people as inherently criminal, these narratives have evolved but remain deeply embedded in the fabric of American society. They serve to justify mass incarceration, police brutality, racial profiling, and the maintenance of a racial hierarchy.

Cleveland's history as a key stop on the Underground Railroad, known as "Hope" for its role in the abolitionist movement, contrasts sharply with the city's ongoing struggles with systemic racism. While slavery was outlawed in Ohio, anti-Black racism persisted, showing that legal reforms alone cannot dismantle deeply ingrained ideological oppression. Narratives that perpetuate stereotypes about Black communities continue to contribute to their marginalization, becoming ingrained in collective consciousness and reinforcing systemic anti-Black racism.

The profiling and subsequent de-arrest of the young boy in Cleveland illustrate how narratives function within systems of power and resistance. While the intentions of individual police officers may be unknown, it is well-documented that Black people are disproportionately profiled and arrested. The false justification that the boy was drunk could have led to his detention, further criminalizing him based on a deeply rooted narrative of Black criminality. He could have died at the hands of police like twelve-year-old Tamir Rice the year before. However, the convening's abolitionist organizers, demanding the police "Let him go!" and resisting their actions, actively demonstrated the fluid and evolving nature of ideological oppression and resistance.

As the boy and his mother left, someone played Kendrick Lamar's "Alright," a movement anthem that echoed the collective will and power of the coalition. The lyrics symbolized more than hope—they declared the power and resilience of a new coalition determined to bring abolitionist arguments and reparations into mainstream discourse. As the organizers dispersed, a butterfly fluttered overhead, a fitting symbol of the transformative magic and power that had been unleashed.

This chapter explores how the Movement for Black Lives, through decentralized organizing, policy making, electoral justice efforts, and a narrative power strategy, effectively challenged and delegitimized the narratives of Black pathology that have long been used to justify racial profiling, criminalization, and the militarization of police in Black communities. By reframing Black suffering as "state-sanctioned violence"—harm institutionalized by the state against Black communities—the movement shifted the blame squarely onto the state, demanding accountability and justice.

Shattering the Postracial Myth: Broken Promises of the Obama Era

The Black Lives Matter movement emerged as a forceful challenge to the narrative of a "postracial America." This narrative gained traction with the election of Barack Obama, the nation's first Black president. As Obama entered his second term, the disconnect between the promises of his campaign and the lived realities of Black communities became glaringly apparent. Frustrations ran high among movement leaders in Ferguson and beyond, who demanded that Obama fulfill his pledge to "insist on a full measure of justice in every aspect of American life." Despite the overwhelming support Black voters had shown for both of his presidential campaigns, many in these communities felt that little had changed.

Princeton University professor and historian of social movements Keeanga-Yamahtta Taylor observed this in her book *From Black Lives Matter to Black Liberation*: "While it may be surprising that a Black protest movement has emerged during the Obama presidency, the reluctance of his administration to address any of the substantive issues facing Black communities has meant that suffering has worsened in those communities over the course of Obama's term of office. , , , African-Americans under Obama are experiencing the same indifference and active discrimination; in some cases, these have become worse."[1]

The myth of a "postracial" America—one where race no longer mattered—was shattered as police violence and systemic racism continued unabated. From the 2009 killing of Oscar Grant by a transit officer in Oakland to the 2012 shootings of Rekia Boyd and twelve-year-old Tamir Rice, the 2014 deaths of Mike Brown and Eric Garner, and the 2015 deaths of Sandra Bland and Freddie Gray in police custody, it became clear that the promise of hope and change had not materialized for ordinary Black people.

The postracial myth perpetuated a harmful deception by gaslighting Black Americans, whose firsthand experiences of systemic violence—whether through police brutality, medical neglect, economic disenfranchisement, or narrative oppression—reflected the persistent and deeply rooted nature of anti-Black racism in America. This myth attempted to obscure the reality of ongoing anti-Black racism by controlling and manipulating stories and maintaining the existing racial hierarchy. Many U.S. Black organizers rallied to elect Obama, donning "Ba-ROCK the vote" T-shirts and passionately supporting the Democratic Party to spread a message of hope and change. Simultaneously, we were confronted with the harsh reality that Obama was escalating drone strikes in our home countries, targeting our people—actively perpetuating and overseeing violence against diasporic Black communities both within and beyond U.S. borders. Black organizers were forced to grapple with the difficult truth that the first Black president, whom many hoped would be a natural ally, instead became an adversary of the movement. This marked a pivotal moment of emotional and strategic growth, as parts of the Black liberation struggle had to recalibrate its approach, learning to hold even those who share kinship accountable when they uphold oppressive systems.

As state-sanctioned violence claimed Black lives across the country, the postracial illusion disappeared, and "Black Lives Matter" became a rallying cry that transcended borders, regimes, languages, and cultures. The movement echoed through the streets, airwaves, digital spaces, and the halls of Congress, making it clear that Obama could not be—and never intended to be—the savior of Black people. Only Black communities themselves could lead the fight for their liberation.

Oppressed African diasporic communities worldwide have developed, tested, and amassed a wealth of tools, resources, strategies, and wisdom to fight for their liberation and construct alternative realities in opposition to white supremacist, settler-colonial agendas. This collective accumulation is what political theorist Cedric Robinson terms the Black radical tradition—a rich tapestry of cultural, intellectual, and action-oriented labor rooted in anticolonial and antislavery efforts.[2] This tradition is not defined solely by resistance against oppressive forces but also by the joy, embodiment, and love that sustain and empower these communities.

Narrative Power and the Black Radical Tradition

George Lipsitz describes the Black radical tradition as "the culture of opposition that has emerged and thrived within everyday life, evolving through expressive culture and underground activism."[3] Central to this tradition is the discipline of narrative power building, which has been instrumental in shaping and socializing Black liberation struggles. Narrative power refers to the ability to shape and control the stories told within a society, including who tells them, what stories are told, and how they are interpreted. Building narrative power is about the capacity to influence perceptions, beliefs, and behaviors through storytelling.

The role of narrative power and communication strategies in advancing a Black liberatory agenda in the United States is deeply rooted in history. Practically, during the era of chattel slavery, enslaved Africans, known as the "Borderland Maroons," established covert communication networks between plantations. These networks were crucial in assisting runaways, helping them navigate the difficult path from slavery to freedom. They forged a powerful means of resistance and survival by operating within the margins between bondage and liberation.

The Underground Railroad, though symbolic, was a vital communication network among runaways and the enslaved, delivering lifesaving information that guided many to freedom. The metaphor was instrumental in keeping people safe. The railroad operated in secrecy in the early to mid-1800s, using coded language, signals, and symbols to communicate and coordinate efforts without being detected by authorities. "Conductors," like Harriet Tubman, were crucial in guiding people. When teased out, this metaphor serves as a powerful framework for understanding and organizing resistance to oppression.

In the early twentieth century, abolitionists like Ida B. Wells harnessed the power of the printing press to expose the horrors of lynching, challenge the legitimacy of white supremacist tools of terror and control, and awaken the conscience of those unaware of or indifferent to the gruesome reality, urging them to demand its abolition. By the 1960s, civil rights organizers innovatively used Wide Area Telephone Services (WATS) to circumvent telephone companies complicit with police surveillance. Today, movements like #BlackLivesMatter and #SayHerName leverage digital platforms to spread contemporary counternarratives, amplifying the voices of communities routinely excluded or vilified by mainstream and elite media.

Traditions like the Black radical tradition guide us and anchor our actions to core values and historical roots. They are essential for building narrative power, offering a foundational and shared story that shapes our movement's objectives and identity. With deep cultural and historical significance, traditions reinforce collective identity, foster connections, and provide continuity with our past and future. For communications workers, traditions are invaluable, often involving storytelling and symbolism that create meaning in our liberatory efforts. They offer resilience, remind us of our long-term goals, and lend legitimacy to our movement, rooted in culture, history, and an unwavering commitment to freedom.

For the past decade, the Movement for Black Lives has strategically deployed a spectrum of tactics rooted in the Black radical tradition to disrupt entrenched power structures and construct a counterhegemonic reality where all Black lives are valued. From time-honored methods like direct action to contemporary content creation and distribution approaches, six chapters in this book contextualize the diverse strategies that define the Black radical tradition in the twenty-first century—Tutashinda and Faison, pp. 331; Black LGBTQIA+ Migrant Project, pp. 165; Steeze, pp. 321;

Fuller and Beek, pp. 127; Brutus, Torres, and Smith, pp. 101; and Cotta and Saavedra pp. 361.

These essays highlight the innovative strategies deeply rooted in the Black radical tradition that have been, and continue to be, crucial in confronting oppressive systems and carving out spaces where all Black lives are affirmed and valued. As the Movement for Black Lives steps into its next decade, the lessons and insights presented here are a powerful testament to the ongoing struggle and the creative resilience inherent in Black resistance. The narratives and analyses within these chapters reflect the movement's historical challenges and victories, offering inspiration for future actions that will further advance Black liberation and self-determination. The essays grapple with a complex interplay of power, morality, nationalism, identity, place, faith, misogynoir, sexual violence, harm, and repair.

From Black Pathology to State-Sanctioned Violence

Black Pathology

Central to these discussions is a deeply ingrained and harmful belief: that Black people are inherently dysfunctional and diseased. This narrative casts Black communities as perpetual outsiders—"othered" and not truly American, as evidenced by the frequent admonition to "go back to where one came from." Black people are often depicted as morally inferior, criminally inclined, or sexually voracious, making them unworthy of recognition as victims of state or sexual violence, crime, or coercion. This distorted view serves to justify oppression and the denial of justice, accountability, and reparative measures for the harm inflicted upon them.

The persistence of the declaration that Black Lives Matter challenges the notion of a postracial society, highlighting the ongoing subjugation of Black people, from which oppressive forces continue to profit. Racial capitalism exemplifies this dynamic: it is the fusion of racial subordination with exploitation, production, and capital. Historically and presently, Black labor has been central to fueling the engine of capitalism. The dominant or hegemonic group gains from this subjugation because it sustains social and racial hierarchies, preserving their power and privilege. Such subjugation is inherently immoral in a democracy, a system that claims to provide equal treatment under the law.

Oppressive forces justify this subjugation by constructing a mythology of Black pathology—blaming Black people for their suffering and depicting them as dysfunctional, inherently unwell, and subhuman. This narrative casts Black communities as the "other," a pariah to both the nation and the world. It allows white people (and, to some extent, non-Black people of color) to maintain a false sense of moral and racial superiority. This propaganda is coordinated across multiple domains of power, reinforcing these oppressive structures.

By pathologizing Black women as sexually promiscuous and impervious to pain, society absolves the medical-industrial complex of its role in perpetuating anti-Black racism in delivery rooms, doctors' offices, and health clinics. This narrative also shifts blame onto Black survivors of sexual violence, protecting their abusers from accountability. Similarly, far beyond being exploited for entertainment or the commodification of culture for profit, Black trans and queer people—who often serve as the blueprint for popular culture—are consistently marginalized, criminalized, and penalized simply for existing. Despite their profound cultural influence, they remain relegated to the edges of American society, facing systemic oppression for living authentically. By disparaging poor Black people and attributing their socioeconomic conditions to personal failings, society ignores the centuries of racialized economic exploitation, including slavery and indentured servitude, that have shaped their circumstances.

Imperialist, white supremacist, and capitalist propaganda serve to reinforce the status quo by assigning blame to individuals, ensuring that existing power structures are seen as the most reasonable and legitimate. By shifting responsibility onto individuals and promoting a culture of moral, social, and economic hierarchy, these systems obscure the deeply entrenched hegemonic and toxic frameworks that shape our lives, allowing them to continue operating unchecked. This strategic deflection ensures that societal and moral failings are attributed solely to the individual, diverting critical attention from the structural forces driving inequality and injustice. Thus, the status quo remains unchallenged, while individuals bear the burden of systemic failures, preventing any meaningful challenge to those in power.

This ideological contest is not new. The Black radical tradition is a generations-long project in which narrative and storytelling play crucial roles in challenging the hegemonic narrative and envisioning a prophetic society where Black lives truly matter. Picking up where our predecessors left off, the twenty-first-century Black liberation movement, through the use of narrative power building, delegitimized narratives of Black pathology that were used to justify the wars on poverty and drugs and the militarization of police in Black communities. In turn, the movement put the blame for Black suffering where it belongs—on the state—recasting Black pathology as "state-sanctioned violence," which includes "any forms of harm produced, promoted, and/or institutionalized by the state to the detriment of Black women, their families, and communities."[4] Through decentralized organizing, policy making, electoral justice, a narrative power strategy, and other tactics, M4BL—an ecosystem of Black-led organizations—uses symbolic resources to reframe how we understand Black suffering in America and offer a vision for reducing it.[5]

The state is fundamentally a violent apparatus—manifesting through systems like chattel slavery, economic deprivation, mass incarceration, family separation, medical neglect, and police violence. Not only does the state engineer these forms of violence, but it also legitimizes them by manipulating ideologies and belief systems, making control, law, and order appear as common sense. To maintain power and authority, the state shifts the blame for sociopolitical issues like addiction, crime, and homelessness onto individuals or marginalized communities. This, in turn, makes those individuals or communities responsible for addressing the problems, diverting attention from structural causes.

The antidote to this cultural and material domination—reinforced by the hegemonic beliefs of the capitalist and political elite—lies in the creation of counternarratives. These narratives, grounded in the lived experiences of those subjected to exclusion and oppression, challenge the status quo. By sharing stories of dispossession and disenfranchisement, we can expose the state's role in perpetuating violence. This process delegitimizes the notion that individual responsibility alone is the cause or solution to societal issues, making state violence visible and comprehensible to the general public, rather than hidden behind ideological constructs.

While an essential and foundational function within movement and power

A demonstrator dances during the Defund the Police march in Minneapolis, MN, on June 6, 2020. Photo by Teddy Grimes, Extensive Knowledge Productions

building, narrative power alone cannot change the material conditions of the lives of hundreds of millions of oppressed Black people in the United States and globally. While narrative power shapes how people perceive and engage with the world, structural power shapes the realities within which these perceptions are formed. Given that the carceral state is responsible for inflicting massive violence on Black communities, it stands to reason that ensuring Black people's safety requires a significant reduction in the size, scope, and budget of the carceral system. These resources should instead be reinvested in life-affirming policies and infrastructure. The approach of divesting from systems that harm Black communities and investing in alternative systems of care has deep roots in social justice movements and was powerfully reinforced during the 2020 global uprising against racialized oppression and police violence.

Defund the Police: A Radical Legacy of Abolitionist Rhetoric

In the summer of 2020, following the brutal murders of Breonna Taylor and George Floyd by police, millions of people across the country took to

Demonstrators march from Bottineau Field Park to the home of Mayor Jacob Frey in Minneapolis, MN, on June 6, 2020. Photo by Teddy Grimes, Extensive Knowledge Productions

the streets, transforming urban rebellions into powerful mobilizations that demanded not just justice for the victims but a complete reimagining of public safety. An urban rebellion is an unplanned outpouring of collective outrage, while mass mobilizations channel this outrage into organized opposition against specific policies and practices.[6]

The slogan "Defund the Police" emerged as a rallying cry, calling for the reduction of police power, budgets, and influence and for investing in new community infrastructures that would ensure proper safety and sustainability for Black communities.

Persuasive discourse hinges on the consistency and resonance of the frames used in public debate. The debate around abolition is not unique to our time; it has evolved over centuries, with abolitionist movements continually adapting to their eras' social and political contexts. Early movements often relied on moral persuasion and gradual legal reforms, such as the Quakers' seventeenth-century opposition to slavery on religious grounds.[7]

By the eighteenth century, abolitionism became more organized, with efforts focused on legal changes, public awareness campaigns, and colonization projects like Liberia. The nineteenth century marked the peak of abolitionism in the United States and the British Empire, with calls for immediate

emancipation and civil rights for Black Americans. This period saw abolitionists increasingly seek political solutions, culminating in the Civil War
and the passage of the Thirteenth Amendment. Global efforts also played a
significant role in the abolitionist cause.[8]

The "divest-invest" frame has emerged in the contemporary context, advocating for reallocating resources from punitive institutions to community-
centered ones. The concept of divest-invest has its roots in enduring criticisms
of excessive policing and the call for more comprehensive approaches to public safety. Scholars, activists, and everyday people have contended that large
police budgets divert resources away from vital services like mental health
care, education, housing, and community development, which are more effective in addressing the underlying causes of crime and social issues.[9]

The Cultural Resonance of "Defund the Police" as a Meme

However, it was *not* the "divest-invest" slogan that animated people and political activity in 2020; it was the "defund the police" slogan, and that matters if
we understand four things:

1. *Defund the Police is a meme, and memes endure because they resonate deeply with people and fulfill specific functions within a culture*:
   Meme is a concept introduced by Richard Dawkins in *The Selfish
   Gene* (1976), which draws an analogy between how ideas spread in
   society and how genes transmit biological traits. Dawkins proposed
   that just as genes carry biological information, a meme carries cultural
   information—such as behaviors, ideas, or beliefs—that spread from
   person to person.

   Ideas and symbols that strike a chord with people become embedded
   in cultural practices and passed along, much like inherited traits. Memes
   that serve a purpose or resonate deeply with a community find ways to
   thrive. In the Black radical tradition, memes can be seen through key
   symbols and ideas passed down and adapted over generations.

   For instance, the slogan "Power to the People," popularized by the
   Black Panther Party, became a meme that represented the fight for
   Black self-determination and resistance against systemic oppression.

The raised fist, a gesture symbolizing solidarity and defiance, has been replicated across various movements, from the civil rights era to Black Lives Matter protests. Likewise, Malcolm X's phrase "By Any Means Necessary" spread as a call for freedom and justice, inspiring generations of activists to pursue liberation without restraint. These examples highlight how crucial ideas and symbols within the Black radical tradition spread like cultural memes, evolving while remaining deeply embedded in the collective fight for liberation and justice.[10]

2. *Not all slogans are equally compelling*: Slogans are crafted to make a lasting impression and provoke emotional responses. They not only justify actions but also wield significant emotional influence, serving as potent tools for mobilization. "Defund the police and invest in Black communities" is a powerful, incendiary offshoot of the divest-invest slogan. It is designed to provoke strong reactions and emotions, something the more neutral phrase "divest-invest" does not achieve with the same intensity. "Defund the Police" captures the urgency and radical shift that today's movement demands, making it a potent rallying cry in the fight for justice. By nature, effective slogans encapsulate complex ideas and values, making them accessible and appealing to a broad audience.

3. *The currency of story is not truth but meaning*: In their 2010 book *Re: Imagining Change*, Doyle Canning and Patrick Reinsborough argue that the value of a story or narrative lies not necessarily in its factual accuracy but in the significance and understanding it conveys to its audience.[11] Meaning lies in the interpretation of the reader or listener; different people derive varied meanings from the same narrative based on their personal experiences, beliefs, and values. A slogan like "Defund the Police" is meant to provoke or inflame emotions, reactions, or conflict, trigger intense anger, passion, or opposition, or incite action. It serves as an on-ramp to broader discourse, whereas "divest-invest" is insider, left jargon that does not have the same rhetorical power with broader audiences.

4. *Effective slogans have a priming effect*: Ideas that seem "impossible" or "extreme" might not be adopted immediately, but history demonstrates that people often seek out innovative and unconventional

solutions during times of crisis. By presenting ideas with a long-term vision for change, you lay the groundwork, and eventually, a significant event or shift will make these once-fringe ideas appear newly achievable. In 2021, in Uvalde, Texas, after children and teachers were massacred in a school shooting, public discourse showed everyday people questioning the utility of the police and speculating where resources for public safety could be more effective.

Leveraging Mainstream Platforms for Revolutionary Purposes

In the twenty-first century, media discourse is increasingly dominated by brief, catchy, and easily digestible information. Complex issues like "divest-invest" are often distilled into short, memorable phrases that can be quickly shared and consumed, particularly on digital platforms. This trend prioritizes speed and simplicity over depth and nuance, frequently leading to oversimplifying critical topics. As a result, messages are crafted to capture immediate attention, often sacrificing the context necessary for a fuller understanding. However, contemporary tactics can also serve as vehicles for revolutionary ideas, helping movements penetrate the hegemonic media apparatus that seeks to obscure or erase narratives of the oppressed.

Nina Simone's journey with protest music exemplifies this tension between simplicity and substance. Initially resistant to the genre, Simone felt that much of protest music lacked the imagination and dignity necessary to truly honor the struggles it aimed to represent.[12] But the brutal murders of NAACP organizer Medgar Evers and the "four little girls" killed in the Sixteenth Street Baptist Church bombing—Addie, Carol, Denise, and Cynthia—compelled her to use her platform to challenge the dominant narratives of racial supremacy. With her 1963 song "Mississippi Goddamn," Simone painted a vivid picture of anti-Black violence and the resistance against it, using music as a counterhegemonic tool.

During the civil rights and Black Power movements of the 1960s and 1970s, protest music became an essential, culturally relevant vehicle for subversive ideas, also serving to solidify movement groups further. Solidification is a crucial process within agitating groups, aimed at uniting followers and fostering a strong sense of community that is essential for the movement's success.

This involves rhetorical tactics that reinforce group cohesiveness, making members more responsive to the group's beliefs, values, and ideologies.[13] Though challenging, solidification is vital, particularly in decentralized and highly energized dissent movements.

As a form of solidification, music serves as a powerful rhetorical tool because it entertains and raises consciousness by resonating with those who already support the movement or those open to persuasion. Protest music creates a shared social reality through language, rhythm, and tone, strengthening in-group solidarity, political resolve, and a sense of belonging.[14] Simone recognized that while protest music might be imperfect, it was a strategic mobilizing vehicle for its time, one that could make the invisible visible to the masses. She continued to use her gift to shine a light on the injustices the dominant culture sought to hide, demonstrating the enduring power of art as a tool for resistance and solidarity.

Provocation and Persecution

In his critique of the defund movement, former president Obama argued that "snappy" slogans like "Defund the Police" can alienate people, diminishing their intended impact.[15] However, Obama's historical stance on anti-Black racism and policing has consistently prioritized appeasing law enforcement over confronting systemic injustice. His support for toothless reforms, the creation of ineffective task forces, and the rhetoric of gradualism have failed to address the root causes of state violence against Black communities. This approach perpetuates the false notion that incremental reforms or symbolic Black representation in office will lead to meaningful change. In reality, the refusal to engage with the material conditions faced by everyday Black citizens is a privilege of the rich and powerful—a privilege that Obama himself embodies. He was not the audience for this message then, nor is he now. Instead, he is an adversary in the fight for a radical new vision of public safety that protects all Black lives.

The demand to defund the police is rooted in a long history of abolitionist organizing that has adapted to different eras and contexts. Different eras demand different strategies. Today's movement uses provocative and emotionally charged slogans like "Defund the Police" to capture public attention and drive the conversation. While the slogan may be incendiary shorthand, it emotionally communicates the urgency of the demand and the need for a fundamental shift in how society approaches public safety.

The defund movement encountered a well-coordinated campaign by state governments to suppress and stigmatize its demands. In a blatant abuse of power, the federal government, under the direction of the disgraced former president Donald Trump and former attorney general William Barr, deliberately targeted supporters of the movement for Black lives. This state-sponsored persecution aimed to disrupt and dismantle the movement by criminalizing its leaders and participants. As a result, hundreds of organizers and activists were hit with severe federal charges, leading to years-long prison sentences without the possibility of parole.[16]

The state's crackdown in 2020 marked a significant escalation in the use of policing and prosecution as tools of repression. The federal government spread anti-BLM propaganda, vilifying protesters as "violent radicals," and imposing inflated federal indictments that carried far harsher penalties than local charges. This tactic was a deliberate attempt to wrest control from local communities that had risen up in protest nationwide, further entrenching state power and silencing dissent.

The left also experienced significant internal conflict as progressive forces criticized defund organizers for being "divisive" and "unstrategic," even as they reaped the benefits of the bold rhetoric. The radical flank effect—where a more extreme faction within a movement strengthens the position of more moderate elements—was pivotal in the defund campaign. Though some tactics and rhetoric were seen as controversial, they succeeded in amplifying the movement's demands, enabling more moderate voices to gain legitimacy and broader support by comparison.

According to research by GenForward and the Movement for Black Lives, close to 55 percent of Black people in the United States support (25 percent "strongly," 30 percent "somewhat") divesting from police departments and investing their entire budgets in other areas, such as health care, education, and housing. Two-thirds of Black people express support (31 percent "strongly," 36 percent "somewhat") for reallocating part of police budgets toward such investments.[17]

In 2020, we secured over $840 million in direct cuts from U.S. police departments. More than twenty major cities reduced police budgets in some form, and in twenty-five cities, officials removed police from schools, saving an additional $34 million.[18] In Minneapolis, 44 percent of voters supported a 2021 ballot measure to replace the police department with a "public-health oriented" Department of Public Safety. Although the measure did not pass, it demonstrated that a significant portion of the public understands and supports the deeper meaning behind the call to defund the police and invest in Black communities. In fact, more Minneapolis residents voted for this new vision of safety than they did for the incumbent mayor who opposed it, indicating the people's desire for something new rather than the existing status quo.

While some of our gains have been rolled back, others remain intact, and we've successfully brought global attention to the abolitionist argument that the only way to prevent more deaths at the hands of police is by stripping them of power and funding and reinvesting those resources into alternative public safety measures. Initiatives like the Dream Defenders Healing and Justice Center and the Movement for Black Lives' People's Response Campaign: Emergencies in Better Hands exemplify this shift, advancing public safety solutions that prioritize the needs and experiences of Black communities by treating safety as a public health issue. The persistence of the movement in keeping this issue on the political agenda, despite fierce opposition, demonstrates the power of narrative to shift public perception and create lasting change.

As we continue to reimagine public safety and advocate for investments in people rather than policing, the defund movement has already made a significant impact by challenging dominant narratives and pushing for bold, destabilizing demands. What the empire dismissed as a "snappy slogan" was, in fact, a deliberate and strategic decision made by organizers gathered in someone's living room the Memorial Day of George Floyd's death, two blocks away from Cup Foods where Darnella Frazier took that fateful video. The chronic underestimation of Black strategy and intelligence stems from deeply ingrained narratives of Black inferiority. Yet, it is precisely this underestimation that provides movement workers the cover to craft strategies that thrust radical ideas into public discourse and prime people for revolutionary political approaches. Underestimate us at your own peril, empire, for we will shake the foundations of this oppressive regime until a new dawn breaks, and the people lay claim to what is rightfully ours.

Conclusion

The Cleveland convening was not simply about strategies and slogans; it was about building a community capable of intervening in anti-Black violence and living out abolitionist values. This collective action continues as the Movement for Black Lives (M4BL) and its allies consistently reframe Black suffering as a consequence of state violence, not inherent pathology. The de-arresting moment captured the movement's vision of protecting, uplifting, and freeing Black lives, offering a glimpse into the abolitionist future M4BL is fighting for.

M4BL embodies the twenty-first-century continuation of the Black radical tradition, fiercely committed to dismantling the intertwined systems of white supremacy, capitalism, and state-sanctioned violence. When we rallied to protect that young boy from wrongful arrest, we demonstrated the movement's core values: rejecting state violence and caring for the most vulnerable. This act of "de-arresting" the boy symbolized a broader fight against systemic oppression, as M4BL challenges the deep-seated narratives that have pathologized Black communities for generations.

By exposing Black suffering as a product of state-sanctioned violence, M4BL flips the script, holding the state accountable for its role in perpetuating harm. This narrative reclamation is not just rhetorical but a radical resistance demanding a global reckoning challenging the legitimacy of the carceral state and making clear the urgent need for abolitionist futures. The fight for Black liberation is a call for the complete transformation of the systems that oppress, exploit, and kill Black people. The movement's strength lies in its ability to control the narrative, mobilize communities, and confront the entrenched powers that maintain the status quo.

Like the butterfly that fluttered overhead, symbolizing transformation, M4BL continues to evolve. We are driven by the understanding that not just narratives but the material conditions of Black people worldwide must change. Anchored in the Black radical tradition, the movement presses forward, determined to create a future where all Black lives truly matter.

Reframing Environmental Justice in the 21st Century: Movement Convergence in the Wake of the 2020 Uprisings

By Cameron Oglesby and Dr. Benjamin F. Chavis Jr.

The Birth of a Movement

In autumn 1982, a predominantly Black and poor community in Warren County, North Carolina, found itself at the center of a burgeoning movement for environmental justice. The state government had decided to locate a hazardous waste landfill in their area to dispose of soil that had been illegally contaminated with polychlorinated biphenyls (PCBs). The decision not only to place these cancer-causing, immune system suppressing chemicals just seven minutes from the county seat, but also to exploit the situation to build a permanent toxic waste facility in one of the state's poorest counties, was indicative of a larger, underrealized injustice of the previous decades: the disproportionate placement of hazardous substances and polluting industries in the disinvested, racially minoritized, and impoverished centers of rural America. The state government, like so many institutions before it, presumed a lack of political will and willpower from Warren County residents would make it easy to establish this new landfill; they were instead met with a revolution.

As word of the state's decision spread—a selection made without community buy-in or notice—the residents of Warren County organized. This was a congregation steeped in communal values: a community birthed centuries earlier out of the remnants of slavery that had decided to organize again to maintain their freedom. Spearheaded inside the hallowed halls and pews of Coley Springs Baptist Church, just down the street from the landfill

The Rev. Leon White, Evelyn Lowery, Dr. Joseph Lowery, Walter Fauntroy, Ken Ferruccio, Rev. Curtis W. Harris, and Dr. James Green lead a march on September 27, 1982. Photo by Jenny Labalme

site, the community orchestrated a massive protest for their right to clean air and water.

For six intense weeks, the streets of Afton in Warren County became the battleground for a fierce campaign of civil disobedience. Men, women, and children marched and lay, vulnerable, in the road, blocking the passage of trucks laden with toxic soil. The fervent tune of "Ain't Gonna Let Nobody Turn Me Around" and similar chants set a tone of righteous fury and hope against all hope. Residents were eventually joined by civil rights activists and environmentalists who, in a show of solidarity, were cuffed and processed alongside the over 500 individuals who were arrested during the protests. It was from a jail cell in Warren County that the term "environmental racism" was first coined, bringing national attention to a town that, previously, barely received a passing thought.

The Warren County PCB protests brought to the forefront of public consciousness the interconnectedness of lived environments and racism in the United States, revealing the systemic inequities faced by historically

Children and teenagers lie on a North Carolina road on October 4, 1982, to protest and block trucks hauling PCB-laced soil to a nearby landfill. Photo by Jenny Labalme

disinvested populations in many of this country's unknown neighborhoods and townships. The impact of these protests was profound. This grassroots activism was the precursor to the formalization of a movement that finally intersected environmental issues with social justice. In fact, the greatest progress in environmental justice movements has occurred when they've aligned with other social justice and human rights movements—rather than with traditional environmentalism.

Although the protests in 1982 were only the first step in what would be a long-term, concerted campaign to limit pollution exposure in Warren County, this story represents one of the most famous examples of the power of movement convergence. The second major moment came in 2020, when the uprisings for racial justice reinvigorated the contemporary environmental justice movement and highlighted the narrative power made possible by the convergence of human-centered movements. This chapter explores the intersections of Black liberation and environmental justice—and how together they are able to grow in power and salience.

A Light Background on the Environmental Justice Movement

The Environmental Justice (EJ) movement was born in the United States as a counterfactual to the modern environmental movements of the 1960s and 1970s. At the time, leaders like Rachel Carson emphasized a "Silent Spring"[1] that positioned humanity in opposition to vulnerable natural systems and creatures, while Nixon's presidency set a precedent for a whitewashed version of environmentalism through Earth Day. In response, the EJ movement sought to highlight the overlooked intersections of environmental and social justice by challenging the predominantly white narrative that had dominated American environmental consciousness since the days of John Muir[2] and President Teddy Roosevelt's[3,4] expansion of the national parks system.

The movement's primary goal has been to ensure that all people and the planet are viewed as interconnected, emphasizing ecosystems' and individuals' collective health and well-being as inseparable. EJ has called for fair treatment of all individuals concerning the benefits and harms of environmental degradation and conservation efforts. This concept has been present in the United States for centuries, often undergirded by Indigenous practice and ancestral wisdom, rooted in a long-standing respect for both people and the planet. However, the EJ movement—as an internationally recognized effort to combat the systemic disenfranchisement of people of color, economically disadvantaged individuals, and historically disinvested populations in the United States and often in the global South—did not become institutionalized until 1982 in Warren County.

People of all colors in Warren County came together and used civil rights–era tactics to draw clear connections between clean air, a healthy environment, and social justice. The PCB protests were the first EJ protests to have national appeal, tugging differently at the heartstrings of the masses, as children lay in the streets and young protesters sang songs reminiscent of the freedom chants of the Student Nonviolent Coordinating Committee just a couple of decades earlier.[5] These protests painted environmental racism as systemic racism, connecting back to civil rights–era righteousness in a way that spurred decades of additional action.

Following Warren County, communities across the country began marching under the banner of the EJ movement. The United Church of Christ worked with young EJ organizers to develop the Toxic Waste and Race Report of 1987,[6] the preeminent study documenting the traceable strategy of placing of toxic facilities in Black, Indigenous, and people of color (BIPOC) communities in the United States. This substantiated the claims of communities like Warren County: that race, rather than class, was the number one indicator of toxic exposure.

The Environmental Justice movement became officially institutionalized in the 1990s.

In 1991, the same individuals who launched these local movements across the country established the seventeen principles of Environmental Justice[7] in Washington, D.C., formalizing and attempting to institutionalize EJ as a movement comparable in size and power to Rachel Carson's modern environmental movement.[8] In 1994, then-president Bill Clinton established EO 12898, enshrining environmental justice into government and mandating a whole-of-government consideration in the equitable assessment of environmental harms. Although the tangibles of the policy were limited to agency incorporation of EJ, the new mandate substantially informed the way the Environmental Protection Agency (EPA) in particular considered environmental hazards, attempting to bridge existing laws such as the Clean Air and Water Acts with an equity lens.[9]

Despite these national efforts, the EJ movement has, for decades, existed and persisted in silos, consisting of intentionally hyperlocal actions in response to industry pollution, lack of toxic waste remediation, and infrastructure and energy disparities. These silos have kept the movement focused, but have also kept it segmented. There are a few incidents that galvanized national calls for environmental justice: the Warren County PCB protests of 1982 as the initial example, as well as the water crises in Flint, Michigan (2014–2015)[10] and Jackson, Mississippi (2022–2023),[11] which respectively highlighted both long-standing infrastructural gaps and the disparate exposure of climate change impacts on Black people in the United States.[12,13] In all cases, these crises were emblematic of a more significant structural charge at the time: correcting the decades-long tendency for city officials to place superfund sites and toxic waste dumps in neighborhoods where BIPOC communities live, work, play, and pray, as well as addressing the simultaneous failure of government to put funding toward critical infrastructure in those communities.[14] These were—and still are—communities hit twice by environmental hazards and other forms of systemic inequality, now triply impacted by the additional threat of climate change.

Despite the mass coverage, one could argue that even those two powerful instances of national attention in the twenty-first century were not necessarily nationally galvanizing. That is to say, they didn't reshape the established public consciousness around environmental issues and the criticality of centering people and justice in national philanthropic and socioeconomic efforts for environmental protection and climate policy. These were tragedies that, to an extent, momentarily acknowledged the matter of fact that is environmental racism, but didn't ingrain the language, the processes, or the passion into institutions of power—and the narratives those institutions uphold.

It wasn't until 2020, a more significant year of "racial reckoning," that the hyperlocal movements for environmental justice were collated into a national call to action. This call was met by environmental nonprofit organizations and the federal government with a fervor not seen since Bill Clinton's 1994 EO 12898. The year 2020 brought something new—or technically old—to the table for the EJ movement: it nationalized and connected narratives of environmental justice and Black liberation, where previously, the movement had trouble communicating how each instance of agricultural disenfranchisement, petrochemical pollution, and lack of diversity in outdoor spaces was connected to the singular system of racism across the United States. It wasn't just one example of a polluting facility, or one community contending with asthma and elevated cancer cases; it was once again emblematic of something more widely spread and systematic.

You Can Work the Land, but You Can't Enjoy It

May 25, 2020, was the day movements converged. George Floyd's and Breonna Taylor's murders by police put a face to years of contemporary state-sanctioned violence against Black people at the hands of law enforcement in the United States.[15,16] However, another viral incident of violence happened earlier that morning that rattled the nation and also sparked discourse about anti-Black racism. In the Ramble, the wildest part of New York City's Central Park, Christian Cooper, a Black birder and naturalist, informed another parkgoer, Amy Cooper (unrelated), that park rules said she couldn't have her dog off-leash. Amy told him she was going to call the police to report that "an African American man" was "threatening" her life.[17] She called the NYPD and used racially coded language to incite the police to come to her rescue. Christian's crime? Being a Black man in the outdoors who dared confront a white woman.[18] The incident uncovered for the public a lesser-known reality of being Black in America: the threat of existing in nature.

Like they have in other public spaces, white separatists have historically made outdoor spaces inhospitable to Black people and justified their actions with mythologies and stereotypes about how Black people don't like being outside, don't enjoy nature, do not touch the dirt or work the land. In many cases, these stereotypes combined the historical trauma of slavery, sharecropping, and racialized violence to firmly ingrain these fears and understandings in the Black psyche and experience. This has led to the systematic exclusion of Black people from spaces like national parks, the Forest Service,[19] beaches,[20] public pools,[21] and green spaces in urban contexts.[22]

Stereotypes often form part of the broader narratives that societies tell about groups of people, and narratives shape how people understand the world and their place in it. For example, the stereotype that Black people don't belong in the outdoors perpetuates existing power dynamics and social structures by normalizing a simplified view of Black people and their interests, hobbies, and lives. Such stereotypes form the foundation for discrimination, prejudice, and dehumanization. When any group is dehumanized, it compels perpetrators to justify committing hate crimes against them, tragically highlighted by the murder of jogger Ahmaud Arbery in early 2020.[23] These stereotypes are also perpetuated by historical narratives that depict Black people primarily as laborers, meant to cultivate the land but not to enjoy it.[24]

The events of 2020 were pivotal in connecting the EJ movement and broader racial justice issues. Christian Cooper's experience inspired community events such as Black Birders Week, which celebrated and acknowledged the presence of Black people in outdoor professions and hobbies from which they have historically been excluded. This marked a significant narrative shift: that Black people not only belong in outdoor spaces but thrive in them.

2020: Revitalizing the Environmental Justice Movement

George Floyd's murder inspired massive funding commitments for racial justice and statements of support that attempted—in some small fashion—to bridge the histories of environmental justice and environmental rights.[25] In July 2020, the Sierra Club, one of the nation's oldest and most well-known environmental institutions, released a statement[26] "taking down" their monuments, their first acknowledgment of the racist legacy of their founder John Muir and the exclusionary principles that have undergirded the organization since its founding in 1892. There was an outpouring of public statements and commitments to diversity, equity, and inclusion (DEI) and EJ across the big green nonprofits, like the National Wildlife Federation, the Audubon Society, the Waterkeeper Alliance, the League of Conservation Voters, and Earthjustice; many established committees, bolstered their DEI funding, and increased their hiring of EJ-specific staff to an extent not previously seen.[27] Perhaps, for the first time, the white-led environmental movement was, at least publicly, coming to terms with its racist past.

Throughout the history of the climate and environmental movement, white advocates spread dominant narratives that separated people and the planet, often prioritizing a "pristine" nature concept tied to white supremacist notions of racial purity and "perfection." In 2020, Black environmental activists and influencers countered the people-versus-planet narrative with the socialization and nationalization of "intersectional environmentalism," built on the intersectional and justice frameworks of the BLM protests. Environmental justice reentered the national consciousness by tying itself explicitly to broader civil rights discussions. Rather than standing alone or countering traditional environmentalism, it became a submovement within the larger national call for racial justice.

The resurgence of environmental justice at a national level in 2020 mirrored the conditions that gave rise to the Environmental Justice movement in Warren County in 1982, which was the last time we witnessed a similar convergence of movements with narrative momentum behind it. Back then, there was a pervasive narrative suggesting that Black and Brown communities lacked the political will, capital, clout, and, therefore, the voice to oppose corporate and government institutions that would dump the country's pollution into their neighborhoods. This narrative has long perpetuated the idea that Black people are less deserving of land, clean air, water, and trees, using economic convenience as a justification for systemic environmental racism.[28]

This was not a new narrative; similar judgments have historically extended to other facets of Black life: inequitable education systems, unjust housing conditions and displacement, and exclusion from economic processes that might allow Black people to transfer wealth to their children. But this was the first time a nationally-reaching and explicit connection was made between environmental harm and other social injustices.

However, despite the amazing research, direct policy engagement, and capacity-building work of organizations like We ACT for Environmental Justice and the Deep South Center for Environmental Justice, the EJ movement lost momentum heading into the turn of the century. One could argue this is because the movement has not adequately tapped into the collective Black American consciousness as it did during its twentieth-century ramp-up. Focuses splintered, critical submovements such as climate justice, food justice,[29] and energy justice rose to individual and hyperlocal prominence, as each community turned its eyes to its own issues, and as the movement on the whole grew more independent of the civil rights language that it drew inspiration from.

For a long time, EJ strove to legitimize itself against whitewashed ecological systems rather than exist as a subsidiary of the civil rights movement. It constantly had to prove itself to an environmental movement whose very foundation was deliberately exclusionary of BIPOC communities. Even intersectional environmentalism in 2020, though influential, was limited as an appeal to an environmental movement that has continued to fail Black and Brown communities,[30] trying to use the system to dismantle the system.

It's critical that we don't discount the foundations of this movement. Legends like Charles Lee, Vernice Miller-Travis, Peggy Sheppard, Beverly Wright, Robert Bullard, and so many more have been consistently and passionately fighting for decades and at every level to center EJ in national environmental conversations. But it took reframing environmental injustices as connected to the fight for Black lives—rather than something separate—to build salience for the movement to grow.

Striving for Change: Intersectional Environmentalism Is Environmental Justice

With the emergence of the twenty-first-century iteration of the Black Liberation Movement came intersectional environmentalism, a term popularized in 2020 to show solidarity between the institutionalized, modern environmental movement and grassroots activism. This narrative shift proclaimed that Black and Brown people not only belong in environmental institutions but will also enhance them. According to environmental influencer Leah Thomas, intersectional environmentalism suggests taking a proactive rather than a wait-and-see approach to dismantling systems of white supremacy within ecospaces.

Intersectional environmentalism overlaps with the intentions of EJ as a movement. It is indicative of the intergenerational nature of this work: a generational marker that, according to movement elders, doesn't signify anything new in what's been established but instead provides a new frame to popularize existing principles. Each generation has rallied against the continued failure of modern-day environmentalism to develop solutions with and for communities disproportionately burdened by environmental injustice. Although major green organizations stepped up after George Floyd's murder in 2020, one must question what took them so long, despite receiving the same message decade after decade? Have they truly been listening? By some accounts, this effort of trying to reform the mainstream environmental movement is futile, because environmentalism, as it currently stands, not only deprioritizes human beings but also fundamentally rejects the well-being of nonwhite communities—regardless of the number of statements these organizations put out.

In the early twentieth century, National Park enthusiasts like John Muir and founders of the Forest Service like Gifford Pinchot described an ideal nature experience as one devoid of people of color. The outdoors were to be protected independently, outside of the Indigenous stewards who had managed them for generations, an untouched marvel for the wealthy and white. Many of today's major environmental nonprofits were birthed with similar ideals: land, water, and wildlife without people of color. Despite landmark bills, such as the Clean Air and Water Acts of the 1970s, designed to redress the health harms of pollution across the country, the policies' focus on regional air and water quality often leaves hyperlocal, predominantly BIPOC hotspots in harm's way.

The most insidious part of environmental harm is the claim of equity. Because environmental movements tend to focus on nature, excluding human impacts altogether, they often fail to acknowledge the historical issues of disparate impact, separating themselves from conversations of race and politics in favor of nonhuman conservation. Ironically, the only recourse EJ communities have truly had to fight the disparate impact of environmental hazards has been through the Civil Rights Act, not through the numerous environmental laws that exist to protect communities and ecosystems in this country. If that litigation gap does not highlight the blatant exclusion of historically unjust environmental conditions in this country, then what does?

Environmental justice, climate justice, and intersectional environmentalism —all concepts developed to address environmental racism—aim to shift the dominant narratives within environmental systems by placing emphasis on people. The greatest progress in these movements has occurred when they have aligned with other social justice and human rights–focused movements, rather than with traditional environmentalism. The narrative shift that made the Warren County PCB protests so impactful in 1982—connecting them with the broader movement for Black lives—allowed environmental justice to be revitalized in 2020. In these contexts, the narrative shift does not require a fundamental overhaul of priorities; instead, it builds on ideals of common decency, life, liberty, health, wealth, and the pursuit of happiness for all, regardless of skin color.

Maintaining the Momentum: Justice40

The impact of 2020's racial reckoning on environmental justice was embodied not only socially but politically. Coming off of a summer of clear and strong commitment to DEI and EJ across governments, corporations, and the social sector, then–presidential nominee Joe Biden centered the language of environmental justice in his campaign in an unprecedented way. Suddenly, Biden's platform was not just a calling card to young people passionate about the climate crisis or an increasingly educated electorate committed to a more equitable economy, but it was also an explicit response to calls for EJ.[31]

The language piece is critical. Biden was not the first president to discuss climate change or to enshrine environmental protections into law, but there was an unprecedented refusal to shy away from the terminology of environmental justice in his campaign.[32] Through the Justice40 Initiative, he became the first president to enshrine environmental justice in executive policy since President Bill Clinton's EO 12898. While far from perfect, Biden's policy went further than the Clinton administration to make EJ a transfer of economic benefits rather than only a generic whole-of-government consideration,[33] and to develop the first ever White House Environmental Justice Advisory Council. Although it's difficult to know whether EJ would have taken hold of the 2020 political conversation if the racial reckoning hadn't occurred, there is a clear continuity between the national resurrection of EJ through BLM and the subsequent commitments of the Biden administration.

A key feature of the 2020 uprisings was the question of economic benefit and reparations: Where does peace in the community intersect with community investment? How does historical disinvestment impact community infrastructure and a community's sense of self? Justice40 was an attempt at a type of reparations: a promise that the billions and trillions of dollars that were to flow into the United States from climate, infrastructure,[34,35] and inflation-fixing bills[36] would represent a community investment very rarely seen by those most impacted by environmental burdens. The process has been slow going, often delayed by, among other factors, a reliance on state governments that are either politically averse or without appropriate distribution infrastructure, as well as by an inability of historically disinvested communities to gather the capacity necessary to take action on such large pots of money.[37] Time will tell if the sum of this investment will truly impact the disinvested BIPOC communities that have lived adjacent to polluting facilities, in the backwaters of rural America, and in the heart of our urban centers.

What we're seeing from 2020 is a repeat of history. Just as occurred in the nationalization of EJ in the 1980s, and the institutionalization of it in the 1990s during the Clinton presidency, we've found ourselves in a moment of great momentum. If history repeats itself, the 2020 resurgence could spill over into policy for several more years. We've already seen the long-term infrastructure being built through the establishment of programs and entities like EPA's Department of Environmental Justice and External Civil Rights in Autumn 2022. However, the historical decline of EJ should also serve as a warning: if we don't continue to build this movement as a fight for Black and Brown lives rather than as the opposition to institutionalized environmentalism, we may very well lose all that we've fought for.

The fight for environmental justice must exist and persist in deep collaboration with broader social justice movements. Grounded in social justice principles, strategies, and symbols and iconography, environmental justice sees its greatest successes when integrated into larger social justice conversations. Just as the 1982 Warren County protests were pivotal, 2020 was another crucial moment for environmental justice. We must not squander this opportunity; the solution partly lies in narrative and priority shifts. It is no longer about proving that environmental racism is real or systemic—we are past that. Environmental justice is social justice, and the movements must intersect and co-conspire.

Just as environmental justice has often failed to leverage larger social justice spaces, many social justice movements are only recently starting to incorporate environmental and climate justice into their programming. We should do more to highlight the collective histories that support us: spotlight the synergies between our freedom songs and marches, recognize that environmental justice is not just about pollution but also about land ownership and resource access—principles that civil rights leaders have championed for decades—and continue to highlight moments like 2020, where our movements beautifully converge.

More Than a Check: Building Narrative Power for Black Reparations

By Jean-Pierre Brutus, Joseph Torres, and Trevor Smith

> *For all the land you took, for all the rapes, all the Rosewoods and*
> *Black Wall Streets you destroyed. All the mis-education, jobs loss,*
> *segregated shacks we lived in, the disease that ate and killed us,*
> *for all the mad police that drilled us. For all the music and dances*
> *you stole. The styles. The language. The hip clothes you copped.*
> *The careers you stopped. All these are suits, specific litigation, as*
> *represent we be like we, for reparations for damages paid to the*
> *Afro-American nation.*
>
> —*Amiri Baraka, "Why Is We Americans?"[1]*

The theft, shackling, and importation of the first enslaved Africans to what is now known as the United States not only marked the inception of an evil system that dehumanized, traded, and sold Black people for centuries, but also normalized a culture of anti-Blackness in the United States. Anti-Blackness has thrived through a web of interlocking narratives and substantiates the pervasive system of racism that persists today.

One movement organizing to contend with the harms of slavery is the Black-led movement for reparations, which has long championed expansive narratives of liberation transcending the confines of colonialism and capitalism. We define reparations as a process to redress acts of gross violations of human rights, as outlined in the United Nations' "Basic Principles and Guidelines on the Right to a Remedy and Reparation for Victims of Gross Violations of International Human Rights Law and Serious Violations of International Humanitarian Law."[2] They offer five components of reparations, including restitution, compensation, rehabilitation, satisfaction, and guarantees of nonrepetition, as a comprehensive approach to implementing reparations programs.

Before these guidelines were created, formerly enslaved Black people, whether explicitly or implicitly, were calling for comprehensive reparations to address the harms of slavery, seeking to transform the system of racial capitalism.[3] Racial capitalism, according to historians Destin Jenkins and Justin LeRoy, is

> the process by which the key dynamics of capitalism—accumulation/dispossession, credit/debt, production/surplus, capitalist/worker, developed/underdeveloped, contract/coercion, and others—become articulated through race.[4]

One cannot discuss the history of the political and social order of the United States without discussing the history of capitalism. Similarly, one cannot discuss the history of capitalism without delving into the history of Indigenous land theft, the enslavement of Black people, and how these colonial practices shaped our economic system.

However, neoliberal economic ideologies—exemplified by the false promise of the American Dream, which posits that anyone can achieve upward mobility with enough hard work—have more recently reframed reparations as merely a financial project that seeks to close the Black/white wealth gap. While most Americans acknowledge the harms of slavery, this neoliberal ideology has led to increased arguments rooted in *bootstrapism* (the cliche that people can pull themselves up by their bootstraps with existing resources to get out of an undesirable situation and into a desirable one) and asserted that reparations are too costly and impractical. To make matters worse, as the reparations movement has gained traction across the country, our media system has only deepened this narrow understanding of reparations—often framing the issue through a zero-sum lens, with white people having to give up something in order for Black people to gain.

Today's modern movement for reparations—which has made significant progress, particularly in the wake of the 2020 uprisings after the murders of George Floyd, Breonna Taylor, and Ahmaud Arbery—is repositioning reparations outside of the neoliberal ideology.

The twenty-first-century reparations movement is actively expanding our collective understanding of what repair should look like on an economic, political, and cultural level. Across the country, cities and states are examining reparative proposals that address not only the massive wealth and income inequalities within Black communities, but also systemic solutions that seek to transform our education, housing, cultural, and criminal-legal systems, as they did in California, where the California Reparations Task Force recommended establishing a Freedman Affairs Agency, providing direct cash payments to eligible Black Californians, implementing policies to address housing discrimination, a public apology from the state of California, and offer tax incentives for Black-owned businesses.[5] The narrative driving today's movement seeks to extend its impact beyond economic realms. It highlights the imperative for a profound cultural shift in society's perceptions, understanding, and treatment of Blackness and Black people.

This chapter argues that, for the contemporary reparations movement to be successful, we must contend simultaneously with anti-Black racism and the gross inequity of capitalism, and not allow neoliberal politics to co-opt our efforts. We must also popularize a national narrative that inspires and persuades people of all backgrounds to support reparations for Indigenous and Black communities on the road to repair, healing, and transformation for all of us.

Ideologies of Harm: From White Supremacy to Racial Capitalism

The broader vision of reparations encompasses establishing structures and systems that affirm Black sovereignty, dignity, and the right to self-determination. It has always been a call to fundamentally rethink and rebuild our social fabric in a manner that eradicates the legacy of colonialism and anti-Blackness. Remembering this is crucial for the reparations movement today, as it underscores the ongoing struggle for not just financial compensation but for the creation of a society in which equality, freedom, and justice are not mere ideals but the lived realities of all.

Embedded in the tradition of Black radical thought is the sustained interrogation of the systems entrenching our racial hierarchy and the impact of those systems and hierarchies on Black communities. Central to this is the exploration of the role of colonialism and slavery in undergirding the exploitative and extractive economic system of capitalism and the modern global system of race governance they birthed.[6]

White supremacy isn't just about beliefs and attitudes; it's a system of governance rooted in the sixteenth-century European colonial project, which created and enforced racial hierarchies. This system actively constructed race as a means of domination. Through a series of violent acts, white Europeans established their rule over subjugated African and Indigenous peoples. This involved the forcible removal of languages, cultures, territories, religions, behaviors, and dispositions. These were then amalgamated into the categories of whiteness/Europeanness and nonwhiteness/non-Europeanness.[7]

Racial subjugation, according to legal scholar Angela Harris, "is not a special application of capitalist processes, but rather central to how capitalism operates."[8] As Sven Beckert, author of *Empire of Cotton: A Global History*, writes:

> Slavery was crucial to the establishment of American capitalism. The capital accumulated from slavery both financed industrial development and sustained an expansive, often reckless capitalism that would not have existed without enslaved African American labor.[9]

Since capitalism and racial subordination in the United States are so intertwined, any efforts to address the ills of capitalism must bring along with it a critical racial lens.

As Ruth Wilson Gilmore notes, every form of capitalism is racialized because the capitalist mode of production was always entangled with the colonial project.[10] Building on the pioneering work of Eric Williams, the first prime minister of Trinidad and Tobago, and many others, contemporary scholarship has consistently demonstrated the emergence of capitalism not from the sooty factories of Western Europe but from the colonial matrix of factories of enslaved people—more aptly, plantations in the Americas.[11] Since their emergence, racial rule and capitalism have evolved, but they have consistently maintained their core functions of exploitation, predation, and governance. Therefore, any reparations effort that doesn't also seek to dismantle the structures of racial capitalism will be insufficient to prevent future harm to Black people.

Up from the Ground: A Brief History of the Movement for Reparations

From the outset, Black activists and abolitionists advocating for reparations mobilized Black communities to demand both financial compensation and systemic change. This call was not just for the labor stolen from them and their ancestors, but also for the cultural and spiritual losses endured.

In 1898, with the country just a few decades removed from the abolition of slavery, amid the nadir of "race relations,"[12] a formerly enslaved woman named Callie House, alongside others, birthed what would become one of the longest-standing movements in U.S. history. Through an organization called the National Ex-Slave Mutual Bounty and Pension Association, House was able to organize around 300,000 dues-paying members[13] and, according to historian Dr. Mary Frances Berry, inspire "the old ex-slaves to exercise their rights as citizens to demand repayment for their long suffering."[14]

House, like many who struggle for the liberation of Black people, became a target of the U.S. government. She was charged with "sending misleading circulars through the mail, guaranteeing pensions to association members, and profiting from the movement."[15] Her conviction, in conjunction with the rise of racial terrorism through radical vigilantes like the Ku Klux Klan, eventually caused the movement to lose its momentum.

The struggle was picked up in the 1920s by other movements for Black liberation, including the Universal Negro Improvement Association (UNIA), led by Marcus Garvey and Queen Mother Audley Moore. Both were fierce supporters of the return of Black dignity and culture, with Garvey stating that reparations must return "us to our own civilization."[16]

Martin Luther King Jr. spoke on the debts that the United States owed to Black America, stating, "But they never realize the debt that they owe a people who were kept in slavery 244 years." He went as far as to say that Black people were coming to Washington, DC, to "get our check." He noted that after the abolition of slavery, Black people were not provided with any resources, while white Americans were succored with the Homestead Act—

which encouraged westward expansion and settlement by providing free land to American citizens and immigrants willing to cultivate it.[17]

In 1968, Black nationalists committed to narratives of Black sovereignty, empowerment, and liberation started the Republic of New Afrika, to create a new Black nation composed of Alabama, Georgia, Louisiana, Mississippi, and South Carolina.[18] The following year, James Forman, a prominent voice in the civil rights movement, walked into a New York church and delivered the collectively written "Black Manifesto," which demanded $500 million from Christian white churches and Jewish synagogues for the role they had played and continued to play in the subjugation of Black people.[19] Many activists call the delivery of the Black Manifesto the birth of the modern-day reparations movement.[20]

The manifesto, led by Forman and the National Black Economic Development Conference, stated:

> We are so proud of our African heritage and realize concretely that our struggle is not only to make revolution in the United States but to protect our brothers and sisters in Africa and to help them rid themselves of racism, capitalism, and imperialism. . . .[21]

As evident, the calls for reparations have never focused solely on financial compensation or economic empowerment; they have always intersected with the Black liberation movement's broader calls for freedom, decolonization, sovereignty, self-determination, and justice.[22]

The manifesto's demands for repairing the harm caused by the media were bold, advocating for the establishment of major publishing and printing industries controlled by Black communities. These proposals aimed to address the imbalance in media representation and empower those in the Black community to narrate their own stories.[23]

These aspirations, however, had been met with resistance, manifesting as a racist backlash fueled by anti-Black narratives propagated by the media. Berry highlighted how the movement was derided by the white press and labeled as "ridiculous and fraudulent," calling the members of the association "misguided."[24] This climate of opposition was further exacerbated by the media's hostile response to the Black Manifesto and its proponents. The media accused Forman of striving to exacerbate racial divisions, a criticism later directed at other Black leaders, such as Malcolm X.[25]

Of course, the narratives of transformation uplifted in the Black Manifesto were supplemented by many Black abolitionists, Pan-Africanists, and freedom fighters, like Angela Davis, Huey Newton, Frank Hampton, Bobby Seale, Stokely Carmichael, Malcolm X, Walter Rodney, Amilcar Cabral, Imari Obadele, Nkechi Taifa, and Ericka Huggins during the 1970s, 1980s, and 1990s in both direct and indirect ways. Today, this tradition is carried on by modern-day reparations organizations, such as N'COBRA, December 12th Movement, Equity and Transformation, Media 2070, Get Free, and a number of others.

The Twenty-First-Century Movement for Reparations: Building Local Power for National Transformation

The twenty-first-century reparations movement in the United States has gained enormous momentum, particularly after the public execution of George Floyd in 2020, which led to what many have called the largest public uprisings in our nation's history, as millions of people took to the streets in protest against police brutality nationwide. The movement is currently contending with the array of narrative challenges outlined earlier here while addressing a phenomenon that we and other activists call the *hope gap*: the large divide that exists between support of reparations within the Black community (over 80 percent) and the belief that it will happen in this lifetime (less than 10 percent).[26]

Yet the realm of possibility is shifting. For decades, HR 40, a bill that would create a commission to study the effects of slavery and legal discrimination, and provide recommendations for reparations, stood alone as the only national proposal on reparations. In 2023, supported by advocates and coalitions like the Why We Can't Wait coalition, Congresswoman Cori Bush introduced a resolution that called for a $14 trillion down payment to close the Black/white wealth gap, transforming the realm of possibility for reparations.

This power for national change has grown locally, partly led by the efforts of First Repair, based out of Evanston, Illinois, to support local organizing for reparations across the country. By positioning local reparations as the first step toward a national effort, First Repair has grown the movement, bringing the issue closer to communities grappling with inequities in education, housing, income, and wealth. Local efforts have given Black communities and advocates the space to contend with what reparations could look like in their communities, from both a financial and nonfinancial perspective. The new addition of organizers and organizations to the movement has allowed it to challenge the notion of meritocracy more directly in the way that it has damaged Black communities—and to actively replace it with notions of morality, debt, and collective responsibility.

As such, both statewide and municipal efforts have continued to grow. California, the largest state in the United States and fourth-largest economy globally, launched a state reparations task force that issued its final report with findings and recommendations in June 2023. In December 2023, the New York State Legislature signed its own version of a reparations task force into law. The New Jersey Institute for Social Justice convened the New Jersey Reparations Council as a civil-society response to the lack of movement of the state legislature on a state task-force bill that the chair of the Legislative Black Caucus introduced.

Various municipalities nationwide have launched commissions; these include Detroit; Fulton County, Georgia; Boston; and San Francisco. Some municipalities—notably Evanston, Illinois—have gone beyond task forces and have begun enacting reparations measures. Evanston was the first modern municipality in the United States to embark on a reparations program for slavery and its aftermath. Asheville, North Carolina, is not far behind and has begun to canvas the local community for proposals on how to embark on reparations for slavery and its legacies.

Beyond legislative change, entities such as Media2070 have underscored the media's complicity in perpetuating slavery and anti-Blackness. Reparations Finance Lab, which sheds light on the financial industry's influence on slavery, is strategically illuminating the culpability of private industries in perpetuating anti-Black harm. Organizations like the BLIS (Black Liberation-Indigenous Sovereignty) Collective are braiding narratives and movements across Black and Indigenous spaces to give rise to a stronger nationwide decolonial movement.

Beneath the surface of this movement lies a strategic and potent force of grassroots organizing, applying immense pressure on elected officials to catalyze initiatives that challenge the conventional narrative surrounding reparations.

In New Jersey, the Say the Word campaign has emerged as a bold endeavor to dismantle the negative narratives surrounding reparations, aiming to redefine it as an essential part of our racial justice discourse.

In Chicago, organizers from Equity and Transformation have launched a groundbreaking drug-war reparations campaign, skillfully weaving in the UN Basic Principles and Guidelines on the Right to Reparations by centering the principle of "satisfaction" in their campaign. Organizers note that "the survivors of the war on drugs are not satisfied" with a previous bill that legalized marijuana across the state and are demanding that "cannabis tax revenue go directly to the survivors in the form of direct cash payments." [27]

In New York, the December 12th Movement, which had long underscored the role of Wall Street in the trafficking of enslaved people, galvanized a statewide coalition of New Yorkers for Reparations. The coalition rallied organizers across criminal justice, climate justice, economic justice, and other issues to translate collective momentum into tangible policy advancements.

What we have witnessed in recent years is a strategic shift reminiscent of successful campaigns, such as the legalization of marijuana or recognition of gay marriage at the federal level. Like those movements, local and issue-specific reparations campaigns are emerging, strategically designed to accumulate the necessary influence for the eventual passage of a federal reparations bill. They are instrumental in reshaping the narrative by highlighting the complicity of state and local governments in upholding slavery and sustaining anti-Black policies after its abolition.

Together, these localized efforts serve as policy laboratories, experimenting with reparative measures and demonstrating to the broader public that substantial progress in dialogue about reparations is achievable and offers viable policy solutions. By shifting the focus from the federal government to placing more responsibility on the historical roles played by state and local entities, these campaigns advance the conversation on reparations, and inform and refine potential policy approaches at the federal level.

The history is clear. The movement for reparations has always acknowledged that the financial aspect of reparations is just a singular part of what must be a greater effort. As the movement progressed and evolved, so did the system of racial capitalism in the United States. Now, not only does it face the same anti-Black narratives and systems previous iterations of the movement faced, but it's confronted with a new version of capitalism that has allowed a sliver of the Black population to attain financial upward mobility while relying on the illusion of the American Dream to prey on Black people in new ways.[28]

Narrative Challenges: Reparations Through the Neoliberal Ideology

The reparations movement faces significant narrative challenges under neoliberalism. This section focuses on three major obstacles: the *American Dream*, *racial progress*, and the *Lost Cause*. These interconnected narratives reinforce each other, necessitating a broader liberation movement that positions reparations and other freedom demands as essential to realizing the nation's ideals.

Meritocracy and the American Dream

National identity is formed through narratives, and the so-called American Dream suggests that anyone can achieve success through hard work. However, this "dream" has historically excluded anyone who is not a white Anglo-Saxon man, masking deep-rooted systemic inequalities. Neoliberalism, emphasizing market primacy and individual freedom, has further obscured structural racism, making it challenging to combat this particular persistent myth.

A False Sense of Racial Progress

Claims of a postracial society, often highlighted by the election of President Barack Obama, obscure the structural dimensions of racial capitalism. Figures like Minority Leader of the U.S. Senate Mitch McConnell argue against reparations by citing civil rights progress, which ignores ongoing systemic issues. Studies show significant racial disparities in income and wealth, contradicting the myth of racial progress and meritocracy. This narrative misleads the public into believing that hard work alone is enough for the attainment of success, negating the persistent barriers faced by Black communities.

The Lost Cause and America's Antihistory Movement

The Lost Cause mythology, which downplays the role of slavery in the Civil War, has shaped racial attitudes and historical understanding in the United States. This whitewashing of history is perpetuated by media, pop culture, and education, affecting collective memory. Modern efforts to restrict discussions of race and racism in schools continue this tradition. Attacks on diversity, equity, and inclusion (DEI) and critical race theory foreshadow similar opposition to reparations, labeling them as *reverse racism*. The reparations movement must counter these narratives to foster honest discussions about historical injustice and systemic inequities.

The Road Ahead: Building a Transformative Narrative at the National Level

As this chapter is being written, the stakes for democracy have never been higher. The reparations movement stands at a pivotal juncture, tasked with creating a transformative national narrative, sustaining momentum at the local level, and integrating the conversation into broader political discourse. The goal is to challenge and reshape the prevailing myths underpinning the American Dream, making the idea of reparations an integral part of the national consciousness.

Today, national support for reparations stands at about 30 percent, in sharp contrast to the 80 percent support among Black people. This disparity highlights the enduring influence of foundational myths—such as meritocracy, Manifest Destiny, American exceptionalism, and racial superiority—on the American psyche. These myths create narratives that legitimize the systems perpetuating modern inequality. This inequality is further exacerbated by ongoing racist attacks on Black studies, critical race theory, intersectionality, and queer studies. These attacks, often framed as opposition to "woke" ideas, are part of a coordinated right-wing effort against all forms of antiracist thought and expression—to which the narrative for reparations is central. To garner white support for the reparations movement, it is essential to counter these policies with narratives illustrating how a nation with a history of profound injustice can take responsibility for its actions, hold itself accountable, and transform itself. For movement workers, this means adopting a strategic narrative approach that helps skeptics understand why a contemporary reparations movement is necessary and how it benefits all of us.

Crafting a narrative that envisions a future free from racial injustice is crucial. This narrative must inspire people to adopt a liberatory social identity that prioritizes collective liberation and justice as core values. Through this transformative narrative, the movement can begin to reshape the national dialogue, making the case for reparations an integral part of our collective pursuit of a multiracial democracy.

While the road ahead holds challenges, it is not devoid of compromise. Crafting this transformative narrative necessitates radical solidarity within the Black liberation and reparations movements. Through this intricate narrative weaving of alliances, the movement can amass the power to popularize a new narrative about repair, healing, power, and reparations.

We live in an empire that divides people along class and racial lines, breeds intolerance, and pits us against one another to prevent collective power building. Thus, combating neoliberal narratives of meritocracy, which often obscure the severe impact of market capitalism and greed, is incredibly challenging. As narrative organizers, we must ask ourselves how we can tell stories that delegitimize neoliberalism, divisiveness, and zero-sum thinking.

Reparations is a movement for transformation—the transformation of systems, thinking, and people. We must remain vigilant about how these systems must change to meet contemporary challenges and opportunities. From the abolitionist movement to today's Movement for Black Lives (M4BL), Black radical thought has always asserted that, in order for a nation to be in right relationship with its people, it must make amends and change. This change manifests itself in the contemporary reparations movement, which must not be co-opted by forces seeking to maintain the status quo of power and privilege.

Liberation Is Coming: The Fight for Indigenous Sovereignty

Interview with Linda Black Elk and Eryn Wise

By Shanelle Matthews and Marzena Zukowska

Linda Black Elk is an ethnobotanist and food sovereignty activist special-izing in teaching about culturally important plants and their uses as food and medicine. She is eternally grateful for the intergenerational knowledge of elders and other knowledge holders, who have shared their understand-ings of the world with her, and she has dedicated her life to giving back to these people and their communities. Linda works to build relationships and ways of thinking that will promote and protect food sovereignty, traditional plant knowledge, and environmental quality as an extension of her work as a gardener, forager, fisher, hunter, and gatherer. Linda and her family spear-head a grassroots effort to provide organic, traditional, shelf-stable food and traditional Indigenous medicines to elders and others in need. Thus far, they have fed and healed thousands of people. She has written numerous articles, book chapters, and papers, and is the author of Watoto Unyutapi, *a field guide to edible wild plants of the Dakota people, which is now out of print. Linda proudly serves as the educational programs and community engage-ment director at NATIFS, a Native-led nonprofit in Minneapolis, Minnesota. She also sits on the board of Makoce Ikikcupi, a reparative justice project on Dakota lands on Mnisota Makoce. When she isn't teaching, Linda spends time with her husband and three sons, who are all members of the Oceti Sakowin—the Seven Council Fires of the Lakota.*

Eryn Wise comes from the Jicarilla Apache Nation (Ollero clan) and Pueb-lo of Laguna (Paguate Village, Shaasrk'a). They are a community advocate centering their work around the liberation of Indigenous nations of Turtle Island—that of all people of the global majority. Ensuring a future for gen-erations to come is a duty and responsibility to them, and they honor the traditional teachings of their predecessors by continuing to build intersectional communities in the spirit of kinship and Indigenous resurgence. They aim to do all their work in homage to their ancestors whose radical queerness, unapologetic stewardship of land and lifeway defense, and commitment to cultural preservation continue to serve as both a lighthouse and a call to action. They are a human being, just like you.

What are the dominant or hegemonic narratives that Indigenous people contend with, whether in the media, within communities, or in progressive or left spaces?

Eryn: In the media, people are still contending with the idea that Indigenous people exist in real time—and that we're not just historical characters playing backdrop to the present day. No matter how many various representations—movies, television shows, curated art galleries, or frontline spaces—are created to show we exist in the present or how many times we place ourselves in current media as curators, thought leaders, key strategists, movement organizers, or as people in positions of power—all to be respected—we are often not taken seriously. The dominant narratives in settler-colonial, so-called America are that we either exist in history books to supplement the tobacco or gaming industries as tragic victims who live heartbreaking lives, or we're those "goddamn activists" who won't shut up about things like "Land Back" and fossil fuels.

The erasure and invisibilization of Indigenous people come from a commitment to concepts rooted in a continuation of colonial projects and the ongoing genocide of Indigenous peoples not just on our lands but globally. Here, the narrative of assimilation was the only means of survival, as manifested in Capt. Richard Henry Pratt's nineteenth-century speech wherein he used the now infamous phrase "Kill the Indian, save the man" to describe a need to civilize and Americanize first peoples. It was also a founding ideology of the development of Carlisle Indian School and other boarding schools nationwide. Over 523 schools were created with the same sentiment, and hundreds of thousands of Native children were forced to not only assimilate physically but were stripped of their languages and denied their voices. How terribly powerful is that? How much worse is it that Sterlin Harjo—a Seminole filmmaker—created an episode in 2023 called "Deer Lady" on *Reservation Dogs* that showcases this horror, and people still think it happened so long ago?[1] In almost every city I've ever lived in, there is almost always an "Indian School Road." That's a powerful PR campaign, and people don't even realize what violent histories they tread across daily.

There's also an unyielding desire to make Indigenous peoples uphold religious ideologies that are not in alignment with the way we, as multidimensional, intersectional, and intertribal beings, commune and interact with the natural worlds we've stewarded since time immemorial. These unreputable desires have looked like the ostracization of third-gender, two-spirit, trans, or gender-expansive relatives from communal spaces through forced enslavement; sexual submission to their capturers; sexual, physical, and mental abuse; and later, a complete erasure of their meaningful existence and contributions to cultural abundance and connection.

Even looking at the story of Lozen, a Chiricahua Apache historical figure, told to me my entire life as the story of a female Apache warrior who fought valiantly with her brother Victorio as part of Geronimo's band, I didn't know until researching as an adult that she was not just a fighter; she was admired by all others because she was stronger than them. And not only that, she had a wife named Dah'tes'te, and they *respected their relationship.* She died in Alabama of tuberculosis, and her wife, who had later remarried and been relocated to Oklahoma, would later tell of her lifelong love for Lozen. If I had heard that version of the story earlier, can you imagine how my queerness could have felt empowering instead of yet another thing that othered me from everyone—especially being raised by a post–boarding school, hyper-Christian grandmother who likely was so because of the dominant narratives that compounded within her to the point of compunction? It's heartbreaking, but it also makes narrative shift and reclamation work necessary.

The stories commonly accepted or portrayed by the media about my communities often remind me of how Palestinians are depicted in ways that exploit Western racial biases. For instance, regardless of personal views on Hamas, it is the governing body in Gaza, so its presence is expected. However, those with little media literacy see terms like "Hamas-run" or "Hamas-controlled" and have their biases triggered, being led to conclusions rather than forming them logically.

At Standing Rock, local media spread uniform and baseless claims about the leadership within our camps. Instead of recognizing us as autonomous individuals with a shared goal—to stop the Dakota Access Pipeline—people were led to believe we were causing harm. These false narratives strained relationships between Indigenous tribes, local farmers, businesses, and communities, fueling settler violence against the original peoples. While there's no direct comparison to the relentless violence Palestinians face from the Israeli regime, as Indigenous people, we remember how our communities were forcibly relocated, made to move permanently from our lands.

We share a common experience of facing the pervasive, extractive tactics of the media. Even in progressive or leftist spaces, our Indigenous knowledge systems and data sovereignty are often disrespected. This manifests itself in the misuse of our cultural traditions—people reciting the words of our visionaries to us as a form of control, documenting our cultural events or ceremonies without consent, or using drones to surveil our unceded, sovereign lands. Recently, I saw my friend, artist Jackie Fawn, have her work used by a nonprofit as an AI prompt to generate "Indigenous art," instead of simply commissioning Jackie, a recognized expert and representative of her people.

If we aren't being outright stolen from, we are often tokenized—expected to become symbols for movements that may not be ours or seen as the sole authority on Indigeneity, even when we don't consent to the circumstances. Tokenization began when settlers tried to "collect" pieces of us, including our skin, hair, or even children. Photographers like Edward S. Curtis, who misrepresented us on film and hunted us for images, are still regarded as experts on Indigenous peoples. While some say we posed willingly, in reality, many were offered small payments to help buy essentials after being forced onto reservations. What parents wouldn't swallow their pride to feed their child? And many of those photographed were never paid at all, systematically exploited for the gain of others.

Linda: It feels like there are two versions of Native people: the ones portrayed in movies, and the real, living, breathing Native people of today. Unfortunately, many don't connect the two. A widespread issue is that non-Native, non-Indigenous, and non–people of color often prefer the performance—the spectacle of us in regalia—over engaging with the real issues. They shy away from discussing the deep-rooted trauma our communities have endured and continue to face. They want the image, but not the conversation or the truth behind our ongoing struggles.

Who has been behind amplifying these types of narratives? Which groups or institutions of power?

Eryn: Dominant narratives aren't just driven by progressives, corporations, or governments that have historically oppressed us. Sometimes, they're perpetuated by Indigenous people themselves, many of whom have been indoctrinated into colonialism. Some have tried to assimilate, avoiding the painful realities of colonial trauma, part of a genocidal project that was, in many ways, alarmingly successful. Until June 2, 1924, it wasn't even legal to be Native. We've only recently passed 100 years since the Indian Citizenship Act, and it's only since 1972 that we've had the right to vote on issues impacting our unceded lands.

These legal nuances, along with the settler classification system that determined who was considered a "civilized American" and who was still a "dirty Indian," led many to avoid the label of Native altogether. Some families chose to identify as Mexican on census forms or even as white, taking on English surnames given in boarding schools, because it was easier than explaining the trauma no one wanted to hear about. My grandmother, for instance, rarely spoke in Jicarilla, even though she understood it perfectly. Boarding schools had instilled so much fear in her that she avoided using her mother tongue.

This exploitation of tribal nations has never been justified, but like a rotten seed, it has taken root in times of extreme hardship. The forced separation of families, lands, and languages; the disruption of our diets; and the inability to even speak about what happened for so long are central to the Indigenous experience. Yet this painful narrative is also part of the myth of what "makes America great." As we approach another election year, we do so knowing that those in power are fully aware of these truths—and stand on them proudly.

Additionally, in a twenty-first-century context, influencers often visit Native lands or cultural sites without doing meaningful research beyond what they see on Instagram or TikTok. They treat these places like pretty backdrops, failing to approach them with cultural understanding. Then, they speak to their large audiences, framing their personal experience as more important than the voices of the people and lands they visited.

What kinds of counternarratives or narratives from your community have you embraced in your work?

Eryn: In 2016, tens of thousands responded to the call of tribal members at Standing Rock Reservation in North Dakota, who were deeply concerned about a pipeline that threatened their water, people, and sacred lands. The grassroots movement began in 2014 and was led by those who had fought the Keystone XL pipeline.[2] After years of inaction from the Obama administration, in 2016 the youth took matters into their own hands, running from Standing Rock to Washington, DC, to directly appeal to President Obama to protect their people and those downstream.

The rallying cry: "Water is life," spread across borders and resonated with people far beyond Standing Rock. What was most powerful was how we came together because the community called, and we answered. Today, I see some of the youth from the Standing Rock encampments now leading, creating

The view of the Oceti Sakowin camp from atop "Media Hill" at the Standing Rock resistance camps on September 16, 2016. At the time this image was captured, there were already thousands present at the camps. Photo by Liminal Films LLC: Jonathan Klett, Sara Lafleur-Vetter, Romin Lee Johnson

music, and sharing stories of their experiences. They have become beacons of the movement. This growing awareness among young people, who are using technology and research innovatively, is one of the most significant political shifts happening right now, and those in power aren't even aware of it.

We also fought against the Line 3 pipeline in Minnesota, a movement similar to Standing Rock. It challenged the idea that Indigenous people can safeguard biodiversity for everyone but not for ourselves. We proved we still have so much advocacy within us. Our strategies evolved to push back against the narrative that our lives are disposable so that colonizers and their descendants can thrive. This belief persists, even in places like Minnesota, known for residents' "kindness." We had to rely on scientific data, supported by a STEM educator, to get people to take our call to protect the waters seriously.

We taught young people to test the water as they paddled from the Mississippi headwaters to Big Sandy Lake. Along the way, we witnessed the environmental impacts of fossil fuels on remote regions. Despite visible gas bubbles in the marshes and crude oil where it didn't belong, pipeline corporations denied the need for testing. But the youth documented water samples over 250 miles, revealing the river's degradation. We could assert our data sovereignty and challenge corporate claims through their work. It was empowering to confront Enbridge employees, publicly declare, "We don't believe you," and back it up with proof. Hearing the youth speak out about the trauma they witnessed on the land was even more inspiring.

Linda: I work a lot with Indigenous scientists and Indigenous science. Every year, I've been going out to do a plant walk with young Natives learning how to code. I went with one group of brilliant Lakota kids who are just as passionate about their culture, ceremony, language, and food as they are about writing code. This narrative of walking in between worlds doesn't apply to them because they are just making it all one world, one narrative for themselves. I've worked with Native scientists who are interested in their traditional plants for ceremonies they've grown up with. One day, they ask themselves, why is this tea from this plant so hydrating? And this question leads them down a path of research. We've always done research as Indigenous people, answering questions methodically and intelligently.

What I love and appreciate about young people and the narrative they're pushing is that we don't have to be respectful to people who are oppressing us. When you're growing up, there's this respectability narrative that you need to be peaceful and nonviolent. I still believe in nonviolence. But we don't have to be kind and nonviolent when people are hurting us. I see all of these fierce young warriors who could go out there, stepping up to defend our Palestinian relatives, and are, like, "No, I'm not gonna fucking sit by and watch genocide happen." Young Indigenous people and young people of color all over the world are done with an overly kind narrative while people in power are spitting in our faces.

Eryn: I still deeply respect my elders and hope our movements achieve victory—for our liberation to come in many forms for people, the land, and our languages. But there's also a dignified rage present right now. I think of those standing up to Stop Cop City, who've faced live rounds and felt the weight of resistance. The narrative often suggests we are in an insurmountable situation, but we are the global majority, and it's time to act from that perspective with continued, educated action.

We saw this narrative shift during Standing Rock. The core belief then, as it is now, is that we're not the minority—we're the majority. We are more aligned than the supposed dominant powers. We've proven we can rely on each other: we can feed, house, and care for ourselves. We can return to ancestral ways, have our ceremonies without asking permission, and experience liberation in our homelands. There is enough for all of us.

At Standing Rock, we built schools, health care centers, kitchens, healing spaces, homes, and more. For a time, we were the twelfth-largest city in North Dakota because we showed up. We created a space saturated with our story and the truth we needed people to see. Tools like Facebook Live were pivotal in sharing our narrative with the world in real time, but now, that tool feels irrelevant. People see injustice happening daily, but they've become numb to it.

What is a chronic argument or tension that shows up again and again in this movement?

Eryn: It feels like there is a generational divide. Having been raised by elders, I deeply respect their wisdom, so when an elder says, "We're not doing that," it's difficult for me to push back. It's not just a tension; it's a profound internal conflict between honoring our diverse ways of knowing and the urgent need to reclaim and assert our voices.

For a long time, it's felt that our stories can *only* be heard if they're told through the lens of trauma. The funding *only* exists if you can see our pain first. We need to perform our anguish and our joy. They need to see us at Missing and Murdered Indigenous Women (MMIW) marches or find us in movie theaters only when we're the protagonists of horrible stories. Even with the show *Reservation Dogs*, many felt like it hadn't been awarded an Emmy for the first two seasons because there is no way we can exist and be respected in the now. We can only be fetishized, infantilized, and put back in the box in our place, only taken out when they want to play with us. Add a few lines here, and young people are coming forward and saying fuck that.

Drop us into a moment where you felt disoriented in the work. Has there been a moment for you when you've been, like, "What's happening?" "Why am I here?" "What's going on?"

Eryn: In Indigenous communications, navigating the complexities of multiple valid ways of knowing can be particularly challenging. For example, I might hear my aunties or clan mothers say, "We need to fight back, take action, burn the house down, blow up a bridge—do whatever it takes." At the same time, other elders might advise, "No, we're going to sit this one out and pray." This dissonance can be disorienting as I work to ensure that everyone feels represented and heard. It's a deeply painful struggle, especially given that, as a larger Indigenous community, we've endured generations of erasure, with our voices systematically stripped away.

Many don't realize that these inner tribal dynamics exist for Native people. They see us as one group, not understanding that when we're having conversations or making decisions, we are doing so with multiple leaders, knowledge keepers, and healers, all bringing their own wisdom and perspectives to the table.

How do you build trust and rapport with Indigenous communities to ensure their narratives are accurately represented and respected?

Linda: I prioritize finding someone from the community to speak for themselves rather than me speaking on their behalf. I often say, "I really can't speak to that because I'm not a part of that community." If I share anything, I clarify, "This is my perspective and my perspective only." When I was younger, I considered myself a storyteller and would sometimes tell stories that weren't mine to tell. As I've matured, I've become more disciplined, learning to step back and allow people to tell their stories instead of overstepping. I now make it a point to avoid telling other people's stories and work hard to respect their voices and experiences.

Eryn: There has been such an extractive approach to storytelling and archiving our conversations in the media. I remember a *New York Times* article that covered the youth council at Standing Rock, and as I read through it, I saw stories that had been explicitly off the record. That experience, among others, made me feel exploited. Since then, I've worked hard to create a space where people can change their minds at every stage of the storytelling process. It's a question of ownership—who should steward these stories, and how do we ensure they are treated respectfully?

My regionally based communications work now involves collaboration and acknowledgment that a deep level of cultural competency is needed when working with people of the global majority. It's about understanding that my way of knowing may not be their way, and that's okay. This cultural competency leads to trust building and a deeper, more accurate understanding of each community's ideas, values, and vision on a tribe-by-tribe, community-by-community basis.

Colonialism is still deeply embedded in today's society—whether through Native mascotry, white families attempting to steal Indigenous children, or the efforts to overturn the Indian Child Welfare Act.[3] Even the idea that non-Natives can claim to be "native" to a place shows a lack of understanding of the history of dehumanization, theft, and exploitation of our people. The harm I see most often comes from people unwilling to learn or be corrected.

Trust building takes time, accountability, and reciprocity. I understand deeply how it feels when trust is broken, and I've also had to reckon with times when I've broken trust myself. In those moments, I had to evaluate my actions and realign with ways of knowing that may not be my own, depending on where I am. Now, I move with the understanding that I am a guest in different spaces, and I work to be the best guest I can be. I hope others adopt that same mind-set when moving through lands that aren't theirs.

In 100 years, what do you want people to know about this work? What is extinct because of the success of this work? And what exists?

Linda: To me, the future looks liberated. I feel privileged to be alive during a time when we're witnessing the death throes of white supremacy and colonialism. It's a painful process, and it can become violent as those in power cling desperately to maintain their order and the status quo—the life of white supremacy and their rigid, binary world. They want a world that's black and white, male and female, one that doesn't acknowledge other genders or identities. People are afraid of change and losing control, so they hold on to these outdated, racist, sexist, and ableist ideas.

There's a group of people who are comfortable with the ongoing violence in Indigenous Gaza because it reinforces their sense of supremacy. While I see the future as liberated, I understand that liberation will look different for each community and person. And while I can't define what it will look like, I'm committed to fighting for whatever it means to them.

Eryn: I look forward to the day when the fight for Indigenous sovereignty becomes irrelevant—when the struggle is no longer necessary. A time when people can go to institutions of higher learning and be taught about us the right way. A future where our writing and narratives aren't just pleas for our existence. I dream of an end to homelessness and to the feeling of being unwelcome in our homelands. I want a day when people can go home without explaining why they want to be there. I think a lot about your work, Linda, and how you always say that seeds and plants tell their own stories, sharing their wisdom.

I look forward to a time when knowledge and culture can no longer be possessed, extracted, and held.

And you know what will be extinct? All of us. We won't be here. I gave my nephew the book *We Are Water Protectors* by Carole Lindstrom and Michaela Goade, and I wrote in it that all of us went to Standing Rock knowing that people like him were coming. We stood for those we knew would come after us. At the Seven Council Fires at Standing Rock, Uncle Arvol Looking Horse said that all our prayers were like seeds planted, and we wouldn't see them sprout. I believe in the next hundred years, we'll see a new landscape of those prayers blossoming. I'm excited to be the planter, even if I can't be the harvester. Part of my vision is no longer needing to be a voice in the room. I hope to be just an echo—comforting and supportive but no longer needed.

Linda: I've seen so much change in the seven years since Standing Rock. It feels like some of those seeds are already sprouting. I feel like we prayed for the way youth are standing up for each other and organizing without fear at Standing Rock. It's hopeful and beautiful to see us moving in that direction, even if we won't be here to witness the full results. Liberation is coming.

Eryn: Land back, water back, languages back, lifeways back. And I think—Y'all are gonna mess with these kids? They'll be of voting age soon, and they're gonna shake things up. By then, we won't have the same kind of democracy or this two-party system that has never worked for us. We'll shape it into something that works because that's what we do. We're not just resilient anymore; we're disrupting in meaningful ways. We're forcing a world that thinks it controls us to reflect on how much it needs us. People may have said it before, but we truly are the dreamers of dreams.

GENDER JUSTICE AND VIOLENCE PREVENTION

Narratives of Resilience and Resistance: The Evolution of me too. and Survivor Justice

By Chelsea Fuller and Denise Beek

Today, the phrase *me too* is inseparable from the movement to end sexual violence popularized in the 2010s by activists, internet communities, and Hollywood. In just one year, between October 2017 and October 2018, the #MeToo hashtag was used more than 19 million times,[1] kindling global deliberation about sexual violence experienced by everyone from sanitation workers to A-list celebrities. But more than a decade before the phrase catapulted into primetime, a little-known organization in Selma, Alabama, founded by a Black organizer named Tarana Burke, used the expression to help survivors of sexual violence contend with and discuss their experiences.

When #MeToo went viral, it not only sparked a nationwide debate about power and privilege in the workplace, it resurfaced a conversation about whose stories are shared and valued, and whose are erased, in the fight for social justice. Throughout history, patriarchal and racial violence have been interconnected and mutually reinforcing. In the United States, Black women are subjected to both racial and gender-based violence, and any movement committed to the safety and liberation of Black women and girls must contend with both.

The #MeToo hashtag capitalized on the network connectivity of social media to allow many survivors to come forward and share their stories. However, the viral nature of this hashtag, while intended to open the discourse to survivors of all races, risked disrupting and co-opting the already established work of the "me too." movement started by Burke.[2] The anti–sexual violence movement has historically erased or obscured Black women's stories, resulting in incomplete narratives and policy solutions not attuned to Black women's and girls' unique needs and experiences. Yet, thanks to narrative interventions by Black survivors, rooted in years of organizing and intergenerational storytelling, #MeToo became a gateway for new intersectional discourse about dismantling sexual violence globally.

This essay explores how "me too." narratives rattled the foundations of patriarchal violence.[3] It traces how Black leaders straddling movements of Black liberation and anti–sexual violence intervened to create an unprecedented opportunity for intersectional storytelling that bucked centuries of erasure and obscurity of Black women's and girls' experiences.

The Origins of me too.

In 1996, Tarana Burke was working as a camp counselor for a youth leadership organization in Selma when she met twelve-year-old Heaven, whose story of sexual abuse stunned her into silence. The delicate details of this child's experience dredged up Burke's own trauma as a survivor. Burke directed Heaven to another counselor, but she never forgot her. Over the years, Heaven was one of many girls who disclosed to Burke that they were being abused. The organization, however, focused on youth development and didn't address gender-based violence or abuse. Instead, sexual violence was rampant within the community and among leaders, some of them with high profiles, who were committing heinous, unlawful acts toward children under their tutelage.

Years later, Burke started Just Be Inc., an organization designed to build a sense of self-worth in Black girls by giving them tools to counteract feelings of worthlessness the world would inevitably push onto them. Just Be Inc. supported Black girls' leadership skills, helping them determine how they wanted to contribute to their community and also supporting them in their goals. The organization was not initially created to combat sexual abuse, assault, or exploitation,[4] but the girls in the program were experiencing all three. Like Heaven, many were survivors of sexual violence and abuse. Some were gang raped, others were new mothers to the babies of their rapists, and some were pregnant—growing a life they did not consent to or choose. Burke knew these girls needed somewhere to tell their stories, commiserate about their experiences, and start their healing journey.

The organization's first campaign was the me too. movement.[5] This is an affirmation Burke would have shared with Heaven back then, "if she had the courage and could find the words."[6] Thankfully, me too. created a soft landing place for Black girls to experience empathy, be empowered, and share their stories safely. Unbeknownst to Burke and her team, their work would soon intersect with fights against state-sanctioned violence and inequity in ways that would create new narrative, social, cultural, and political terrain.

How Emerging Movements in the 2010s Built Momentum for Survivor Justice

Occupy Wall Street

By 2011, a separate movement was percolating that was not focused on survivor justice itself but would help set the national stage for the work of Burke and other Black women to elevate the voices of survivors of sexual violence. In September of that year, Occupy Wall Street challenged the capitalist class and policy makers by addressing growing economic disparities through mobilization, encampments, and storytelling. Global protests emerged as activists constructed encampments in several major cities, including Zuccotti Park near Wall Street in Manhattan—the headquarters of U.S. capitalist activity.

The Occupy movement mobilized people in the United States who were frustrated with economic inequality, corporate influence in politics, and favoritism of the financial industry, which spurred the 2008 financial crisis. This crisis depleted billions of dollars in Black wealth[7] when predatory lending companies exploited poor Black families, hungry to give their children a better life, by peddling faulty loan contracts.

A swell of media coverage during Occupy's peak documented white protestors clashing with violent police. These instances of protestors being beaten, harassed, and tear-gassed led to critical reporting and research highlighting the misconduct displayed by the New York Police Department.[8] What was less covered were reports of sexual violence occurring in the Occupy camps. Multiple women inside Zuccotti Park reported incidents of groping and sexual assault. Men in the camp organized patrols and reported chasing away harassers, but those efforts were insufficient.

Occupy foreshadowed the protest movements that emerged in the latter half of the 2010s, highlighting the deep-seated frustrations of younger generations who felt disillusioned and neglected by the country's systems and institutions. Additionally, it exposed the internal divisions within these movements, particularly along racial and gender lines. This underscored a significant issue: Many people felt these movements failed to provide an inclusive space that addressed their specific concerns and needs.

Black Lives Matter

Public awareness and discourse around police violence and racism surged between 2010 and 2012 following the deaths of Oscar Grant, Aiyana Stanley-Jones, Rekia Boyd, and Trayvon Martin. The reality on the ground, as evidenced by numerous recorded incidents of police violence, often contradicted familiar police narratives claiming their role is to protect and serve. The Black Lives Matter (BLM) movement gained significant momentum in February 2012, after the tragic event in which seventeen-year-old Trayvon Martin was harassed, attacked, and fatally shot by George Zimmerman, a neighborhood vigilante, while walking in his Sanford, Florida, neighborhood with Skittles and iced tea. The acquittal of Zimmerman on murder charges sparked widespread protests, drawing millions to demand justice and challenge the systems that continue to oppress and endanger Black communities.

Martin was not the first or last Black person to be killed by white vigilantes or police. The list of such killings by law-enforcement agencies was so long, and so obfuscated, that it led Wesley Lowery, a journalist who often covered these murders, to organize his employer, *The Washington Post*, to create a database in 2014.[9] By March 31, 2024, the *Post* tallied more than 9,473 deaths since 2015 at the hands of U.S. police officers.[10] The killing of Trayvon Martin and subsequent mass mobilizations across the country led to the creation of BLM in July 2013. Black Lives Matter Global Network—a formation founded by Patrisse Cullors, Alicia Garza, and Opal Tometi—had more than a hundred chapters in the United States and globally at its organizing height.

BLM created one of the most significant narrative opportunities in decades. Hundreds of thousands of activists took to the streets to dismantle the systems that perpetuate and condone anti-Black violence. Of equal significance is how BLM forced a global conversation about whom those in power view as most deserving of safety and dignity. Narrative strategists inside the movement worked with others across the progressive left, uniting fights with interconnected goals and values to craft new, impactful narratives about justice, power, accountability, privilege, class, the value of Black and Brown lives, the role of the state, and bodily autonomy.

As a movement committed to the protection of Black lives, BLM often stumbled where the mission intersected with Black women's fights against sexual violence. As with Occupy Wall Street, there were multiple accusations of sexual assault at the sites of BLM protests.[11] In 2016, some organizers boycotted a Seattle BLM protest in the police killing of forty-seven-year-old Che Taylor because Taylor was convicted of rape in 1992.

The conflicts around sexual violence in the BLM movement were a continuance of similar conflicts in the civil rights movement. Not often mentioned in discussions is the extent to which the civil rights movement was motivated by addressing patterns of sexual violence[12] against Black women that existed alongside lynching, extrajudicial killings, and segregation.

Rosa Parks herself was a survivor of sexual violence and worked to center its elimination in the movement.[13] While the civil rights movement was animated by the harrowing experiences of women like Parks, most protests did not include narratives about sexual violence against women. Prominent male civil rights leaders attributed instances of patriarchal violence within the movement as a distraction from the broader fight for Black civil rights. Still, there were Black women and queer and trans activists who were fighting against patriarchal violence from inside the movement. Across Black-led movements today, a commitment to ending sexual and gender-based violence must be interconnected with the fight to end all forms of systemic violence.

As movements like Occupy and BLM surged in the 2010s, they not only highlighted systemic economic and racial injustices, but also set the stage for a significant focus on survivor justice. The visibility of Occupy, which exposed incidents of sexual violence and racial and gender divisions within its ranks, laid the groundwork that movements like BLM would later navigate. BLM propelled a robust dialogue about the enduring impacts of racial injustice and police violence. It also underscored the complexities of addressing sexual violence within activist movements. This challenge echoed conflicts from the civil rights era, during which sexual violence was often sidelined in the broader racial-justice narrative.

Both movements were transformative, driving the narrative that justice must be intersectional and inclusive of fights against all forms of violence, including sexual and gender-based violence. This perspective has catalyzed a shift, urging today's Black-led movements to integrate a staunch opposition to sexual and gender-based violence alongside their broader systemic aims. As we move forward, the lessons learned from these movements stress the importance of crafting narratives that fully reflect the multidimensional realities of those most impacted, ensuring that no aspect of the fight for justice is left behind.

Women's March and the Election of Donald Trump

The presidential election of Donald J. Trump, whose sexual misconduct was well documented during his campaign,[14] represents one of the most prominent examples of how one figure could embody both individual weaponization of wealth and influence against women's safety and bodily autonomy, and institutional privilege, as Trump ascended to the highest elected position in the wealthiest country on Earth.

Trump, who ascended to the presidency without ever retracting his incendiary comments, faced his own reckoning over allegations of sexual misconduct. Despite a recorded admission of sexual harassment, he won the 2016 presidential election. His presidency sparked an uproar among feminists and activists, reinforcing their resolve against a system that tolerated sexual violence and undermined women's autonomy—a resolve symbolized by his election and the subsequent overturning of *Roe v. Wade*.

On January 21, 2017, the day after Trump's inauguration, the Women's March set a tone that women and gender-expansive people were ready to speak truth to power. Where other iterations of the feminist movement had often employed heteronormative and binary articulations of how patriarchal violence harms and dehumanizes women, the Women's March's proximity to people of color and queer, trans, and nonbinary-led formations enabled it to push more intersectional narratives around who is impacted by sexual violence.

In addition to directly confronting Trump and the rhetoric espoused by his base, the Women's March focused on dismantling oppressive systems that leave vulnerable communities without the resources they need to build the lives they deserve. Their Unity Principles centered on interconnected issues, such as ending violence, protecting reproductive and LGBTQIA+ rights, and environmental justice. As such, the Women's March sought to shift the political conditions that allowed Hilary Clinton, the most qualified presidential candidate in years, to lose to a known racist who took pride in flaunting his long history of harassing women.

While the Women's March set the stage for a host of women candidates to run for public office and win, as well as established women as the leaders of Trump's opposition, it garnered criticism for whitewashing and the erasure of Black and Brown voices. Organizers of the march, many of whom were white women, dubbed the 2017 mobilization the "Million Women March," co-opting a title that had already been used by Black women twenty years prior. Black women and women of color grew concerned that the march wouldn't represent their needs, and that the appointment of women like Tamika Mallory and Linda Sarsour was an attempt to sweep the feminist movement's racist history under the rug without white women being held accountable for their decisions. Public responses by Black women sparked much-needed dialogue about racial dynamics and led to the creation of the Unity Principles.

Ultimately, the Women's March became a testing ground for how to mobilize women, gender-expansive people, survivors, and anyone impacted or threatened by misogyny and sexual violence in opposition to the normalization of far-Right politics.

The resistance to Trump unified various progressive groups, including those involved in Occupy Wall Street, BLM, and what would become the #MeToo movement. These groups saw in Trump the embodiment of the patriarchal and white-supremacist structures they opposed and organized to abolish. For the movement against sexual violence, the backlash against Trump cracked open a political opportunity. It reached a boiling point when, months later, several accounts of sexual misconduct in Hollywood started making international headlines. There would be no turning back.

In October of 2017, actress Alyssa Milano tweeted, "If you've ever been sexually harassed or assaulted, write 'me too.' as a reply to this tweet."[15] In twenty-four hours, 12 million people turned "me too." into #MeToo, sharing experiences of sexual violence with others. Many said they were disclosing their survivor identity for the first time, exposing their abusers, and affirming other survivors seeking commiseration.

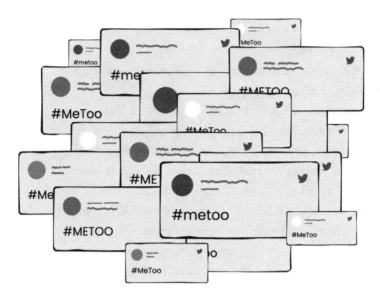

The viral #MeToo moment.

People, especially Black women, who knew about Burke's work organized online, drawing connections to Just Be Inc.'s me too. campaign that began years before. However, according to philosopher Olúfẹ́mi Táíwò, people were primed for the celebrity-focused approach because the world is organized along systems crafted by and for elite interests. In his book *Elite Capture: How the Powerful Took Over Identity Politics (and Everything Else)*, he defines elite capture as a process where "the advantaged few steer resources and institutions that could serve the many toward their own narrower interests and aims."[16]

Anti-Black narratives are gendered, meaning they target Black women differently. In particular, they have consistently stereotyped Black women as sexual deviants and unfit mothers. Such narratives have accumulated power over time and hold sway over our capacity to empathize with Black women and our perceptions of who does and does not deserve to benefit from being protected from sexual violence.

Today, more than a third of Black women experience some form of sexual violence in their lifetime. Yet, according to a Brandeis University study, prosecutors file charges against just 34 percent of attacks reported by Black women, compared to 75 percent of attacks reported by white women. The police are often perpetrators of sexual violence against Black women, according to research by the African American Policy Forum. For example, former Oklahoma City police officer Daniel Holtzclaw raped and/or sexually assaulted at least thirteen Black women over several years.[17]

Because Black women are subjected to racial and gender-based violence, any movement committed to the safety and liberation of Black women and girls must contend with both. According to Shanelle Matthews, Distinguished Lecturer of Anthropology and Interdisciplinary Studies at the City University of New York:

> At present, Black boys and men remain the face of police brutality and state-sanctioned violence in the US. Their deaths and the organizing that follows have given rise to powerful mass uprisings for racial justice and Black liberation. Oscar Grant, Trayvon Martin, Philando Castile, Alton Sterling, Eric Garner, Mike Brown, George Floyd—we know their names. This is important. Black women and girls deserve the same recognition, rage, and people-powered response. As Professor Brittany Cooper smartly asks, "Why does it remain so difficult for outrage over the killing of Black women to be the tipping point for national protests challenging state violence?"
>
> The relative invisibility of Black women's experiences of policing in the US is a product of Black women's social positionality: Black women sit at the intersection of patriarchal misogyny and anti-Black racism. Patriarchy deploys ideological and physical violence to objectify and repress women in the interest of male dominance, denying women's fundamental humanity. Anti-Black racism, an essential part of the racial capitalism that structures US (and global) society, involves, as a professor of African American studies Dr. kihana miraya ross[18] explains, "society's inability to recognize our humanity—the disdain, disregard, and disgust for our existence."[19]

While Milano's viral tweet brought widespread attention to the issue of sexual violence, it also highlighted the long-standing efforts of activists like Burke, who have been advocating for marginalized survivors long before the hashtag existed. To achieve true liberation and safety for all, social movements must acknowledge and address the dual layers of violence faced by Black women, ensuring that their struggles are met with the same urgency and solidarity afforded to other victims of systemic oppression.

From #MeToo to "me too." International

In the wake of the #MeToo movement, different organizations emerged to address sexual violence and advocate for workplace respect. Time's Up, led by high-profile figures in Hollywood, aimed to tackle sexism with a focus on cisgender women, backed by celebrities and wealthy industry professionals. In contrast, me too. International, guided by Black survivors and funded by philanthropy, sought to broaden the national conversation about sexual violence with a focus on marginalized communities.

While both aimed to challenge a culture of misogyny, their approaches and constituencies differed markedly. Time's Up often didn't reflect the narratives of Black and Brown survivors or those from queer, trans, and disabled communities. Meanwhile, me too. became unfairly associated with cancel culture due to public confusion between #MeToo and me too., which led to a need to distinguish them clearly. To maintain focus on survivors of color, Burke collaborated with Blackbird,[20] a capacity-building project, to realign the narrative. Burke's proactive engagement with the media emphasized the systemic nature of sexual violence and the mission of me too., keeping the movement's core message and the people it serves in the spotlight.

In alignment with its commitment to survivors, me too. International guided the creation of the Survivors' Agenda,[21] a platform with a cultural analysis and policy recommendations developed by survivors. More than forty organizations came together with a mission to: (1) listen deeply to survivors about what they need and how they want to use their voices; (2) expand and shape a constituency of survivors that is rooted in healing and political action; and (3) call for a change in the rules, so that elected leaders would be held accountable to the needs of survivors by passing laws in support of their survivor base. The strength of the Survivors' Agenda could be measured in its ability to organize survivors around pressing issues, and build narrative and political power with nuanced messaging about sexual violence as a nonpartisan issue.

The legal and carceral-centered orientation around sexual violence was also missing the mark when it came to everyday survivors seeking healing and safety in their daily lives. Accountability can take the shape of prosecutions, prison sentences, and lifelong placement on sex-offender registries. Still, all of those measures focus the resources and power of the state on the perpetrator rather than the victims. Once punishment is meted out, the survivors of sexual violence still need safety and support. Neither are the provinces of local law enforcement.

A Future Without Sexual Violence

When #MeToo took off, hundreds of thousands shared survivor stories to commiserate across time and space. This opened new gateways to discourse about how to solve an epidemic that has hurt so many people. This intervention was made possible because of years of organizing and advocacy from survivors with small platforms, reach, and resources. It was possible because of online community building, offline advocacy, and intergenerational storytelling.

The history of organizing against sexual violence is long and storied. It did not start with twentieth-century white feminists, Tarana Burke, or Alyssa Milano, but with women whose names we may never know. Women who fought patriarchal dominance and norms that perpetuated violence against women and others at a time when it was criminal to do so. Women on plantations and under colonial rule. Women on slave ships and refugee vessels. The me too. movement exists in a long lineage of the Black radical tradition: "The culture of opposition born, nurtured, and sustained within everyday life, honed and refined through expressive culture and underground activism."[22] Today, it's hard to imagine a world without the me too. movement and the millions of survivors it has reached. Few interventions in the twenty-first century have led to such swift political, social, and cultural change.

Still, there is more work to do.

Who deserves safety? This question binds the interconnectedness of the systemic issues that plague Black people—like poverty, limited health care and education, safe housing, and livable wages—and create a breeding ground for violence in our communities.

Suppose we aim to build a world where public safety includes the welfare of Black people, particularly Black women, girls, and gender-expansive people. In that case, we have to examine how narratives about race and identity determine whom public safety is *for* and whom the public is being kept safe *from*.

In this current moment, survivor-justice organizations like me too. are working across the movement ecosystem, taking up the mantle with reproductive-justice organizations to defend bodily autonomy in the face of sweeping legislation that bans abortions and criminalizes those who seek them. This suppression of choice, access, and agency unravels decades of progress. It underscores the reality that the systemic oppression survivors face is inextricably linked to all other injustices born from patriarchal violence and white supremacy.

In the years since the viral #MeToo moment, survivors have been forging a path to freedom and fighting for safety while creating space for questions like: How do we build staying power for me too. and the fight for survivor justice? Through the work and the lessons learned from those who fought before us, one of the many answers to this critical question is through coalition building and shared narrative strategies that weave together the stories, experiences, and solutions of those who suffer yet have been silenced and subjugated.

The collective work we've done—and must continue to do—has aided the power building of other progressive movements working across systemic issues, not because they are all doing survivor-justice work per se, but because me too. taught us that all justice work is survivor-justice work. Survivors are in every crevice and cranny of our communities—living, contributing, and leading every day. That acknowledgment alone moves us one step closer to a world where the threat of sexual violence is merely a memory instead of our present reality.

De-carceral work is survivor-justice work.
Economic-justice work is survivor-justice work.
Education-justice work is survivor-justice work.
Faith work is survivor-justice work.
Environmental-justice work is survivor-justice work.
The fight for Medicare for All is survivor-justice work.
Abortion-access work is survivor-justice work.

The me too. movement demonstrated how collective healing and action begin with empathy and a determination to convey sexual violence as a systemic and, therefore, solvable issue. It also demonstrated that narratives are one of the most essential tools for legitimizing the movement for survivor justice and weaving it into the fabric of our world, history, and future.

Burke and those who have since rallied to fuel the global movement to end sexual violence over the past decade are stewards of a venerable legacy. They are griots carrying the stories, strategies, and dreams of survivors and allies who fought to ensure that the experiences of survivors—namely survivors of color, those impacted by poverty, and gender-expansive survivors—were not erased from the broader feminist movements throughout history. Their role in that legacy and the parallels between what their predecessors experienced and the conditions they have navigated in creating new frames, messages, and storytelling strategies about survivorhood make their offerings both familiar and one-of-a-kind.

Root Causes and Radical Change: Reimagining Gun Violence Prevention in America

By Trevon Bosley and Rachel Jacoby

As organizers in the gun violence prevention movement, we both share stories of trauma and the profound impact gun violence has had on our lives, families, and communities. While we represent different entry points into the gun violence prevention movement—and different positionality with respect to race, class, and lived experiences in the Chicagoland area—the work that we do to reduce and prevent gun violence is inextricably linked. This is why we have chosen to introduce this essay with our firsthand accounts.

As a child growing up in a city like Chicago, many days I woke up and went to sleep to the sounds of gunshots and police sirens. I thought of this as just a way of life. In December 2005, when I was seven, I first experienced gun violence when my cousin Vincent Avant was shot and killed down the street from his home. A year later, violence hit even closer to home when, on April 4, 2006, my brother Terrell Bosley—a prominent gospel bass player and college student—was shot and killed at church while getting ready for band rehearsal. Terrell was at a place of worship—a place thought to be safe. Yet his shooting was immediately labeled gang-related. And his character was investigated by police long before they investigated his murder. Terrell's case remains unsolved, and his story is not foreign to this city, state, or country.

My violence prevention journey started after the loss of my brother. My parents had me attending marches since the age of eight, and by age eleven, I joined a youth-led violence prevention organization called the B.R.A.V.E. Youth Leaders (Bold Resistance Against Violence Everywhere). It was a group of youth from different communities around Chicago coming together to create real change through action outside of solely legislation.

I eventually served as board co-chair for March for Our Lives national violence prevention organization. My goal in this fight represents a far too often ignored and overlooked community whose lives have been deemed unimportant to the violence prevention conversation. Whether their lives were ignored because of the color of their skin or their lifestyle, I work to make sure their impact lives on.

   —Trevon Bosley, 25

I vividly remember completing my first active shooting drill when I was seven years old, cowering under my desk, jaw trembling, trying to breathe normally. Throughout my schooling, I completed more active shooter drills than fire drills. Young people across the country—members of Generation Lockdown[1]—recognize that my story is not unique as we have grown up under the constant threat of gun violence. After finishing college, I decided to work in the gun violence prevention movement to do everything I could to end the scourge of gun violence in our country. I spent just under two years working at Giffords, the gun violence prevention organization founded by Gabby Giffords after she survived being shot in the head. My time at Giffords served as a crash course in the history of the gun violence prevention movement and introduced me to the narrative and structural challenges that persist in the movement today.

   After an eighteen-year-old shot and killed nineteen students and two teachers at Robb Elementary School in Uvalde, Texas, in June 2022, I organized a rally with March for Our Lives in my hometown of Highland Park, Illinois. The rally called on elected leaders to pass legislation and invest in community violence intervention to prevent gun violence. Three weeks after the rally, the same streets we marched through became the site of another mass shooting, where seven people died and forty-eight others were injured in our city's July 4 parade. I jumped into action to support my community, leading vigils, rallies, and ultimately, the grassroots organizing effort for the Protect Illinois Communities Act (PICA). PICA became the most comprehensive piece of gun violence prevention legislation ever passed in state history, making Illinois the ninth state in the country to ban assault weapons. Following graduate school, I returned to my hometown of Highland Park, Illinois, where I currently work in a local office of gun violence prevention in my home county.

—**Rachel Jacoby, 28**

Gun violence ranks as one of the top concerns for residents in major U.S. cities. Every day, more than 120 people are killed and 200 are shot and wounded.[2] Despite the ubiquity of gun-related deaths and injuries, dominant media narratives tend to obfuscate the root causes of gun violence. On the one hand, the media overrepresents mass shootings[3] while ignoring the persistent pattern of mass shooters as men with a history of violence and white supremacist views, who have been radicalized by the far Right. Instead, shooters are framed as troubled lone wolves with mental health issues,[4] which disregards systemic racism and the proliferation of guns as the main drivers of homicides and violence.[5]

When reporting on gun violence goes beyond mass shootings, prevailing narratives often portray it as a cultural issue within Black and Brown neighborhoods that can be addressed through increased policing and incarceration, while incidents involving predominantly white perpetrators are viewed as aberrations. In both cases, news stories tend to invisibilize the experiences of communities directly impacted by gun violence, especially communities of color. The ideological roots of these dominant narratives are steeped in white supremacy, date back to racist gun laws underpinning the Second Amendment, and directly intersect with present-day housing shortages, trauma center deserts, mass incarceration, and poverty.

It's imperative to address the root causes of gun violence on a structural and narrative level if we are to build lasting power within our social movements. In this chapter, we will not only trace the history and dominant narratives that have shaped responses to gun violence in the United States but also shed light on a new generation of young organizers who have shepherded a turning point in the gun violence prevention movement. By deploying counternarratives that center a diversity of voices, debunk racist stereotypes, and address the root causes of gun violence, movement organizations have been able to secure electoral wins and pass hundreds of state-level legislative actions on gun safety. As the gun violence prevention movement continues to grow, investing in narrative power and movement building will be critical to long-term change at a national level.

Roots Causes of Gun Violence

We're going to fight racism not with racism, but we're going to fight with solidarity. We say we're not going to fight capitalism with black capitalism, but we're going to fight it with socialism. We say that we will work with anybody and form a coalition with anybody that has revolution on their mind.[6]

—Fred Hampton

In 1969, Fred Hampton, then deputy chairman of the state of Illinois Black Panther Party, founded the Rainbow Coalition in Chicago. The coalition, comprised of diverse member organizations—including those led by Black radicals, Latinx and Indigenous revolutionaries, white Southerners, and militant leftists—became one of the first formations to address the root causes of gun violence, such as poverty, substandard housing, and systemic racism. Members formed alliances across race and ethnicity in one of the most segregated cities in the United States, building power and leftist political analysis in the face of rampant police brutality and systematic community disinvestment. Although the movement was cut short due to the FBI's assassination of Fred Hampton and its ongoing harassment of local organizers, the coalition's comprehensive approach became a model of modern-day violence prevention efforts.

Decades later, gun violence continues to disproportionately affect Black communities due to the same historic and present-day root causes the Rainbow Coalition had tried to address. One of the major issues has been redlining by the Federal Housing Administration (FHA), which had deemed Black neighborhoods "undesirable," locking residents out of bank loans and insurance and limiting their geographic and economic mobility. In Chicago, the FHA redlined nearly one-third of Chicago neighborhoods, all of which were predominantly Black.[7] Research shows that neighborhoods that were redlined in the twentieth century have higher levels of firearm violence today.[8]

Fred Hampton, left, chairman of the Black Panthers, speaks during a press conference with the Young Lords, a Puerto Rican civil and human rights group, on October 10, 1969, at Holy Covenant United Methodist Church in Chicago. With Hampton are, from left, Pablo "Yoruba" Guzman, a Young Lord from New York; Jose "Cha-Cha" Jimenez, founder of the Young Lords of Chicago; and Mike Klonsky, a spokesman for Students for a Democratic Society. Photo courtesy of *Chicago Tribune*/Tribune News Service via Getty Images

The firearms industry has recognized this trend, using racist marketing strategies and fearmongering to convince people in both Black and Brown and white communities that they are not safe without the protection of guns. This narrative of fear has increased the number of guns in circulation, and by extension, the likelihood that a firearm ends up in the hands of persons looking to harm themselves or others. These same guns can be misplaced, stolen, or improperly used, leading to an increase in gun violence that disproportionately affects Black communities and the cycle begins again.

Today, Black communities bear the brunt of gun violence. Black people account for approximately 14 percent of the U.S. population yet 60 percent of the homicide victims.[9] This translates to Black people being 11.5 times more likely to be victims of firearm homicide than white people. Black people also face the greatest increases in firearm suicide rates: from 2018 to 2021, the firearm suicide rate for white people rose by about 4 percent compared to an increase of about 44 percent for Black people.[10] The effects of this violence permeate into the broader community, leading to collective grief and trauma.

How the World Perceives Gun Violence

The root causes of gun violence—and efforts to curtail gun violence prevention measures—are upheld by deep-seated dominant narratives, including the idea that guns keep us safe and stories that pathologize Black cities and Black people. These narratives feed into divide-and-conquer tactics that attempt to segment the issue of gun violence based on how it affects different communities, sowing division among those in our movement. Understanding how these dominant narratives operate is central to building cohesion among organizers and movement actors.

Guns Keep You Safe

In the 1970s, the gun lobby and conservatives launched efforts to broadly reinterpret the Second Amendment to emphasize twofold narratives of individual freedom and protection of people and property. First, they began funding a far-reaching movement of judges and scholars to broadly reimagine the Second Amendment and reinforce the idea that a "good citizen" is an "armed citizen." This shifted the public's perception of the Second Amendment from one focused on preventing the disarmament of state militias to one rooted in the idea that owning firearms promotes safety and self-defense. Nevertheless, recent research demonstrates that firearm ownership is associated with increased suicide, homicide, and unintentional deaths and injuries.[11]

Although this radical shift may have been initially spurred by ideology, the NRA's positions in the last two decades have been inextricably linked to the financial interests of the gun lobby, including gun manufacturers.[12] The expanded reinterpretation of the Second Amendment has corresponded to an increase in the sale of firearms and guns in circulation, leading to record-high profits for gun manufacturers.[13] For example, about 132 million guns had been produced in the United States in 1975. That number rose to an estimated 494 million guns in 2023.[14] This is not surprising given the millions of dollars gun manufacturers invest in the NRA to support Republican politicians, who create the conditions that enable easy access to firearms.[15]

The rise in gun ownership,[16] particularly among BIPOC (Black, Indigenous, People of Color) communities and women,[17] reflects the power of these dominant narratives, as well as the deep-seated mistrust of institutions that should keep us safe. While white people, especially white men, have histori-cally been the primary demographic represented in gun ownership, Black people, and Black men in particular,[18] are the fastest-growing group of gun owners in the United States.[19] In recent years, the gun lobby has gleefully capitalized on fear of violence following racist shootings to sell more guns. In 2022, the gun lobby ramped up marketing to Black Americans following a shooting in Buffalo by a white supremacist.[20] They did the same to Asian Americans the following year after two mass shootings in Half Moon Bay and Monterey Park.[21]

The increased levels of gun ownership among BIPOC communities repre-sent a failure by the gun violence prevention movement to counter narratives from the gun lobby about firearms, violence, and safety. It is not enough to simply utilize data and facts to combat the very real fear that many mar-ginalized groups feel. Rather, the gun violence prevention movement must acknowledge fear and mistrust in institutions and counter these narratives with investment, community support, and an influx of resources.

Racist Dog Whistles

From "Black on Black crime" to "What about Chicago?" conservatives often use racist dog whistles as a justification for opposing racial justice measures or investment in community violence intervention (CVI) programs in Black and Brown communities. Dog whistles serve to code insidious narratives in messages that seem, on the surface, innocuous.

"Black on Black crime" is a phrase used to pathologize Black commu-nities, signaling that Black people are more likely to commit crimes than white people. Despite this myth being debunked (the overwhelming majority of white people are killed by other white people), its persistence in public and political discourse signals the pernicious strength of white supremacist ideology as a staple in the American psyche. In a 2020 article for *Teen Vogue*, columnist Jameelah Nasheed wrote, "Using language like 'Black-on-Black crime' perpetuates the myth that intraracial violence is specific to the Black community—a myth that implies Black people are inherently more violent. This tactic has been used to justify the mistreatment of Black people since the abolishment of slavery."[22]

The city of Chicago has similarly been used as a racist symbol for out-of-control violence in Black and Brown communities. The phrase "What about Chicago?" has fueled conservative justification for why gun violence prevention legislation does not work, as Illinois has the third strongest gun violence laws in the country.[23] Chicago is not unique: it ranks 10th among major U.S. cities in terms of homicide rates.[24] This narrative ignores the reality that more than half of guns used in crime in Chicago come from neighboring states with weaker gun laws, which correlates with higher rates of firearm fatalities.[25,26] This narrative also ignores that eight of the ten states with the highest homicide rates have lax gun legislation, rates higher than Illinois.[27] With Chicago home to one of the largest Black populations in the United States, this racist narrative has been used to dehumanize victims of gun violence and misdirect away from the root causes driving high violence rates in cities across the country.

Debunking these dog whistles, and the underlying racist narratives that drive them, we must recognize that everyday gun violence is fueled by decades of disinvestment and a lack of resources, particularly in Black and Brown communities. Policy responses must address the varying root causes of gun violence, from poverty to underfunded educational institutions to economic neglect, rather than further criminalize people of color by pouring more money into law enforcement. Jameelah Nasheed of *Teen Vogue* summarizes this well: "White supremacists will justify colonization, slavery, and the confederacy, all while saying Black people are an inherently more violent race. . . . Crime within Black communities is comparable to crime within white communities, but white people aren't being killed by police at the alarming rate that Black people are."[28]

Seeding Counternarratives: Bridging the Divide

One of the greatest challenges to shifting the narrative on gun violence in the twenty-first century has been bridging two sides of the same movement: those addressing the rise in mass shootings and those focused on the impact of everyday gun violence. Often, funding and legislative strategies do not center on the people most impacted by gun violence, leading to solutions that do not address the root causes. Following, we examine the shift from the

1990s and early 2000s, when community violence intervention (CVI) organizations were often invisibilized by the media, to the 2010s, when the mass shooting at Sandy Hook reignited national momentum for the gun violence prevention movement. In 2018, March for Our Lives marked an opportunity to recenter radical values within the gun violence prevention movement and build momentum toward grassroots change.

Recentering Community Investment (1990s–2000s)

During the 1990s and early 2000s, violence in urban communities grew as the effects of redlining, systemic racism, the crack epidemic, and mass incarceration became more prevalent. More local organizations and initiatives directed efforts toward violence prevention such as Operation Ceasefire in Boston, Life Camp in New York, Cure Violence, and the Faith Community of St. Sabina in Chicago.

All of these organizations were confronted with dominant media narratives that stoked contempt and fear toward Black communities, leading to policies that promoted mass incarceration. However, these local organizations knew that addressing the basic needs of their communities was the only way to counteract the growing violence. This first generation of CVI organizations utilized multiple tactics to prevent violence, such as offering mediation services to address interpersonal tension and conflict; investing in case managers to support individuals with drug treatment, employment, and housing; and creating activities for community members to come together. Their messaging centered on unity and investment in the community, recognizing that violence is driven by disinvestment and neglect. These efforts by local organizations, however, were frequently ignored by society and the media.

Following the deadly mass shooting at Sandy Hook Elementary School in December 2012, several national gun violence prevention organizations formed, such as Moms Demand Action, Everytown, Newtown Action Alliance, and Giffords. These organizations originally focused heavily on legislation particularly to address mass shootings, such as universal background checks and the assault weapons ban. Narratively, they framed the problem as a matter of restricting access to high-powered firearms by those who are at risk of harming themselves or others.

Although this new energy in the movement brought more funds and organizations into violence prevention, these new efforts and legislative strategies often excluded and ignored Black communities and local Black-led organizations like Cure Violence and Operation Ceasefire, who had been most impacted by everyday gun violence and had already been working on increasing access to community violence intervention funding and addressing the root causes of violence.

One of the primary challenges in the movement has been the disproportionate amount of media, resources, and public attention focused on mass shootings. When the American public thinks of gun violence, they may think about shootings like Sandy Hook, Parkland, or Uvalde. These mass shootings are devastating, especially because they involve children. However, the majority of mass shootings—defined by the Gun Violence Archive as an incident in which four or more people (not including the shooter) are shot and killed—occur in Black communities outside of the national media spotlight.[29]

For example, a decline in media attention during the COVID-19 pandemic gave the false perception that mass shootings had declined, while people were quarantining and children were in virtual, rather than in-person, school. In reality, data from the Gun Violence Archive showed that mass shootings rose during the pandemic, especially in Black neighborhoods.[30] This matters because media attention brings financial resources to support survivors, an influx of funding for violence prevention efforts, and an acknowledgment of the problem from elected officials. During COVID-19, legislative debates on gun violence prevention legislation were often pushed to the back burner despite gun violence victims increasing the strain on overcrowded hospitals.[31]

The data reflect this disparity in media coverage. A study of coverage of homicide victims in Chicago found that Black people killed in predominantly Black communities received about half as much media attention as white people killed in predominantly white communities.[32] One of the authors of this study stated, "The most newsworthy shootings seem to break an assumption that a particular place is safe." The implied conclusion of this statement is that shootings in predominantly Black neighborhoods do not seem to break this assumption, particularly for people living outside of these communities. That is a narrative problem that the gun violence prevention movement—and our country more broadly—must address. Every child and every person in every community should feel safe going to school, playing in the park, or simply walking down the street.

Birth of March for Our Lives (2010s)

In the 2010s, several CVI organizations tried to bridge the gap between the two sides of the gun violence prevention conversation. Larger organizations, however, continued ignoring the needs of communities of color, so tensions grew and attempts at unity stopped short. It was not until the 2018 Parkland, Florida, shooting that the discourse around gun violence prevention shifted. With the birth of March for Our Lives (MFOL), society saw not only a nationally recognized youth movement in the violence prevention space, but a more inclusive approach to violence prevention.

MFOL was hardly the first youth-led organization to mobilize around gun violence. Yet it received outsized attention from media, elected officials, and society more broadly, primarily because of its whiteness. After meeting with some of Chicago's Black and Brown youth organizers, from organizations like B.R.A.V.E. Youth Leaders and North Lawndale Peace Warriors, some of

The first March for Our Lives demonstration took place in Washington, DC, on March 24, 2018. The mobilization was attended by over one million people, with solidarity events taking place across the United States and the world. Photo courtesy of March for Our Lives

MFOL's founding members took the opportunity to share the spotlight with many of us who had been in this fight but whose stories and actions were being ignored by the public. Together, we organized the first MFOL rally in Washington, DC, with over a million people in attendance and speakers not only from Parkland, but from Chicago, Baltimore, Atlanta, and more. Young people in large cities and small towns organized hundreds of sister marches across the country. Black, Brown, and white youth all spoke about their different relationships with gun violence. Although far from perfect, this was the beginning of a different approach and response to gun violence.

In response to the movement's growing power, the gun lobby perpetuated narratives that the young people leading this movement were crisis actors, who were pawns of the Democratic Party and liberal billionaires plotting to take away guns from law-abiding citizens.[33] MFOL created a narrative that rejected the scarcity mind-set, demonstrating that there are enough resources to address legislative solutions to gun violence *and* invest in violence prevention in historically underserved communities. MFOL gave youth of all backgrounds the opportunity to be at the forefront of the national conversation to counter decades-old false narratives. The unfiltered youth voices, revitalizing energy, and lived experiences of young people led to a change in legislation and political power as well as the beginning of a more inclusive approach to gun violence prevention from major organizations.

The birth of March for Our Lives coincided with record-breaking youth voter turnout around the country, the creation of multiple youth-led progressive organizations, and diverse voices shifting the strategic direction of national gun violence prevention organizations. As young and diverse faces moved to the forefront, many communities felt more inclined to get involved in the movement. This diversity provided strength, leading to wins such as the Bipartisan Safer Communities Act, the first piece of gun violence prevention legislation to pass in thirty years. This law included over $250 million in violence prevention funding, a key priority to address gun violence in Black communities. Additionally, pressure from advocates led to the creation of the first White House Office of Violence Prevention. At the state level, over 250 pieces of gun safety legislation have been passed since the founding of March for Our Lives. The movement also solidified electoral wins, outspending the

NRA in the 2016 and 2018 elections, and electing Maxwell Frost, the first Gen-Z member of Congress.

Toward a More Radical Future

Despite the progress of the gun violence prevention movement, 327 people are shot every day in the United States.[34] This is approximately one person every five minutes—or the time it takes to read this chapter.

In recent years, organizations like March for Our Lives have accelerated the progress and direction of the gun violence prevention movement, bringing it back to its more unified roots. Fighting with solidarity, as Fred Hampton said, should form the foundation of the movement, as we continue to deconstruct racist dominant narratives driven by mass media and the ever-growing gun lobby.

As the gun violence prevention movement continues to grow, investing in narrative power and movement building is critical to ensuring that there is an inclusive approach to gun violence prevention centered on addressing root causes. It is easy to feel hopeless as shootings continue, people die, and more and more people in the United States live with the trauma of gun violence.

Moving forward, we must recognize that where institutions have failed our most vulnerable communities, community trust and resources are the antidote. To shut down and work in silos would be to repeat the mistakes of past generations—rather, we must invest in narratives that center on the people closest to the issue and lift up the solidarity between different segments of the gun violence prevention movement.

Guiding Principles: March for Our Lives

The success of March for Our Lives has been rooted in a set of guiding principles that have shaped and will continue to shape the trajectory of work. These are principles that harken back to the radical moments of the Rainbow Coalition and communities themselves, on their own terms, setting the strategies for violence prevention. We hope these principles will inspire others across progressive movements.

People most proximate to the pain should be the most proximate to the power.

Only in recent years have major gun violence prevention organizations begun to center on the voices of young people and Black and Brown people. We have often felt that decisions on policy and strategy are made in the ivory towers of Washington, DC, while the lived experience and expertise of those who are not in traditional positions of power are relegated to sharing personal stories of trauma. Whether it is youth, mothers, formerly incarcerated people, or survivors of gun violence, the movement has an obligation to those who have felt the devastating effects of gun violence most intimately. This approach also helps build movement power and provides survivors the agency to regain control over personal narratives. Too often, these organizations will parade survivors of gun violence and the most marginalized for their own purposes, regardless of how retelling their stories can force survivors to relive the most traumatic moments of their lives. The days of performative press conferences and social media posts are over. The movement must fundamentally restructure and redistribute power to those who have been most deeply affected.

Legislation without investment is an incomplete answer to a systemic problem.

For too long, legislation has been viewed as a panacea in the gun violence prevention movement. Although bills such as an assault weapons ban, universal background checks, or safe storage would play an important role in curbing the devastating effects of gun violence, this legislation would not make a significant impact on the everyday gun violence that continues to plague underserved communities throughout the country. Gun violence is an inherently intersectional issue—it is impossible to make progress without recognizing its intersection with the criminal legal system, systemic racism, redlining, historic disinvestment, and more. Accordingly, legislation passed in a vacuum without corresponding easily accessible investment in community violence intervention programs and a redistribution of resources to balance decades of disinvestment will not end gun violence.

There are no permanent friends and no permanent enemies— only permanent purpose.
This principle is based on the fact that those in positions of power—particularly elected officials—must continue to earn the trust and goodwill of this movement. Regardless of who is in power, who has allied with the movement before, and who has opposed key bills, our commitment to ending gun violence remains consistent. And remains in service to the grass roots first and foremost.

The Best Defense Is a Good Offense

What the 2016 Campaign Against the North Carolina Bathroom Bill Can Teach Us About Today's Narrative Battles for Trans Liberation

By hermelinda cortés and Jess St. Louis

Today, we are in an environment that's increasingly hostile to LGBTQ+ people. In 2023 alone, more than 500 pieces of anti-LGBTQ+ legislation[1] were introduced by local and statewide elected leaders[2] across the United States—attacking gender-affirming care and banning trans people from education, athletics, and the basic right to exist. This has led to not only threats but real-world violence, targeting school districts[3] and Pride demonstrations.[4]

This anti-LGBTQ+ climate does not exist in a vacuum: It has been upheld and amplified using a coordinated narrative attack by right-wing actors[5] with trans people at the center. Through fear-mongering stories[6] about trans people, these right-wing actors have rehashed long-standing and harmful narratives about LGBTQ+ people, casting us as a threat to children and society. Meanwhile, trans athletes have been used as a wedge to divide communities and deploy language that connects trans people to sexual assault and "grooming."[7]

To understand the success of this renewed moral panic, we must go back to 2016, when the North Carolina state legislature passed the Public Facilities Privacy and Security Act, better known as HB2, or the Bathroom Bill. Through it, the Right not only succeeded in demonizing LGBTQ+ communities, but opened the door to broader attacks on good governance and our democracy.

North Carolina: A National Testing Ground

For some, it came as little surprise that antitrans narratives and policy were leveraged in North Carolina (NC) in 2016 as a testing ground to advance right-wing narratives and governing power.

North Carolina has occupied a particular narrative position as "more progressive" than other Southern states, making it a good testing ground to shape the national conversation. Yet, by 2010, the state was feeling the ripple effects of six years of right-wing takeover. The North Carolina Republican Party (GOP) had captured both houses of the state legislature in 2010 and secured a political trifecta when they won the governorship in 2012.

Over the years, the national and state-based GOP learned they could win policy victories by using anti-LGBTQ+ narratives. The passage of the state-wide ballot initiative Amendment 1—targeting same-sex marriage [8]—acted as proof of concept for that strategy. However, after the Supreme Court ruled same-sex marriage bans unconstitutional in 2014, the state party needed to try a new approach to retain and expand their power.

In March 2016, North Carolina GOP legislators and Governor Pat McCrory passed HB2 after Charlotte's city council passed an antidiscrimination ordinance that included trans people. The bill did three things: (1) It stripped local governments of the right to adopt more antidiscrimination laws for at least five years; (2) it prevented local governments' ability to raise the minimum wage above $7.25 an hour; and (3) it restricted trans people from using public bathrooms that match their gender.

The Narrative Battle of HB2: Dominant Narratives

The North Carolina and national GOP were the anchors of the right wing's narrative strategy, supported by networks of conservative leaders and organizations spanning religion and business.

Governor McCrory was a primary spokesperson in support of HB2, whose messaging of "government overreach" was applied to both the local[9] and federal government,[10] the latter of which sued the state in a civil rights lawsuit in response to the bill. This messaging drew upon long-standing narratives that elected officials should protect states' rights from the federal government, the belief that "outsider" progressive views in big cities do not reflect the true values of the whole state, and the persistent view that big government is bad.

Governor McCrory and others flanked their antigovernment narratives with talking points about trans people in bathrooms being a public-safety concern,[11] with messages like "Keep Women Safe" and "Protect NC Women."

By misgendering and scapegoating trans women as a threat to public safety, right-wing narrative actors leveraged the historically racist narrative about "dangerous men being a threat to women and children," often used to attack Black people in the South. Despite the "women" and "children" in these stories being implicitly coded as "cis" and "white," a multiracial constellation[12] of spokespeople in the state advanced these narratives, with Black and Latinx pastors speaking out in support of HB2.[13]

Narrative Resistance to HB2

Because HB2 attacked trans people, antidiscrimination practices, and fair wages, the campaign against HB2 brought together a set of unlikely allies who had not always worked side by side. Grassroots organizations, coalitions, and formations working inside and outside North Carolina—such as Southerners on New Ground (SONG),[14] the Moral Monday movement,[15] and NC Raise Up[16]—came together to activate people and groups organizing across voting and faith communities. Together, they rallied in support of workers' rights, LGBTQ+ liberation, and racial justice. As momentum built, large national LGBTQ+ organizations, such as the Human Rights Campaign[17] and the National LGBTQ Task Force,[18] as well as the statewide and national Democratic Party and political communication firms, joined the fight, pouring in greater financial resources than local grassroots formations were able to leverage. As a result, these mainstream progressive bodies shaped and impacted the campaign's strategies and tactics.

The core narrative questions that leaders working to defeat HB2 were grappling with included:

- Do we lead with communicating about trans people and issues affecting them?
- Do we lead with communicating about the economy?
- Do we lead with the values of privacy and self-determination or the value of antidiscrimination?

The national LGBTQ+ organizations and Democratic Party formations shared internal polling data that found that leading with trans people and issues impacting them would not lead to greater success. Instead, they determined that the coalition should focus on HB2's economic consequences in order to sway the "moveable middle." Millions of dollars were leaving the state as businesses, conferences, musicians, film productions, and high-profile sporting events like the Atlantic Coast Conference men's basketball tournament organized to boycott North Carolina—as long as HB2 remained on the books. As a result, focusing on economics and boycotts to move a wide range of audiences living inside and outside of North Carolina quickly expanded to become the dominant conversation.

Many grassroots groups were upset by this strategy, as some felt this messaging was not centering on trans people or North Carolinians as spokespeople. Others wanted messaging to focus on how HB2 was an attack on trans people in a way that resonated with the audiences most impacted by the bill. The debate over messaging strategy was presented as a zero-sum game, when in reality, a more intersectional approach was possible.

At the time, working as communications director at SONG, co-author hermelinda cortés and her team worked behind the scenes to coordinate with national LGBTQ+ organizations to make sure that they were including and developing trans spokespeople who lived in North Carolina. SONG trained people on talking points that aligned with the values of liberation. They positioned messengers to center the inherent value of trans people as humans who deserve dignity no matter what, while also touching on the economic fallout of the bill.

Despite attempts to course correct, both messengers and audiences remained stuck in frames the Right had created, focusing primarily on the use of bathrooms. This narrow focus relied on narratives of individual and interpersonal solidarity by communicating such messages as "I deserve to pee," alongside "I'll go pee with you," rather than the inherent humanity of trans people or the economic argument around poverty wages.

While these personal and individual messages sought to reinforce a narrative about trans people's dignity, the "Bathroom Bill" frame obscured the attacks on local government's ability to combat discrimination and cultivate a more equitable economy through municipal authority. This further entrenched public safety and government overreach as the two dominant narratives by communicating privacy, safety, and self-determination as key values.

The Complex Outcomes

The Win: The pivot to focus the bulk of messaging on the economic and cultural impacts of the boycotts against the Bathroom Bill generated a political majority that dismantled the North Carolina GOP's political trifecta by unelecting Governor Pat McCrory. Roy Cooper, a Democrat who opposed HB2, replaced him. Under Governor Cooper's leadership in early 2017, the portion of the bill restricting trans people's access to public restrooms was removed.

The Loss: The Bathroom Bill was replaced by HB142, which kept the parts of HB2 that prevented local governments from raising the minimum wage and enacting antidiscrimination laws for five years. Ultimately, the North Carolina and national GOP succeeded in using antitrans narratives as a doorway to broader attacks on good governance. Moreover, they strengthened the narrative threads around trans people, public safety, and government, seeding the ground for the defensive fights in support of trans rights that we find ourselves in today.

Building Narrative Power to Win a Protrans Future

Our opponents are scapegoating trans people as a key doorway into advancing a version of governance and family values aimed at decimating public education, access to comprehensive health care, reproductive freedom, racial-justice efforts, and more. With this reality, no matter the social movement we build power within, we must have the narrative discipline to consistently and persistently reinforce trans people's inherent value and dignity as human beings in the communities we call home. Here's how we can do it:

Unapologetically affirm the dignity and humanity of trans people.

This must be a central value and narrative that's echoed across our stories, messages, and content so we can grow our narrative power while weakening the power of antitrans narratives.

Plan ahead and invest in a vast, resourced, and vibrant protrans narrative infrastructure working across identities, issue areas, and geographic regions.

In addition to strengthening trans-led formations, such infrastructure must fortify nontrans organizations' understanding of the antitrans-narrative Trojan horses the right wing is using; they must also know how to skillfully respond.

Engage narrative actors both within and beyond the choir.

We can and should amplify the voices of those who already agree with us and craft narrative strategies to reach people in the "moveable middle." To do this, we must use messaging from the narrative actors best positioned to reach the full range of audiences needed to win.

Together, we can cultivate a broad-based narrative ecosystem that is willing and able to fight back against the use of our communities as wedges to divide collective efforts for liberation. We must build a "bigger we" toward a multiracial democracy and economy that works for all.

IMMIGRANT JUSTICE

Beyond Borders: Building Power and Counternarratives in the Black LGBTQIA+ Migrant Community

Interview with the Black LGBTQIA+ Migrant Project (BLMP)

By Shanelle Matthews and Marzena Zukowska

The Black LGBTQIA+ Migrant Project (BLMP) envisions a world without forced migration, where no one is forced to give up their homeland and where all Black LGBTQIA+ people are free and liberated. BLMP builds and centers the power of Black LGBTQIA+ migrants to ensure the liberation of all Black people. BLMP is led by a directly impacted steering committee and staff and operates organizing networks in regions throughout the United States while connecting to the fight for Black liberation in its members' home countries.

Rose Berry is a Black, queer, migrant organizer with more than twenty years of experience in racial, migrant, and gender-justice work. As a co-founder and co-director of BLMP, Rose focuses on empowering Black queer, trans, and nonbinary migrants and first-generation people to achieve Black liberation through organizing, strategic communications, and sustainability. Rose is deeply committed to the belief that Black liberation is possible within our lifetime.

Ola Osifo Osaze is a formerly undocumented trans migrant of Edo and Yoruba descent, born in Nigeria and now based in New York City. With decades of experience in organizing, movement building, and fund-raising for LGBTQ+, BIPOC, and migrant communities, Ola serves as the cultivation strategist at the Trans Justice Funding Project. Ola was the founding director of BLMP and co-founded the Black Migrant Power Fund. Ola's work centers on co-creating and sustaining movement-led initiatives through a Black, queer, and trans-liberatory lens.

Oluchi Omeoga (any pronouns) is a Minnesota-born organizer who still lives and organizes in Minneapolis, Minnesota, today. Born from Igbo immigrants from Nigeria, Oluchi is a co-founder and founding Core Team member of Black Visions, a black-led local organization that centers on Black queer and trans folks in Minnesota. In Oluchi's role at Black Visions and together with other abolitionist organizations, over $1 million has been diverted from the police budget in 2018. Oluchi also co-founded the Black LGBTQIA+ Migrant Project, or BLMP, and still works there to this day as the co-executive director.

Shanelle and Marzena: What narratives have Black LGBTQ+ migrants historically faced and continue to face in various contexts—whether in the media, within neighboring communities, or in progressive and left movements?

Oluchi: Many of our members are first-generation migrants, children of migrants, or those who immigrated very young. In the Black migrant community, LGBTQ+ identity is often not discussed, leaving many of us feeling isolated and disconnected from our cultural roots. Traditionally, migration is understood as a collective journey undertaken with family and community. I was drawn to BLMP because, for a long time, I felt that I couldn't be both Nigerian and queer. This struggle is common among us—we must often sacrifice one aspect of our identity to prioritize another.

The narratives we encounter often suggest that being queer is "not African" or "not Black." Or [they determine] for us that we are not queer. We've had to challenge these ideas and demonstrate that we exist and have existed for a long time. This has been a significant struggle for us. Within other communities, especially on the left during the early days of BLMP, it felt like we were often an afterthought in LGBTQ+ spaces—brought in at the last minute just to fulfill the need for someone Black and queer. Similarly, in Black spaces, we were included only when something related to immigration arose and they needed to talk to Black immigrants. For a long time, our organizing strategy focused on entering spaces where our people were present but not being centered in the way we should have been.

Ola: During my time at BLMP, working on detention-related cases for queer

Black migrants was always more challenging than any other campaign. Finding an attorney and raising awareness and funds felt like an uphill battle. I recall BLMP's first case—Zack Mohammed and I struggled to find a lawyer for a detained brother. Even established gay immigrant legal organizations turned us down, saying the case was "too hard." They preferred more uncomplicated cases, like affirmative asylum, where the person isn't detained.

In detention, our community faced extreme scrutiny. To prove their credibility, they had to relive trauma before asylum officers, only to still be doubted by judges simply because they were Black and queer. Even when we secured an attorney and a judge granted release, bonds were astronomical—sometimes as high as $30,000. The predominant narratives we faced were clear: our cases were "too hard," and our people were seen as disposable. The system seemed designed to deny them any legal pathway. This was the reality for every case we handled.

Rose: BLMP recognizes the impact of U.S. imperialism on dominant narratives. It's no coincidence that, as antitrans violence and legislation increase in the United States, similar issues arise in our home countries. In February 2024, Ghana passed an anti-LGBTQ bill. In places like Uganda and Honduras, people are denied the right to change their name and gender on their identification to reflect their true identity. United States–dominant narratives that dehumanize LGBTQ people here directly influence both social and legislative impacts in our home countries.

In our strategic communications work, we aim to reshape narratives—not just about Black migrants being migrants but also about how harsh legislative reforms impact people with intersecting identities. These realities are often excluded from mainstream media, and that's intentional; our experiences are made invisible.

Organizations like Black Alliance for Just Immigration (BAJI) helped lay the groundwork by fostering discussions within Black communities, bringing together Black migrants and Black Americans to address how they've been pitted against each other—often by design. They helped us dissect the internalized white supremacist narratives around what it means to be Black, whether as a migrant or as an American. For instance, as a first-generation migrant who's been in the United States for thirty-eight years, I see myself as both a Black American and a Black migrant. We must have nuanced discussions reflecting multiple identities when discussing the impacts of oppressive systems. Black people worldwide face displacement and forced migration, and it's crucial to learn the histories and parallels that connect these experiences. The same oppressive tools are used against Black communities everywhere.

Our work builds on BAJI's foundation by using strategic communications to shift the narrative and make the realities of Black migrant experiences more visible globally. That's the direction we're moving in.

Shanelle and Marzena: What kinds of groups have been responsible for spreading oppressive narratives about Black LGBTQ+ migrants?

Oluchi: One group responsible for the oppressive narratives that dehumanize Black queer migrants are Christian nationalists who often cite the biblical story of Sodom and Gomorrah to condemn homosexuality, portraying it as sinful and deserving of divine punishment. This narrative has been used to justify the persecution of LGBTQ+ individuals, particularly in African countries where Christian missionary influence is strong. It dehumanizes Black queer migrants by portraying them as morally corrupt and deserving of discrimination or even violence.[1]

A second and perhaps more innocuous group is liberals, who use the "good immigrant"/"bad immigrant" narratives to argue for more inclusive immigration policies. This narrative praises immigrants who contribute economically, assimilate culturally, or serve in the military, implicitly reinforcing the idea that only these immigrants deserve rights and protections.[2] Our communities often internalize and reinforce these narratives. My parents and I participated in a documentary with Translash Media, in which they said things that reinforced the idea that there are good immigrants and bad immigrants, as well as the narrative that there is a right way to immigrate.

Yet, as I reflected on the experiences and stories of those closest to me, I was reminded that many of us didn't even immigrate the "right way." Growing up in an immigrant community, you are constantly reminded of the fallacy of the American Dream. You are reminded of your uncle, who was deported with all of his family members because a form was filled out incorrectly; you are reminded of the times we had to silence our culture because of fear of surveillance and policing. As a Black or nonwhite migrant, there is never a right way to immigrate because racial animus and profiling permeate all facets of our society. We are taught very early on that the United States thinks we do not belong here.

All people deserve autonomy and agency to determine if they stay or leave the homelands in which they were born. At BLMP, we believe in a world free of nation-states, where migration is not just a global reality but an inherent right for all living beings. In the current landscape that we live in, that means access to and expansion of true immigration, allowing for folks to have rights and privileges afforded to any other person who lives on that land. The model-minority myth—the racialized idea that there is a perfect way to be an immigrant or minority in America that all minorities should aspire to—has plagued Asian communities for decades. In my experience, some Nigerian people play into this mythology, which requires assimilation, the quieting of identities, and the disregarding of what you deserve as a human being. This mythology pits us against one another and separates us from our collective power.

But this mythology is not a coincidence. The Scramble for Africa—whereby European nations conquered, colonized, and nationalized many African territories to build their empires in response to the Second Industrial Revolution—created new groups, labeled them nation-states, and pitted them against one another for resources and land. This division put the vision of a global Black identity out of reach, making our counternarrative of immigration being a Black issue harder to socialize.

Ola: Because of the legacy of colonization, slavery, and white supremacy, there is an intentional disconnection from—as well as a willful ignorance about—the realities of African and Black-majority nations, especially relative to oppression and trauma caused by U.S. and Western imperialism. The U.S. left acts like they can only focus on one international crisis at a time. That crisis is rarely one that happens in a Black-majority context outside of the United States. I have been gently calling in my comrades to make connections to diasporic liberation struggles that are also long-standing. Illustrating how white supremacy and colonization operate across borders and nation-states makes our collective work more impactful. So, at BLMP, we are leading work around making the global analysis of anti-Black racism, white supremacy, and colonization more pronounced and more concrete by creating alliances and movement building across borders in Honduras and Jamaica, and building with queer and trans organizations.

Rose: In addition to spreading harmful narratives, Democrats often use immigration as a scapegoat to appeal to conservative and right-wing voters. Obama and his policies are a prime example of how structural power can shape our realities. Despite claiming to be progressive, Obama deported more migrants than any president before or since, reinforcing the harmful myth that migrants are dangerous and should be kept out of the country. BLMP rejected that narrative and, through organizing and strategic communication, created interventions that emphasize the human right to migrate. We led campaigns to close detention facilities where migrants are housed in horrifying conditions and expanded the abolitionist narrative to include Immigration and Customs Enforcement (ICE) as an extension of the carceral state.

Shanelle and Marzena: Can you describe a specific moment when BLMP seized a political opportunity or leveraged a crisis to advance the counternarratives you mentioned and build power for your community?

Rose: When Trump referred to African diasporic countries like Haiti as "shithole countries" in 2016, it presented an opportune moment for us to assert a strong counternarrative. We saw it as a chance to highlight how this anti-Black rhetoric leads to structural and systemic violence. We wanted to make it clear to everyone paying attention that his remarks were an attack on all Black people—Black, queer folks from Haiti, the African continent, Jamaica, Honduras, and beyond.

Coming from a Black Caribbean background, I wasn't fully out for a long time, even though it was obvious to my family that I was queer. It wasn't until I felt safer after moving out of my family home that I could be openly out. This experience resonates with the broader issue of feeling pressured to separate different parts of our identities within our communities and families. This moment allowed us to appeal to the broader Black migrant community by highlighting that Trump's words were directed at all of us, including Black queer folks. By inserting this narrative into the conversation, which was previously unrepresented, we helped foster a sense of solidarity that hadn't been fully recognized before.

Oluchi: In Albuquerque, New Mexico, in 2018, BLMP co-hosted a convening with trans, queer, migrant justice organizations like the National Queer Asian Pacific Islander Alliance, Detention Watch Network, Mijente, and Familia: Trans Queer Liberation Movement (Familia: TQLM). During this convening, we engaged in political education on issues at the intersection of immigration and the criminal-legal system, otherwise known as crimmigration—specifically, how LGBTQ+ migrants are treated when seeking asylum.

While together in Albuquerque, we organized a direct action and occupied the intersection where the justice center and immigration detention center stood. It was the first time I was with other LGBTQ+ migrant folks building power toward ending detention for transgender asylum seekers. That moment was the birth of our End Trans Detention campaign and our effort to free a trans-Jamaican woman named Sza Sza, who spent more than ten years in immigration detention—longer than any other detainee ever documented. In collaboration with the Transgender Law Center and Familia: TQLM, we freed Sza Sza, but sadly, two others died inside because they were denied health care.

Ola: We organized two transnational campaigns, collaborating across borders to build solidarity among Black LGBTQ+ migrants. In 2020, during an uprising in Cuba, Black Cubans were organizing against racism and capitalism, which had deeply infiltrated Cuban society. We hosted an informational webinar in partnership with Afro-Cuban organizations to highlight Black queer perspectives and connect the struggles in Cuba to similar realities here. Simultaneously, in countries like Ghana, anti-LGBTQ+ fervor was intensifying, with legislation being passed to criminalize LGBTQ+ identities. BLMP collaborated with our Ghanaian members in the United States and organizations in Ghana to uplift and draw connections between our shared struggles against homophobic and transphobic empires that justify their hate with Christian nationalist narratives.

Shanelle and Marzena: How do you build trust and rapport with Black LGBTQ+ migrant communities to ensure you accurately represent their stories?

Rose: We're a base-building and member-led organization with more than 300 nationwide members participating in various programs, training and leadership opportunities, and regional convenings. During those convenings, we talk strategy and organizing, but we also tell our stories, making a big difference in relationship building. Still, we don't assume that because we have similar identities we have the same stories, experiences, or backgrounds. Instead, we make room for a diversity of [all those things]. Not making assumptions about people's realities helps build trust.

We distributed a national survey to Black migrants, asking questions about their experiences, migration journeys, and interactions with various systems—health care, policing, criminalization, etc. By creating opportunities for people to tell us exactly what their lives are like and what they need to feel safe, we build trust and have a more precise direction for our work.

Shanelle and Marzena: In the next hundred years, what else, aside from prisons and police, is extinct because of this work? And also, what exists?

Oluchi: Liberation [would exist]—which, to me, means a world in which we intentionally recognize that our individual actions have consequences, not only on an individual level but also on interpersonal, communal, and global levels. [We would] respond in ways that center agency, autonomy, and collective wholeness. Liberation is not a destination but a never-ending journey of individual collective actions that centers the wholeness of every being in our ecosystem. It won't happen in a hundred years, but if I were to dream, forced migration wouldn't exist. People would not be oppressed or forced to leave their homes. If they did want to go, migration would be free and self-expression would not be criminalized. We understand that community is prolific, and in a hundred years, if BLMP is successful in our organizing work, we will have a global Black identity. I dream of the days when I am traveling between Black-predominant countries, and there is a sense of identity that's grounded in Black queer feminist ideals. Punitive and retributive justice would also be extinct, and we would be well on our way to a regenerative economy rather than an extractive one.

Rose: Capitalism would be abolished and replaced with care, wellness, and accountability systems. I believe that's the only way Black people can indeed be free. These new systems would be centered around people, allowing humanity to thrive by providing all the necessary resources to support it, because it's entirely possible. While people would still be free to migrate, there would be no forced migration. Individuals could choose to remain in their home countries because we would have addressed the systems of power that have historically made it impossible for people to meet their basic needs.

Climate change will likely be the catalyst for a global uprising, forcing the imperialist state to reckon with the harm it has caused. As a result, the state will have no choice but to confront the people. Many of our homes may no longer exist, making migration a necessity rather than an option. This will lead people to rise up and do whatever it takes to survive—it's an innate human function. So, I envision a world where people have risen up, reclaimed our right to exist, and done what's necessary to create that reality.

Asserting Humanity: Lessons from the Drop the I-Word Campaign

By Rinku Sen and Roberto Lovato

In April 2013, the Associated Press (AP) removed the phrase *illegal immigrant* from its stylebook—the result of nearly three years of pressure from readers, journalists, and immigrants themselves. Thousands of news outlets around the world immediately implemented the change, replacing a dehumanizing characterization of immigrants with fair and accurate alternatives, such as *undocumented* and *unauthorized*, as these didn't carry the emotional impact of *illegal*. Donald Trump normalized the i-word again in political discourse, but even during and after the Trump years, this narrative victory against racial bias in immigration coverage remains in place.

The Drop the I-Word campaign was part of a strategy to popularize racial-justice ideas, organizing, and solutions—the central goal of Race Forward (then called the Applied Research Center). Rinku Sen was appointed executive director in 2006, and Roberto Lovato was a strategic advisor for several years. The organization, already twenty-five years old, transitioned from an action-oriented think tank to a multidisciplinary home for racial justice. We had a training program, produced timely research, hosted the biennial Facing Race conference, and shaped collective thinking through a quarterly print journal called *Colorlines* that had 1,200 subscribers.[1]

With these assets, we started dreaming of mainstreaming concepts like racial equity. The organization had been working on immigration issues since 9/11, and immigrants were a large portion of Race Forward's constituency, staff, and board. We saw immigration as a matter of racial control and, therefore, as a part of racial justice. We routinely met people whose lives were degraded by the ubiquity of the word *illegal* in the context of immigration. Various expressions of "somebody should do something about the use of *illegal immigrant*" started to arise at our meetings. Lovato, having designed and led Presente.org's successful campaign to get CNN to drop anti-immigrant show host Lou Dobbs,[2] presented the idea of a similar campaign targeting the i-word.

The AP emerged as a high-leverage target early in our exploration process. The potential for a clear demand backed by a large constituency directed at a specific target brought a path to change into focus, including potential partners and pressure tactics.

In this case study, we will analyze the strategy and tactics of the Drop the I-Word campaign targeting the AP and its impact on racial-justice discourse in the United States. The campaign revealed the power that cultural and media interventions can have when paired with grassroots and digital organizing.

Why It Mattered

There were plenty of compelling reasons to take on such a campaign. Chief among them was the correlation between dehumanizing language and deadly hate crimes. A couple of years before we launched, the world learned the tragic story of Marcelo Lucero, an Ecuadorian immigrant murdered by a group of teens who repeated the word *illegal* in the course of their assault. The Southern Poverty Law Center reported that hate crimes against Latinos had risen by 40 percent between 2003 and 2006; these were the most recent data available when the campaign started.[3]

Using the i-word was not a natural occurrence driven by "common sense," as immigration conservatives pretended. It was a key element of their narrative strategy. A 2004 words-that-work memo from pollster Frank Luntz, who has said that he was wrong about immigration in recent years, instructed conservatives to use legality as their primary frame and to repeat *illegal immigrant* as much as they possibly could.[4] Mainstreaming this language was a central tactic of the anti-immigrant movement so that only the breaking of increasingly punitive immigration laws had any place in the discourse.

We saw the terrible consequences of the conservatives' success in drawing this boundary when the Obama administration broke deportation records and failed to advance any significant liberalization of immigration policy. This is the period in which comprehensive immigration reform ("comprehensive" because it would normalize undocumented peoples' status, as well as demilitarize the border) began a decade-long slide off the negotiating table.

Luntz noted that people should never use *illegal* as a noun because that would, in fact, be objectifying and racist, dropping the veneer of accuracy that it had as an adjective.

Of course, immigration has many other dimensions; family, economics, and freedom are just a few. Even if we lost, we believed the campaign could insert these dimensions into the debate. But we also knew we could win.

Reading the Moment

There were excellent political (make new policy) and social (prevent hate crimes) reasons to launch Drop the I-Word. Still, these reasons wouldn't have been enough to warrant investing nearly half a million dollars and thousands of human hours in the campaign. The timing would have to be right. We noted important developments in the body politic to read the moment.

- A constituency for such a campaign had grown dramatically over the previous generation. Because Congress failed to create a sensible and smooth immigration system, the actual number of undocumented immigrants grew again after the Immigration Reform and Control Act of 1986 led to the legalization of some three million people. By 2008, the estimated number of unauthorized immigrants ranged from 8 to 13 million, depending on whom you asked.[5] Many immigrant families are mixed-status and include citizens, green-card holders, and undocumented members. The country had grown browner over the same period, so the constituency of people who could be slapped with the label, regardless of their actual status, also grew. The numbers of Latine and Asian organizations, journalists, and outlets expanded.
- This constituency, including the generation of young immigrants we now know as Dreamers, felt the harm of the i-word deeply, and was eager to take action at a time when policy momentum was stalled. This generation came of age, politically speaking, fighting off conservative legislation like the Sensenbrenner Bill of 2005, which threatened to criminalize even humanitarian support for undocumented people.[6] By 2010, though, the immigration debate in

Congress and the Obama White House were not just stalled but actually moving toward greater border militarization and more restriction.

- We could point to precedents. We collected lessons from many people and movements to inform our strategy. Rashad Robinson, who had been the director of media programs at the Gay and Lesbian Alliance Against Defamation and campaigned for journalists to replace *homosexual* with *gay and lesbian*, helped us identify assets to leverage. Feminist icon Gloria Steinem told us the story of getting *Ms.* into newspapers,[7] and warned us to not expect timely, or any, pickup by *The New York Times*. She shared her failed effort to make "crimes of entitlement" a common way of talking about sexual violence. We took heart from disabled activists' successful effort to vilify the "R-word."[8]

- We could build on previous efforts to drop the i-word, reaching at least as far back as the Carter administration, which explicitly avoided it in White House communications. In the mid-1990s, the National Hispanic Journalists Association adopted a resolution condemning its use.[9] In 2009, the National Alliance of Latin American and Caribbean Communities (NALACC, now Alianza Americas) launched the Somos/We Are campaign to get *The Boston Globe* and other outlets to drop it.[10] That same year, undocumented attorney Prerna Lall and DreamActivist.org delivered a petition to *USA Today*, challenging the phrase *illegal students*.[11]

Race Forward was hardly the optimal organization to take on such a campaign. We weren't a campaigning organization; many staff were former organizers, but we had no organizing program. We also weren't part of the core leadership of the immigrant-rights movement and had no dedicated grants for our immigration work.

However, Race Forward also had important assets. Through colorlines .com, we had access to hundreds of thousands of readers and substantial journalistic credibility. *Colorlines* could post a challenge to reporters and editors from inside the sector. We had enough money to devote to general-support funds, partly due to a game-changing general-support grant from the W.K. Kellogg Foundation and the recent sale of the organization's office. Most important, we were willing to absorb the risk of launching such a campaign. Willingness counts for a lot.

Partners and Tactics

Victory hinged on our ability to generate debate about journalistic ethics, with partners representing the breadth of the constituency backing the demand. The National Hispanic Media Coalition produced key research on the effects of the i-word; Presente.org generated and delivered petitions; and local immigrant-youth organizations like United 4 the Dream in Charlotte, North Carolina, ran campaigns to pressure local outlets. Even if the answer was always "We follow the AP's *Style Guide*," these tactics built local leadership and added to the pressure within journalism.

We made the constituency visible, asking outlets and individuals to sign a pledge to drop the i-word. Nearly 20,000 people shared that pledge on Facebook, by far the most enthusiastic response to a post we had experienced. Inspired by NALACC's Somos/We Are campaign, we published *I Am* stories submitted by readers to show undocumented people in all their glorious complexity. The mother of a fourth-grader sent us her child's video about undocumented children. Artists like Favianna Rodriguez, Julio Salgado, and Ernesto Yereña contributed images, poetry, fiction, videos, and beauty.

We then started criticizing current practice in journalistic venues—columns, conferences, and social media. One of the earliest interactions occurred between Rinku and Adam Serwer, who was then a reporter at *The American Prospect*. After some back-and-forth, Serwer dropped his position that *illegal* was bad as a noun but acceptable as an adjective, essentially repeating the Luntz memo. Organizations that shape journalism made space for the argument, including the Poynter Institute, the Nieman Fellowship, the Society of Professional Journalists, and Unity (the alliance of associations of color). In September 2011, about a year into the campaign, journalist José Antonio Vargas, having won a Pulitzer Prize while undocumented, implored 1,000 reporters and editors to drop the i-word at the Online News Association conference.[12]

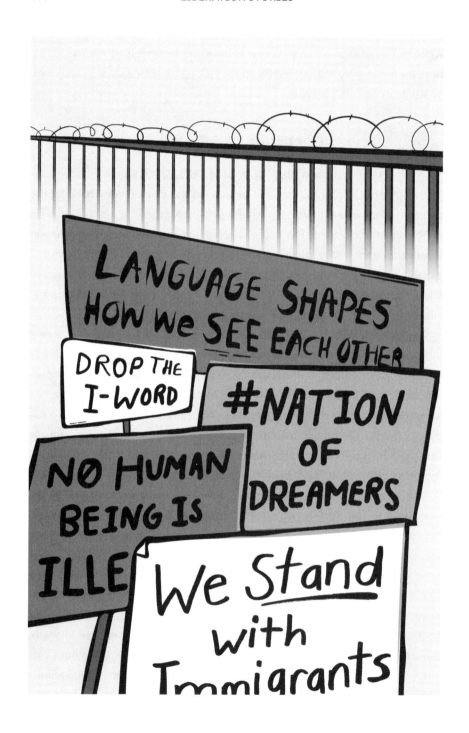

Activists haunted the AP's Twitter feed. The campaign reached into cultural and social spaces, as when *New York Times* crosswords editor Will Shortz used the i-word to answer a hint referencing border crossers; he apologized after the campaign called it out.[13] In a tweet, San Francisco Giants manager Bruce Bochy called out Fox radio announcer Tony Bruno for using the term *illegal alien*.[14]

The 2012 election was a turning point. That March, we met with the managing and stylebook editors at the AP. Human-rights attorney Chandra Bhatnagar of the ACLU joined our meeting to describe the legal ramifications of using an imprecise term to cover so many different kinds of status. Vargas and the National Hispanic Media Coalition had their own meetings as well. The National Hispanic Media Coalition poll had produced a jaw-dropping data point: one-third of their sample assumed that most Latinos were undocumented.[15] In October, the AP issued an update urging sensitivity in using the word but did not ban it.[16]

The actual ban came six months later. The AP titled their blog post about the decision "Illegal No More."[17] Outlets with independent style guides followed, including the *Los Angeles Times*,[18] *USA Today*,[19] and the *Chicago Tribune*.[20] Usage plunged from appearing in nearly 100 percent of AP stories on immigration to 0 in one month.[21] Just as Gloria Steinem had warned us, *The New York Times* held out and, to our knowledge, has never changed its style.

Looking Ahead

If narrative organizers are observant, wise, and lucky, we recruit millions of people to walk the path to a new culture. The arenas of cultural struggle vary, but some overlap with the arenas of political struggle. Institutions shape both culture and politics, and institutions can be challenged and changed. The Venn diagram of cultural and political concerns produces campaigns like Drop the I-Word.

As proud as we are of this history, we must acknowledge that this and other isolated cultural interventions, however successful, did not prevent the rightward shift in immigration policy now embraced by Republicans, Independents, and Democrats alike. This is a big country, and we own few media assets. True saturation of just narratives on immigration will take the entire movement to understand the relationship between culture and politics to craft breakthrough strategies. The lessons from Drop the I-Word can support such a leap.

Relief for All of Us or Relief for None of Us

By Alejandra Pérez and Julie Feng

In March 2020, as the coronavirus pandemic began to ravage Washington State, Daniela Murguia saw her world fall into crisis. Working as the case manager for low-income students at an education nonprofit, she witnessed firsthand how the pandemic fragmented the lives of young people she worked with, many laboring tirelessly in "essential" jobs.

Yet for undocumented immigrants[1] like Murguia, her students, and her community, this precarity was deepened by preexisting dominant narratives of exclusion, tokenization, and victimization rooted in ideologies of racism, xenophobia, and capitalism. These narratives have historically cast undocumented people in limiting roles—either as heroes self-sacrificing for the capitalist state, victims always dependent on institutions, or villains blamed for the scarcity of resources. During the pandemic, this compounded precarity caused disproportionate layoffs and lost work hours among undocumented immigrants, in addition to increased work on the front lines of the most hazardous jobs while not getting access to health care or financial government assistance.

The federal and state governments' failures to protect the more than 240,000 undocumented immigrants across Washington State during the pandemic was not unique but by design. For decades, many of those who are undocumented have not had access to critical resources upon arrival in the United States, including federal financial aid, driver's licenses in many states, unemployment benefits, health care insurance, food-stamp programs, and Earned Income Tax Credits. During the pandemic, undocumented people and their families were excluded from stimulus payments under the Coronavirus Aid, Relief and Economic Security Act (CARES) enacted March 27, 2020 and its expansion in December 27, 2020.[2]

Daniela and her community turned to grassroots organizing to provide relief for the community in the absence of government support. Within weeks of the outbreak, Daniela and four other organizers[3] who were part of the Washington Dream Coalition (WDC), a grassroots group of undocumented and formerly undocumented immigrants who started as youth organizers, launched the COVID-19 Relief Fund for Undocumented Individuals and became part of the Washington COVID-19 Immigrant Relief Fund coalition. More than 19,000 undocumented people in the state applied for the one-time fund, ranging from $500 to $1,000, requesting a total of $16.6 million in aid. Alongside twenty-two immigrant organizations and with the support of the community, WDC raised more than $7.1 million in six months from more than 3,400 donors. To date, it remains the largest grassroots-led, undocumented-specific fund in the United States.[4]

This change in material conditions for undocumented people was made possible due to years of building trust and authentic relationships, centering individual stories, providing community care and political education, and advocating for change at multiple levels of government. Yet it was grassroots narrative strategy that built the foundation for the campaign—an approach that young undocumented organizers have used for decades of advocacy and resistance. The fund launched a listening campaign that sought to better understand the immediate needs, supports, and obstacles faced by undocumented people during the pandemic. Organizers heard directly from individuals about inequitable and inadequate support as well as the need for longer-term statewide efforts that center on equity and economic justice. These individual stories and demands provided the framework for policy recommendations and state-level relief.

The turning point came on August 10, 2020, after two momentous events: Farm workers went on strike in Yakima, Washington, to protest working conditions during COVID-19, and a Deferred Action for Childhood Arrivals (DACA) Supreme Court victory press conference with DACA recipients was publicly disrupted. This led to Governor Inslee announcing a commitment to a state relief fund for people who cannot access federal aid or unemployment insurance due to their immigration status. Taking control of the narratives around worker and community power, more than 400 community organizations mobilized to create a state-funded program that secured $62.6 million in relief aid from Inslee. This money fed into countless relief funds across

Washington, including the Seattle Immigrant and Refugee COVID-19 Disaster Relief fund for $8 million.[5]

The grassroots network that formed made it possible for the Washington COVID-19 Immigrant Relief Fund coalition to conduct outreach across 226 cities and towns throughout every county in the state. They mobilized the state to provide education, outreach, application assistance, and follow-up support for more than 10,000 applicants per week. In the end, they requested over $82.5 million dollars in aid for more than 94,000 undocumented people.[6]

The efforts by WDC and others won tangible policy change, while helping transform the larger dominant narratives that months prior made COVID-19 relief for undocumented people seem impossible. At the same time, crisis moments can offer narrative openings that drive a range of new policies, from gaining unemployment and health care insurance for undocumented workers to universal basic income for all. Grassroots organizers recognize that building toward narrative change is not a step-by-step process, but a complex web that requires nuanced understanding of power, story, and culture. The balance between messaging for short-term policy wins versus narratives for long-term cultural shifts is evident in strategies like the DREAMer narrative, which helped build pressure for policies like DACA, yet have been criticized by undocumented organizers for perpetuating long-term harm through narratives of deservingness.

Below, we offer seven practices that help untangle these complexities and provide a road map for building narrative power in times of crisis.

Appeal to Connection, Not Production

Advocacy for the rights of undocumented immigrants often focuses on the benefits to national, state, and local economies. Messages from the media, government, and pop culture remind us that "immigration built this nation" and "Immigrants: we get the job done!"[7] The phantom of the *economy* hovers over this messaging. Critical to the success of WDC's campaign efforts was the disruption of the idea of a mythologized economy by elevating the reality of human lives.

When farmworkers in Yakima, Washington, went on strike to bring attention to dangerous working conditions and lack of protection from COVID-19, they were declaring that their health and their lives were important. One worker asked, "Y sus manzanas valen más que nosotros?"[8] *Are their apples worth more than our lives?* These messages disrupt the narrative of undocumented people as self-sacrificing for the capitalist state. While it is true that many undocumented immigrants are essential workers, taxpayers, and contributors to the economy, relief during a pandemic should not be contingent on production. It should focus on humanity: Undocumented immigrants are neighbors, friends, family, teachers, students, and community members.

Reject Binary Narratives

In the drama triangle,[9] a narrative tool used by many communicators and storytellers, social groups are cast as specific characters (hero, villain, victim), whose roles determine the framing of the narrative.

In current public discourse, the media and politicians often cast undocumented immigrants in one-dimensional roles. Those who oppose equity cast undocumented people as villains, using dehumanizing metaphors likening people to floods, animals, or disease, or attempting to connect groups with images of crime. However, the well-intentioned narratives about undocumented immigrants as victims, charity cases ("they came as children without choice"), or heroes ("essential workers") are also problematic. These narratives are patronizing and strip away agency.

Instead, we subvert the dichotomy to uplift multidimensional stories about who undocumented immigrants are. None of these categories are enough to capture the fullness of their stories. During the campaign for COVID-19 relief, WDC used data to show the diverse interconnected backgrounds, experiences, and identities of undocumented immigrants, sharing stories from their own voices and positioning them as experts of lived experience.

Disrupt Scarcity Narratives

The underlying and deeply entrenched narrative that upholds neoliberal capitalism also upholds scarcity: the narrative that there is not enough for everyone. If you do not have enough, it is because you do not deserve it and did not work hard enough. Inherent in this idea are myths of a functioning meritocracy within the American Dream—the ability of anyone to pull themselves up by their bootstraps. However, this is the reality for only a few.

The hoarding of resources by the wealthy and powerful shut many out of opportunities, undermine labor protections, and drive down living wages. At

WDC, we argue that when we care for one another, there is always enough for everyone. That's why we uplift narratives of collective care. In our campaign, we shared perspectives from undocumented community members like Ana, who told us: "When the United States talks about undocumented immigrants in this country, they usually tend to focus on two things: what they 'take,' and how fast can we get them out? Not many people are willing to see past a status into the daily lives of actual hardworking and contributing families. WDC's fund was not just a direct result of the COVID-19 pandemic, but of decades of this community's striving to be seen as contributing, hardworking, and deserving."

Center Community Desire

In "Suspending Damage: A Letter to Communities,"[10] Unangax̂ scholar Eve Tuck calls on us to reconsider the long-term impact of "damage-centered" frameworks, which document peoples' pain and brokenness to hold those in power accountable for their oppression. These frameworks are "often used to leverage reparations or resources for marginalized communities yet simultaneously reinforce and reinscribe a one-dimensional notion of these people as depleted, ruined, and hopeless."

Tuck proposes an alternative of "desire-centered" frameworks, which focuses on the wisdoms, strengths, and complexities of marginalized communities rather than their pain and trauma. Inspired by this notion, WDC ran listening sessions throughout 2021, asking undocumented immigrants, "What does your ideal world look like?"[11] Thirty-four community members spent hours with us sharing their visions of a world with systemic supports, long-term stability, no barriers to medical care, no fear, and care for them and their families. This provides the foundation for our advocacy for years to come—to build the world we desire.

Follow the Lead of Those Most Impacted

As criminal-justice reform advocate Glenn E. Martin said, "Those closest to the problem are closest to the solution."[12] It is simple: To advocate for undocumented people, follow the lead of undocumented organizers. Not only do they hold material stakes in the outcomes of our campaigns, but they have deep expertise in what is needed to win.

WDC brought on documented allies to support this work, but as a team, everyone understood that lived experience is key to leadership. Lived-experience organizers provide nuanced knowledge of circumstances, having already learned many of the consequences and possibilities needed to take action. For instance, they know what language to use to assure fellow immigrants that we will truly protect their privacy if they decide to share something with us. We also practice having transparency in individual and collective positionality. For example, those of us who are documented immigrants, have DACA, or are the documented children of undocumented immigrants recognize that while our struggles are valid, we cannot equate our situations with those who are undocumented. We must be vocal about all of the layers and spectrums of what it means to be undocumented.

Uphold Community Power, Not Institutional Power

Our stories are not about showcasing trauma to get "those in power" to empathize, but about showing how people at the margins—how undocumented immigrant communities—create ways of thriving.

In June 2020, Governor Inslee held a press conference to celebrate DACA's victory in the Supreme Court. Rather than allow politicians to use those with DACA as feel-good stories, DACA recipients Kamau Chege and Alejandra Pérez disrupted the flow by asking why there was not yet state-funded relief for undocumented communities and protections for those without DACA. The dominant narrative is that DREAMers should be grateful for the chances they have been given. Organizers wanted to shift the public narrative to remind the audience that not everyone in the community has been given the same chance. The goal is not to beg or pander to policy makers, but to show that immigrant communities already have power to speak up and organize. As a result, on August 10, 2020, Governor Inslee announced a commitment to a state relief fund for people who cannot access federal aid or unemployment insurance because of their immigration status.[13]

Co-Create Solutions and Deep Relationships

To spread the news of the first grassroots fund and advocate for a larger state fund, WDC tapped into a whole network of "trusted messengers" across the state. These were community leaders, nonprofit workers, labor organizers, and others who could spread messages and collect stories. This trust had been built by years of organizing. It was further strengthened by community participatory feedback loops. This took place through listening sessions, mass text mechanisms, and social-media engagement. It relied on recruiting community members for various organizing supports, including language interpretation, art, and data coding.

Meaningful collaboration means embedding intentional feedback loops at every stage of the campaign: project design, data analysis, creation of recommendations, and dissemination. We hired undocumented college students to sort through recordings of listening sessions and label the patterns and themes they found. Meanwhile, those with the lived experience of being undocumented advised at every stage of the process. This was one way to hold these invaluable stories with care.

HEALTH AND DIGNITY

"They Don't Care About Us, But We Care"

The Narrative Power of Community Love, Grief, and Resistance from HIV to Long COVID

By Jennifer Johnson Avril and JD Davids

In the past year, we have become self-educated experts on "Long COVID," the term patients prefer for long-term symptoms related to COVID-19. Not all of our doctors believed us, but together with thousands of other people we met online, who were all experiencing similar symptoms, we researched our conditions, lobbied for treatment, and formed a support group. . . .

A year later, we still struggle to be taken seriously by friends, family members, clinicians, and policy makers. People are sympathetic, yet few think Long COVID can happen to them, or that it will affect their postpandemic life. But Long COVID is not a footnote to the pandemic or a curious human-interest story. It is America's next big health crisis, and we should prepare for it now.[1]

In March 2021, Fiona Lowenstein—journalist and founder of feminist, queer health-justice organization Body Politic—and Hannah Davis co-wrote an article for *The New York Times* in which they identified as living with Long COVID.[2] In the article, they not only detail the struggle to have their lived experiences taken seriously by communities and institutions around them, but they also hone the importance of building collective power, insisting that those impacted by this chronic illness are the best people to speak on how it should be handled.

Through this framing, Lowenstein and Davis, both queer white people in their twenties, carrying on the legacy of HIV/AIDS activism—specifically, the *1983 Denver Principles*, a foundational document created by people living with AIDS that established the rights of people with a health condition to speak for themselves.[3] Much of Long-COVID advocacy has echoed the lived narrative practices of ACT UP and other formations of people living with HIV.

ACT UP rose to prominence nationally and internationally as a grassroots activist organization during the height of the HIV/AIDS crisis in the late 1980s and early 1990s. With a membership of primarily out, visible, and vocal LGBTQ+ members, ACT UP used direct action and civil disobedience, among other organizing tactics, to demand better access to treatment and funding for research, and to counter stigma that devalued and marginalized individuals living with HIV/AIDS.

ACT UP rooted its praxis in community care, even as those with lived experience fought to develop and expand public health care systems.[4] Meetings were not only for decisions about direct-action strategies; they also prioritized sharing information about possible experimental remedies, creation of affinity groups that became circles of care for those who grew sicker, and commitments to honor last wishes for memorials, including confrontational political funerals in the street.[5]

Rarely, however, have media narratives around illness reflected this power of community care. Instead, they perpetuate narrower, victim-driven framing. For example, early AIDS reporting focused almost exclusively on young, white gay men in the final stages of the disease, excluding nonwhite queer men, all women, transgender people, and people who inject substances.

While it is true that homophobia and hatred of all queer people drove government inaction and the overall cultural response to the AIDS crisis, racism and anti-Blackness also fueled narrative exclusions that have had devastating impacts. Today, the highest rates of HIV and AIDS are among Black gay and bisexual men, and they rarely elicit media coverage.

Despite the groundbreaking *Denver Principles* during the HIV/AIDS epidemic—and subsequent decades of "patient-led" movements—many stories about Long COVID have similarly conformed to hegemonic victimhood narratives, tending to profile young, previously "well," white people who were suddenly felled by mysterious symptoms. Their youth, race, presumed class,[6] and lack of visible preexisting conditions have made their sickness one that was acquired, at least within the media lens, through no fault of their own. In this sense, the reporting around Long COVID skipped to the "innocent victim" stage of AIDS-related media, akin to the imagery of babies who acquired HIV from parents in pregnancy or childbirth.[7] Through this lens, both movements have contended with the complexities of care "as a modality of power dynamics," as recognized by disability scholar Akemi Nishida. She notes that

> Care is used to enforce top-down dominant power as much as care is exercised at the grassroots level to enable resistance against such dominant power and enact transformative power for a more just world and way of living.[8]

These complexities have been explicitly embraced by Long-COVID advocates faced with caring for one another in a nation and world slow to acknowledge and address the frequently chronic nature of COVID-19–triggered illness. Any movement led by those closest to the oppression, in this case by disabled or chronically ill people, must contend with this modality of power dynamics—caring for one another while advocating for the expansion of care by a state that deems those outside of hegemonic power structures as disposable.

As narrative practitioners, we believe that the patterns of media reporting and of omission, including which stories are made visible and how they are circulated, have wreaked narrative damage and neglect on communities most impacted by chronic illnesses, from HIV/AIDS to Long COVID. Further, we believe that these narrative harms can be confronted with intentional care through narrative itself[9]—those that center care not only as a fundamental responsibility of the state, but also as an integral component of community and movement resilience.

Ungrievability: Who Is Deserving of Care?

Our analysis is informed by Judith Butler, who in their 2009 book *Frames of War: When Is Life Grievable?* discusses how the media portrays victims of war as "ungrievable" to serve state interests.[10]

Applying Butler's framework to the dominant narratives of HIV/AIDS, COVID-19, Long COVID, and other chronic illnesses, we see the presence of ungrievability, which has required activists to craft and deploy alternative, or counter-, narratives and media strategies that reassert individual and collective grievability alongside demands for change. This narrative struggle starts from the baseline that one's life holds value.

For example, in 1997, the state of Pennsylvania instituted the first phase of HealthChoices, a mandatory managed-care program for Medicaid recipients that put a level of care restriction over most people living with HIV, beginning in the heavily affected southeastern region of the state. John Bell, an African American Vietnam veteran living with AIDS, was one of ACT UP's leaders of a HealthChoices-focused protest at the State Office Building in Philadelphia. During the funeral procession of primarily Black mourners, activists bore mock coffins under a looming giant puppet of the governor as the Grim Reaper. Bell addressed the impassioned crowd, centering on ACT UP members' right to care and their caring for one another: "We want to live.

HIV activist John Bell, speaking at an ACT UP rally targeting the presidential campaigns of George W. Bush and Al Gore. This was one of many coordinated rallies organized in 1999 and 2000 to make global access to HIV treatment a presidential campaign issue. Photo courtesy of Philadelphia FIGHT Community Health Centers

We will make a noise until we are heard. They don't care about us, but we care. Our friends are dying and dead."[11]

Perceptions of people with chronic illness are deeply tied to disability. While not all individuals with chronic illnesses necessarily consider themselves disabled,[12] much of the discrimination, prejudice, and bias against individuals with chronic illnesses stem from the stigma of *ableism*—a belief in the superiority of nondisabled or neurotypical individuals. Ableism functions to deny grievability to disabled and chronically ill people, and thus justifies narrative neglect. This perspective is based on and elevates narratives of disposability and individualism, which reduces individuals coping with chronic illness to faulty cogs in a necessary societal machine. They are dependent at best and blamed or invisible at worst.

The denial of grievability is strengthened by the harmful narrative—interwoven with deep, racist narratives of capitalism—that a person's health is a matter of their own choices, with no connections to the social determinants of health, such as economic stability, access to quality health care, community support, exposure to environmental contaminants, and interpersonal violence. The material impacts of these narratives include direct calls for mistreatment, oppression, apathy, or even the deaths of people with chronic illness.[13]

Depictions and assertions of narrative damage and erasure are recirculated and reconstituted through all forms of mass media every day, creating a 24/7 news cycle of harm. At times, it is a visible process, as in the platforming of people who believe that transgender people can be legislated out of existence, or in the use of criminalizing terms like *illegal* to describe millions of undocumented immigrants, who are often depicted solely as racialized minorities.

In other cases, it can also be a lack of presence, which we call *narrative neglect*. The first years of the COVID-19 pandemic included a near-absence of public acknowledgment and grieving of the deaths of more than a million people in the United States, including disproportionate numbers of Indigenous, Latinx, Pacific Islander, and Black people, when adjusted by age.[14] Furthermore, COVID-19 deaths among those who were incarcerated were undercounted.[15] As of this writing, we have found only one example of mainstream media reporting on Long COVID among people in congregate living, jails, and prisons.[16]

In the lead-up to the COVID-19 pandemic in the United States, proof of the relative ungrievability of disabled and chronically ill people, along with seniors, came time and again in major news reporting. Outlets asserted that the novel coronavirus would not necessarily constitute a major problem, as it was predicted that only the elderly and previously ill would be killed by SARS-CoV-2. In these assertions, the audience is an imaginary "general public," per the words of Gregg Bordowitz,[17] that is somehow devoid of disabled and chronically ill people or vulnerable seniors. Communities affected by HIV and AIDS were conceived by mass media as not even being part of their audience.

Nearly two years later, Centers for Disease Control and Prevention (CDC) chief Rochelle Walensky cheerily told *Good Morning America* that "the overwhelming number of deaths—over 75 percent—occurred in people who had at least four comorbidities. So really, these are people who were unwell to begin with."[18] Her statement drew a swift response titled "Letter from the Disability Community to CDC Director Rochelle Walensky," in which a broad range of groups noted that "the dismissal and devaluation of people with disabilities has been our daily experience throughout this pandemic."[19]

Care as a Demand and a Practice

As of early 2024, Long COVID has affected nearly six million children[20] and 7 percent of adults in the United States, with one in four of them reporting significant limitations on daily activities.[21] It remains a threat to anyone infected or reinfected with SARS-CoV-2, with bumps in reported cases after more recent COVID-19 surges. Women continue to be disproportionately affected, similar to other complex infection-associated chronic conditions,[22] while federal funding for prevention and care has been nearly eliminated.

In this context, it is crucial for our narrative and media practices to counter ungrievability, deliberately introduce counternarratives of care, and hone best practices from decades of HIV/AIDS activism. Long-COVID patient-led movements have waged narrative campaigns for basic recognition of the condition, facing overt and diffuse opposition, ranging from medical cost-containment groups; politically motivated COVID minimizers; and harmful deep narratives on gender, productivity, and worth. While our primary audiences for these counternarratives are those of us living with HIV/AIDS, Long COVID, and/or chronic illness, as well as those who love us, we recognize that most people will be impacted by disability and chronic illness throughout the course of their lives. Focusing on our target audiences allows us to strategically activate our surrounding communities toward change.[23] One of the most powerful examples from the era of HIV/AIDS activism is the years-long campaign to force the CDC to change the definition of AIDS in 1993 to include symptoms most frequently seen in women and injection-drug users. The campaign included protests at CDC headquarters in 1989 and 1990, and was rooted in the national ACT UP Women's Network, whose leadership included Black and Latina woman who led HIV education efforts in New York state prisons.[24]

Forcing a narrative shift in the understanding of who was affected by AIDS, the activist community rallied around the phrase "Women don't get AIDS, they just die from it," which was reflected in a series of graphics from the Gran Fury collective, including bus-shelter posters. The campaign succeeded not only in changing the definition of AIDS itself—a key to getting benefits and care—but established a more powerful presence of women in the narrative of HIV/AIDS and within often male-dominated HIV advocacy.

One of the shortcomings of communication analysis of health-justice movements is that they largely focus on demands of the state. Yet, in the absence of state recognition of the right to health and life-saving information, movements like ACT UP have focused their efforts on providing community care and harm reduction. In the 1990s, ACT UP Philadelphia produced fifteen editions of its own *HIV Standard of Care*,[25] a photocopied document designed for people living with HIV to take to medical appointments to educate their providers, until the federal government created guidelines and provider education that took responsibility for this vital information. The group, like many formations of HIV activists across the country, also initiated a needle-exchange project to enable injection-drug users to access sterile syringes and information for HIV prevention, operating the exchange until they won a city-funded program to expand access.[26]

Like activism during HIV/AIDS, disabled and chronically ill people have led efforts during the COVID-19 crisis to expand definitions of symptoms and conditions, fill gaps in information and resources, and combat mis- and disinformation.[27] On March 7, 2020, before the emergence of widespread stay-at-home orders, an ad hoc group of chronically ill, disabled, and former ACT UP members (including chapter co-author JD Davids) hosted a national webinar on one week's notice: *COVID-19 (Coronavirus) Preparation for People Living with Chronic Illnesses in the United States.*[28] In May 2020, members of the Body Politic support group, later formalized as Patient-Led Research Collaborative, released the first survey data documenting and detailing Long COVID in hundreds of people,[29] which helped ensure that the interim CDC definition of Long COVID was inclusive of a wide range of symptoms and conditions. [30]

Four years on, and after many mutual-aid efforts of 2020 have evaporated, "mask bloc" groups, often started by or largely made up of disabled and chronically ill people, are running their own media and communications networks. These networks serve to distribute information, masks, and COVID-19 tests to gig workers and others at high risk of exposure in low-income neighborhoods, as well as find access to Paxlovid and other treatments for people when they are sick. Formations of chronically ill and disabled people, such as PeopleHub and SIQ (Sick in Quarters) are holding online space for one another. This comes after most groups that shifted to remote programming, and the funders that assisted that shift, have abandoned online offerings.

The media created from and for these grassroots community–based actions show the so-called ungrievable asserting their own and others' grievability through active, visible, and tangible care. Activist and writer Chimére L. Sweeney, who testified at the first congressional hearing on Long COVID and is creating a documentary film centering on the lived experiences of Black people with Long COVID, roots her work in a lineage of care and advocacy by Black enslaved people, stating:

> Advocacy usually starts because one person wants to fix a problem that impacts them, and that's okay. We don't have to wholly reinvent the wheel. But we must acknowledge that our enslaved ancestors left us tools that will illuminate how we approach Long COVID healthcare and community care right now. We just have to learn and then be willing to use them.[31]

Rejecting the False Binary of Sick vs. Powerful

HIV/AIDS activists notably broke through the false binary segregating the sick from the powerful, creating public and often impolite spectacles that simultaneously took up public space while demanding very specific policies or practices necessary to their survival. In doing so, they often overtly referenced the lack of concern that forced their actions.

Long-COVID advocates have significant barriers to turning to the recognized ACT UP playbook of visible, edgy direct action. Many people with Long COVID have extreme fatigue and/or myalgic encephalomyelitis/chronic fatigue syndrome (ME/CFS); may be fully homebound; and face the risk of additional COVID infection bringing new, worsened, or potentially irreversible symptoms or medical consequences. This challenge has been long noted by disability advocates and scholars, including Johanna Hedva in their "Sick Woman Theory":

> If being present in public is what is required to be political, then whole swaths of the population can be deemed apolitical simply because they are not physically able to get their bodies into the street. . . . So, as I lay there, unable to march, hold up a sign, shout a slogan that would be heard, or be visible in any traditional capacity as a political being, the central question of Sick Woman Theory formed: How do you throw a brick through the window of a bank if you can't get out of bed?[32]

The September 2021 Millions Missing protest, hosted by ME/CFS advocacy group MEAction in collaboration with newer Long-COVID advocacy groups,[33] harnessed years of caring, disability-focused organizing and strategic narrative interventions to address these obstacles. Participants from around the world contributed to digital advocacy, engaging in tactics ranked from the least to most energy-intensive. A highly visible group of around fifty people with ME and Long COVID, including caregivers/family members, gathered at the White House with walkers, wheelchairs, and other mobility devices in coordinated red shirts, saying, "Still sick, still fighting," as they blocked the sidewalk.

Demonstrators living with myalgic encephalomyelitis/chronic fatigue syndrome (ME/CFS) and Long COVID gather at the White House to advocate for disability justice protest in September 2021. Photo by John Zanta

The narrative return on the day of protest was unprecedented in ME and Long-COVID advocacy. Digital-media stories on Long COVID or ME that had previously been illustrated by stock photos of a tired woman with a laptop and a cup of coffee in a bland living room now showed disabled and chronically ill people as a politically relevant, organized force, gathered to demand change.

The nascent years of Long-COVID advocates, just like those in HIV activism decades before, have brought tension and conflict, as newly ill and disabled activists—who may also be more likely to be white and from privileged classes than the many millions facing these conditions—confront their own lack of information, biases, and political understandings within a deeply ableist society rooted in racial and gender bias. For example, in her *Long COVID Lessons* videos on TikTok and Instagram, longtime Black disability-rights activist and author Imani Barbarin speaks directly to newly disabled people with Long COVID.[34] She explains the importance of learning history from previous movements, turning to people with similar conditions for support rather than expecting answers from the medical system. She underscores that our struggles for justice today may not benefit us directly, but may create a better future for those who come after us.

As a communicator, Barbarin holds online space as a form of the commons: a public space that asserts and nuances individual and group politics as a counterpoint to the narrative tyranny of the ostensibly well. Interventions such as Barbarin's place people living with chronic illness and disabilities directly in the frame, affirming their grievability and serving as a prime example of the potential of care through narrative, amid a landscape of institutional narrative neglect.

Going Full Circle in an Ongoing Pandemic

At the time of this writing, COVID-19 narratives have, in some ways, gone full circle in just four years. With the May 2023 ending of public-health emergency declarations that funded much of the COVID response and undergirded mitigation policies, we are once again told that SARS-CoV-2 primarily endangers the sick, the disabled, and the elderly. Our communities are still often absent from deliberation of COVID-19 policies and still not afforded the protections we need in an ongoing pandemic. Moreover, COVID-19 continues to be a pandemic of weaponized mis- and disinformation, purposefully used to bolster right-wing forces.[35]

Long-COVID advocacy is still in its early years. However, it will be vital in determining the path of not only this health crisis but others likely to come in a time of environmental peril and predicted future pandemics. People with HIV/AIDS and their loved ones won huge social, policy, and medical victories, weaponizing their own mortality and grief in the face of tremendous public fear, scorn, and callousness.[36] We believe in the potential power of a similar narrative pathway both by and for people with Long COVID but also, crucially, by and for all disabled and chronically ill people, as well as the COVID-bereaved.[37]

We must also recognize patterns of societal and narrative neglect—particularly structural white supremacy, entrenched racial injustice, and gender bias, all of which drive health disparities—that can limit or undercut movement strategies and outcomes. To quote Body Politic president Angela Meriquez Vázquez:

My comrades in Long COVID justice work do indeed work to make space for the voices of advocates of color in their respective efforts. Still, as an advocate of color, I feel I am participating in political theater rather than driving systemic change across all the systems that impact marginalized communities.[38]

Recognition of care as both a demand and practice in HIV activism shows us how internal and network communications forged powerful bonds across people with HIV and their loved ones, generating heat and light to overturn dominant narratives of disposability. As those most at risk of COVID-19 harms continue to face disabling and deadly consequences of unaccountability for an ongoing airborne pandemic, intercommunity narratives of group identification, care, and collaborative dissent are vital to any hope for policies to support survival.

In this era of a mass disabling pandemic that falls most heavily on women/femmes, transgender people, and racialized minorities, we urge substantive institutional and organizational communications investment in the interpersonal health of disabled and chronically ill people. Bolstered by authentic caring through narrative, our movements will be more fully enabled to love, care, and mourn for one another as communicative acts that simultaneously demand systemic changes and affirm and honor our lives.

From "Safe, Legal, and Rare" to "Everyone Loves Someone Who Had an Abortion": How We Shifted the Abortion Conversation

By Renee Bracey Sherman and Regina Mahone

Just days before the 2022 midterm elections, actress and comedian Cecily Strong declared before millions of *Saturday Night Live* viewers, "We all love someone who's had an abortion."[1] Strong said she didn't want to talk about abortion on live TV, but "these are scary times. They don't want to just take away access to health care; they want to criminalize it, too."[2] Strong affirmed the genuine fears of activists in states that banned abortion outright following the Supreme Court's ruling in *Dobbs v. Jackson* a few months earlier, overturning the federal constitutional right to abortion.

Eighty percent of Americans believe abortion should be legal, an opinion that hasn't changed in decades.[3] This has not stopped politicians from exploiting the issue to polarize and mobilize voters. Indeed, just after *Roe* legalized abortion in 1973, conservatives exploited people's fears of a liberal society that normalized homosexuality and feminism and threatened traditional family values. They lumped abortion into the argument, which became a proxy for radical or perverse behavior. Democrats further stigmatized abortion by arguing the procedure was *safe, legal, and rare*, even though it was not rare, given that one in four cisgender women have an abortion in their lifetime. Radical-left factions demanded that abortion access be *on demand and without apology*—messaging that was exploited by the opposition and increased support for more moderate asks.

For decades since, a narrative battle over abortion has raged on between political groups. Some of these battles have been between activists and the state, others between abortion rights activists and antiabortion activists; and even some have been intramovement, where activists in the same movement contest for power against one another. The shift from popular messaging that labeled abortion as "safe, legal, and rare"[4] to a message that affirms that "everyone loves someone who had an abortion"[5] did not happen overnight. It resulted from strategic and radical communications efforts by social-justice organizers, activists, policy advocates, and everyday people. Media allies engineered the elevation and amplification of these stories and messages centered on love, self-determination, and community care.

Safe, Legal, and Rare

"Safe, legal, and rare" as a message to describe abortion was popularized by then-president Bill Clinton and First Lady Hillary Clinton in the early 1990s.[6] Abortion is not rare, but the message was a compromise that allowed the administration to pacify pro-choice voters while courting more moderate Democrats who only agreed abortions should be legal in instances of rape or incest.[7] Politicians who were uncomfortable with abortion used "safe, legal, and rare" as a political workaround to indicate their support for abortion rights while not putting forth any substantive policies to make abortion more accessible or affordable.

The overemphasis on "rare" allowed politicians to cast abortion as necessary only in dire circumstances, which meant that abortion was still stigmatized. The mainstream pro-choice movement endorsed this, allowing only certain kinds of abortion stories to be publicly told, particularly those from wealthy, white, married, heterosexual couples—excluding everyone else.

This compromise the Democrats made came with grave consequences. By being dishonest about how prevalent abortion was, they missed an opportunity to normalize abortion care as routine reproductive health care. This is a demand progressive and left proponents of abortion, including Black feminists, knew was essential to the self-determination of all people who needed abortions for any reason.

There was a lesser-known and more insidious reason why Democrats pandered to pro-choice voters by fighting to keep abortion legal: eugenics. President Clinton campaigned on "ending welfare as we know it," a bipartisan message that tapped into old, racist tropes by implying Black women were "gaming the system" to access housing vouchers or food stamps. Although the mythology was largely untrue, liberals and conservatives argued that Black women should not have children they "could not afford." For elected officials, abortion—and forced sterilization—provided mechanisms to curb the Black birth rate legally, reducing the number of poor, Black children.

Those fighting for access to abortion splintered off into multiple factions. The abortion-rights movement was led by lawyers and physicians who pushed for complete control of abortion access to be solely in their care and within a legal framework outlined in the *Roe v. Wade* decision. Renee Bracey Sherman and Dr. Tracey Weitz wrote for *Rewire*:

> This new legal framework allowed advocates to distinguish themselves from radical activists who wanted abortion "on demand and without apology" and full decriminalization. From this distinction, the pro-choice movement was professionalized, institutionalized, and legitimized. The new pro-choice movement did not seek the radical transformation of power; it sought to become part of the power, creating new political messaging and frameworks for understanding when, where, and how pregnancies should happen and which are deemed worthy of protection.[8]

Those abortions they were willing to defend should be safe, legal, and rare.

The pro-choice framework narrowed the scope of the reproductive-rights movement and limited its imagination for Black and Brown liberation and queer and immigrant families. It was unresponsive to reproductive atrocities outside of contraception and made abortion legalization only possible for white women who could afford it.

What radical activists knew was that there was no choice if people could not access abortion because there is no clinic in their county or they don't have a car or access to public transportation. Ultimately, their reproductive decisions were narrowed because of systemic inequities created by bad policy and justified by racist ideologies. If some women could not freely decide if, when, and how to grow their families without the fear of state-sanctioned violence or reproductive coercion, the pro-choice framework did not have the teeth to liberate all pregnant people.

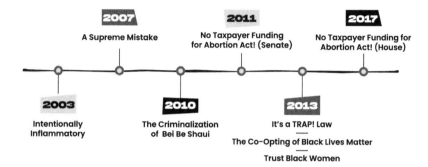

In response to abortion stigma and racist welfare reform policies from the Clinton administration, a multiracial, big-tent coalition of activists organized. They called out the racism and racist language in the lawmaking, pointing out that these policies would plunge Black families deeper into poverty if implemented.

Narrative Flashpoints in the Twenty-First-Century Reproductive Justice Movement

With the intervention of the reproductive-justice framework in 1994, Black, Brown, Indigenous, queer, and trans movement leaders entered the twenty-first century, breaking free of the limitations set by moderate, white-led reproductive-rights organizations, and bringing a vision of what reproductive freedom and liberation truly means to the mainstream.[9]

The goal was to shift the message from "safe, legal, and rare," which stigmatizes abortions, to one that unapologetically supports and amplifies the experiences of those who have had abortions—no matter when or why. This effort was not without its challenges. Key flashpoints between 2003 and 2022 demonstrate the state of reproductive politics in this century, and where the movement needs to head in order to normalize the stories of people who have abortions.

Intentionally Inflammatory (2003)

In 2003, President George W. Bush signed the Partial-Birth Abortion Ban Act, which banned a standard procedure for later abortions.[10] *Partial birth* was an intentionally inflammatory, medically inaccurate phrase left unchallenged by pro-choice advocates.

Rather than defending later abortion as critical to all people who need abortions—no matter how far along their pregnancy is or how delayed they become because of financial and logistical barriers—the pro-choice movement only safeguarded access for defensible cases, such as rape, incest, and health contraindications. They were reinforced by stories from married, straight, white women who wanted their pregnancies but feared the health risks to their lives.

In the eyes of the pro-choice movement, this effectively erased and delegitimized the stories of Black and Brown people who obtained abortions every day without a sympathetic reason for doing so.

A Supreme Mistake (2007)

The judiciary is crucial in normalizing or delegitimizing abortion narratives. For example, even today, the media and some advocacy groups frame abortion as a "heartbreaking"[11] and "difficult" decision.[12] This framing was not popularized by medical professionals but by Supreme Court Justice Anthony Kennedy through his 2007 opinion in *Gonzales v. Carhart*. This Supreme Court decision upheld the ban on later abortion procedures. He stated:

> While we find no reliable data to measure the phenomenon, it seems unexceptionable to conclude some women come to regret their choice to abort the infant life they once created and sustained. Severe depression and loss of esteem can follow.[13]

This narrative became popular in messages about abortion, leading to thousands of state-level restrictions based on the idea that abortion damages our bodies and mental health.

In protest, abortion proponents used stories to counter Kennedy's narrative. Stories can transport people, build empathy, and change beliefs over time. While abortion storytelling was not a new strategy, sustained organizing around it breathed new life into the movement. The stories illustrated that abortion allowed us to move forward with our lives and create our families on our own terms, should we choose to. It was not a source of mental duress, as Justice Kennedy and antiabortion advocates asserted. Some abortion sto-rytellers spoke out to challenge these false narratives. However, the abortion-rights movement—still cowering to abortion stigma—chose to elevate the socially acceptable stories of married white storytellers or the composites of people who needed abortions for "acceptable" reasons.

The narrative did not begin to change until state abortion restrictions piled on and more abortion storytellers of color began to speak out, demanding that ordinary abortion stories be heard. This moved the discourse beyond cherry-picked stories to advance a message steeped in respectability politics, elevat-ing white and/or middle-class couples with justifiable decisions.

Bei Bei Shuai and Purvi Patel (2010 and 2013)

In the 2010s, antiabortion advocates escalated efforts to criminalize preg-nancy, evidence of which can be found in the cases of two Indiana women, Bei Bei Shuai and Purvi Patel.

Shuai was thirty-three weeks pregnant when she attempted suicide by ingesting poison. She survived, but her premature baby died a couple of days after being delivered by cesarean section. Shuai was charged with murder. After significant public pressure from activists and the public, the prosecution offered her a plea deal, but not before she'd served fourteen months in jail.[14]

Shuai's case set a precedent for further prosecuting pregnant women for behaviors that could endanger their fetuses. However, reproductive-justice advocates knew that because of rampant racist and xenophobic narratives, which justify oppression and reproductive violence, immigrants and other ostracized communities are more likely to be targeted and criminalized by law enforcement. At the same time, they're less likely to get adequate and culturally appropriate health care services.

The consequences of that precedent became apparent in 2013, when thirty-three-year-old Purvi Patel was accused of illegally inducing her own abortion and of giving birth to a baby she then allowed to die. She was charged and convicted with feticide and sentenced to twenty years in prison. She was the first woman to be charged under Indiana's feticide law, initially imple-mented to protect pregnant women from violence.[15]

Shuai and Patel are of Asian descent, which did not go unnoticed by abor-tion proponents and movement workers. South Asian American physician and writer Sayantani Dasgupta wrote for *Salon* in 2015:

The fact that Patel is of Indian origin, a brown woman in the heart of the American Midwest, a South Asian face in the era of post 9-11 racial profiling, is in fact critically important in this narrative of criminalized reproduction.[16]

It's a TRAP! Law (2013)

In 2013, the Texas state legislature introduced the Targeted Regulation of Abortion Providers (TRAP) law. This bill proposed closing more than half the abortion clinics in the state and banning abortion even when the fetus was too premature to survive outside of the womb. Texas state senator Wendy Davis famously filibustered a version of the omnibus bill for thirteen hours, reading abortion stories from people all over the state who had been shut out of testifying against the law.[17] The Supreme Court later ruled that two significant portions of the law, Texas HB2, were unconstitutional.

Throughout national coverage of the Texas legislation and Supreme Court case, the media and policy makers used biased abortion stories that would drive their political agenda. By sharing the most tragic abortion stories, they exploited people's emotions to sensationalize abortion instead of normalizing it. Those of us who had abortions demanded the media tell a complete story about who gets abortions, how, and why.

Local communities in Texas spoke out by sharing their abortion stories and elevating the voices of abortion providers in their communities and the growing left movement in Texas. However, the larger narrative driven by nonprofit organizations focused on the safety of abortions in clinics and debated the illegitimate merits of the case. While the legitimacy of the merits were important, they did not address the rising political fascism, voter suppression, and overarching discrimination and racism that were fueling the growing antiabortion movement's motives to break the *Roe v. Wade* decision and democracy writ large.

The Co-Opting of Black Lives Matter (2013)

The Black Lives Matter (BLM) movement emerged in 2013 after a Florida jury acquitted vigilante George Zimmerman for the murder of seventeen-year-old Trayvon Martin. It did not take long for the antichoice movement to co-opt BLM by trying to link abortion to anti-Black racism. In Missouri, after uprisings demanding justice for Michael Brown (who was killed by Ferguson,

Missouri, police officer Darren Wilson), policy makers attempted to draw upon protesters' outrage to advance a repressive "pro-life" agenda. They introduced the All Lives Matter Act,[18] legislation that defined a fertilized egg as a person, and in doing so, compared terminating fetal tissue to the death of eighteen-year-old Michael Brown. All Lives Matter builds upon earlier antichoice messaging, which implies Black women who have abortions contribute to "Black genocide."

The *abortion is Black genocide* myth tugs on real fears about scientific racism, which is the practice of co-opting science to justify racial inequality. As more overt racialized violence became less acceptable, scientific racism flourished in the twentieth century. For example, thirty-two states participated in a government-mandated program to involuntarily sterilize Black, Brown, and Indigenous women so they could not have children. Today, antiabortion advocates tell stories that attempt to associate abortion with this gruesome behavior, or even with slavery.

Trust Black Women (2013)

The reproductive-justice and BLM movements formed alliances to illustrate how police and state violence are a threat to building healthy and thriving Black families. Trust Black Women, a coalition of Black-led organizations and individuals, coalesced in response to racist, antichoice billboards in 2010. The coalition's name was also a mandate and counternarrative. It asserted that Black women must be trusted to decide when, whether, and with whom to have a family, and should not be shamed, coerced, or forced into motherhood by antiabortion zealots. In a solidarity statement, Trust Black Women acknowledged how the work of racial justice and reproductive justice go hand in hand.

Interventions like this take time to become popular in public discourse. The normalization of ideas—the process by which wisdom becomes conventional and part of our "common sense"—requires activists to put the issue on the political agenda, make it relevant to everyday people, and defend it against co-optation and delegitimization. As a 2023 poll of Black youth ages eighteen to thirty-five by HIT Strategies revealed:

> Phrases such as "reproductive justice" . . . were unfamiliar to participants. Once described, participants understood their importance; but on their own, these terminologies do little to motivate

Black voters. . . . Instead, putting these issues into the context of how they impact Black voters . . . is key before introducing the terminology without context.[19]

One example of reproductive and racial justice in mainstream discourse can be found in media narratives about the death of George Floyd and the subsequent uprisings in the summer of 2020. When Floyd was suffocated by police, he called out for his mother before taking his last breath. Fundamental to reproductive justice is the ability of Black people to parent their children in safe, healthy neighborhoods free from state violence. Although Floyd's mother had died two years earlier, his plea demonstrated how police violence is also an issue of reproductive justice.

"Saving Roe"

In the decade leading up to the *Dobbs* decision, reproductive-rights organizations set their sights on "saving and protecting *Roe*." For this group, codifying abortion through the lens of law and policy was the ultimate goal. If *Roe* were passed as a law by Congress, abortion would be federally protected and binding for all states without excessive government restrictions.[20] To do that, they would have to make heavy concessions that would leave out important provisions for vulnerable communities, such as young people. To codify *Roe*, advocates abandoned conditions that ensured that people who were under eighteen and living under the guardianship of someone else would not have to ask a judge for permission to get an abortion.

This singularly focused strategy edged out people for whom the promise of *Roe* was never a reality because of state-based restrictions, economic hardship, and other factors relevant to the systemic conditions of their lives. Although abortion was legal, it was not guaranteed to be geographically or financially accessible. For poor people, Medicaid recipients, and those incarcerated or detained in immigration detention centers, abortion was a right in name only.

No Taxpayer Funding for Abortion Act! (2011, Senate, and 2017, House)

In 1977, four years after the *Roe v. Wade* decision, Congress passed the Hyde Amendment, which bars federal funds from being used to pay for abortion. This has been a policy attached to the annual budget every year since.[21]

In 2011, Republicans introduced and passed the No Taxpayer Funding for Abortion Act, which denied abortion care to poor people enrolled in Medicaid by eliminating government insurance coverage for abortion.[22] This decision making was fueled by entrenched mythologies about Black women's sexuality, which originated during the colonial period. The Jezebel stereotype characterized Black women as oversexed and rationalized this lawmaking, which went beyond controlling what American tax dollars were spent on. It was a mechanism to control and regulate Black women's sexuality, sexual freedom, and reproduction.

Rather than rejecting the inhumane stance that this policy took, some pro-choice policy makers appealed to moderate voters by contending that their current federal policies did not allow for the funding of abortion care.

The word *taxpayer* invokes several racist stereotypes—namely, that taxpayers are hardworking, law-abiding white people who are having their money taken by people who are undeserving of it, including immigrants or Black women on welfare. Because Democrats refused to challenge these racist assumptions, they allowed the racist myths to live in the minds of voters. This ensured that people enrolled in Medicaid were unable to afford an abortion and that Black and Brown women remained the scapegoats. They refused to challenge the outright lies that people on Medicaid do not pay taxes and are therefore undeserving of health care. These myths made it clear that abortion bans for low-income people were not worth fighting for. Thus, they would remain the status quo in order to save political face.

To counter, the National Network of Abortion Funds took a bold stance declaring that funding abortion was a way to redistribute wealth.[23] Abortion funds nationwide began to use the organizing slogan "Fund Abortion, Build Power!" while donors of abortion funds proactively declared that they *wanted* their tax dollars to fund abortions. Led by primarily Black women and people who have had abortions, reproductive-justice organizations took on a defiant message demanding that abortion be spoken about, loud and proud, and revealing that people were indeed "pro-abortion."

Black and Brown leaders in the reproductive-justice movement led with messaging that spoke to the fullness of our experiences, including and beyond abortion access. They made clear how the barriers to abortion also existed in health care overall and led to high Black maternal mortality rates.[24] It became increasingly apparent that legal doesn't mean accessible, and that Black and Brown people had been left behind throughout the decades and centuries of abortion-access efforts.

Imagining a New Future

Today, many people who have had abortions openly share their stories to achieve reproductive justice—the human right to maintain personal bodily autonomy, have children, not have children, and parent the children we have in safe and sustainable communities.[25] "Everyone loves someone who had an abortion" is a counternarrative to the decades of stigma and judgment of abortion care. It also reinforces the reality that abortion is not rare and people who have abortions are the same people you love—and they deserve respect. Despite 80 percent of the nation believing abortion should be legal, perceived polarization makes phrases such as these seem radical rather than normal and true.

Despite progress in building narrative power for reproductive justice, in 2022, the United States became one of only three countries to overturn federal protections for abortions in the last century. The fight for abortion access, dignity, and power is raging on in most states. Activists, medical practitioners, and legal experts are working together to safeguard in-clinic and medication abortion, and to keep pregnant people and those taking abortion care into their own hands from being criminalized. We have our work cut out for us.

Still, being in control of our narrative has allowed for a generational shift in who is showing up to demand abortion rights and access and to make the movement more inclusive. We need all of us to win. This radical communications work depends on our network of advocates and activists to achieve the incremental gains at the local and state levels, where the fight is playing out. We must continue pushing the bounds of what is considered socially and politically possible, and invite opportunities for imagining a future that uplifts a range of abortion stories.

Building People Power: How to Shift the Health Care Narrative in the United States

By Ben Palmquist and Anja Rudiger

The movement for Medicare for All, long at the margins of political debates, burst into national prominence in 2016. Vermont senator Bernie Sanders, a longtime proponent of universal, publicly financed health care, recognized that millions of people were ready for political revolution. Most political histories start and end there, with elected leaders. While Sanders deserves enormous credit for his role in extending the horizons of national politics, he was hardly acting alone.

In 2008, as politicians in Washington, DC, began formulating plans to reform health care markets by subsidizing and regulating for-profit insurance, the Vermont Workers' Center launched a different kind of campaign—one that would shift the narrative away from health care as a privilege and a commodity toward recognizing it as a human right.

Within a few short years, the Workers' Center's Healthcare Is a Human Right campaign won the first legislation in the country committing a state to creating a universal, publicly financed health care system. It demonstrated to Sanders that the time was right to make Medicare for All the centerpiece of his presidential campaign. Although both policies remain unfulfilled, the impact of the Workers' Center's campaign is ripe with lessons for other movements. While most stories about health policy center on politicians, the real story of what upended U.S. health care politics in the last decade is a different story. It is a story about people joining together, rising up, and changing what is politically possible. It is the story of the Healthcare Is a Human Right campaign.

The Neoliberal Health Care Model

The dominant model of health care in the United States is market-based, which requires people to purchase private-insurance plans directly or through an employer. Despite sizable public subsidies, this private-insurance system is highly inequitable and leaves 30 to 40 million people entirely uninsured and more than 100 million technically "covered" but still unable to afford the care they need.[1] These injustices are normalized and reproduced by the dominant promarket ideology of neoliberalism, which shapes policy, law, and public opinion.

The Vermont Workers' Center rejected the standard neoliberal prescription for health care, which treats health care as an individual responsibility and a for-profit commodity. This model effectively turns patients into "consumers" who make choices between competing insurance plans, hospitals, and prescriptions, and who are responsible for securing their own insurance coverage.

Implicit in this is the assumption that not everyone deserves care. If you are uninsured and cannot afford care, it is ostensibly because of a choice you made—-a choice to take a job without health benefits, to be unemployed, or to be poor. Rarely is it seen as the fault of an unjust, exclusionary system. Yet U.S. health care programs exclude tens of millions of people without full-time formal employment, immigration papers, and other markers of economic status from Medicare, Medicaid, the Affordable Care Act, and private insurance.

Though superficially race- and gender-silent, these exclusions are constructed in ways that disproportionately affect people of color, women, transgender people, poor people, and others at the bottom of social hierarchies. This produces a self-reinforcing logic: People who are seen as "undeserving" cannot get needed care, while people who are excluded from care come to be seen as "undeserving." By dividing and ranking people according to an imagined moral hierarchy and treating health care as a privilege, the neoliberal worldview shatters social solidarity and stifles collective demands to protect everyone's health. Instead, it forces people to suffer in individual isolation and self-blame, and encourages the political scapegoating of Black, immigrant, and poor people.

President Barack Obama's health care reform—the Affordable Care Act (ACA)—perpetuated this model, even as it sought to improve access to and affordability of private insurance through correcting perceived market failures. It increased public subsidies for private-insurance companies, while also expanding Medicaid, an essential public program for millions of lower-income people and those living in poverty. While these measures released just enough political pressure on elected officials to stave off popular demands for universal health care, the ACA's piecemeal interventions quashed more radical proposals, co-opted large segments of health care advocates, and pre-empted systemic change.

Changing the Frame to Human Rights

Universal, publicly financed health care is in operation in countries all around the world, but in the U.S. political context, the Vermont Workers' Center had to develop a new way of thinking and talking about health care. They teamed up with Partners for Dignity & Rights (then called the National Economic and Social Rights Initiative, or NESRI) to create a narrative of health care as a human right and a public good. Health care, they said, was not an individual responsibility but a collective responsibility that encompasses caring for each other and our government caring for us. In place of freedom of choice between market options, they called for a more expansive freedom: the freedom from want and freedom from fear we would all enjoy if we could live our lives without worry of losing insurance, being denied care, or winding up in medical debt.[2]

Grounding health care in human rights demands a completely different role for government. In the neoliberal model, government regulates and subsidizes health care industries to promote market competition and sustain private profits. As a universal human right, health care must be guaranteed by government as a public good to all. This means government is obligated to finance health care publicly, distribute resources equitably, and govern health systems democratically—with transparency, accountability, and participation from patients, workers, and communities.

With this narrative shift, the Workers' Center believed they could chip away at the hegemonic neoliberal worldview and supplant it with a collective, liberatory vision of health care framed through the lens of human rights and rooted in equity, solidarity, interdependence, government responsibility,

THE VERMONT WORKERS' CENTER'S HUMAN RIGHTS PRINCIPLES:

UNIVERSALITY:
Everyone must have guaranteed access to comprehensive, quality health care.

EQUITY:
Healthcare resources and services must be distributed according to people's needs, with no systemic barriers, such as costs, to accessing care. Everyone gets what they need and contributes what they can.

ACCOUNTABILITY:
Government has an obligation to establish a healthcare system that meets human- rights principles, and that is accountable to the people it serves.

TRANSPARENCY:
The healthcare system must be open with regard to information, decision-making, and management.

PARTICIPATION:
The healthcare system must enable meaningful public participation in all decisions affecting people's right to health care.

and public goods. The campaign that made this possible was Healthcare Is a Human Right (HCHR), whose story begins with a hotline.

Building People Power

In 2007, while the Vermont Workers' Center was supporting workplace organizing, its workers'-rights hotline was ringing off the hook. Hundreds of callers sought help with hospital bills, prescription co-pays, and insurance claims. Their grievances were overwhelmingly about health care, not workplace issues.

Around the same time, Workers' Center leaders were reflecting on the future of their organizing. For ten years, the organization had partnered with unions in worker-organizing campaigns in a couple of Vermont's rural towns. What would it take to engage a broader base of people, to expand into a statewide organization, and to build a mass movement with the power to effect systemic change?

Hotline callers drew attention to a vast battleground beyond the workplace: the struggle to access and pay for health care, which affected almost everyone in the state. Here was an opportunity to expand the organization's base, engage a broad spectrum of people, and widen the focus from defending workers' rights to demanding a new right for all: the human right to health care.[3]

HCHR originated from a bold strategic vision of mass movement building, with a carefully orchestrated narrative shift at its core. By concentrating on health care, an issue of universal resonance, and repurposing the liberal human-rights frame for progressive social and economic demands, Workers' Center leaders assembled components of a new hegemonic narrative, one that upends the capitalist market ideology and turns health care consumers into rights holders. Just as workers'-rights campaigns develop through collective awareness and action, HCHR transformed individual consumer complaints about health care into collective human-rights claims. It debunked the bootstrapping myth of individual responsibility and brought people together around the values of universal rights, to be won in a popular struggle.

Across the state, people told Workers' Center organizers of their harrowing experiences with the health care system. One man reported losing his house to keep up with medical bills, another refrained from getting care until his cancer had metastasized, and an immigrant worker suffered a ruptured appendix while trying to obtain the paperwork demanded by the hospital. Using a survey tool, organizers went into working-class and rural communities, knocking on doors and visiting local markets to talk with people about their health care struggles. These conversations served as entry points to political consciousness and engagement. People connected with each other in local organizing committees; shared video recordings of their health care stories in the People's Stories Project; participated in speakers' training; and contributed to the campaign's first report, *Voices of Vermont's Healthcare Crisis*.[4] Woven together, these stories documented the human-rights violations perpetrated by the market-based health care system.

As the campaign matured, leaders and members used human-rights norms to envision a different health care system, one that provides quality health care to all, publicly financed and free at the point of service—not unlike the universal health care systems implemented in other countries. Collaboratively, leaders and members agreed on the campaign's foundational human-rights principles—universality, equity, transparency, accountability, and participation. With these principles as cornerstones, the HCHR narrative emphasized values that resonated broadly, including with people concerned about injustices beyond health care. The campaign cast a new light on unmet needs, ranging from health care to food to housing, by reclaiming the idea of public goods removed from the market.

This approach marked a critical departure from standard health care advocacy models, embodied by "single payer" activists. For years, Vermont single-payer groups had sought to repurpose the neoliberal efficiency frame, touting the cost savings the state (and the country) could achieve if they only had one payer, the government, handling all insurance and payments. Led by physicians fed up with the bureaucratic maze of insurance administration, these groups focused on reducing administrative complexity and, by extension, costs. This made perfect sense to physicians drowning in paperwork, but reinforced the notion that health care and other resources were scarce and failed to connect with people unable to access care.

HCHR directly counters this dominant scarcity frame, which rations access to health care and other public goods, and prioritizes those who can pay. Instead, the campaign coalesced around personal stories that illuminated shared problems, and agreed-upon principles that guided toward a common solution. Centering on the experiences of those most impacted by health care injustice and connecting people across geography, race, age, gender, sexuality, and employment status enabled the campaign to build collective agency where a ready-made class identity that could unite workers against their bosses was lacking. The campaign's free clinics, held in reclaimed public spaces, showcased a culture of abundance produced by collective strength and solidarity. This solidarity and unity held firm throughout the campaign. For example, a Catholic funder had asked the Workers' Center to remain silent about reproductive rights in their health care demands; the campaign refused. The Workers' Center lost that funding but gained credibility and broadened its membership.

The campaign also built unity by learning from workers' struggles. Both the stories and the human-rights frame highlighted a clear antagonism: On one side were people unable to afford health care and denied their rights; on the other were profiteers who built an industry around commodifying a human right. HCHR's People's Media Project turned this antagonism into a "battle of the story," guided by the communications tool developed by the Center for Story-Based Strategy.[5] They produced a simple but effective contrast between people claiming their rights and corporations denying them. This oppositional frame served to reinforce a sense of collective political identity and set the stage for supplanting neoliberal market fundamentalism with collective rights and public goods.

The Winning Recipe

On May Day 2009, HCHR staged the largest rally in Vermont's recent history. From this moment onward, the annual human-rights rally would become a barometer of the movement's vibrancy and the outward expression of power and unity.

Tangible wins followed surprisingly quickly. In 2010, the campaign inserted human-rights principles and a requirement for public participation into a health-reform study bill, thereby opening further political and organizing opportunities. During the following election season, the campaign held a series of statewide People's Forums during which the candidates listened and the people spoke. It assembled a People's Team to work the legislative chambers in lieu of professional lobbyists. Armed with the People's Toolkit, a comprehensive communications and engagement guide prepared by those directly impacted by health care injustice, many campaign members set foot in the statehouse for the first time. In public hearings, they wove their own stories into a collectively agreed-upon People's Agenda. The mantra of health care as a human right—previously foreign to public discourse in the United States—permeated legislative and media circles.

The year 2011 brought the biggest victory. Vermont became the first state to enact a universal health care law, Act 48, requiring the establishment of a publicly financed health care system based on human rights principles. At the last moment, the bill's passage was threatened by an amendment that would have excluded undocumented people from the new health care system. But HCHR members were unwavering in their commitment to universal rights. Assembling jointly with migrant justice organizers on the steps of the statehouse, they demonstrated their solidarity on banners reading "universal means everyone." This show of unity pressured legislators to reject the discriminatory amendment.

HCHR leaders took the lessons they learned on national tours,[6,7] sharing the People's Recipe they had developed.[8] Narrative strategies are both a specific ingredient, as well as multiple ingredients interwoven throughout the recipe in internally facing organizing and political education and externally facing public messaging and coalition building. The recipe metaphor clarifies that neither narrative power nor any of the other ingredients—such as base building and leadership development—is sufficient on its own to effect systemic transformation. The better all ingredients are combined, the greater the potential for building complementary facets of power.

The Struggle Continues

By the end of 2014, the combined power of corporations and state government had stopped universal health care in its tracks. The governor, pressured by business interests, refused to adopt a financing plan for Act 48, the health care law, and legislators followed his lead.[9] Despite the governor's own calculations showing that nine in ten Vermont families would be financially better off if the state transitioned to universal health care, he steered the debate back to spurious fiscal and macroeconomic considerations.[10]

This sleight of hand was not unexpected: The universal health care law featured a built-in delay of five years, designed to meet federal requirements and allow time for fleshing out a financing plan. HCHR had adjusted its narrative strategy accordingly by inoculating its members against austerity arguments. This included unpacking false assumptions behind scarcity tropes and applying human-rights principles to fiscal issues.[11] They even launched a complementary initiative, the People's Budget Campaign, to demand that spending and revenue policy be based on the principles of universality and equity.[12] The vision of a state budget that meets everyone's needs and distributes resources equitably struck at the heart of the scarcity paradigm. It recast annual budget debates in human-rights terms, framing the state budget as "a moral document." Both campaigns operated under the Workers' Center's new "Put People First" umbrella, designed to build alignment with other social-justice forces.

In retrospect, what was missing was the ability to translate narrative power and legislative wins into lasting changes to the state's political and economic power structures. This is no easy feat. It requires clearly identifying how dominant power is produced and reproduced. The HCHR narrative largely cast the health-insurance industry in the role of the villain, yet in Vermont, which lacks for-profit insurers, the most organized opposition ultimately came from businesses wary of taxation, along with the political groups they fund. This sustained the institutional inertia of a government steeped in market ideology. To prevail against these dominant political and economic forces protecting the status quo, the campaign's level of countervailing power was insufficient.

National Impact

For decades before Vermont's HCHR campaign, a small but steady circle of advocates had been pushing for Medicare for All (or, as they called it, "single payer" health care), but were never able to generate significant popular power. HCHR's victory in 2011 struck like lightning, sparking new energy within health care advocacy organizations and, importantly, among a much broader set of unions, community organizations, and everyday people.

Even before the stalled implementation in Vermont, the Workers' Center

recognized that systemic change is a relay race, not a sprint, and supported others to take the baton. Within a few short years, groups in Maryland,
Maine, Oregon, and Pennsylvania launched campaigns directly modeled after
HCHR. Strong organizing and narrative strategy drove legislators in twenty states to introduce at least fifty-nine bills proposing state-level universal
health care,[13] and the Campaign for New York Health and Healthy California
have both passed their bills through one legislative chamber and are close to
winning majority support in the second.

Even more famously, Vermont senator and longtime friend of the Workers' Center Bernie Sanders waged historic runs for the presidency in 2016
and 2020 that fully embraced health care as a human right, centered on
the goal of Medicare for All. As Sanders is the first to say, his campaigns
were not about top-down change directed by him, but were reflections of a
people's movement.

The Healthcare Is a Human Right campaign was central to this movement.
It helped crack the hegemonic neoliberal health care dogma and put a radically different, rights-based vision squarely on the national agenda. HCHR
reshaped the political imagination through popularizing human-rights principles and combining them with personal storytelling that empowered, embold-
ened, and connected people. It forged a new collective political force through
broadening the Workers' Center's organizing strategies and aligning people
across differences into a popular movement.

The future of health care politics in the United States is yet to be written—
that story is up to all of us to shape. But as the Vermont Workers' Center has
shown us, if we convey a transformative vision rooted in shared values and
human experiences, and if we can back that narrative up with real organizing
and movement building, we can create the people power to make the politically "impossible" possible.

Building a Fat-Positive Future: Strategies for Advocacy and Change

By Tigress Osborn, Amanda Cooper, and Pamela Mejia

No one could have anticipated that a politician who wrote a diet book would become a key figure in changing the narrative about antifat discrimination. But on May 26, 2023, a coalition of community leaders working to end size discrimination sat in New York City Hall's historic and picturesque Blue Room while Mayor Eric Adams hosted a public signing ceremony for legislation making it illegal to discriminate based on height and weight in employment, housing, or public accommodations in New York City.[1] Adams, whose own weight loss has been widely covered in the media, told a room full of city leaders and journalists that fairness outweighs assumptions about weight when it comes to New Yorkers being treated inequitably. The mayor was clear: "When you talk about a person being discriminated against because of their body size, it's not [about] fighting obesity," he said. "It's just being fair."

It was a great win for New Yorkers of all sizes and a great win for fat rights.

However, Eric Adams is not the leader we would have chosen for this moment. The controversial mayor had already demonstrated at the time of the press conference that his unrelenting support of the New York Police Department (NYPD) under all circumstances, as well as some of his other politics, were misaligned with liberatory values. Months after this crucial moment for our movement, he was accused of corruption and sexual harassment. Yet, that morning in the Blue Room, his allyship with fat rights created ripple effects beyond the signing ceremony, advancing civil rights for New Yorkers of all sizes. The legislation he signed that morning made New York City one of the most populous places in the world to name height and weight as protected categories under the law. That day, New York City became the largest of only eight cities in the United States, and of two states at the time, with explicit legal protections of any kind for body size. Size discrimination is legal almost everywhere in the world.

Long before launching the Campaign for Size Freedom[2] to elevate the struggle for legal protections against size discrimination, organizations like the National Association to Advance Fat Acceptance (NAAFA) and Solovay Law's Fat Legal Advocacy, Rights, and Education Project (FLARE), as well as local organizers and individual activists,[3] have supported antidiscrimination legislation in many jurisdictions where it now exists. This advocacy has led to notable successes in places like Santa Clara and San Francisco, California, and New York City. Despite their efforts, achieving state-level laws has proven more challenging. At the time of this writing, New York and Massachusetts advocates have been pushing for state laws for years, with bills attempted or introduced in several other states.

Protective laws are one tactic to improve fat people's lives—and to change the narrative about fat rights. The damaging perceptions of fat people must be challenged to encourage new understandings of how body-based discrimination harms people living in bigger bodies. As world-renowned body liberation activist and author Sonya Renee Taylor reminds us in her acclaimed book *The Body Is Not an Apology*, "To varying degrees and without much thought, many of us have accepted what we have been told about our bodies and the bodies of others based on what our government allows, sanctions, ignores, and criminalizes." [4]

Body size remains overlooked as a social-justice issue among movement workers who regularly push for change in government policies and procedures. Even among those who understand the personal to be political, antifatness is often classified as *only* personal. To address systemic challenges faced by fat people, we have to see antifatness, not fatness itself, as the problem to be solved. This requires an incredible shift from our current cultural thinking, which treats fat people as fat first and people second.

One way we can create this shift is through strategic narrative-change work. The government and its policies cannot and should not determine everything about how we see fat people. Yet changes in how the law allows us to treat fat people raise broader questions about why we've been treating fat people so poorly in the first place. These questions and the answers they demand create opportunities to tell a new story about fat bodies.

The National Association to Advance Fat Acceptance and its supporters rallying before the public hearing to End Size Discrimination in New York City at City Hall. Photo by Jackie Molloy

The Harms of Pervasive Antifat Attitudes

Fat people are part of every population but are often discriminated against without repercussion, compounding other forms of injustice. Antifat attitudes and systemic oppression are a direct result of concerted efforts to elevate thin, white bodies and to enshrine white supremacy and patriarchy in every one of our systems. Both colonization and the slave trade created many of our ideas about which bodies are ideal and which must be forced into conformity or treated with disregard. The historical roots of antifatness can be traced to explicit messages about racial purity, designed to create contrast between white people and the supposedly out-of-control, unrestricted appetites of the "savage" other.[5]

While the organized fat-liberation movement has existed for more than fifty years, antifatness still dominates personal, professional, and political spaces. Today, body size criteria are often used to deny health care: everything from organ transplants to trans and gender-affirming care. Antifatness also limits access to sexual and reproductive health care, including abortion, birth control, and fertility treatment. Parental rights are diminished based on assumptions about parents' or offspring's body sizes. Being a worker in a larger body means facing bias in hiring, pay, and advancement opportunities. Fat children are the most likely to be bullied,[6] and fat students of all ages see their educational attainment limited by unaccommodating desks, inaccessible learning spaces, bullying and ostracism by peers, and the attitudes of faculty and staff that fat students cannot be successful.

These realities are magnified for fat people who are Black, Indigenous, and people of color (BIPOC). BIPOC fat people find antifatness used as a proxy for racism, with many parallels between negative stereotypes about fat people and those about race, especially narratives related to laziness or lack of discipline. Racial and class-based disparities within the justice system—whether in the streets, the courts, or carceral systems[7]—are compounded by size discrimination, which labels fat people as everything from dirty to dangerous.

Weight Loss Dominates the Media Landscape

News shapes public opinion and policy agendas. How an issue shows up in the news is an entry point for the public conversation about that issue—and it has implications for how movements like ours can best implement strategic narrative change and generate more productive coverage to advance liberation. Much of the injustice faced by fat people because of body size goes unreported in the media. From microaggressions to life-risking limitations, weight stigma takes a backseat to weight loss in the current narratives about fat. To learn more about the current news narratives about larger bodies, NAAFA engaged a new partner, Berkeley Media Studies Group (BMSG), whose researchers study the news to gather insight into the public narrative about various issues.

BMSG examined print news media to discern how fat is being talked about in news stories. BMSG's findings supported what we suspected based on lived experience: There is much more print news content about weight loss than antifatness or advocacy for fat rights. For example, from February to July of 2022, there was nearly fifty times as much coverage of weight loss (5,302 articles) compared to fat liberation (108). During the same period in 2023, even as fat-rights advocates were most engaged in changing the law in New York, there was still nearly twenty times as much news-media coverage of weight loss (7,265 articles) compared to articles that referenced "fat libera-tion" (373).[8]

We expected an imbalance, but even those of us highly experienced with antifat bias in the media were surprised at how lopsided the results of BMSG's analysis were. The vast majority of news articles about fat people focus on health-related research or new "miracle drugs" to eliminate fat people, with very little nuanced reporting that challenges what is often considered com-mon knowledge about body fat and fat people. Fat people are shown as a problem that needs to be solved—reflected in the number of stories that raise debates about the health harms of fatness, even in stories that are ostensibly about other issues. As a result, readers are introduced to fat people as fat bod-ies without personality, community, or any hopes beyond changing their bod-ies. This kind of coverage is dehumanizing, disheartening, and destructive to the pursuit of fat people's civil rights.

Of course, we want fat people recognized as complete human beings with hopes and joys and families and complications in their lives that have little to do with their size. We also want a narrative that accurately depicts the reali-ties of size discrimination. Fat people face life-limiting and life-threatening discrimination in almost every area of life. Research by Dove showed that weight discrimination affects 34 million people across the United States and costs $206 billion every year.[9] That is equivalent to the combined population of the twenty biggest U.S. cities. How is so little attention paid to the harm that impacts a community this populous?

To start a new conversation about civil rights related to body size, society must recognize that we do not live in a world where fat people are safe, valued, or have access to all that life has to offer. We live in a world where it is *not* illegal to discriminate against fat people, as evidenced by the disheartening story of a Texas medical resident who lost her job due to her body size.[10] This doctor-in-training was meeting standards, but her fellow residents singled her out, citing "concerns" that her lack of fitness would make her unable to treat patients. Their concerns were based on imagined scenarios rather than actual incidents, showing us that our narratives about fat people are even more pow-erful than our actual experiences.

Her lawsuit challenging the discrimination was unsuccessful and revealed that when size discrimination goes to court in a locale that has no explicit laws about protecting fat people, it is almost impossible to win the case. By working to enact legislation and using newsworthy moments to tell diverse and authentic fat stories, we can drive and sustain conversations about how our laws and practices can reflect our values—of what it means to be free now, in the actual bodies we are living in today.

"A Little Justice in the Big Apple"

The New York City bill[11] offers a glimpse of what narrative change driven by legislation can look like when on-the-ground advocacy and organizing drive national and global news coverage. The bill was sponsored by Council Member Shaun Abreu, who had an "a-ha moment" after gaining weight at the beginning of the pandemic.[12] When he noticed that people treated him differently, he began to think of size discrimination as intersecting with housing, reproductive rights, and other issues he was working on for his constituents.

Abreu soon introduced a new version of a bill previously introduced by Brad Lander and co-written by District Leader Lydia Green. Abreu's personal narrative helped energize the bill, and his willingness to talk candidly about size discrimination with colleagues, constituents, and the media brought more attention to the issue. The bill received immediate support from the Retail, Warehouse, and Department Store Union (RWDSU) and Retail Action Project (RAP), whose members had experienced job loss, demotions, and pay reductions due to size discrimination. NAAFA and FLARE connected with these labor partners, and together our organizations became the primary advocates for the bill, working closely with Council Member Abreu's team.

The bill came up for a hearing in February, on the first snowy day the city had seen all winter. Transportation and traffic were affected all over the city, and some folks we expected that day simply couldn't make it to City Hall. The rest of us showed up with brightly colored "Yes on Size Freedom!" signs and handmade posters bearing slogans like "My body is perfect! It's your laws that need to change!" We had effective chants: "What's the solution? Size inclusion!" and spirited speakers. Only thirty of us were there, but our small group made a big impact. By the time we headed into the hearing, news stories were already being prepped about the feisty fatties and friends who showed up to push New York City to become one of the few places in the world with explicit civil rights for fat people.[13]

Heading into testimony, we were prepared for the pushback our organizations have heard over the years—that accommodations for fat people are too costly and that protecting fat people from discrimination is "glorifying obesity" and enabling poor health. One council member decried the bill in the media, writing antifat discrimination off as a lack of personal responsibility from people who should lose weight if they want to end the discrimination they face. Business leaders told the press that the bill would lead to frivolous lawsuits.

But none of the naysayers bothered to show up to testify against the bill. Meanwhile, thirteen people gave testimony in person or virtually, and another six submitted written statements of support.[14]

Opera singer Tracy Cox spoke to the reality of hostile work environments for larger-bodied performers. "Weight stigma and discrimination is a sanctioned strategy in the performing arts. On behalf of all of the fat artists in New York City, I ask for our basic right to be able to show up at work without our bodies being fair game for criticism and derision," she said. "Let me do my job without being casually encouraged to develop an eating disorder or have bariatric surgery, which has happened to me countless times in the workplace."

In her testimony, recent college graduate Victoria Abrams shared the difficulties of getting size-accessible seating on her campus. "My choice is being sat at the special desk at the back of the class, serving as a reminder to the room that I don't fit, or suffer in silence with wood digging into my side, hoping that I remember the lecture because, at that angle, there's no way I would get a pen to paper. Something as simple as being able to sit in my seat and take notes like my peers, I did not have the privilege of doing."

These and other heartfelt personal testimonies at the hearing cemented support for the bill, moving undecided council members from curious to inspired. Attorney Brandie Solovay said in her testimony, "Passing legislation in New York City won't fix all of the wrongs, but it is an important start. It's about time that fat people have a little justice in the Big Apple!"

It also moved journalists to hear more from those testifiers, many of whom were quoted in media pieces that reached a broad audience in local and national print, television, and radio. Fat and allied perspectives dominated the narrative.[15] *The New York Times* did a thorough and thoughtful piece and promoted it via a push notification on subscribers' phones.[16] It even gave NAAFA the final word, ending with Tigress Osborn's challenge to legislators nationwide: "It's time for lawmakers across the country to ensure that everybody and every body is protected under the law and has equal opportunity."

The media attention continued as the bill moved toward a final vote. Once the bill passed the City Council with a vote of 44 in favor to 5 opposed, the question was how the notoriously vegan and "health-conscious" Mayor Eric Adams would respond. We did not fear his veto because we had enough votes to override it, but we feared it would slow us down and dampen the enthusiasm for other pending bills. We hoped he would quietly let the bill go into effect. Then—surprise!—we received a call in mid-May 2023 inviting us to New York City for a signing ceremony. Not only was the mayor making it official, but he was also making it a media moment, offering us another public opportunity to shift narratives about antifatness and why it matters.

We should not have been surprised that the mayor's team was swayed by the ongoing media attention to the matter. We know that news coverage is a critical source of information that influences public-policy agendas. When a proposed policy is discussed in the news, the coverage legitimizes it to the public as something worth knowing about—perhaps more important, something worth *doing something about*.[17] Mayor Adams's decision to sign the bill ceremonially activated the press in ways a quiet bill passing never could have. But it was still up to us to capitalize on the moment by continuing to engage with the media to produce coverage that focused on our civil rights and not on efforts to change our bodies.

News Stories Lead to New Stories

In the wake of the mayor's signing ceremony, we elevated stories about other places poised to ban size discrimination, some with even more protections than the New York City legislation offered. A story from *The Boston Globe* explored how the New York City bill would affect efforts to pass similar legislation in Massachusetts,[18] and NPR's nationally distributed *The Takeaway* series featured a segment on fat rights as civil rights,[19] with Osborn explaining how changing laws can change hearts and minds. There were numerous other features, and those caught the attention of popular podcasters, including Aubrey Gordon and Michael Hobbs of *Maintenance Phase*, who chose the passing of the New York law as the fat-liberation highlight of 2023 in their year-in-review episode heard by thousands of Patreon subscribers.[20] Features like this helped us reach new supporters and continue the dialogue long after the signing ceremony.

Movement Momentum

While we haven't (yet) tipped the scales away from weight-loss coverage, we have added an entirely new conversation to the dialogue. As discussed earlier, the difference between 2022 and 2023 in the coverage of fat rights is dramatically improved, with the ratio of weight loss to fat-rights coverage shrinking from 50:1 to 20:1.[21] Even with a marked increase in the coverage of fat rights, stories about the movement are still dramatically outnumbered by the media coverage of weight loss. The juggernaut of news and viral social-media coverage about weight-loss drugs in 2023 and 2024 continues nearly unabated. This is aided by significant marketing investments by pharmaceutical companies that stand to gain billions, regardless of any health or social harm caused. Still, change is happening, and we can build on and maintain the momentum.

What lessons can other movement communicators take from our campaign?

- Analyze media to understand what dominant narratives you are up against. This will help you track progress to see if the needle has moved.
- Collaborate with people with decision-making power, stories to tell, and good messengers, like Council Member Shaun Abreu.
- Use various forms of media to normalize your message—photo ops through public actions with signage, testimony, print media, etc.
- Use the news-making nature of legislation as a tool to build narrative power.
- Make sure you have a diversity of spokespeople, from those with lived experience of the issue to those who can lend credibility to a marginalized group.

We also hope you are inspired to ensure your organizations and campaigns support narrative change for fat liberation. This could include any or all of the following:

- Put body size on the list of diversity areas you are recognizing and celebrating. Add height and weight to your internal antidiscrimination policies.
- Deepen your understanding of intersectional antifatness.
- Hire fat people and support fat professionals in other ways—for example, by ensuring that your rallies, protests, and events have accessible seating and other facilities for bigger bodies.
- Tell our stories, show our pictures, and create spaces where we are welcomed and accommodated to tell our own stories—on our terms and in our voices. Stories are still one of our strongest currencies for helping people relate to and care about those who face discrimination.

With this momentum, we can invigorate a conversation about body size that differs from what people in the United States know. We can use fresh tactics to pave the way for new stories that omit the narratives we want to divest from. The New York City story is about advocates who seized on a critical moment with an unlikely supporter to tell an entirely different story. We can kick-start new narratives that ensure that everybody and every body is protected under the law and has equal opportunity.

ECONOMIC EQUALITY AND WORKERS' RIGHTS

The Power to Win: Occupy Wall Street, the Fight for $15, and Multidimensional Power

By Dorian Warren and Katherine Ollenburger

When we began writing this chapter in the summer of 2021, the country was experiencing a once-in-a-generation strike wave. The COVID-19 pandemic had upended all our ideas of normalcy, and workers from Amazon to Starbucks were demanding better pay and a union. Progressive politicians and mainstream economists had come to agree on the need to raise the federal minimum wage to $15 an hour—at least.

Ten years earlier, Mary Kay Henry, president of the Service Employees International Union (SEIU), began organizing the conversations that would birth the "Fight for $15 and a Union" campaign. She asked Dorian Warren, then an associate professor at Columbia University, to organize some progressive economists to support the idea of a $15 minimum wage. He couldn't find a single one.

Their arguments against a living wage mirrored the economic common sense of the prior half century: neoliberal capitalism. The markets, economists argued, once unencumbered by government interference, would deliver the socially optimal minimum wage; doubling wages from $7.25 to $15 would "hurt the very people you want to help."

Neoliberalism's fundamental faith in markets to organize the economy was undergirded by three ideological pillars: the transfer of public wealth to private control through privatization, corporate freedom from accountability through deregulation, and the starvation of government services through low tax rates.[1] The dominant narrative reinforced the economic theory's common sense. It was a story of individual responsibility, the low value of physical versus intellectual labor, and the erasure of social difference to uphold long-standing forms of social stratification[2] based on race, gender, ability, and other identities. It also connected market fundamentalism with social conservatism, refocusing government intervention on protecting traditional, Christian family structures for their stabilizing effects.[3]

What caused the consensus to unravel? The real pillars of the economy: people.

Ordinary people built power through organizing and called forth a future beyond neoliberalism.[4] Through the emergence of Occupy Wall Street in 2011 and the Fight for $15 a year later, ordinary people—organized into labor unions, community-based organizations, and social-justice movements—advanced an alternative story in which economic productivity does not determine human worth and dignity. Scholars refer to this alternative as a "solidarity economy," which prioritizes people and the social good of economic activity. Its elements include the dignity of work, a positive role for government regulation and rule setting, the rejection of zero-sum thinking, a "bottom-up" or "middle-out" economic framework,[5] and equity in our institutions, policies, and politics.[6]

This new narrative developed over the past decade because of the narrative power that emerged from Occupy Wall Street and matured in the Fight for $15. Power is the ability to achieve purpose, as Dr. Martin Luther King Jr. defined it. Narrative power is the idea that the stories we tell and the values they transmit can change mind-sets and behaviors by setting the public debate and, ultimately, reshaping notions of common sense. Occupy Wall Street flexed narrative power that changed the American conversation on economic inequality, while Fight for $15 built on that narrative power with the multidimensional *movement power*[7] of grassroots organizing, ideas, and politics.

Narrative and movement power unraveled the neoliberal consensus and transformed people's lives. The Fight for $15 campaign delivered material change in numerous places around the country and proved that our economy can function with a different way of valuing workers. Twenty-seven million workers won roughly $150 billion dollars in raises over a ten-year period.[8] The campaign's victories, however, would not have been possible without the narrative groundwork sparked by the Occupy Wall Street movement. Over the last decade, these movements have demonstrated the importance of narrative power—and its catalytic impact when connected with movement power. In many ways, Occupy Wall Street busted open the narrative door toward an alternative to neoliberalism that the Fight for $15 expanded and kept open for over a decade.

Occupy Wall Street's Narrative Power Puts Income Inequality on the Agenda

On September 17, 2011, a group of protestors in Manhattan's Zuccotti Park forced policy makers to put economic inequality on the national political agenda. Their action—and the Occupy Wall Street movement that emerged around it—reset the agenda by using two strategies: effective, compelling stories and disruptive action.

Stories are the building blocks of narrative, and the way we construct each story can create the scaffolding for a broader, more inclusive narrative. Social-justice communications strategists, including Anat Shenker-Osorio[9] and Doyle Canning and Patrick Reinsborough,[10] have developed a set of principles for this narrative change, including naming villains and heroes in a story. Occupy Wall Street named villains: the 1 percent who extracted their wealth from the rest of us. The rest of us were the heroes—the 99 percent, David to the CEOs' Goliath. We were the small but many against the mighty few.

Protest on the anniversary of the Occupy Wall Street movement in Zuccotti Park, New York, NY (2015). Photo by Cindy Trinh (@ActivistNYC)

Meanwhile, disruptive action is the hallmark of social movements in American history, and Occupy Wall Street used it to bring public attention to their David and Goliath story. They made visible the economic pain of the Great Recession. Between 2007 and 2012, financial institutions foreclosed on four million homes, and 9 percent of job seekers couldn't find work.[11] The publicly visible Occupy protests, which spread to hundreds of locales around the country, made the individual experiences of job losses, declining wages and household income, and skyrocketing debt and foreclosures into a visible, collective story that demanded conversation. It was a collective response that eased the shame of neoliberalism's "personal responsibility" narrative.

Occupy Wall Street used these strategies to build and wield the four dimensions of narrative power:

Agenda setting

It put economic inequality on the agenda through disruptive collective action that captured and sustained public attention to force a political response. The 112th Congress, dominated by Tea Party Republicans elected during the 2010 midterm elections, had shown no interest in addressing the root causes of the financial crisis or rampant inequality. They had narrowly avoided both a government shutdown and a default on the U.S. government debt. It was also the first Congress in which half of the members were millionaires.[12] The Obama-Biden administration had expended most if not all of its political capital on modest economic rescue packages and passing the Affordable Care Act. Politicians were not speaking to the economic concerns of working people, and their lack of leadership created a vacuum and an opening.

The Occupy movement filled the void.[13] By putting inequality in the news, they forced the Democratic establishment to speak to the problem protestors raised. By October 15, 2011, the White House was aligning with Occupy Wall Street's demands and messaging, with White House spokesman Josh Earnest describing President Obama as fighting to make certain that the "interests of 99 percent of Americans are well represented."[14]

Salience

Occupy Wall Street framed the concept of economic inequality in a salient way that resonated with the experiences of a significant segment of the population.

FOUR DIMENSIONS OF NARRATIVE POWER

Narrative power is a type of persuasion based on four abilities:

AGENDA–SETTING:

the ability to put an issue onto the political agenda despite opposition from political elites.

SALIENCE:

the ability to make an issue relevant to and resonant with the broader public.

PERSISTENCE:

the ability to keep an issue on the agenda over time with the narrative infrastructure to embed new stories that change what people believe and value.

PERMANENCE:

the ability to reset the perception of "common sense" in a permanent shift away from existing worldviews.

Rather than an esoteric concept based on data, statistical correlation, and historical trend analysis, Occupy Wall Street spoke to a *feeling*: I can't get ahead. The vast majority of Americans had felt the impact of the recession directly, through job losses, foreclosures, loss of equity in their homes, and rising household debt. Occupy Wall Street connected those experiences in a compelling story—a game has been rigged in favor of the 1 percent—that shunned the contrived, confusing acronyms of policies like the Troubled Assets Relief Program (TARP) that never "trickled down" to ordinary people.

The first visual call to Zuccotti Park evoked David versus Goliath imagery with a ballerina balanced on the head of Wall Street's iconic charging bull statue.[15] From street art[16] to *The New Yorker*,[17] designers caricatured the villains as Monopoly-man bankers and politicians held hostage to Wall Street's interests. Organizers' imagery drew battle lines between the wealthy 1 percent and the rest of us, and it helped to elevate the growing critique of neoliberalism. The public could recognize the protestors might have a point without joining them in the park, and social scientists could use movement disruption to make their critiques politically salient and powerful.

Persistence

They persisted. Occupy Wall Street was not a single news cycle or a local story. Targeting the center of the financial markets helped the protest to break through the noise, and generated ongoing media coverage that was sympathetic, describing protestors as "a generation of lost opportunity" and reflective of the views of most Americans.[18] What began as a 1,000-person protest on September 17, 2011,[19] grew to a two-month-long takeover of Zuccotti Park, with occupations across the country and the world in solidarity. Even as New York City police officers cleared Zuccotti Park in December 2011, and ended the Occupy movement's most visible period, its impact was just beginning.

Transformation

Occupy Wall Street transformed the politically acceptable discourse, permanently changing the way organizers, politicians, economists, and the general public talk about inequality. It opened the Overton Window, which is a model that political scientists use to describe the scope of political possibility based on evolving social norms and ideas.[20] By opening the Overton Window—by expanding the boundaries of political possibility—Occupy Wall Street created space for a politically viable progressive economic agenda to emerge. Bernie Sanders's 2016 presidential campaign, for example, carried the Occupy movement's narrative and connected it with progressive narratives like "health care is a human right." His campaign built on Occupy's momentum and drew from its alumni.[21]

Social Science, Movements, and Narrative Power

The Occupy movement was free to tell its story—and advocate for an alternative worldview—in a way that social scientists were not. In fact, they lacked the narrative power that Occupy Wall Street brought to Zuccotti Park. Within academia and progressive think tanks like the Roosevelt Institute, social scientists had begun to assemble data and analysis over the first decade of the twenty-first century, but their advocacy was constrained by the rigor of the scientific process: frame your hypothesis, objectively present competing views, gather evidence, and evaluate your hypothesis based on the data. Conventional social science—dominated by a relatively conservative economics profession—relies on the researcher acting as an unbiased observer, trained to minimize lived experience so as not to contaminate objective truth or theory. It is designed to produce objectivity and to present the evidence without privileging or advocating for any one hypothesis. Numerous scholarly formations like Scholars for Social Justice, Institute for New Economic Thinking, and Scholar Strategy Network, among others, have begun calling academics into a new activist role—one that is sorely needed.

The Limitations of Occupy's Narrative Power

Occupy Wall Street's narrative power changed what was possible to imagine. As one of the Occupy protestors, Cecily McMillan, reflected: "It drew a line. It was the beginning of a cultural movement."[22] It did not, however, deliver material change to realize the alternative vision it put forward. It lacked two elements of successful social movements: roots and infrastructure.

Successful social-justice movements are rooted in the lived experience of the people most impacted by injustice. They are sustained by social bonds between people, built over time and gathered in organizations and formations that deepen an understanding of shared fate across lines of difference. Community-based groups form the movement infrastructure to sustain campaigns for change over time and amid adversity.

Occupy Wall Street was disconnected from the people most impacted by the system it challenged. The people who responded to the initial call—made by the glossy, anticapitalist magazine *Adbusters*—represented a relatively elite, young, and white subsection of the 99 percent. Their privilege impacted the coverage of and response to their protest—in many ways to Occupy's benefit. It won narrative victories, but it did not aim to build infrastructure to advance a grassroots movement. In particular, the lack of *narrative infrastructure*, as Color of Change's Rashad Robinson terms it,[23] limited Occupy's ability to carry messages deeper than awareness and into a new common sense.

Narrative infrastructure refers to the spaces in which we find and create meaning—the channels where stories build on stories to create narrative over time. It is the structure that takes the raw material of stories, headlines, and focus-grouped messages and makes them real for people.

People are the most consistent and powerful form of infrastructure because we trust and make meaning with other people. As the Ad Council found in its most recent "Trusted Messenger" survey, the majority of Americans look to those much closer to them—their partners, family members, and friends, to better understand and make decisions on the issues that impact their lives.[24]

Strong and well-resourced narrative infrastructure exists as part of the wider culture. The film and movie industries produce and distribute enormous amounts of content that tend to support dominant narratives. Channels like TikTok are creating new, democratized forms of narrative infrastructure, though still plagued by the inadequacies of corporate profit-making algorithms.

Brands are a third form of narrative infrastructure. Companies, campaigns, and even people construct brand narratives to engage the world around them and build relationships that influence the way people think, feel, and act. A politician like Senator Bernie Sanders has a brand that captures both his issue agenda (uncompromising hero of the working class) and his personality (a curmudgeon with a heart of gold). These brand narratives make us feel like we know and relate to Bernie, and viral moments like the "mittens meme"[25] reinforce and strengthen those associations.

The Fight for $15's Movement Power Delivers Material Change

Just over a year after the first tents went up in Zuccotti Park, on November 29, 2012, 100 fast-food workers walked off their jobs in New York City and publicly launched the Fight for $15 and a Union.

The Fight for $15 built on Occupy Wall Street's narrative victory, and it backed up Occupy's demands with the power and infrastructure of movements. Although it may have seemed as spontaneous as Occupy Wall Street, the organizing of fast-food workers and their demand for a $15 minimum wage and a union began nearly two years earlier. Nine months *before* the first protestors set foot in Zuccotti Park, the executive board of the Service Employees International Union (SEIU) gathered in Puerto Rico to approve a new strategy: the Fight for a Fair Economy (FFE).[26] SEIU and its partners saw narrative and worker power as the key components to "changing the climate," as SEIU International president Mary Kay Henry described it, for the issue of income inequality.

Their new strategy began with two ambitious goals: change the public debate and rebuild the labor movement's power.[27] A campaign to organize fast-food workers served both these goals. It created the opening to build the power of millions of workers, and the industry offered an ideal case study to rebut neoliberal values and narratives.

Where Occupy Wall Street critiqued the neoliberal system and its harm to society, the Fight for a Fair Economy focused on wages and worker power. They rooted their campaign in the value of human dignity and in the idea that all people, regardless of the type of work they do, deserve a living wage. One job should provide enough to survive and thrive in the richest country in the world.

The dominant neoliberal narrative was a story about markets, and its façade of cold economic theory papered over the moral and political narrative of neoliberalism. In that story, wages are low because the people who prepare our food, for example, lack the education, skills, and work ethic to "command" a higher rate of pay. They are replaceable, interchangeable, and lucky to be employed.

This dominant narrative frames morality in a way that subordinates and denies the dignity of working people, while lifting up corporate wealth as the necessary reward for innovation and risk taking—a moral good for society. It erases the unique value of individuals while paradoxically casting them as solely responsible for their current conditions. It ignores the imbalance of power between worker and employer, and it masks the economy's brutal origins: slavery. As sociologist Matthew Desmond writes, American capitalism dehumanizes workers and casually accepts obscene disparities between those with wealth and those whose labor creates their wealth because "American capitalism was founded on the lowest road there is."

Against this backdrop, and as Occupy Wall Street protests grew in Manhattan, Oakland, and hundreds of cities in between, Fight for a Fair Economy organizers and union members were organizing behind the scenes. The organizers challenged neoliberalism's assumptions and built support for a different idea of how the economy should operate. They capitalized on the narrative power of Occupy Wall Street and told a story where workers are full people, work is dignified, and we have better alternatives to the low-road capitalism that has defined the United States thus far. They publicly launched the campaign in November 2012 with a clear, bold demand: $15 and a union.

Protest by the global movement to fight for a $15.00 minimum wage in Midtown West near Columbus Circle, New York, NY (2015). Photo by Cindy Trinh (@ActivistNYC)

Building the Strategy

As the Occupy Movement pushed open the Overton Window, the Fight for $15 organizers stepped into the public debate with a story where workers are the heroes who create the real economic value that powers every corporation, financial markets, and the country as a whole. They built on the narrative opening that Occupy created, and they added a clear and affirmative demand, which grounded their power analysis. A critical difference: The Fight for $15 centered on directly impacted people. Below we outline their strategy.

Power Analysis

The Fight for $15 organizers grounded their strategy in an analysis of their relative power. They recognized that:

- *People power was low.* The percentage of U.S. workers belonging to a union had steadily declined from its height in 1954, and private sector union membership had plummeted from 16.8 percent in 1983 to 6.7 percent in 2013.[28] State legislatures were also attacking public sector unions, with states like Wisconsin severely constraining unions' collective bargaining rights and limiting their power.[29]

- *Corporate power was high.* In the years following the Great Recession, financial institutions faced few consequences and corporate profits soared, reaching an annual rate of $1.659 *trillion* in the third quarter of 2010. This was the highest level in the sixty years of the U.S. Commerce Department's tracking.[30] With an unemployment rate hovering at 10 percent, the corporations had significant leverage.[31]

- *The federal judiciary threatened worker power.* With Justice Samuel Alito on the U.S. Supreme Court and a strong conservative bloc around him, labor leaders anticipated judicial threats to New Deal–era labor organizing protections that would further erode union density. These attacks culminated in the court's 2018 decision in *Janus v. AFSCME.*[32]

Based on their power analysis, organizers developed innovative strategies to change corporate behavior and enact policy change where they had power and leverage—at the local and state level. They also sought to change the power dynamic, framing their demands from the beginning as $15 *and a union.* They understood that low wages were not solely responsible for income inequality—weak labor market institutions and declining union density *allowed* corporations to keep wages low, and unequal political power further limited workers' ability to compel shifts that would keep policy at pace with changes in the economy.[33] In its early years, the campaign increasingly focused on $15 and de-emphasized building worker power in new sectors. It sought early wins and knew that organizing a new sector would be a decades-long project.

Clear Demand

Although support for a $15 wage was ubiquitous in 2023, economists perceived it as laughably high in 2012. In conversations within progressive think tanks and among those economists Dorian Warren could reach, the $15 minimum wage was a joke. It was well outside the Overton Window. Congress had increased the federal minimum wage from $6.55 to $7.25 in 2009, which was the kind of incremental growth that economists believed the market could bear. They viewed the market as *the* mechanism to set the price for labor (i.e., wages). Artificially inflating wages, they argued, would accelerate the forces holding wages down, which were primarily companies' access to a global labor supply and increased automation of "low skill" functions.[34] Even in hindsight, the real impact of wage increases on unemployment and inflation is difficult to parse.[35] The story in 2012, however, was unambiguous: $15 is impossible.

The role of organizers is to change what is possible. That work starts with listening, defining shared values, championing new ideas, and telling a different story that builds support for a clear demand.

Directly Impacted People

The campaign did not choose its $15 demand in a vacuum. Its organizers and advisors were steeped in the prevailing, dominant narrative, and they were cautious about how far they could push. What if the economists were right?

However, because the campaign centered on the leadership of directly impacted people—minimum wage workers—they adopted the $15 demand. They listened to workers rather than settling for what the political strategists said was winnable or what the economists said was optimal for the time being. As Derrell Odom, a cook at KFC, testified before the Atlanta wage board: "I can't even afford to put a roof over my child's head with the amount of money that I'm making. . . . We need 15. We deserve 15."[36]

In 2012, and continuing today, workers earning the minimum wage or lower were most likely to be employed in the food service industry and more likely to be Black, Latinx, and women.[37] Organizers focused on Black and Latinx fast-food workers, particularly women, to shape the demand and lead the fight. This is a core tenet of community organizing, as Amanda Devecka-Rinear, executive director of the New Jersey Organizing Project explains: "It's so critical to keep stories at the front and center because not only did they really humanize what we're going through but those stories tell us what our work needs to be."[38]

Taking Action

The Fight for $15 had two routes to achieve the goal of a wage increase: compelling corporate actors to establish a higher wage as part of their corporate practice, or enacting a minimum wage increase through local, state, or federal policies. The campaign pursued both strategies.

Corporate Behavior and Narrative Power

To change corporate behavior, the Fight for $15 targeted the narrative infrastructure. Organizers recognized that the traditional shop-by-shop, company-by-company, sector-by-sector drumbeat of union organizing would be a long, expensive, and difficult fight. Building the level of organization necessary to sustain a long-term, sector-wide strike capable of inflicting real financial pain would take decades.

The carefully crafted brand narratives of fast-food companies are more fragile. The McDonald's brand, for example, was valued at over $42 billion in 2014 and is consistently ranked among the top ten globally.[39] It seeks to convey values of family, community, and inclusion: "At our best, we don't just serve food, we serve moments of feel-good, all with the lighthearted, unpretentious, welcoming, dependable personality consumers know and love."[40]

Brands are strongest when their narratives are authentic. As the brand narrative moves further from reality, the more vulnerable to threats it becomes. A one-day walkout, one of the most common tactics of the Fight for $15, can generate enough media coverage to crack the expensively curated image of "Lovin' it." Associating McDonald's with starvation wages, for example, undercuts the "feel good moments" they aim to serve alongside a Big Mac.

The Fight for $15 leveraged the narrative infrastructure that these companies had created, brought to bear other forms of movement power, and compelled some actors, like the Target Corporation, to change their policies.[41]

Policy Change and Movement Power

To enact policy change, the Fight for $15 campaign took the approach of progressive federalism.[42] Progressive federalism is a strategy of enacting model policies in cities or states that can demonstrate the viability of an idea and create meaningful change without holding power at the federal level.[43] It reclaims the states as the laboratories of democracy, using a similar approach for progressive policy change as conservatives have adopted with their "states' rights" ideology. Lacking sufficient power to make federal changes, start local, legitimize the idea, and land early wins.

They started in Seattle. In less than a year, Seattle's Fight for $15 won tangible improvements in workers' lives and transformed what was considered politically possible. The campaign built on the narrative shift that began with fast-food worker organizing and walkouts in May 2013. Their organizing leveraged the people power and coalitional strength that groups had built in Seattle in the years leading up to the campaign, and they aligned their strategy with the electoral calendar. Political victories in November 2013 created the opportunity to pass the $15 minimum wage ordinance in June 2014.[44] The three dimensions of movement power—organizing, ideas, and politics—delivered the policy change that fueled the national movement:

Movement Power Is Three Dimensional

1. Organizing: the people power of individuals directly impacted by injustice recognizing their agency and finding common purpose and solidarity within organizations.
2. Ideas: the bridge between abstract values and concrete policies that ground narratives and create the architecture for the just world we aim to build.
3. Politics: the muscle to elect leaders and champions who advance and enact the people's agenda and vote out leaders who don't.

Organizing

Seattle's campaign drew on strong organizing infrastructure that built individual and collective power. Labor unions mobilized their members and moved early flexible funding. Crucially, because few fast-food workers were part of a union,[45] the campaign also relied on Seattle's community-based organizing infrastructure to draw on existing people power built by organizations like Main Street Alliance, ONE America, Washington CAN, and Working

Washington. The key organizations in this coalition had a history of collaboration, and alliances existed among labor unions and community organizations that expanded the capacity, reach, and influence of the policy campaign.

Ideas

In Seattle, the conversation on income inequality that started with the Occupy movement collided with local coverage of the fast-food workers' walkouts and worker organizing at Seattle-Tacoma International Airport (Sea-Tac). Highly visible actions, such as a fifteen-mile march from Sea-Tac to Seattle,[46] built power behind the idea that working people should make enough money to feed their families.

The campaign also used research produced by campaign partners Puget Sound Sage and the Washington State Budget and Policy Center, as well as credible outside researchers at the University of Washington and University of California, Berkeley. Sage calculated impacts of a $15 minimum wage on jobs, which helped to counter arguments from opponents, gain the support of potential partners, and make decisions about campaign strategy and actions.[47]

Politics

The campaign aligned with the electoral cycle, and organizers made the minimum wage fight the political issue for Seattle's 2013 mayoral race and for the one city council race that was truly contested. Kshama Sawant, a socialist who challenged the incumbent Democratic Party candidate for the city council seat, was a political outsider and academic who made $15 the centerpiece of her campaign and won. By demonstrating the political viability of a $15 minimum wage, the campaign was able to persuade the city council to enact every key demand of Seattle's Fight for $15.

Narrative and Movement Power Are the Keys to Transformational Change

The final aspect of narrative change is transformation—the ability to reset the perception of common sense in a permanent shift away from existing worldviews. Occupy Wall Street used its megaphone to build narrative power and call attention to the issue of income inequality. The Fight for $15 bolstered this narrative power and brought movement power to advance a bold demand rooted in an alternative set of values. Together, they created the conditions for a paradigmatic shift in our economic common sense.

This narrative power does not sit alone or outside of grassroots organizing of people. By winning a $15 minimum wage in cities and states across the country, the Fight for $15 changed the lives of 26 million workers and won $150 billion in wage increases.[48] It also shifted notions of expertise, deservedness, and human value. It demanded an economy that values workers as full, dignified human beings.

Politicians see which way the wind is blowing and test the conditions to see how much political capital a certain position will require. Organizing shifts the wind. Occupy Wall Street and the Fight for $15 permanently changed American perceptions of income inequality and the minimum wage. They were catalysts for an overdue public conversation about the neoliberal economic consensus. They critiqued more than starvation wages; they indicted the system and called for a different economic paradigm. Because the demand for a $15 minimum wage expanded the limits of what is perceived to be possible, movements could politically push further in their demands.

By 2020, with the $15 minimum wage accepted as a comfortably mainstream idea for the center left,[49] the layered crisis of COVID-19, economic catastrophe, racial reckoning, and ascendent authoritarianism broke open the deep cracks in our economic and political system. Felicia Wong of the Roosevelt Institute argued in May 2020 that the COVID-19 pandemic had disproved neoliberalism's tenets, particularly in underlining the critical role of government in structuring health markets, providing economic security, and leading societal transformation.[50] With direct cash payments to families and trillions of federal dollars flowing to communities, movements seized the opening to shift the political winds. Policies like the Child Tax Credit reduced Black, Latinx, and Native child poverty rates to the lowest levels on record in just six months. We have evidence that a new set of values can create an economy where everyone can thrive.

How we bring that opportunity to fruition remains to be seen. After every period of progressive gains in the United States, we have seen retrenchment and backlash from those in power. Today, "zombie neoliberalism"[51] continues to stumble alongside rising authoritarianism and white nationalism. We see differences exploited and scapegoats offered. Reflecting on the task of building multidimensional power, the poet Gwendolyn Brooks wrote that: "We are each other's harvest: / we are each other's business: / we are each other's magnitude and bond."[52] The future that we create together depends on what we make of each other.

Reframing the Retail Apocalypse: Narrative Strategies for the Future of Worker Organizing

By Aliya Sabharwal and Asha DuMonthier

When Toys 'R' Us shuttered its last stores in May 2018, leaving 33,000 workers unemployed, the leveling of the seventy-year-old toy retailer was attributed to the "retail apocalypse" claiming its next victim. *Retail apocalypse* is a term commonly used to describe the sharp increase in closures and bankruptcies of brick-and-mortar retail stores in the late 2000s that was accompanied by the growing popularity of online shopping. Retail experts and economists saw the rise of online shopping pioneered by companies like Amazon as a warning sign that the retail sector needed to adapt to consumers' changing preference for an online experience or face its demise.[1] This narrative was powerful but fundamentally inaccurate to explain the scale of retail bankruptcies at the time, as e-commerce accounted for about 10 percent of all retail sales in the United States in 2018.[2] The destruction of Toys 'R' Us was actually due to another formidable factor: Wall Street greed.

Wall Street firms have been responsible for a wave of bankruptcies in the retail sector, including Toys 'R' Us, yet they have been absent from the retail-apocalypse narrative. Wealthy investment firms known as private-equity firms buy companies like Toys 'R' Us in deals that saddle the acquired company with untenable debt. Private-equity firms profit from these highly leveraged buyouts, but the debt often leads acquired companies into bankruptcy. In the wake of these bankruptcies, laid-off workers and indebted creditors are left with limited options to hold private-equity firms responsible, despite the great financial gains these firms often walk away with.[3]

Wall Street private-equity firms and hedge funds can legally get away with behavior that most working people in the United States cannot—taking out debt under a different entity's name, reaping the benefit, then walking away without repaying what is owed. This contradiction is unsurprising, given that many well-known private-equity firms and hedge funds have direct financial and political ties to prominent politicians, shielding them from scrutiny or being held to stricter federal regulations.[4] As a result, Wall Street greed, which harms workers, communities, and the economy overall, has been growing unchecked. Private equity is now growing its influence over numerous key industries—buying out hospitals, apartment buildings, prisons, and more.[5]

This chapter tells the story of the Toys 'R' Us workers who pulled the curtain back on Wall Street greed and reframed the narrative of the retail apocalypse to hold some of the most powerful players in our financial system accountable. Workers connected their deep knowledge of the retail sector and the changes they tracked in their workplaces with their resonant personal stories to build a winning truth-telling campaign that revealed Wall Street's predatory patterns in the sector. Workers demonstrated that Wall Street's involvement in retail has led to a more precarious industry with worse conditions for hundreds of thousands of workers while they lined their pockets as the richest investment firms in the world. The campaign underscored that the rules of our economy are rigged against workers for the benefit of the most powerful and well-resourced. Workers' counternarrative led to transformational change at the individual and collective level of workers in the movement, which grew to be multigenerational, multilingual, and multiracial. Toys 'R' Us workers won a historic $20 million severance-pay fund from the Wall Street firms that had killed their jobs, and built the foundations for a movement of retail workers advocating for Wall Street accountability that continues to this day.

Dominant Narrative: Retail Apocalypse

Ann Marie had more than twenty years of experience in retail when she learned that Toys 'R' Us was going bankrupt. She had begun her career at her local Toys 'R' Us in Commack, New York, when she was a new mother. Ann Marie grew to be highly respected in her store and described herself as part of the retail family—a phrase many workers used to describe their relationship to co-workers. For Ann Marie, she meant it quite literally: Her son and former daughter-in-law met at their Toys 'R' Us jobs. After being laid off, Ann Marie and her family were left without enough money to pay for adequate health care, and she struggled to find a new job in Durham, North Carolina. "After being so loyal to the company, to be let go without our promised severance is disrespectful," Ann Marie said.[6] She expressed her frustrations online, was contacted by a United for Respect organizer to share her story with a reporter, and soon became one of the leaders in the fight for severance pay. Her passion and sense of justice was infectious, and she went on to be one of the most recognizable faces of the campaign.

When Toys 'R' Us filed for Chapter 11 bankruptcy in 2017, the company was described by major news outlets as the latest casualty in the retail apocalypse, a narrative that resonated with many who noticed the shift to online shopping. However, there were three major problems with this narrative.

It Marginalizes and Ignores Workers

The retail-apocalypse narrative abstracts and underestimates the harm experienced by workers by treating them as overhead costs, not as valuable stakeholders or experts of their industry. It fails to account for the impact of store closures on workers' livelihoods and the broader impact of job loss and displacement on the economy. This narrative assumes that all retail jobs and workers are interchangeable, which erases the skill building and hard work that many workers spend years developing to build long-term retail careers. This narrative perpetuates the misconception that retail jobs are low-skilled, homogeneous, and, ultimately, disposable types of work—which, in the context of the Toys 'R' Us bankruptcy, undermines the harm workers experienced by losing jobs they had built for decades. Numerous workers we spoke to, like Ann Marie, had to reenter the job market for the first time in decades, only to find worse-paying and more physically demanding jobs. These workers, many of whom were women, bore the brunt of the growing precarity of the industry, where stable, full-time careers are becoming increasingly rare.[7]

It Avoids Accountability

The retail-apocalypse narrative omits Wall Street firms' roles in destabilizing the retail sector and instead confers a high level of influence on consumers' taste and preference as the driving force behind retail bankruptcies. In reality, private-equity firms and hedge funds have made a play for the sector and have spent hundreds of billions of dollars to take over retailers since the early 2000s.[8] Private-equity firms buy out retail companies using a common playbook: They purchase companies with large quantities of leveraged debt they raise from their investors, putting in very little of their own money. As part of the buyout deal, they charge fees to the acquired company, and the funds used to buy out the firm are tacked on to the acquired company's existing debt. When the excessive debt becomes untenable, the company declares bankruptcy and the private-equity firm walks away unscathed because it is not legally liable for the debt because it is now associated with the acquired company. Companies like Toys 'R' Us enter into these buyouts because they are promised a leaner, streamlined company. Private-equity investors put up the money for these deals because they are promised high returns on their money. Everyone stands to lose, except the private-equity firms. Hedge funds can use a similar investment strategy to take control of companies and drain them of value, as occurred with Sears.[9]

Many Toys 'R' Us workers told us that their stores remained lucrative and successful leading up to bankruptcy, but it wasn't enough to dig the company out of the massive debt imposed by the private-equity owners of the company. This is because private-equity firms win, even when companies and workers lose. In the Toys 'R' Us case, owners Bain Capital and KKR had already collected more than $470 million in fees and interest from the company when it entered bankruptcy proceedings in 2018.[10] The ability of private-equity owners to legally dump debt on the company they simultaneously extract fees and profits from was the driving factor leading to the bankruptcy of Toys 'R' Us. Consumer behavior, the "Amazon effect," or any shortcoming of employees did not have the same outsized impact on the company's demise.

Toys 'R' Us workers would often ask us: "How can private equity get away with this sort of behavior?" While some workers were able to secure small portions of their severance pay through bankruptcy court, the vast majority of workers whose companies went bankrupt because of private-equity and hedge-fund buyouts found that the law did not protect their interests.[11] Weak federal regulations regarding private equity, as well as bankruptcy laws that are stacked against everyday people, create an accountability vacuum for the wealthiest firms.[12]

It Promotes the Inevitability of Inequality

A powerful underpinning of the dominant retail-apocalypse narrative is the belief that inequality is natural and no one is at fault. It collapses the imagination, making the idea of an equitable future an impossibility. A formidable challenge we faced as organizers was challenging members to imagine an alternative to a system, and world, that seemed too deeply unjust at times to overcome. The retail-apocalypse narrative understands the rise of online shopping, the emerging influence of Amazon, and the deterioration of the quality of retail jobs as rational outcomes of a modernizing and changing economy. In this rationale, everyone will ultimately benefit, even though workers are negatively impacted in the short term. Throughout the campaign, we had to constantly push back on the claims that Toys 'R' Us's demise was inevitable, and work even harder to imagine what a better future looked like and meant to United for Respect members and us.

Building a Counternarrative: Wall Street Greed

Adrianna worked at Sears for thirty years in El Centro, California, a small city close to the U.S.–Mexico border. Adrianna and most of her bilingual co-workers worked in the appliances section of her store and spent the majority of their adult lives at Sears. They celebrated their children's and grandchildren's births, supported each other through separations, and experienced all of life's in-betweens together. Working at Sears offered financial independence that changed their lives. Adrianna and her co-workers bought houses and put their kids through college on Sears salaries. They often worked long hours and missed time with their families, but they thought they had good jobs with decent benefits. Adrianna was looking forward to a pension and eventual retirement until hedge-fund manager and billionaire Eddie Lampert took over the company. Like Toys 'R' Us, Sears and Kmart were sold in the early 2000s to a hedge fund owned by CEO Eddie Lampert called ESL Investments. ESL took the company apart, sold off the valuable pieces, and left the remnants to flounder. When women like Adrianna were robbed of their jobs, severance pay, and pensions, they didn't just lose a job. They lost the family of co-workers they had come to rely on, the respect they commanded at work, and the sense of freedom that financial independence can offer. Some lost the possibility of retirement, and others struggled to support their families. The decision to get involved in the movement for Wall Street accountability was rooted in fighting for self-respect and dignity.

One year before Adrianna found out she would be losing her Sears family, Toys 'R' Us workers were hearing that they were going to be denied their promised severance pay. Outraged, they did what any group of wronged co-workers would do: They started talking to each other. In break rooms and online groups, they began sharing their stories, voicing different reactions to the bankruptcy news.

Workers' stories varied widely: Some shared how losing their job would affect their everyday lives, whether in falling behind on rent and mortgage payments or their anticipated trouble paying for their children's medical expenses. Workers who had been with the company for a longer time told newer co-workers how Toys 'R' Us had deteriorated as an employer over the years. For these workers, their job satisfaction had been on a steady decline since 2005, when a conglomerate of private-equity firms, including Bain Capital, KKR, and Vornado Realty Trust, purchased Toys 'R' Us for $6.6 billion.[13] They noticed raises and employee benefits diminishing, less investment in technology in stores, and a deprioritization of customer service and product

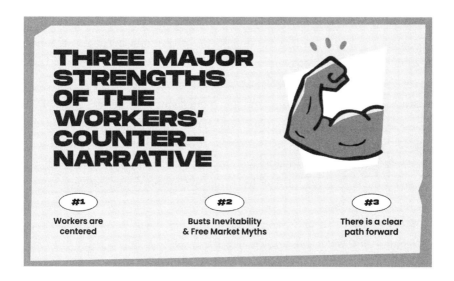

quality. Many were emotional about losing a job they loved and talked about their fond memories of Toys 'R' Us. These perspectives countered the common misconception that retail jobs are dead-end, meaningless jobs, which is used to justify the low pay and lack of dignity afforded to retail workers. In contrast, some expressed no sympathy for themselves or fellow Toys 'R' Us workers, and spoke instead on the practicalities of needing to get new jobs.

In 2019, a wave of retail-store closures followed the bankruptcy of Toys 'R' Us: Thirty-three retailers planned to close 6,683 stores, 70 percent of which were owned by private-equity firms.[14] Our team spoke with workers at newly bankrupt companies, including Sears, Kmart, Gymboree, Payless, Shopko, and Art Van, all of whom had been denied their severance pay. These workers quickly saw the similarities in what they had all been through. Workers' stories made two truths clear. First, Wall Street greed is responsible for millions of job losses; second, without workers' intervention, the Wall Street firms were going to get away with it, facing no accountability. These two truths became the backbone for the new narrative that workers put forward with organizers, media, politicians, and investors. Over time, it developed into a simple, united message: *Wall Street greed is destroying jobs, and we need to change the rules so that Wall Street can't do this anymore.*

The workers' counternarrative had three major strengths:

Workers Are Centered

The counternarrative centers working people on multiple levels. It is grounded in retail workers' lived experiences of witnessing and living through Wall Street takeovers and bankruptcies. It is based on countless conversations between co-workers and across multiple retail chains. As stories were shared across the country in break rooms and online, a collective consciousness shaped the narrative, inspiring workers to speak out. The counternarrative is also worker-centric in its method of delivery. Retail employees who had been impacted by Wall Street–driven bankruptcies spread the narrative by sharing their stories with reporters, elected officials, and pension-fund trustees. Workers with decades of experience talked about the families they supported, the homes they were able to buy with these jobs, and their paths to financial stability. Workers could speak to the concrete, often devastating, impacts of being laid off on their and their families' physical, mental, and financial well-being.

The counternarrative centers and places value on retail workers who are often undervalued and disrespected. Retail workers earn a median hourly wage of $13 and are increasingly forced to work part-time; in addition, many have limited or nonexistent benefits.[15] As a result, major retail companies can afford to treat them as disposable.[16] By placing working people, not corporations, at the center of our economic analysis, our counternarrative respects workers and casts them as the experts we need to trust. It empowers workers and allows for solidarity to build across the industry. For example, Toys 'R' Us workers who had been active in the fight for severance pay joined Sears workers as they called on Eddie Lampert for accountability.[17] Together, they joined Shopko workers demanding their severance from private-equity firm Sun Capital and Art Van workers confronting Thomas H. Lee Partners—thus growing the movement.[18]

Inevitability and Free-Market Myths Are Busted

The counternarrative also busts the myth that the destruction of retail jobs is inevitable, a reflection of societal and technological progress, or the result of individual consumer preferences. It clarifies that declining working conditions and job losses are attributable to two factors: Wall Street greed and the current laws and regulations that do not hold Wall Street firms accountable. This includes the lax regulation and oversight of the excessive amount of debt Wall Street firms dump into the companies they buy, and the lack of scrutiny of the overblown returns on investments private-equity firms claim to produce for their investors.[19]

By busting the myth that the injustices endured by retail workers are inevitable, the counternarrative also critiques the myth of the free market. The free-market myth proposes that market structures are organically formed based on preferences, and that workers and firms only agree to exchanges that benefit them. However, the Toys 'R' Us and other retail workers' counternarrative highlights that the structure of the current market is a result of policy decisions and features highly unequal power dynamics. Many of the workers involved in the campaign were forced to take precarious, lower-paid retail jobs after being laid off, and were denied their severance. To propose that working-class people and billionaire firms are entering into economic exchanges on an equal footing exposes the fallacies of the free market. Workers have seen how lax regulations, insubstantial oversight, and tax loopholes favoring private equity have directly benefited these firms and hedge funds at the expense of workers' jobs.[20] This is why, after winning the $20 million fund, workers from Toys 'R' Us, along with other retail workers, helped introduce landmark legislation, the Stop Wall Street Looting Act, to permanently close legal loopholes favoring private equity.[21]

There Is a Clear Path Forward

In the assertion that "we need to change the rules," the workers' counternarrative puts agency and power into everyday people's hands and asserts a collective responsibility to take action against a problem. *We* can change policy so that Wall Street companies are regulated and prevented from continuing their predatory practices destroying retail jobs and the economy overall. The counternarrative identifies organizing targets: Wall Street companies that can be held accountable through media exposure, their investors who can be called on to more closely scrutinize their support of the industry, and policy makers who can change the rules under which Wall Street corporations operate.

Workers took action on multiple fronts. Armed with a growing understanding of private equity, Toys 'R' Us workers visited pension funds that were investing in Bain Capital and KKR, two of the firms responsible for the company's bankruptcy. They educated investors on the personal impacts of the bankruptcy and called them to consider retail bankruptcy as a significant market risk, given its negative impacts on workers and the economy. Workers spoke with the media and shared their stories with elected officials. Their efforts paid off, culminating in the two private-equity firms creating a $20 million severance fund for laid-off workers. It wasn't the $75 million that workers were owed, but it was an unprecedented victory for working people speaking out against private equity. In the subsequent years, retail workers' efforts to advance the Stop Wall Street Looting Act was another vehicle for change.

The path forward illuminated by the counternarrative has created an important healing space for workers living through mass layoffs. After one former Sears employee met with a senator in Washington, DC, she cried while sharing her story. "This whole process of losing my job has made me feel so worthless," she said. "It's been so hard. But I'm glad some people are listening." In a culture that pushes a bootstrap mentality and blames the poor for their lot, losing a job—or more accurately, having one's job destroyed—ignites self-blame and shame. Becoming worker leaders in the campaign to hold Wall Street accountable for its predatory behavior became part of a healing process. It acknowledged that workers did not deserve to feel ashamed, that our value as people does not have to be determined by our work, and that immensely powerful institutions were responsible for choosing to disregard the jobs of thousands as they maneuvered to make a profit.

Conclusion

Ann Marie and Adrianna, the two worker leaders featured in this chapter, were fierce advocates in the campaign for Wall Street accountability. They brought many of their co-workers at Toys 'R' Us and Sears into the movement and advocated for creating more accountability for the predatory behavior of Wall Street. They were experts on the declining working conditions in the American retail industry and helped spread an inspiring, worker-centered narrative to bust the myths of the retail apocalypse. But for retail workers, even those involved in the movement for Wall Street accountability, it is nearly impossible to escape the reach of Wall Street hegemony. Both women eventually found new retail jobs at companies owned by private-equity firms; these companies have filed for bankruptcy within the last few years.

Ann Marie died in February 2021 of COVID-19. Her passing was a huge loss to the vast community of retail workers who respected her as a leader, and is still felt today by those of us who knew her. The COVID-19 pandemic accentuated the precarious working conditions that retail workers endure, and the massive imbalance of power they face. In the same year Ann Marie died, private equity had a record-breaking year, pocketing trillions of dollars and profiting off of the pandemic-related stimulus packages, receiving an estimated $5.3 billion of CARES Act money.[22] The industry has reached far across the economy, entangled in the health-care sector, news media, transportation, and more.[23]

Toys 'R' Us workers proved that it is possible, through a variety of strategies, including narrative change, to achieve a substantial win against corporate titans like private-equity firms. It also grew workers' political awareness and activism on connected issues, leading some to support environmental-justice and immigration-reform campaigns. Workers backed legislation in their home states and became civically and politically engaged. They also experienced a personal transformation as they were invited to sit at the table with policy makers, academics, and other technical experts to inform and educate these decision makers' thinking on financialization.

As of the writing of this chapter, retail workers have reintroduced the Stop Wall Street Looting Act to prevent Wall Street firms from continuing to play games with working people's livelihoods. They have won severance-pay funds from private-equity owners of other retailers, and introduced and won legislation at the state level to protect workers.[24] At the same time, the movement for Wall Street accountability faces formidable odds. Private-equity firms and hedge funds continue to operate with near impunity. These firms' vast financial resources and ties to numerous elected leaders accentuate the scale of the challenge that activists face. These structural factors make calls for accountability that much harder. The Stop Wall Street Looting Act has yet to pass, and although workers won organizing victories at Toys 'R' Us, Shopko, and Art Van, they were owed substantially more than private-equity firms paid out. In the case of Sears, Payless, and others, worker organizing did not result in a fund for workers, despite hundreds of workers lending their voices to the campaign.

Workers who participated in the movement maintain that they are glad they took the risk in sharing their stories, speaking out, and calling for change. Taking part in collective action was a healing and transformative process for hundreds of these workers who, together with us, the organizers, have glimpsed the possibilities for a better, more liberated world.

The Past, Present, and Future Narratives of Philanthropy

By Zaineb Mohammed and Mandy Van Deven

When we consider the narratives that govern our lives, pinpointing their origin or the ideological systems from which they spring is often hard. For example, the narrative of individualism—which governs everything from privatized health care and education to how we structure our families—is so widespread and ingrained that it seems like it's always been this way. Its origins in neoliberal capitalism and Christianity are invisible to most, and this is by design.

In fact, countless unseen forces are fighting to control the narratives that govern our lives, and philanthropy is among those affected. On the progressive side, funders have slowly begun to recognize the importance of pushing back on authoritarian frames and harmful narratives that have pushed an anti-Black, antitrans, antimigrant, misogynist agenda to undermine democracy and justice in our societies. With this realization comes a fundamental question: Who sets the narrative agenda? Is it philanthropic institutions with roots in racial capitalism and colonialism, or grassroots social movements that work in service to those most harmed by these injustices?

As philanthropy's interest in resourcing communications and narrative-change work has grown, so too have capitalist practices prioritizing expediency and reform over radical change. Funders have normalized outsourcing communications work to self-proclaimed experts at corporate communications firms while underinvesting in work done by grassroots communicators. Meanwhile, power brokers in foundations have made unilateral decisions about the direction of messaging and campaigns across areas as distinct as housing affordability, climate policy, and marriage equality.

This paternalistic and scarcity-driven approach has had harmful consequences for social movements, positioning charitable organizations as the best vehicles for solving social problems. Communicators must expend energy providing expertise to funders, while movement groups, often pitted against each other in a race to the bottom, struggle to obtain resources for narrative power building. Ultimately, this dynamic impedes movements from propagating truly liberatory and transformative narratives.

For example, when funders prioritize approaches that appear easy and expedient—such as hiring a corporate communications firm to design a campaign for marriage equality and funding organizations to adopt the firm's goals and messaging—it often comes at the expense of achieving larger, longer-term objectives, such as the recognition of the humanity of all queer and trans people. As more dollars flow into narrative and communications work, movements face the imminent risk of derailment and co-optation if we don't organize to redirect philanthropy's well-meaning yet detrimental behaviors.

Examining philanthropy's history will equip social-justice leaders to more strategically advocate for long-term, at-scale investment in narrative and communications work led by frontline leaders, grassroots organizers, and others whose voices are deliberately suppressed. By understanding the narratives that govern the analysis and actions of those working in philanthropy, we become better positioned to lead successful interventions in resource redistribution and, ultimately, build a world where institutional philanthropy is obsolete.

Roots of Philanthropy: Capitalism, Exploitation, and Reputation Laundering

When professionalized philanthropy began in the late nineteenth century, it was not simply a means for charity but a way for the nouveau riche to insulate themselves from growing unrest over a then-new phenomenon: wealth inequality. The combined forces of colonialism, white supremacy, laissez-faire capitalism, and the Industrial Revolution had starkly transformed the global economy, causing wealth (and the power it afforded) to become highly concentrated in the hands of industrialists such as John D. Rockefeller, Henry Ford, and Andrew Carnegie.

As the elite class reaped the benefits of the Gilded Age, everyone else's quality of life decreased dramatically due to harsh and dangerous labor conditions, low wages that kept people in abject poverty, and steep rises in social ills such as housing slums, malnutrition, disease, pollution, and child mortality. Systemic racism and the vestiges of slavery further entrenched inequality, pushing Black and Indigenous people, communities of color, and immigrants to the margins of society. As collective organizing built worker power and public opinion turned against the capitalist class, the elites manufactured a new tactic to hold on to their ill-gotten gains: institutional philanthropy.

Carnegie's and Rockefeller's foundations were among the first professional philanthropic institutions established in the United States. Both were launched with the stated aim of alleviating suffering by providing charitable contributions to organizations such as the New York Public Library and the American Red Cross, which sought to enable access to education and improve health. However, in their public statements, they strategically omitted how their own corporate practices caused the suffering that their philanthropic endeavors claimed to abate. Moreover, the new codification of charitable giving in the tax code allowed wealth holders to engage in tax-avoidance schemes and control public funds; they did this by taking the tax dollars they would have contributed to our democratically governed financial commons and rerouting that money to the private foundations they controlled.

According to a 2023 Institute for Policy Studies report, U.S. taxpayers lost 74 cents in revenue for every dollar a billionaire donated to charity. This cumulative loss amounted to more than $111 billion in 2022.[1] This means that taxpayers are literally paying for the expanding power of philanthropy and giving up power to make democratic decisions about their lives.

This trajectory, however, was already set in the nineteenth century. In his field-defining essay, "The Gospel of Wealth," published in 1889, Carnegie argued that it is the role and responsibility of the rich to provide for those who are deemed "deserving," thereby serving the public good:

> Individualism will continue, but the millionaire will be but a trustee for the poor; entrusted for a season with a great part of the increased wealth of the community, but administering it for the community far better than it could or would have done for itself. . . .[2]

Carnegie's influential opus originates the idea of philanthropy as a form of reputation laundering. He writes, "The man who dies thus rich dies disgraced,"[3] giving voice to the notion that by giving away their accumulated wealth, the rich are absolved of any sins that came from its extraction and instead leave a legacy of "doing good."

This mind-set remains ingrained in the ways that foundations approach communications work as public relations, a tool for crafting a compelling story about all the good the foundation is doing. Thus, it generates positive associations with institutional philanthropy and the benevolent generosity of the rich. When we consider philanthropy's role in narrative change, we must remember that its underlying goal is to justify its very existence.

Myths That Uphold the Power of Philanthropy

The sector's origin story remains embedded in the shared beliefs and practices that still govern philanthropy today. Deeply held narratives about resource scarcity, the primacy of particular kinds of expertise, and oligarchs as the best arbiters of societal change underpin and uphold these institutions. Their dominance drives funders to operate in ways that ultimately impede the transformative work of social-justice movements.

Scarcity

One of the most deeply entrenched narratives governing philanthropy is that resources are scarce and, therefore, must be protected. This belief is present in the design of foundations as financial holding vehicles that are allowed to exist in perpetuity, even at the expense of the mission, so long as they fulfill the legal mandate to redistribute 5 percent of their net assets annually.

At the end of 2023, FoundationMark estimated that private foundation assets totaled more than $1.5 trillion in the United States alone, and the National Philanthropic Trust put the combined assets of donor-advised funds at nearly $230 billion in 2022.[4,5,6] These figures unequivocally demonstrate the financial abundance that philanthropic institutions are choosing not to redistribute while simultaneously manufacturing the artifice of scarcity.

The practices that foundations employ when designing and carrying out funding strategies reflect this scarcity mind set. For example, many foundations set narrowly defined grant-making priorities that focus on one issue area or geographic region. These artificial boundaries exist partly because of a desire to preserve resources for future use. In addition, onerous grant proposals and reporting requirements that ask organizations to prove their efficacy, often within very short time spans, are practices born of the notion that foundations have limited resources and must be exceedingly judicious in their application.

The scarcity narrative has ripple effects on the entire social-movement ecosystem by setting up a dynamic whereby organizations must compete with each other for funds that are ostensibly few and far between. This competition for resources also creates "donor darlings"—or highly visible individuals and organizations that funders uphold as exemplars of their grant making acumen. Funders then shape their questions and expectations of other organizations within the same ecosystem based on the work of these donor darlings, forcing other groups to contort themselves to fit within an artificial framework.

As a result, communications workers *within* organizations are also caught in the crosshairs, pitted against other areas of critical work that their colleagues are doing. Rather than viewing social-justice work as consisting of diverse strategies (such as organizing, policy, communications, research), philanthropy falsely divides programmatic work and communications. As such, communications work is deprioritized within the organization and as an area for funding. The need to navigate these complexities is one reason communications roles within movement groups have an exceptionally high turnover rate and the communications field struggles with worker retention.

In creating these scarcity dynamics that groups must navigate, philanthropy slows progress and sets movements up to fail, hindering collaboration and cohesion both inside organizations and across movements.

Authority

At the heart of philanthropy is a narrative about whose expertise is legitimate and which data are deemed valid to guide decision making. Most often, funding strategies that seek to solve a social injustice are not designed by those with lived experience of systemic harm and who are intimately familiar with the most needed interventions. Instead, decisions are made by people whose access to and control of capital is the greatest. Through a framework of power and paternalism, foundation workers habitually dictate agendas, strategic priorities, and even the tactics of social-justice organizations and movements—wielding status to produce the illusion of expertise and to bestow undue authority.

An example of this can be seen in grant-making strategies seeking to end criminalization. Most foundations do not fund organizing that advocates for prison abolition or defunding the police because they believe these strategies are not politically savvy or realistic. Instead, most grant making uplifts organizations with more moderate and reformist stances, such as efforts to improve police training or adopt body cameras. In directing resources toward moderate groups, larger foundations legitimize these strategies and set a direction that is often mimicked by their philanthropic peers. This effect is called *movement capture*. It has been well documented in research by political scientist Megan Ming Francis[7] and other scholars, who show how philanthropy persistently derails liberation in favor of liberalism in feminist, queer, racial-justice, economic-justice, and decolonial movements alike.

Philanthropy's work on "capacity building" also reinforces an authority narrative. Grant makers without deep knowledge of communications will, at times, make negative judgments about organizations' communications without knowing the rationale for using specific tactics. After making these determinations about their grantees, funders tend to move in a few predictable directions:

1. They sideline movement groups by hiring corporate communications firms to carry out campaigns in ways that are more appealing to people in philanthropy.
2. They encourage grantees to adopt funder-approved communications methods through training and other capacity-building schemes.
3. They bring the work in-house, build their own capacities, and direct field-level campaigns and "narrative change" strategies.

For example, instead of investing in the expansion of existing infrastructure within social movements, some foundations have established in-house research teams to conduct polling and message testing to determine the most advantageous messages for influencing a given issue area. While some funders consult with grantees on these projects, the knowledge and skills are situated within and owned by the foundation rather than social movements.

They then set the agendas by controlling who has access to the research they produce and how the research is used.

These common inclinations in philanthropy weaken the infrastructure of social movements. They delegitimize decades of proven narrative organizing methods that lack visibility, such as facilitating dialogues among community members to identify shared struggles, cultivating a holistic analysis, building a common cause, and forging a collective strategy.

Throughout centuries of social-movement history, from the abolition of slavery to labor organizing through unions to the civil rights movement, we have seen how organizing makes radical social change possible. At its worst, philanthropy usurps this history, positioning nonprofit and foundation professionals as the core agents of change rather than "we the people."

Foundations often present themselves as serving the public good by moving money to charitable organizations. However, foundations are also run by trustees who have not been democratically elected, are not accountable to the public, and often lack proximity to the communities they claim to serve. Philanthropy is designed to allow the world's wealthiest to determine which injustices are worth solving and which individuals and organizations deserve to have resources to lead us into the future.

Redistributing wealth, not simply moving cash, is what shifts power. When unaccountable institutions that hoard trillions of dollars are setting agendas for how social change happens—or is not allowed to happen—the ability of those most harmed by injustice to determine solutions is threatened.

Prefiguring the Future of Philanthropy

As we have seen, philanthropy is not immune to the narratives that govern the wider world. Yet critiques of the sector have become sharper and louder as the rich are getting exponentially richer. This echoes the Industrial Era, when stark inequality became driven by such factors as the rapid growth of new technologies that revolutionized work; greater economic precarity due to low wages and poor labor conditions; rising fascism and the destabilization of democracy; forced migration as a result of war, genocide, and climate crises; and increased interpersonal and state violence against those who endure the greatest marginalization, including Black and Indigenous people, migrants and refugees, trans and gender-nonconforming people, and religious minorities. Social movements that work toward liberation understand the ways progress is being stifled by funding practices. They have responded by imagining a world where philanthropy is obsolete and by redesigning methods for resourcing genuine transformation, using the following approaches.

Embrace Abundance

Having continuous access to financial resources is a critical part of building and sustaining narrative infrastructure, and, like it or not, our social movements have become dependent on money received from individual wealth holders and institutional philanthropy. As part of the work to move away from scarcity narratives, initiatives such as Solidaire Network, Good Ancestor Movement, Resource Generation, and Ten Years' Time engage wealth holders in a layered process of self-interrogation. This serves to identify and reconstruct the harmful beliefs they've embodied; to provide political education that supports the adoption of solidarity principles and practices; and to facilitate individual and collective redistribution of assets they control in just, accountable, and reparative ways. "We exist to disrupt mainstream practices in the private wealth industry by challenging dominant narratives about the economy, excessive wealth accumulation, tax minimization, and the redistribution of resources and power in society," says Stephanie Brobbey, chief executive of Good Ancestor Movement. "In the next ten years, I would like to see a thriving movement of values-driven wealth holders committed to setting limits on their personal wealth and reducing their wealth over time by redistributing capital back into communities that have been historically harmed by and excluded from benefiting from the economy."

Value Many Forms of Expertise

Funder education and organizing spaces are also growing, with groups such as Justice Funders, Shake the Table, Resource Mobilizers Collaborative, Thousand Currents Academy, and Elemental cultivating the conditions for deep relationship building, politicization, peer learning, and co-investment and participatory grant making experiments that shift ways of being within the philanthropic sector. All of this is to ensure greater alignment with narratives of abundance, reciprocity, cooperation, and power sharing.

"'Moving the money' may be our primary objective, but it's not in and of itself an act of organizing," says Farhad Ebrahimi, founder and president of Chorus Foundation. "If 'organizing' is the process of building collective power and developing leadership to effect structural change, then 'funder organizing' must focus on building power, developing leadership, and effecting structural change within the philanthropic sector."

To advance epistemic justice and norms of shared governance, funder education must occur in close collaboration with narrative practitioners and movement leaders to foreground their expertise and agendas. In ReFrame's Narrative Nexus learning series, grant makers from thirty foundations learned about misunderstood concepts like *narrative infrastructure* and *narrative power* directly from movement strategists hermelinda cortés, Jung Hee Choi, and Joseph Phelan. In addition to learning from case studies at the sessions, funders gain a space to map out current narrative funding commitments, identify sources of expertise grounded in social movements, and find opportunities for collaboration and knowledge sharing.

Contribute to Movement Infrastructure

In 2007, INCITE! Women of Color Against Violence published *The Revolution Will Not Be Funded: Beyond the Nonprofit Industrial Complex,*[8] a collection of criticism penned primarily by Black and Indigenous women whose groundbreaking analysis has since been picked up and popularized by more recognizable philanthropy pundits, such as Edgar Villanueva, Anand Giridharadas, and Robert Reich. In it, prison abolitionist and scholar Ruth Wilson Gilmore writes:

> If people living under the most severe constraints, such as prisoners, can form study groups to learn about the world, then free-world activists have no excuse for ignorance, nor should they rely on funder-designed workshops and training sessions to do what revolutionaries in all times have done on their own.[9]

Part of the work to reclaim power is creating alternatives to systems that don't serve us. This enables movements to take a proactive stance of building durable power through mutual aid, gift economies, and shared infrastructure, among other approaches. We see this in groups that reduce the operational burdens of running an institution through shared subscriptions and hiring workers who contribute their skills and knowledge across multiple organizations.

At the start of the COVID-19 pandemic, groups with greater tech savvy, such as Whose Knowledge? and Numun Fund, lent their specialized expertise to support others in working remotely or engaging in digital organizing. By showing up for each other in a time of need, movements demonstrated what is possible when grassroots communities have their own infrastructure and act in solidarity instead of waiting for a foundation to fund their capacity.

Embracing into Shared Prosperity

For more than a century, the story of philanthropy has served the interests of those who benefit most from white supremacy, patriarchy, racial capitalism, and colonialism. By diverting public money to private financial vehicles that monitor and control dissent through manufactured scarcity and bureaucratic redirection, philanthropy saps the intellectual and energetic resources from activists and movements that seek to transform society.

The ubiquitous permacrisis framework makes transforming philanthropy challenging because many foundation workers operate as saviors who are compelled to prioritize finding and funding solutions to these catastrophes. What they miss is that their actions allow the cycle of wealth holders setting agendas and deciding what's best for our societies to continue.

Social-movement workers know that moments of uncertainty allow us to intervene in radical ways. The interventions identified in this chapter offer a window into what is possible when we organize inside and outside existing systems to shake off the constraints of philanthropy. Some focus on harm reduction, while others lay the groundwork for new structures.

Looking ahead to the decades to come, it is eminently possible for us to rewrite the story about philanthropy and embrace the narratives of our own making.

DEMOCRACY FOR ALL

Refusing the Status Quo: How Narrative Power Can Shape Policy Change

By Eesha Pandit and Verónica Bayetti Flores

In the mid-2000s, we worked at reproductive-health organizations just as the debate around health care reform was beginning. In 2007, before the passage of the Affordable Care Act (ACA), the number of uninsured Americans reached 45.6 million.[1] The country's uninsured could have filled the University of Michigan football stadium, the largest in the United States, about 420 times. Most of those millions were Black, Brown, poor, immigrant, disabled, and transgender people—communities that were often chronically underinsured or uninsured. We noticed quickly that these communities and, most important, the interventions that would most meaningfully address their health care needs were being excluded from health care reform demands in favor of a lowest-common-denominator political assessment—one that favored the art of the politically possible instead of fighting for what communities actually need.

Rather than demand the expansion of a popular, already-existing public health care program for all people (Medicare),[2] a broad sector of progressive organizations rallied around a reform that would allow a public option to compete in the private health insurance market. On the one hand, the demand for a public option seemed to accept that the public sector is uniquely equipped to provide quality, low-cost care; the public option, some argued, could be expanded once it proved itself as a program. On the other hand, the demand immediately accepted private insurers' terms by ceding ground to a sector that profits from people's illnesses and deaths.

Indeed, plenty of liberal organizations' values allowed for the existence of private health insurance, a system that is both profoundly unjust and abysmally ineffective. Yet more progressive organizations—ones that should have challenged the underlying assumptions of this neoliberal capitalist system and sought a single-payer universal health care approach—made a basic mistake: starting negotiations from a place of compromise. Calculating that universal Medicare expansion was not politically feasible in 2008, they traded their true beliefs for a chance to sit at the big kids' political table.

The endeavor was not entirely fruitless. Today, 15 million people have insurance through the ACA's marketplace.[3] And, as of 2023, more than 24 million people received coverage through Medicaid expansion.[4] But we are not meaningfully closer to a health care system that values people's lives beyond what they can pay; in fact, we find ourselves much further from it. The uninsured are still those most vulnerable in our society, and the compromises made were at their expense. Although there have been significant gains in health coverage in "minority communities,"[5] the vast majority of the 25.6 million uninsured nonelderly adults are working low-income families and people of color.[6]

As these compromises were made, we were young green policy newcomers, and it seemed to us that this was just how it was done. "Someday, we will find a way to do policy work differently," we told ourselves. A decade later, we founded the Center for Advancing Innovative Policy (CAIP). In this grassroots, people-focused project, we create innovative policy advocacy strategies that foster progressive policy change and build vital connections across movements.

With the benefit of all this experience, we know how policy making in the health sector leads to only minor adjustments being made within the constraints set by existing power dynamics, thereby perpetuating the status quo rather than challenging it to effect more substantial change. Early in our careers, we knew what we were seeing was wrong, and we knew even then where it went wrong: Demands should be determined in communities based on the needs they identify. The starting point was never in Washington, DC.

We have learned that no policy, communications, or organizing work can be effective unless we pay attention to all of them together. This chapter explores some of our hard-won lessons, best practices, and examples of how to make our work effective and integrative.

Why Policy Making Is a Critical Tool for Power Building

Some people's careers entail communicating policy proposals and wins for ever-campaigning candidates. As it stands in the United States, however, many of these candidates do not stray far from the status quo. As communicators who work in service of radical demands and are interested in left-flank policy, we face a distinct task. It can be summed up in the question: How do we tell stories to craft narratives that are born from and are compelling to the people who are demanding a systemic overhaul toward justice while at the same time convincing those who have the power to make change in our favor?

Many on the social-movement left are understandably disillusioned with their ability to make meaningful change in the halls of Congress or in their city or state houses. As money-backed interests' stranglehold on power achieves an even stronger grip, highly paid lobbyists are tasked with maximizing the profits of their benefactors by any means necessary. Contributions to our elected officials' electoral campaigns serve as roundabout purchases of political favors, so it is not unreasonable to feel disillusioned with American "democracy." Why, then, do we refuse to relent in this arena of activism? And how do we respond to those who say that policy change is where radical ideas go to die?

Practically, we know that decision making regarding the distribution of public resources happens through policy at the federal, state, and local levels. If we are serious about demanding a shift in resources toward our communities, we must engage at each level. While policy is often decided in highly exclusionary spaces with only the perspectives of the powerful, policy that is in service to work on the ground and to the culture shift we demand is possible and up to all of us to push for.

Legislation can sharpen organizing by defining terms and goals rather than diminishing them. What seems impossible today may be doable tomorrow, and our movements must be prepared for these moments. Having grassroots-anchored policy demands is not only just but also strategic.

A policy agenda is simply a list of things a group of people needs; on a basic level, everyone knows what they need. Whether it be safety, financial security, or access to clean water, the communities we work with are clear on what they require to live dignified lives. Policy agendas must be created in tandem with communities because the people closest to a problem are the people closest to the solutions.

So, how does one communicate policy demands for a new world?

Policy Agendas as Narrative Tools

A policy agenda is a powerful narrative tool that shapes public discourse, frames societal issues, and influences public perception and priorities. It functions in this role by defining the problems and proposed solutions. This articulation shapes how issues are perceived and discussed in the public sphere, influencing what people believe to be true and viable. For people who do not spend their time thinking about how to solve pernicious social problems, a policy agenda can also expand our ideas of the kind of world that's possible. This is a crucial aspect of narrative power, guiding public opinion and setting the stage for potential solutions.

Establishing a policy agenda can effectively frame public discourse around specific themes or priorities. This framing can elevate specific issues to the national agenda while sidelining others, directing public attention and resources toward specific goals. Policy agendas often reflect and reinforce certain values and norms, which can shape societal expectations and behaviors. For example, prioritizing health care reform may reinforce the value of health care as a human right, influencing public opinion and potentially leading to broader shifts in how health care is viewed.

A clearly articulated policy agenda can mobilize supporters by providing a clear set of goals and actions. This mobilization builds support for specific policies and galvanizes communities through a narrative that resonates with their experiences and aspirations, transforming passive observers into active participants in the political process. Policy agendas also help legitimize specific issues by bringing them into formal channels of power. These agendas gain legitimacy as serious concerns worthy of public and governmental attention, and attract media coverage, funding, and institutional support.

Over time, the cumulative effect of consistent and strategic policy agendas can shift the overall direction of national policies and priorities. By consistently advocating for specific themes or issues, social-movement organi-zations can gradually shape the policy landscape, aligning it more closely with their visions. A comprehensive policy agenda can also be a focal point for building coalitions between various groups and stakeholders, which can enhance the narrative power of the agenda by combining strengths, resources, and voices.

Methodology

Policy is a precise and potent tool that is most effective when combined with other strategies. We employ a three-pronged approach, synchronizing our policy efforts with narrative and movement power strategies. Achieving policy change that doesn't merely reinforce the status quo is challenging, as our system isn't designed for social transformation. Thus, we must strategi-cally marshal all available resources, strengthening our policy initiatives with movement and narrative power–building efforts. This integrated approach aims for long-term structural change that tangibly improves people's lives. Given the difficulty of achieving meaningful policy change, many activists view policy work as too incremental to effect real change. Still, by aligning these efforts, we increase our potential.

This community-led—or stakeholder-led—process allows for more inter-sectional demands to emerge. However, policy agendas must also be legible to the political class, who have the power to impact demands. So, the role of the policy advocate is to engage an organization's stakeholders, clarify their needs, and translate them into clearly articulated agendas for policy makers who have the power to shift material conditions on the ground.

Critically, having emerged from the reproductive-justice movement—a movement informed by intersectional values and Black feminist abolitionism—we dutifully apply an intersectional framework to the organizing and analysis we were taught. To us, this means that centering on the perspectives of the people who are at the crossroads of the multiple interlocking systems—white supremacy, capitalism, colonialism, ableism, patriarchy, etc.—that shape the ways we can exist in the world will always provide a more elegant, effective, and widespread solution. It also means that we have seen what policing as a system of order has done for people living at these crossroads and that we must abolish this system as we know it, creating new ones for keeping each other safe.

In the end, this means that we arrive at a document that reflects people's needs, contains a set of solutions aligned with a left-flank political analysis of their impact, and details specific mechanisms through which policy makers can seek to meet the needs articulated within it.

When communicating about policy, our goals must be threefold.

1. We illuminate the systems by which daily decisions about our lives and livelihoods are made.
2. We elucidate the mechanisms through which decisions are made within those systems to home in on the places where we can demand changes and improvements.
3. We create the opportunity for people to see that the systems that rule our lives have been built by people, so they can be torn down and re-built for the better.

As is the case for all radical communicators, part of the job is to address a crisis of imagination by painting a clear, concise vision of what a new world could be. And, for policy communicators, this means identifying which political levers get us closer to it.

Communicating Policy Change in Practice

There are many intersections between policy change and building narrative power. If we aim to build strong movements with strong messages, we must find these nodes and attend to them intentionally. Below, we share two examples from our recent work that clarify the intersection between policy and communications.

Abortion and Black Women

In September 2021, as the policy-communications consultant team for the Movement for Black Lives (M4BL), we began to make a plan for the *Dobbs v. Jackson* decision in 2022. We knew that the Supreme Court had agreed to hear the Dobbs case, and we knew one possible outcome was the fall of *Roe v.*

Wade, the landmark 1973 case that legalized abortion care across the United States. We understood the crucial importance of an organization like M4BL, grounded in abolitionist Black power, having a robust and unified response. This response was rooted in a distinctly Black feminist politic: engaging M4BL's ecosystem of Black liberation organizations whose focus wasn't primarily on reproductive-health issues and building alliances with Black-led reproductive-justice organizations within and beyond the M4BL network. In short, we knew that those whose perspectives are centered in communications shape the depth of analysis.

With a solid communications team—and an ecosystem eager to communicate the impact of a potentially massive shift in the legal landscape around pregnancy and bodily autonomy—we had the opportunity to craft resonant abolitionist messages centered around Black people. In the context of the ever-increasing presence of the criminal-legal system in the abortion discussion, being prepared with a strong message against the targeted criminalization of Black people and abolitionist responses to the fall of *Roe* created a powerful opportunity: We had a chance to center Black women during a pivotal moment in the political history of the United States and its legal treatment of women and pregnancy-capable people. This accomplished two goals: (1) It shed light on how the ever-growing police state had already been harming pregnant people, particularly pregnant Black people; and (2) it firmly positioned Black liberation movements as preeminent leaders and thinkers around issues of reproductive rights and bodily autonomy.

Trans Kids

In 2019, we worked with Unite for Reproductive and Gender Equity (URGE), a reproductive-justice organization whose base of young people includes many trans and nonbinary students explicitly concerned with reproductive and gender justice. To build a list of their policy demands, we asked a group of these young organizers what they most needed. We kept hearing one need articulated over and over: Young trans people need safety. And yet, safety is not a singular policy demand.

As in all of our agenda processes, our work is to interpret the needs identified by stakeholders and identify policy demands that address the root of these. We were left with the questions: What would make trans youth safe?

And what is currently making trans youth unsafe? Their answers illuminated the ways trans youth are vulnerable to violence and harassment because of homelessness and housing instability, leaving them without safe havens; how they're targets of police harassment and violence, including sexual violence; and that gender-affirming care is out of reach for many trans young people—and had been even before the rise in antitrans state legislation began limiting access. Together, we determined the conditions that could provide the safety they were seeking.

With their agenda, URGE advocated for access to gender-affirming care for all trans and gender-nonconforming young people; they also advocated for policies that increase economic justice, such as housing access, eradicating student debt, and raising the federal minimum wage. While these economic-justice issues aren't LGBTQIA+-specific, we learned that economic security is a key factor in the safety and stability of young people.

In this way, determining their policy goals revealed a powerful narrative: Safety is central to many of our most radical movements' demands. The process for arriving at this narrative was uniquely rooted in policy and communications: Start with an expansive question about needs, engage the communities most impacted, connect their needs to policy demands, and tell the story of how we got from needs to policy goals.

Challenges

Communicating about radical possibilities in policy work comes with its challenges. Developing a political agenda involves creating lists of demands that closely align with the needs of a specific community. A significant challenge we face is transforming these demands into political realities. This involves employing narratives, stories, and other communication tools to make our radical policy solutions salient and popular.

While policy makers are a primary audience for any policy agenda, it is crucial not to limit our demands to what is currently deemed politically feasible. Instead, we must aim to create the conditions allowing transformative policies to emerge—policies that genuinely shift the status quo. Our audiences extend beyond policy makers; they include our base, which relies on us to advocate for imaginative demands that envision a more just world. They also encompass our movements and organizations that are deeply committed to policy work, even if they sometimes get bogged down in tactical complexities.

We must also persuade our communities—those often systematically excluded from the policy process—that engaging in policy is worthwhile and not merely a graveyard for radical ideas. We need to guide our people through the deliberately complex and winding paths of the policy world, helping them to identify and leverage their points of influence within it. As communicators, we face the challenge of addressing multiple distinct audiences simultaneously. While we may target a specific group, the public nature of policy discourse requires us to recognize and cater to the nuances relevant to all observers.

Consider, for instance, communicating about a particular labor policy to a group of workers who are pivotal in advocating for labor rights. Our primary objective is to explain to these workers how the policy might alter their working conditions. However, it's crucial to acknowledge that other onlookers' perceptions of these communications might influence subsequent actions and shape the environment in which these actions unfold. In this way, while there is a target audience for these messages—a specific group of workers—the messages we use can create alliances or rifts with other communities, such as allied movements, local leaders, and legislators.

Finally, understanding the dominant narratives within our communities often requires us to become students of history. So many harmful narratives have been used in media and movements for decades, and thus have a grip on our audiences and even on us. Some of these insidious tropes include the myth of American meritocracy or the idea that "entitlement programs" in this country exclusively benefit poor people of color. These are false narratives that many years of Reaganomics have normalized.

On a project focused on messaging research in states that had not expanded Medicaid access, we conducted focus groups with low-income communities of color to gauge their perceptions of Medicaid expansion and their general attitudes toward "entitlement programs." The feedback was complex. Many participants who had previously used Medicaid or food stamps insisted they were not the "type of people" who needed government assistance. Some even opposed these programs, fearing they would foster dependency on "handouts" within their communities. Yet they distinguished themselves from others by emphasizing their desire to work.

This reveals a critical insight for radical communicators: Our communities are not immune to internalizing damaging narratives about their identity and essential government support and services. Being students of history, however, can help us understand why these beliefs persist. A common reaction might be to dismiss these views, noting that even beneficiaries do not support expanding these services. However, we must look more deeply and recognize the underlying shame and fear of being seen as undeserving, as these emotions have been instilled by decades of stigmatizing narratives. Thus, advocating for policy change is just a fraction of our task. We must also work to counteract the long-standing, harmful messaging that defines who the poor are and why they are in poverty.

Clear Vision Ahead

To remain grounded in political analysis and values, policy work must be anchored in deliberate accountability to movements. To us, this is about where we ground our demands. A policy agenda is only as powerful as the movement backing it, and our movements require deliberate narrative strategy aligned with our short-, medium-, and long-term goals. We have more narrative work to do, as we are not merely interested in what some believe is politically possible but, instead, in what our people genuinely need.

Policy makers are public servants whose job is to represent us; our job is to make our demands impossible to ignore. We have to make the case that our goals should not be limited to the art of the possible. Instead, we have to tell the stories of what is necessary. If we cannot articulate a clearly defined vision of what we need, our political position will weaken, and we risk spending promising political moments fighting about details. When our vision is clear, we can strategize ways to engage policy makers in service of our demands.

Understanding and Combating Online Racialized Disinformation in the 21st Century

By Jaime Longoria and Jacquelyn Mason

In today's digital landscape, misinformation (referring to false or inaccurate information) and disinformation (referring to intentionally misleading information) threaten social cohesion and democracy. They undermine trust, deepen polarization, and fuel conflict by spreading false and divisive narratives.

Racialized disinformation is particularly pernicious among the many forms of these deceptive tactics. This form of disinformation specifically targets racial groups, with the intent to deceive or manipulate the public—exploiting social-justice issues to further entrench racial divisions. Strategically crafted and disseminated through online platforms, racialized disinformation is used to achieve political gain, financial profit, and the perpetuation of white supremacy.

Despite its profound impact, the study of racialized disinformation is still in its early stages, requiring further research to fully grasp its mechanisms and consequences. This emerging field is at the heart of a political power struggle in which various actors use disinformation to push their agendas. The Disinfo Defense League[1] aims to democratize the study of racialized disinformation, making mitigation strategies accessible to progressive organizers and advocates. We can collaboratively and effectively counteract disinformation by empowering those within our social-movement ecosystems and communities with a deeper understanding of how truth is constructed and manipulated, particularly within communities of color.

In this essay, we delve into the dynamics of racialized disinformation in the twenty-first century, examining how it spreads online, its profound effects on communities of color in the United States, and the strategies used to combat it. By exploring the role of social-media algorithms that amplify sensational content, orchestrate coordinated disinformation campaigns, and manipulate emotional triggers, we aim to illuminate this pressing issue that undermines our democracy. Additionally, we offer practical insights for those committed to promoting truth and equity in the digital age.

How Does Racialized Disinformation Manifest Itself Online?

1. **Inciting hate and promoting "othering"**: This involves using stereotypes and wedge issues to divide groups, fostering hatred and alienation among different communities.
2. **Harassment and slander**: Individuals, groups, or movements are targeted with harassment, defamation, or criminalization, aiming to discredit or undermine their credibility and efforts.
3. **Impersonation and infiltration**: Disinformation agents may impersonate or infiltrate online groups to disrupt solidarity and sow discord from within.

Racialized disinformation perpetuates and amplifies existing inequalities and consolidates power among politicians, wealthy individuals, and media or technology companies. This form of disinformation has tangible, real-world consequences, influencing how communities of color interact, trust one another, and engage with social issues. At its core, racialized disinformation is rooted in power and oppression, strategically targeting racial dynamics to uphold and reinforce systemic inequalities. By understanding its emotional and psychological underpinnings, we can more effectively combat its spread and mitigate its harmful impact on society.

Black People as "Canaries in the Coal Mine"

Racialized disinformation is not a new phenomenon; its roots can be traced back to the history of propaganda and systemic racism. Propaganda has long been wielded to manipulate public perception and sustain power structures, often by exploiting racial and ethnic divisions. During the colonial era, propaganda was used to justify the transatlantic slave trade and the subjugation of African peoples. In the United States, the Jim Crow era saw the use of films, newspapers, and other media to perpetuate harmful stereotypes about Black people, reinforcing segregation and discrimination. The civil rights movement faced disinformation campaigns aimed at discrediting activists and organizations fighting for racial equality.

In the digital age, these tactics have evolved. Social-media platforms have become battlegrounds where false information can be disseminated rapidly and broadly. As highlighted in the *Report of the Select Committee on Intelligence, United States Senate, on Russian Active Measures Campaigns and Interference in the 2016 U.S. Election*,[2] Black Americans were the primary target of the Internet Research Agency (IRA), a Russian troll farm, during the U.S. presidential election. Between 2015 and 2017, the IRA reached more than 120 million people on Facebook and 20 million on Instagram; produced 1.4 million tweets; and uploaded more than a thousand videos to YouTube, all aimed at influencing the election through the spread of harmful disinformation. The Senate Select Committee on Intelligence confirmed that race and related issues were central to the IRA's disinformation campaign, specifically designed to deepen divisions in the country.

Black internet researchers and activists sounded the alarm about such tactics long before the election interference became widely known.[3] They observed that social platforms were being used to undermine the Black vote through disinformation. Despite their warnings, their insights were largely dismissed by researchers and social-media companies. This lack of action allowed disinformation to proliferate, affecting movements like Black Lives Matter (BLM). Notably, platforms like Facebook were criticized for permitting fake pages and events run by trolls to exploit and mislead Black communities. This ongoing issue underscores the need for more research and proactive measures to protect communities of color from targeted disinformation campaigns.

Real-World Harm: Who Are the Most Impacted?

Understanding the real-world impact of mis- and disinformation remains one of the field's central research questions. In the U.S. context, racialized communities' histories of marginalization and violence at the hands of dominant cultures and systems of governance often find themselves at the center of assertions[4] that communities of color are particularly susceptible[5] to mis- and disinformation and conspiracy theories. While these may have a role in communities' truth-making processes, more recent studies[6] have shown that Black and Latino populations, for example, are unsure or skeptical[7] when it comes to information that may be false—as opposed to naive. What has been observed, however, is that ecosystems[8] of racialized disinformation exist specifically to influence or impact people of color. Additionally, these communities' disproportionate reliance[9] on online news and a general lack of opportunities for correction due to a media ecosystem that does not cater to their information needs positions them at a significantly higher risk of mis- and disinformation exposure. This phenomenon ultimately perpetuates the consolidation of power among ruling classes and allows those who uphold oppressive governance structures to skirt accountability.

Here are six ways we can combat racialized disinformation:

Combat Systemic Racism and Invest in Ethnic and Community-Specific Media

One way to combat racialized disinformation is by investing in ethnic and community-specific media. Ethnic media, including Black-owned newspapers and radio stations, historically played a crucial role in providing tailored content that addressed diverse communities' specific needs and interests. These outlets offered a platform for underrepresented voices, promoted cultural heritage, and facilitated informed civic participation. However, financial challenges, consolidation in the media industry, and the shift to digital platforms have led to the closure of many ethnic media outlets.

The rise of news deserts and the decline of Black media have had significant repercussions for information access and community engagement. "News deserts" refers to areas with limited or no access to local news outlets, resulting in a lack of reliable information about local events, policies, and issues. This problem is particularly acute in communities of color, where ethnic media often serve as vital sources of culturally relevant news and perspectives.

The absence of ethnic media and the prevalence of news deserts contribute to data voids—gaps in available information that can be exploited by disinformation campaigns. Without trusted sources of local and culturally relevant news, communities are more vulnerable to misinformation and less equipped to engage in the democratic process. This lack of reliable information can lead to voter suppression and voter depression, where individuals are either misinformed or dissuaded from participating in elections. It is vital to ensure that communities of color have access to resources and support to create and sustain their own media outlets. This includes funding, training, and infrastructure enabling these communities to produce and disseminate accurate information.

Contending with systemic racism in the media industry is another way to combat mis- and disinformation. The Free Press essay called Media 2070[10] is an excellent example of an initiative to address and dismantle systemic racism within the media industry. It seeks to reimagine a future where media systems are equitable, inclusive, and just, particularly for Black communities. By advocating for reparations, investment in Black media, and a transformation of media policies and practices, Media 2070 highlights the importance of equitable media representation and access to accurate information.

Implement Regulatory Reforms for Social-Media Platforms

Social-media platforms thrive on an attention economy, where the primary goal is to maximize user engagement to drive ad revenue. This financial model incentivizes the amplification of sensational content, including racialized disinformation and hate speech, which generates high interaction rates. This model disproportionately harms communities of color, as they become primary targets for such harmful content. The constant exposure to false narratives and hate speech not only perpetuates stereotypes and misinformation but also erodes trust, incites psychological distress, and discourages political participation. This systemic issue exacerbates existing social and economic inequities, further marginalizing communities while platforms profit from the increased engagement. Regulatory reforms are needed to combat this to change these incentives and ensure that platforms prioritize truthful, community-benefiting content.

Localize Our Understanding of Information Ecosystems

Contemporary research on mis- and disinformation often relies on social-web data to understand and articulate the issue. This tendency, however, often overemphasizes social-media platforms' centrality. Mis- and disinformation are not new phenomena, and their drivers predate TikTok, Facebook, Friendster, chain emails, and even dial-up internet. What can be said is that new social platforms have accelerated the spread and availability of information and play an active role in the targeting, curation, profiteering, and amplifying of content based on models that prioritize engagement.

These novel elements certainly add a new dimension to the issue, but researchers often use platform data out of convenience,[11] neglecting offline networked communications and information sharing. This is especially relevant to organizers and advocates attempting to understand their communities' information and narrative needs. However, social-media platforms allow for microtargeting—and those data, more often than not, are not available to researchers. Localizing our understanding of information ecosystems usually requires tapping into communities outside of passive social-web data collection and analysis, understanding their media consumption and community discourse, and providing accurate and appropriate warnings that social media alone cannot measure.[12]

Primary research strategies prioritizing the creation of original data within localized physical communities offer a valuable approach to gaining deeper insights into often overlooked or trivialized spaces. These research tools, such as face-to-face conversations, interviews, door-to-door outreach, phone calls, focus groups, and surveys, already exist and can be effectively employed. While this research can explore online experiences, it should equally emphasize investigating offline sources of information and truth making, such as communal spaces, influential figures, and the social ties that shape an individual's worldview.

Additionally, combining this localized approach with quantitative data gathering, such as data donation from community members, can provide researchers with a more nuanced and detailed understanding of media consumption at a personalized level. This method, which involves asking community members to share years of their personal social-media data for analysis, requires deep trust and careful consideration of privacy and data-security concerns. However, it could reveal insights that conventional mass social-web data analysis alone might miss if conducted safely, systematically, and respectfully.

Be Vigilant About Research and Answering Unanswered Questions

Public discourse often centers on the many unanswered questions at the center of this study area. Critics question the scale[13] of the problem, debating whether the prevalence of online mis- and disinformation necessitates such attention, documentation, and study. Some research suggests the issue is less widespread[14] than it has come to be described. Similarly, whether mis- and disinformation impact belief and behavior necessitates more scrutiny. Of course, researchers have shown how some communities that have mobilized in recent years have shared mis- or disinformation beliefs. Still, it remains difficult to prove that this type of information was at the center of a shift in worldview or whether it played an active role in spurring action on the ground.[15]

The necessity of establishing universal standards for mis- and disinformation research cannot be overstated. A significant challenge in this field is measuring relative amplification:[16] To what extent do platform algorithms amplify specific content over others?[17] This fundamental question is critical to advancing platform-accountability research yet remains complex and elusive. As such, continued study and diversity of expertise—from psychologists to platform analysts—are crucial. Expanding our understanding and addressing these challenging unknowns are essential to a more comprehensive and effective approach to combating misinformation.

We must continue scrutinizing these knowledge, communication, and community control systems. The same technologies, which warp the concept of information sharing in favor of profit maximization, filter and shape our worldviews at their core; contemporary social-media platforms are not neutral modes of communication. Although the extent of their influence and danger may still be up for debate, we know that—just as many other tools, and especially tools built from the roots of colonial-capitalist frameworks—they have been used to wield power and influence, particularly against marginalized communities. Our focus should lie there when considering how to continue to disarm mis- and disinformation while acknowledging the gap in our knowledge. These challenges are larger than simple facts or lies; we must continue to prevent the consolidation of power this technology grants to the few; keep a watchful eye on those who gain unwarranted influence from these technologies; and guard our frameworks and values by telling good stories to underpin the ways in which we view, understand, and relate to each other and the world.

Combating Racialized Disinformation Requires a Multidisciplinary Approach

To effectively combat racialized disinformation, it is vital to recognize that while organizing and advocacy are foundational, they are not sufficient on their own. The pervasive nature of disinformation highlights the urgent need for systemic interventions and material change. A comprehensive *whole of society* approach is essential to address the root causes and manifestations of disinformation.

This approach involves the collaboration of various sectors and levels of society to address complex issues. It recognizes that challenges like racialized disinformation cannot be effectively tackled by any single entity. Combating racialized disinformation effectively requires the joint efforts of government, the private sector, civil society, and local communities. Policy makers must enact and enforce regulations that hold platforms accountable. Tech companies must invest in improved content moderation and transparency. Civil-society organizations need to advocate for these changes while supporting the communities most affected.

Structural reform and material change are indispensable in tackling the underlying issues that enable disinformation to thrive. Beyond addressing surface-level symptoms, we must engage in deep, systemic transformation to uproot the conditions that foster racialized disinformation. Equally important is promoting narrative change and power building. To counteract disinformation, we must actively promote positive, truthful narratives about communities of color. This is critical for dismantling harmful stereotypes and fostering a more inclusive and accurate public discourse.

Local organizing and advocacy are crucial in building community resilience against disinformation. Grassroots movements can drive awareness and mobilize action, but their impact will be limited without the support of broader systemic changes. To be truly effective, these efforts must be part of a larger, coordinated strategy that addresses both the symptoms and root causes of racialized disinformation.

Policy Makers Must Examine and Redress the Corporate-Media Ecosystem's Distortion of Facts and Spreading of Lies

Online platforms have consistently evaded their responsibility and accountability for their roles in propagating dangerous mis- and disinformation. This negligence has enabled falsehoods to spread unchecked, with grave consequences for society. It is imperative that policy makers critically examine how the corporate-media ecosystem distorts facts and disseminates lies, and take decisive action to rectify these harms.

Therefore, we call on policy makers to enact a strategic set of solutions to curb mis- and disinformation and reshape the media ecosystem in order to better serve the public interest. This includes promoting accurate news and information dissemination; safeguarding civil and human rights; and fostering an informed, equitable electorate across all languages. By implementing these measures, we can begin dismantling the structures that allow mis- and disinformation to flourish and build a media landscape that genuinely meets the needs of all communities. By adopting these measures, Congress can help create a media ecosystem that is more transparent, equitable, and accountable, ultimately reducing the spread of mis- and disinformation and its harmful impacts on society.

Comprehensive digital-privacy legislation is needed. As users of social-media platforms, we should be able to control how apps use our data. We should have the right to quickly access, correct, delete, or download our personal information and take it with us when we leave an online service. We deserve to know what kinds of information companies and data brokers are collecting about us, and there need to be strict and transparent safeguards against what is off limits. Congress should ban algorithms that profile users and target content to them in ways that constitute age, racial, and sex discrimination in employment, housing, lending, and e-commerce. They should also investigate voting and other civil rights violations that flow from abusive data practices. These are just the bare necessities; more can be found in the Disinfo Defense League Policy Platform.[18]

Conclusion

Despite the significant strides in understanding and combating racialized disinformation, much more research and targeted action are urgently needed. The experiences of people of color must receive focused attention, as these communities are often the most affected and least protected. Their voices and lived experiences are crucial to devising effective countermeasures that address the unique challenges they face.

Tackling racialized disinformation requires a multifaceted approach that involves concerted efforts at various levels of society. Grassroots community initiatives are vital in fostering digital literacy and resilience and equipping people with the tools to recognize and resist mis- and disinformation. Simultaneously, legislative action is imperative to hold social-media platforms accountable, ensuring they are not complicit in the proliferation of harmful content. Corporate responsibility must also be at the forefront, with technology companies taking proactive measures to design governance structures that are equitable, transparent, and reflective of diverse perspectives.

Advocating for comprehensive, whole-of-society solutions is essential. This means engaging educators, policy makers, activists, and tech industry leaders in a collaborative effort to dismantle the infrastructure that enables disinformation to thrive. By promoting accessible and equitable governance of online platforms, we can cultivate a digital environment that prioritizes truth, justice, and inclusivity for all.

Ultimately, the fight against racialized disinformation is about more than just correcting falsehoods—it's about fostering a more just and equitable society. By understanding the tactics used to spread mis- and disinformation and implementing robust, comprehensive strategies to counter it, we can protect the integrity of our digital spaces and empower all communities to thrive in an informed and equitable world.

Data for Liberation: The Role of Surveys in Social Movement Infrastructure

By Cathy Cohen, Kumar Ramanathan, and Matthew D. Nelsen

In the summer and fall of 2020, millions of people took to the streets in the United States and across the globe to protest the killings of George Floyd, Breonna Taylor, and many others. Part of this mobilization included demands to divest from police budgets and invest in Black communities. These varied and complex demands were quickly misrepresented in media coverage and attacks from opponents as a decontextualized call to "defund the police."

Three years removed from those mobilizations, the question remains: Was *defund the police* a successful frame for mobilizing mainstream publics? Did ideas about divesting from police and investing in alternative policies and programs resonate with Black communities? Do Black people really want to defund the police—or rather, as some pundits have claimed, was it a briefly salient idea that lost support after the summer of 2020? For social movements that have organized against police violence, the answers to such questions have important implications, both for their organizing work and for the media narratives they confront. One way that movement organizations can tackle these questions and inform their organizing strategies is by drawing on survey research.

In this essay, we make the case that survey data can be a critical resource within social-movement infrastructure. We draw on Cathy Cohen's essay "Death and Democracy" to define social-movement infrastructure as the interconnected

organizations, networks, movement halfway houses, and other "political quilters" needed to bring people together to articulate their concerns, sustain collective mobilization, shift power, and hold our precious representational democracy accountable for the systemic change people are demanding.[1]

We discuss the role that survey data can play in this infrastructure, by deepening organizers' and advocates' nuanced understanding of on-the-ground experiences and beliefs of those we seek to mobilize. Survey data can also be used to develop counternarratives meant to challenge the story being disseminated by the mainstream media and provide often-marginalized publics with a story that resonates with their lived experiences. To make this case, we highlight the data coming from the GenForward Survey.[2] We share how GenForward works in collaboration with organizers to develop surveys that are helpful to social movements, and we provide an example of the role of surveys in movement infrastructure by examining survey data on Black young adults' beliefs about defunding the police and alternatives to policing.

Movement Infrastructure

Building a robust movement infrastructure has been essential to the struggle for racial and social justice. For example, sociologist Aldon Morris's seminal study of the civil rights movement points to a broad infrastructure as enabling systemic change. The movement's sustained efforts not only were the result of the work of prominent national organizations and leaders, but relied on a widespread network of organizations and resources in which they were embedded.

Morris writes:

> Mass protest is a product of the organizing efforts of activists functioning through a well-developed indigenous base. A well-developed indigenous base includes the institutions, organizations, communication networks, money, and organized masses within a dominated group.[3]

Today's social movements continue to build a broad infrastructure. For example, as historian Barbara Ransby writes, the Movement for Black Lives (M4BL) coalition includes an ecosystem of organizations that are actively in one another's orbit, having collaborated, debated, and collectively employed an array of tactics together: from bold direct actions to lobbying politicians and creating detailed policy documents.[4]

This ecosystem includes not only national networks such as the Black Lives Matter Network (later renamed BLMGN, or the Black Lives Matter Global Network) and membership-based organizations such as Black Youth Project 100 (BYP100) and Dream Defenders, but also less visible "political quilters," such as the Blackbird team or the BlackOUT Collective, who provide "political education and skills and tactical training" to the wider movement.[5]

We believe that survey research, when conducted thoughtfully and in collaboration with organizers, can be an important resource within the broader movement infrastructure. Effective surveys can support movement work in at least two ways. First, surveys can deepen our understanding of the on-the-ground experiences and beliefs of those we seek to support and organize. By incorporating community-based knowledge into the designs of surveys, we can gather data that shed light on how people and communities, especially those whom movements hope to mobilize, think about complicated issues. Second, drawing from this deeper understanding, survey data can help movements develop effective counternarratives against dominant accounts seeking to dismiss the new and radical ideas that movements advance.

We recognize and acknowledge that movement organizers have good reasons to be skeptical of survey research. Surveys are a core part of the repertoire of the social sciences, which have a long history of extracting knowledge and resources from marginalized communities and social movements. Surveys are also a tool commonly used to establish dominant narratives that defend the social order, and thus can be used to dismiss movements' demands for systemic change.

However, rather than use this experience to reject survey research entirely, we believe that movements can and should use survey data as a means to counter these dominant narratives. This is why we believe that survey research is most helpful to movements when movement organizations have a long-standing and principled relationship with survey researchers and when movement organizations are involved in the research process, from its initial design to the final analysis and dissemination of findings. The approach we advocate here is similar to the tradition of Participatory Action Research.[6]

Survey research is only one of several ways of understanding people's experiences and beliefs. Other approaches include interviews, focus groups, participant observation of community conversations, and social listening (i.e., analyzing social-media discourse). Each approach has advantages and disadvantages. Interviews and focus groups provide room for probing questions and enable a deeper understanding. Participant observation and social listening can show us how people talk with each other in organically formed spaces. Surveys lack the depth that these other approaches can provide, but they enable us to examine experiences and beliefs, and how they vary across groups, on a broad scale. Surveys allow us to measure the opinions of those who are often ignored and silenced. They provide a way to expand the archive and whose voices are included. While all of these approaches can be useful resources within movement infrastructure, we focus on survey research here, since this is our area of expertise as researchers affiliated with the GenForward Survey.

The GenForward Survey

The GenForward Survey was founded in 2016 by Dr. Cathy Cohen, building on the earlier work of the Black Youth Project Survey conducted in 2005. Cohen is a Black queer feminist with ties to movement organizations. Thus, her work to build the GenForward Survey was informed by her work in activist and movement spaces. The GenForward Survey has always sought to expand whose voices, experiences, and opinions are included in discussions of "the public." We do this by focusing on communities that are often ignored in mainstream polling—for example, young adults of color. We also pay special attention to how race and ethnicity influence the ways young adults experience and think about the world.[7]

We are committed to disaggregating the categories of "Millennials" and "Gen Z" because we know there are important differences in lived experiences and political attitudes among young adults of different ages, racial/ethnic, gender, and class backgrounds and positions. What makes GenForward different isn't just the people included in our sample; it is also the types of surveys we produce. In our surveys, we strive to connect with the work of social-justice movements and to generate data that are helpful to movements, advocates, policy makers, politicians, journalists, and academics. We do this by incorporating the ideas of movements into our surveys and, most important, collaborating directly with them when possible.

Our mission is reflected in how we approach two central decisions that are part of the survey-research process. The first decision is *sampling*, which refers to the population that the survey wants to understand. Sampling reveals decisions about who we envision as "the public" and whose voices we value. Most survey and polling efforts focus on being "nationally representative"— that is, constructing a sample of respondents that matches the demographics of the national population. This approach is valuable in that it can provide a snapshot of the average views of the nation.[8] Our work at GenForward is different. We *oversample* young adults of color, meaning that we recruit extra responses from this population.[9] This approach does not mean we are less representative; instead, it allows us to produce a nationally representative sample that is more precise and detailed in our analysis of responses from young adults of color. We find that oversampling is crucial in order to develop a deeper understanding of the voices of young and marginalized people, especially to understand the differences in experiences and beliefs *among* them.

The second decision is *survey design*, which refers to the structure and content of the questions and response options on the survey. When we design and select our questions, we pay careful attention to the issues facing young adults of color and the work of social movements. This means that the questions we ask can look quite different from what mainstream survey and polling firms ask. For example, our 2005 Black Youth Project Survey, which was the forerunner of the GenForward project, asked questions about hip-hop long before anyone else was including rap and hip-hop as topics of exploration in surveys. We did this because, through their lived experiences, the Black young adults who helped construct our first survey understood the significance of hip-hop and argued for its central inclusion in the survey. They were right; the data showed that hip-hop had a strong influence on how Black young adults thought about politics—even more than commonly studied factors like party identification.[10]

When we work with movement organizations as partners, we invite them to collaborate in all stages of the survey-research process. This includes both the sampling and design stages we described earlier. Our collaborations strengthen our efforts to value the voices of communities who have been marginalized, and to design surveys with their lived experiences at the center of our research. Working with our organizational partners can also lead to tailored decisions about sampling and survey design. For example, we have conducted surveys that sample only one ethnic or racial group in order to provide insight about the communities that our partners seek to mobilize. We have also refined our questions to support our partners' campaigns by doing things like using surveys to gauge awareness of and support for specific campaigns or to assess the effectiveness of different communications strategies that our partners are considering. This is the work of being a part of movement infrastructure.

Case Study: Divestment from Policing or *Defund the Police*

The summer of 2020 witnessed massive nationwide protests following the murder of George Floyd and other instances of anti-Black police violence. Many of these protests and related activism were incubated and sparked by the efforts of Black youth-led social-movement organizations. Amid this heightened mobilization, many organizations advanced campaigns to invest in Black communities while divesting from carceral practices and institutions, including the police. The frame of *defunding the police*, which focused on the divestment portion of these demands and emerged from the radical wing of the movement, drew attention to campaigns to radically transform policing and fueled broader discourse about abolitionist strategies. However, mainstream-media coverage focused its attention narrowly on the call to *defund*, rather than the varied and nuanced demands for *divestment* from police departments and *reinvestment* in nonpolicing alternatives targeting the root causes of violence, poverty, and despair.

The idea of defunding the police was quickly subject to intense scrutiny and criticism in mainstream and right-wing media and political discourses. These entities weaponized the decontextualized version of the *defund* slogan popularized in media coverage.[11] Notably, these criticisms often used survey data to back up a claim that defunding the police was not only a bad idea, but that it was opposed by Black communities whom movement organizers sought to support and organize. Pundits seeking to discredit movement organizations argued that movements were out of step with the Black community, which was looking for public safety from whoever could provide it, including the police. As early as the summer of 2020, conservative and libertarian news outlets published articles with headlines like "Black Americans Do not Want to Defund the Police."[12] By 2021, news articles in mainstream publications cited survey data showing a lack of support for decreasing police spending and emphasized low levels of support among Black people in particular. For example, articles in *Insider* and *Slate* cited a Pew survey which found that only 23 percent of Black respondents supported defunding the police.[13]

While the data presented in articles targeting movement organizations and their campaigns for divestment from policing and other carceral practices and institutions were accurate,[14] we believe there was a missed opportunity among movement organizations to use survey data to better understand Black communities' relationship to policing, public safety, and the idea of *defund*. To use survey data to truly enhance the work of movement organizations and the communities they represent—in this case, Black people—it is crucial that surveys are designed with an investment in exploring the nuances of how Black people think. As a case study of how thoughtfully collected survey data could be used to deepen our understanding, we share some findings from surveys of Black young adults (ages 18–36) that we conducted in August 2020 and April 2022. We begin with questions that ask about defunding the police in the abstract, and we show how designing additional questions to ask about specific alternatives reveals more complex beliefs among Black young adults in relation to policing and defunding the police.

In our August 2020 survey, we found that 38 percent of Black young adults expressed support for defunding the police, while 32 percent opposed it and 29 percent were unsure (see Figure 1). By April 2022, amid increasing public opposition to the idea among mainstream pundits and politicians on both sides of the aisle, the percentage of Black young adults who said they supported defunding the police dropped 8 percentage points to 30 percent; 38 percent now said they opposed it, with the percentage of those who were unsure remaining about the same. Interestingly, despite fervent debates in the

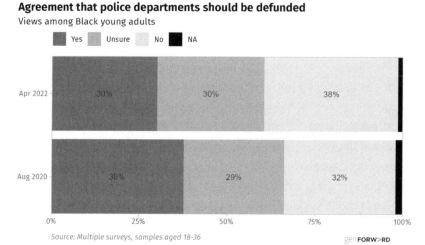

Agreement that police departments should be defunded
Views among Black young adults

Figure 1.

media, these data suggest that by April 2022, more than a quarter of Black young adults still had not formed a clear opinion or were unwilling to share their opinion about defunding the police.

The simple question shown here, however, does not capture the complexity of Black young adults' beliefs about policing. In our surveys, we also asked whether respondents believed police budgets (either for the police in general or for their local police department) should be increased, kept the same, or decreased. When asking about the possibility of defunding the police in this manner, a much larger proportion of Black young adults—52 percent in 2020 and 46 percent in 2022—agreed that police budgets should be decreased (see Figure 2). Only a small minority believed budgets should be increased. The greater support for decreasing police budgets when the question is formulated in this way should give us pause about survey data that simply prompt a response to the politically fraught term *defund the police*.

Notably, there was less support for decreasing police budgets when we narrowed the question to respondents' *local* police departments (39 percent in 2020 and 38 percent in 2022). This difference could arise because some Black young adults disapprove of the police generally but are more willing to accept their local department. The difference might also stem from the immediate need and desire for safety; thus, asking about local departments prompts them to consider the existing services provided by police in their community. This

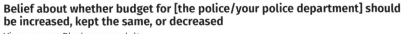

Belief about whether budget for [the police/your police department] should be increased, kept the same, or decreased

Views among Black young adults

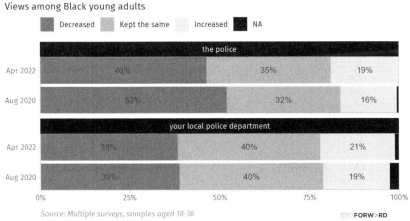

Source: Multiple surveys, samples aged 18-36

Figure 2.

question alone cannot explain the reasons for the gap, but it does prompt us to carefully consider how Black young adults' relationship to policing in general and policing locally can differ.

So far, the questions we have discussed asked respondents to consider changes to funding for the police in the abstract. Social-movement organizations that have advanced campaigns to defund the police, however, have not only argued for divestment, but also *investment*, in alternatives to policing. Reflecting this divest/invest approach, we asked respondents whether they support divesting from police and putting all or part of the police budget into investments in health care, education, and housing. The results are sharply different compared to the previous two questions: 60 percent of Black young adults in 2020 and 74 percent in 2022 strongly or somewhat supported reallocating part of police budgets to these areas (see Figure 3). This support persisted even when we asked if respondents supported reallocating police departments' *entire* budgets to investments in these other areas: 60 percent of Black young adults in 2020 and 67 percent in 2022 strongly or somewhat supported this proposal. Note that the level of support Black young adults offered to the proposed policy *increased* from 2020 to 2022, even as overall support for the abstract idea of defunding the police decreased.

Drawing on other proposals made by social movements, such as the Treatment Not Trauma campaign in Chicago,[15] we asked next about support for a

Support for divesting from police and putting [part of their budgets / their entire budgets] toward investments in healthcare, education, and housing

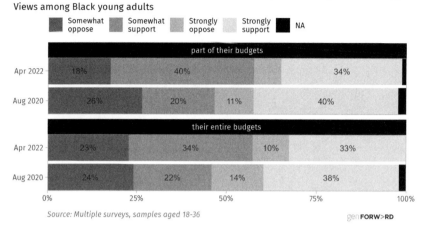

Figure 3.

Support for alternative first responders to replace some police functions

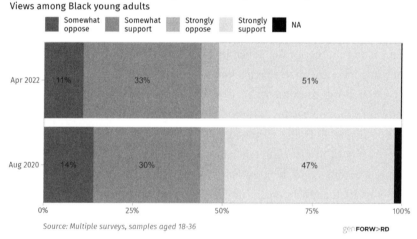

Figure 4.

"new agency of first responders that specialize in de-escalation of violence, providing mental-health support and other social services that would take over these responsibilities from the police." Instead of asking about funding allocations, this question asks about replacing some police functions with an alternative nonpolice agency. Here, we again find overwhelming support from Black young adults (see Figure 4). Specifically, 77 percent said they strongly or somewhat supported this idea in 2020, with agreement with this proposed policy growing to 84 percent in 2022. Once again, we see an *increase* in support for alternatives to policing over this period, even as the idea of defunding the police received intense criticism in mainstream-media discourse.

Examining these results illustrates how survey data can be a useful resource within social-movement infrastructure. First and foremost, survey data can help us deepen our understanding of experiences and beliefs among the communities that movements seek to organize and mobilize. In this case study, we see that Black young adults' attitudes toward the idea of divestment from policing are complex. Only about a third supported the abstract idea of defunding the police, and support dropped from 2020 to 2022 amid intense criticism of the idea. However, when we asked about police budgets without using the terminology of defunding, we found higher levels of support, albeit with important differences, depending on whether we asked about budgets for police in general or for one's local police department. When we turn our questions to the investment side of the divest/invest campaigns pursued by movement organizations, we found *much* higher levels of support. These data can help organizers strategize about their communications—for example, they suggest that organizers should consider emphasizing alternatives to policing when advancing campaigns among Black young adults.

Second, survey data can also help movements develop counternarratives, rooted in a meaningful understanding of the preferences of communities that have been marginalized. In this case, survey data can help respond to claims that defunding the police is unpopular among Black young adults. It may be true that the terminology of *defund* is not widely supported, but the *ideas* of divestment and reinvestment receive broad support in Black communities. Importantly, these data can help counter the constructed message that police divestment was a briefly salient idea that has lost support since the summer of 2020. Our questions about alternatives to policing, whether posed in terms of reallocating police budgets or replacing police functions, found an *increase* in support among Black young adults from 2020 to 2022.

The survey data shared here offer a small slice of GenForward's work on this topic. Our surveys have asked a broad array of questions about individual and communal experiences with policing and violence, beliefs about the seriousness of police violence, and other ideas about alternatives to policing. While we highlight our findings about Black young adults here, our surveys have also examined experiences and beliefs among other young adults of color and compared these with the national population.

Survey Data in Movement Infrastructure

The example of how survey data could be used in the ongoing discourse about defunding the police illustrates at least two ways that surveys can be a critical resource within movement infrastructure. First, survey data can help movements learn about the experiences and beliefs of publics, especially those that they seek to mobilize or support, in a nuanced and detailed way. This is not to say that movements should be beholden to the findings of surveys. Rather, surveys show where people's beliefs are at a given moment, enabling movements with more knowledge to pursue campaigns that can move public opinion.

Second, survey data can also help movements reshape and control the narratives around their demands and campaigns. Mainstream media and opposing interests often use tools like surveys to defend the status quo or dismiss the claims made by social movements. These tools, however, can be used in direct response to such efforts. When survey research is conducted alongside movement work, it can help movement organizations push back against such claims and craft their own narratives.

We reiterate that we do not believe survey research to be the panacea for all that ails movement work. Instead, we understand movements to be most effective and successful when embedded in an elaborate and extensive infrastructure of organizations and resources meant to enhance the work of organizing and power shifting. We believe that the use of survey data is one example of the resources organizers and movement organizations might better use to refine their strategy and let the voices of their communities speak to them. We do not believe that survey research should take the place of other ways in which organizers connect with those they seek to mobilize, such as one-on-ones. Instead, we think that survey research provides another glimpse into the struggles and liberatory ideas of those often marginalized but also willing to resist.

VISUALS AND TACTICS

Storytelling and the Power of Visual Media

By Shadia Fayne Wood and Wambui Gichobi

The year was 2011. People from all over the United States, horrified by the climate crisis and tired of sitting by watching the world burn, were urged to action. On August 20, a group of us—seventy organizers strong—stood proudly in front of the White House, where you could be arrested and fined $50 for blocking the sidewalk. Together, we waited for the police to put us in handcuffs and escort us offsite. Despite the risk, we had developed a plan to turn this small action into a wedge that would open the door on the Keystone XL (KXL) pipeline—an issue that was politically considered a done deal.

The KXL was a massive project that would have expedited climate change, threatened our country's most precious fresh-water aquifers, and cut through tribal and small farm lands. The House of Representatives was controlled by Republicans, making significant action on climate nearly impossible. However, because the KXL crossed the Canadian border with the United States, the project had to be signed off on by President Barack Obama. This was our moment for direct action.

On day one, seventy people kicked off the first of fourteen sit-ins, sitting patiently in the heat. Though we sent press releases out to all press in the area, they grossly underestimated the power of this moment, providing minimal coverage. Our team of photographers, however, had set up shop, uploading the first images through a hot spot from the cordoned-off press area adjacent to the action. Our rapid-response tactics worked: Our images, not those of the press, were picked up and shown live on MSNBC to tell the story of what was unfolding.

Our goal as the photography team was to get an image of every single person who'd been arrested; we wanted to make it easy for folks sitting-in to share what they had done in defense of climate justice. We saw this as a way to organically grow our narrative presence. During that historic period, 1,252

Organizer Kandi Mosset is arrested outside the White House, one of 1,252 arrested during the multiday sit-in to protest the Keystone XL pipeline. Photo by Shadia Fayne Wood

people were arrested. Many online viewers were shocked to see their friends in handcuffs. Our dedicated communications team ensured that the images were picked up by the local press, and our digital team spent the night sharing the photo albums on social media, telling a visceral story of action in the face of disaster.

In the end, the photos served a multifaceted purpose. They became an organizing tool to recruit more participants to Washington, DC, to risk arrest. They were used in the press to reach our target, President Obama. Finally, they served a political-education purpose long after the protests had ended. Our strategy revealed the power of imagery to break through noise and invisibilization, and to seed a counternarrative on a mass scale.

Changing the Narrative Through Imagery

When you hear terms like *suffrage movement*, you may imagine women standing in front of the White House admonishing President Woodrow Wilson. When you hear *the fight for farmworkers*, you likely imagine workers holding signs that read "Huelga, Strike," or "Boycott Safeway." And when you hear *civil rights*, you probably see iconic images of Rosa Parks refusing to cede her seat on the bus, or Dr. Martin Luther King Jr. giving his "I Have a Dream" speech at the Lincoln Memorial.

Imagery, from photography to motion picture and video, has been used by social movements for over a century, and for good reason—it's a powerful tool for memorable storytelling. During the twentieth century, the ubiquity of imagery not only made it indispensable in storytelling, but it also made it easier to put pressure on the press—and, by extension, the political targets of social movements.

With the rise of social media in the twenty-first century, social movements have been presented with yet another opportunity to combine high-quality visuals and storytelling with audience engagement. It was at the height of this cultural shift that we founded Survival Media, a network of global media makers dedicated to using photo and video storytelling in service of social movements. We grew out of the summer of 2011, during which we documented the unprecedented civil disobedience against the KXL outside the White House and recruited a team of creatives with a deep understanding of organizing.

We think of visual media as part of an organizing strategy. We start by learning as much as we can about the campaign our partners are working on and what goals they are trying to achieve. We then dig deeper to understand what hurdles they face, whom they need to build with to overcome this, and what they need those people to do. Then, we create a visual strategy and plan.

We have identified a handful of organizing tactics that video and photo tools are best suited to support. These tactics serve a function, so we create our visual tools with this function at the heart of each piece.

Developing a Visual Strategy

Organizing over Vanity Metrics

Often, organizations are swayed by vanity metrics, such as view counts and website click-throughs, which are disconnected from their ultimate goals. Even when we desire to get as many people to care about our issue as possible, it is critical to remember the context we live in: People are bombarded with content by the day, by the hour, by the minute. We can watch a video of the climate crisis that makes us sob and then scroll to photos of our cousin's wedding. Suddenly, the thing that could've compelled us toward action is gone and the moment has been forgotten.

Virality is not predictable. It is also not a sound predictor that an audience will do much more than watch. Social movements require deep investment in people and their participation. These relationships are not transactional. They are complex and dynamic, and are about more than getting viewers for content. This work should be rooted in engaging new audiences or an already-identified base of supporters to join an event, take bold action, or deepen their investment by assuming greater leadership. We must devise a strategy that connects back to organizing before deploying visual imagery.

Political Education

Movements need to evolve and incorporate new information and understanding. Political education recognizes that not everyone starts from the same level of knowledge and experience. Content within this strategy should speak to your base, or to those adjacent to it, in a way that is welcoming and accessible. This type of media invests in people and inserts campaign strategies and insights into the long game.

This approach works well in making meaning when a big national or global event has occurred and people are glued to their social-media channels. It also works during a civic-participation campaign, when people are fighting unjust legislation through a complex legal system or voting a progressive politician into office. Visuals work well to encourage one's base to participate in important yet often-tedious activities outside of their comfort zone, like phone banking or door knocking.

Invite people to genuinely build with you and they will.

Fund-Raising

To sustain themselves, movements require money. Visual work can propel a people-driven crowdfunding campaign or engage major donors or foundations, who often require a different level of communication. Although how or what you communicate might differ among your various audiences, the goal is the same: We want our audiences to see themselves as part of that movement. We also want to inspire them and give them the confidence to invest in us.

Movement Cohesion

Movements are made up of thousands of individuals in different locations. Many of them are tired, scared, and inspired. Most of all, they have the audacity to hope that we can build a more just and equal world. Visual tools designed with the goal of helping people feel seen and heard can create a shared sense of cohesion, especially when movements are grappling with big issues, such as climate grief or internal power issues. Individuals with different levels of understanding and commitment to the issues are linked through such efforts, culminating in a powerful union. This can be an especially helpful factor, especially when it comes to releasing content during big events, such as annual celebrations, international conferences, and national direct actions.

Political Pressure

Movements work to achieve change at scale, which requires pressure to be placed on existing power structures. The use of press, billboards, creatively placed images, or direct sends to the decision maker can be much more effective than a social-media post. In the case of the KXL, the same images were used across tactics, with our protestors knowing what the end goal was at every stage. Posting images on social media never guarantees that we'll reach our intended target, but having a plan in place to reach and build with our intended audience can make all the difference.

Cultural Engineering: The Use of Design and Creative Strategy in Revolutionary Movements

By Fresco Steez

As a cultural worker who belongs to an oppressed people, my job is to make revolution irresistible.

—Toni Cade Bambara[1]

I've always dreamed that Black communities across the country could look around—on street corners, in laundromats, on front porches—and see a group of young Black folks dedicated to their liberation. You could trust that they held specific values and were trained in organizing skills and leadership. Because of their cultural context, these organizers could activate people and build the infrastructure of any political formation, small or large. Their analysis would always be sharp, elevating any room they entered, and they'd be instilled with a profound love for their people. This league of extraordinary Black freedom fighters would carry stories from the depths of their hearts, with a clear vision for their people's future—rooted in integrity, abundance, and compassion—and armed with the rigor, discipline, and precision needed to fight for that future.

And when you're in the room with them, you feel more free. These Black folks embody a vision of a world and a life free from fear, and they bring a piece of that freedom into every space they enter. Culture isn't just about art or objects; it's about presence and connection.

As a cultural organizer and creative strategist, I have three priorities: first, to help my people make sense of the world in ways that deepen our collective political consciousness; second, to create a sense of belonging and connection for marginalized people; third, to develop and replicate cultural dimensions that mobilize people on a mass scale and inspire them to take radical, political action.

The deliberate use of visual culture and creative strategy has been a driving force in shaping revolutionary movements, particularly within the Black liberation struggle. By examining the intersection of art, culture, and organizing, I will highlight how these elements work together to mobilize communities, deepen collective consciousness, and create a sense of belonging.

Revolutionary Aesthetics: Shaping Movements Through Visual Culture

The role of the artist is exactly the same as the role of the lover. . . . If I love you, I have to make you conscious of the things you don't see.

—James Baldwin[2]

The political commitment of a freedom fighter is deeply intertwined with a creative commitment to redesigning the very fabric of society. History shows us that revolutionary movements are defined not just by their political actions but also by their cultural and artistic expressions. Art and design have always been crucial to the political resocialization of a people, shaping the visual identity and cultural resonance of movements.

When we look back at the history of political resistance, the most impactful movements had strong visual identities and cultural elements that connected deeply with their audiences. We can instantly recognize the Black Panther Party, the Black Power movement, and the civil rights movement by their powerful imagery and cultural symbols. Even non-Black movements, like the antiwar movement or the hippie counterculture, had distinct vibes that were unmistakable. The punk-rock era, the Blitzkrieg, and the struggle around the Berlin Wall all carried unique cultural signatures. Dance, music, fashion, and various art forms were integral to these movements, giving them a visual and cultural identity that amplified their messages.

AfriCOBRA (African Commune of Bad Relevant Artists), a Black artist collective founded on the South Side of Chicago in 1968, is a perfect example of how art was used to politicize and empower Black communities. The

Unite (AfriCOBRA), 1971. Color screen print on ivory wove paper. Artist: Barbara Jones-Hogu (1938–2017). Art Institute of Chicago/Art Resource, NY

philosophical mission of AfriCOBRA was to create images committed to a sublime expression of the African diaspora that would be identified by and reflected on by all Black people.[3] They understood that art and culture are not just accessories to a movement but are essential to its very soul, helping to galvanize and inspire collective action.

As the minister of culture for the Black Panther Party, Emory Douglas played a pivotal role in shaping the visual and cultural identity of the Black Power movement. He was the mastermind behind the political posters, zines, and powerful imagery that made the party's message accessible and compelling. His artwork wasn't just decoration; it was a tool of communication that captured attention, illustrated the struggles, and drew people in to learn more about the issues the Panthers were fighting against. His ability to translate complex political ideas into striking visuals made the movement's message resonate far beyond words alone.

When I reflect on the impact of visual culture in revolutionary movements, I think of the Zapatistas, a movement that, like the Black Panthers, understood the power of imagery in anticapitalist revolutions. The red star, a symbol seen

Paperboy, 1969. Artist: Emory Douglas (1943–). Photo courtesy of Emory Douglas / Art Resource, NY

in many anticapitalist struggles, became a unifying visual marker, signaling resistance and solidarity. I also think of the powerful art that emerged from Russian and Asian communist movements, with their bold use of red, gold, black, and white, depicting slogans like "Workers of the World, Unite" or "Power to the Proletariat." These visuals weren't just art—they were calls to action, galvanizing the working class to rise against the ruling elites.

Across the globe, movements have harnessed the power of visual identity to inspire and mobilize. From the African National Congress in South Africa to the Quilombo Movement in Brazil, these movements developed distinctive cultural aesthetics that were integral to their campaigns for justice and liberation. The propaganda shops of these anticapitalist movements often produced works that resembled superhero comics, imbuing ordinary people with the sense that they could rise up, resist, and, ultimately, transform their societies.

These visual elements weren't just consistent; they were essential. They gave each movement a recognizable and cohesive identity—a culture that spoke to the people, fueled their resolve, and united them in their shared struggle against oppression. In their book *The Rhetoric of Agitation and Control*, John W. Bowers and Donovan J. Ochs argue that this is called *solidification*—a mechanism to unite members to create a sense of belonging and that it is vital to a movement's success.[4]

Unapologetically Black

I remember entering organizing spaces with Black people, especially in Black Youth Project 100 (BYP100), where we deliberately created environments exclusively for Black people to process the Black experience, build solidarity, and strategize on how to advance Black political power. Yet even in those spaces, there was hesitation. Black people would ask, "Are you sure we can do this?"—a question born of a lifetime of being denied spaces where they could authentically connect, process shared experiences, and feel a sense of belonging.

This hesitation mirrored the pervasive dynamics of respectability politics that had long plagued our communities. Blackness and Black identity have been pathologized in every form, so much so that no matter what we do—whether it's wearing a hoodie, like Trayvon, or even putting on a suit—it's turned into something inherently dangerous or negative. We've been conditioned to believe that we must constantly shape-shift to be palatable in a white-supremacist world, walking through life as if we're apologizing for our very existence.

But what does it mean to live without an apology for who we inherently are? To enter a room without a content warning simply because we are Black? For young Black folks just beginning to engage with their political identities, it was a radical and pivotal declaration to be unapologetically Black. This meant organizing with other Black people, building exclusively Black spaces, and embracing Black culture without the need to dilute or make our message vague to appease others. It meant creating something unapologetically for us, by us.

One of the most powerful moments for me was hearing early members of BYP100 reflect on why they joined. It wasn't because they heard a life-changing speech or a grand political manifesto. They saw a group of people in matching T-shirts, hyped and energized, and they felt freer just being around them. They wanted to belong to that group, wear that T-shirt, and be part of something that made them feel seen and empowered. Once they walked through the door, we could radicalize them, engage them in activities that activated their collective consciousness, and deepen their commitment to the movement. This is the power of unapologetic Blackness—it's magnetic, transformative, and the foundation of our continued struggle for liberation.

An action organized by BYP100 on August 26, 2014, to call out the Chicago Police
Department's disproportionate arrest rates of Black people for minor possession of
marijuana. Photo by Sarah-Ji Rhee

Before BYP100 was even established, I coined the phrase "Unapologetically
Black," which resonated deeply with our work. People began wearing a shirt
with that declaration boldly emblazoned on it, and it became a powerful
symbol of our movement. The shirt didn't just make a statement—it
marked the person wearing it as part of something bigger. On the back, it
featured the organization's logo, signaling that if you were seen in that shirt,
you were connected to one of the few organizations at that time that were
unapologetically creating spaces exclusively for Black people. It became a
badge of honor, a visible commitment to Black liberation, and a sign that you
were part of a community dedicated to building power for Black people.

From Propaganda to Persuasion: The Role of Creative Strategy in Movement Building

When I think about the opposition, I think about the power of big data—the
vast investment in big data aimed at reading the minds of marginalized people
and moving them with conservative misinformation and disinformation.

Corporations and political entities spend millions—even billions—just to understand people, build impactful relationships, and influence them to act, often against their own best interests. We need to counteract this with cultural contributions that challenge narratives of conservative misinformation and disinformation. The opposition isn't just the entities collecting data; it's the narrative strategies they deploy through shows that our aunts, uncles, and cousins watch.

For example, decades of films and television shows have portrayed the police as heroic, offering humanizing storylines sympathetic to their struggles on the job. Police procedurals like *Law & Order* and *Cops* have shaped how millions view law enforcement. Meanwhile, we keep saying, "Police and prisons don't keep us safe," but where are people seeing stories that back this up? Where are the illustrations, the concrete examples, that reflect their own lived experiences? We often rely on data and reports, but we know that's not what changes hearts.

We need to create cultural dimensions: art, stories, and designs that resonate on a personal level. As a survivor, I can honestly say that I've seen my experiences reflected more on *Law & Order: Special Victims Unit* than I ever have in movement spaces. We need accessible, relatable storytelling—not a 200-page book or an ugly zine, but stories in which people can see themselves.

Like public schooling, the arts are often the first thing movement organizations divest from. When budgets get tight, the graphic designer, storyteller, or creator is usually the first to go. Even when it comes to campaigns and political projects, creatives are often brought in at the last minute—after the messaging has been set in stone. They're asked to make a banner or a graphic for a flier, but by then, the creative potential to truly enhance the campaign has been limited. Creatives, who are constantly thinking about how to implement and deploy concepts that resonate with people and inspire action, are underutilized.

One valuable lesson I learned from Shanelle Matthews is that the distinction between propaganda and persuasion is consent. We don't want to build propaganda, which is coercive. Instead, we want to persuade and compel people to take action in ways that are genuinely in their best interest and that they fully consent to. We need to develop creative strategies with the same level of discipline and commitment as the opposition uses to build propaganda.

Our goal should be to create cultural work that inspires action by prompting a moral crisis—not one that spirals people into confusion, but one that makes the choice clear. When people see something and instinctively feel that there's a right side and a wrong side, it pushes them to vocalize their stance and take action. This is the moment when people find their entry point into a journey of radicalization and build a political commitment that stays with them for life.

For example, in 2013, the Dream Defenders—an organization founded after George Zimmerman murdered Trayvon Martin in 2012—occupied the Florida State Capitol for thirty days demanding justice for Trayvon. This action not only highlighted Trayvon's story but also fueled the growing momentum around the demand for justice in the face of Zimmerman's lack of accountability.

While BYP100 was strong in political analysis, we lacked the visual impact that Dream Defenders consistently delivered. Dream Defenders had a remarkable team of artists who were always ready to respond to political moments with powerful visuals. Whenever a significant event occurred, their first response, even before drafting statements or building narratives, was to create a sharp, resonant graphic that captured the essence of the moment.

When Dream Defenders adapted the black hands-up emoji with the slogan "Hands up. Don't shoot!" during the Ferguson uprising, it spread like wildfire, becoming a symbol of resistance. This ability to quickly produce and disseminate compelling visuals, integrated with our organizing strategy, generates a momentum for our work that is unmatched by those who overlook the importance of creative strategy.

Divine Purpose: Art, Liberation, and the Black Radical Tradition

The purpose of cultural workers is divinely rooted in using art as a powerful tool for Black liberation. We craft creative strategies that spark curiosity, serving as a catalyst for collective consciousness. Our work visually unifies political movements and fosters a deep sense of belonging, inviting others to join in the struggle for justice.

We immerse ourselves in the study of culture, focusing on how collectives build enduring relationships and strategically create spaces for move-ment building. Through art and culture, we transcend time, creating work that is not confined to the present but is deeply anchored in the principles of Sankofa—reaching back to honor our ancestors and moving forward to build a better future.

Our art consistently elevates the legacy of the Black radical tradition, ignit-ing curiosity in the audience and compelling them to delve deeper into our history. It clearly communicates that those who engage with our work are carrying forward the values and traditions of our ancestors. When we cre-ate for political formations like BYP100 or the Movement for Black Lives (M4BL), our focus is not solely on the present organizers or their immediate impact. We think beyond, to their grandchildren and great-grandchildren—imagining a future where a young person discovers a piece of gear or artwork in their ancestor's closet and asks, "What were these young Black people fighting for? How can we continue their legacy?"

Our work exists simultaneously in history and the future, always in service to the present. If you possess something we've created, it signifies that you are part of something divine, revolutionary, and profoundly impactful. It means that in a time when it was difficult to hold certain values, you did so with courage and conviction, contributing to the ongoing fight for Black liberation and pushing us closer to revolutionary transformation. I hope our work is a hall of fame for young Black organizers.

Progressive art assists people in learning what's at work in the society in which they live.

—Angela Davis[5]

Disrupting the Status Quo: Direct Action as a Narrative Force in Uprisings

By Chinyere Tutashinda and Celeste Faison

On MLK weekend in 2016, the spirit of resistance took a palpable form on the highways that weave the cities of Oakland and San Francisco together. Organizers from the Movement for Black Lives (M4BL) and their allies orchestrated a bold act of defiance that would echo through the heart of the Bay Area. Their stage was the westbound span of the San Francisco–Oakland Bay Bridge—a vital artery connecting two vibrant communities, now the backdrop for a powerful narrative of protest.

As the afternoon unfolded, the organizers and activists transformed the bridge into a living tableau of resistance. They didn't just block traffic; they carved out a space of remembrance and outcry on the tarmac, leveraging symbols and signs to voice their messages. Among these, a wooden shrine emerged, meticulously crafted and bearing the heavy names of those lost to police shootings. This shrine stood not just as a monument but as a beacon of collective memory and mourning, a stark reminder of the lives extinguished by state violence.

This act of civil disobedience didn't arise in isolation. It was the crescendo of four days of fervent protest throughout the Bay Area, a region already pulsating with the urgent call for justice. The divest-invest movement found new vigor in the wake of Mario Woods's tragic death on December 2, 2015, at the hands of San Francisco police officers. Woods's story became a rallying cry, a symbol of the systemic violence and racism that activists and organizers were determined to challenge.

Choosing Martin Luther King Jr. weekend for their direct action was a deliberate and profound decision. The activists sought to reclaim and honor Dr. King's radical legacy—a legacy too often sanitized and stripped of its revolutionary vision. They sought to remind the world of King's true vision, which challenged injustices and demanded radical change.

The bridge shutdown was a master class in using symbolism in direct action. Every element, from the handmade signs to the protesters' physical presence, from the mobilizing songs to the unified chants for justice, was meticulously chosen to disrupt the status quo. These organizers understood the power of their actions to command attention, disrupt the comfortable rhythms of daily life, and compel the broader community to confront the harsh realities of systemic anti-Black violence and oppression.

Through their actions, they sent a clear message: The fight against state-sanctioned violence and anti-Black racism demands more than passive acknowledgment—it requires direct, bold, and unyielding resistance and radically transformative change. On that day, the San Francisco–Oakland Bay Bridge became more than a conduit of concrete and steel; it transformed into a symbol of struggle, a testament to the power of collective action and the enduring demand for justice.

That action, and many others in the Bay area and across the country, were supported by The BlackOUT Collective, a full-service, Black direct-action organization supporting and training groups in direct action. Direct action is a testament to the enduring spirit of revolutionary organizing. It is a method through which individuals, groups, and communities use their bodies and actions to enact the change they wish to see.

According to the BlackOUT Collective, direct action is a tactic used to make an immediate intervention that stops business as usual. The purpose is to cause a crisis of conscience for the public, a crisis for the state, the elite, or corporations. It is transformational for those utilizing the tactic and aims to transform the practitioner, the material conditions, the target, and the oppressed/working classes' relationship to power.

This chapter delves into two case studies of direct action within the United States, showcasing its pivotal role in shaping the narratives of various movements. Direct action is not merely about disrupting a system but about challenging its foundational assumptions and questioning its legitimacy.[1] From demonstrations that confront and disrupt to strategies that create crises and compel negotiation, direct action dramatizes issues to the extent that they cannot be ignored. In his Letter from Birmingham City Jail, Martin

Luther King Jr. reflected on this strategy: "So we had no alternative except that of preparing for direct action, whereby we would present our very bodies as a means of laying our case before the conscience of the local and national community."[2.]

Direct Action in the Ferguson Uprising and the Formation of the BlackOUT Collective

In 2008, the myth of a "postracial America" spellbound the nation. Major media outlets like *The New York Times*, *The Economist*, and the *Los Angeles Times* perpetuated this idea, capitalizing on the election of Barack Obama as the country's first Black president. The narrative was straightforward: America, a nation founded on the violent expropriation of Indigenous land and genocide and built on the backs and blood of enslaved Africans, had supposedly moved beyond race. This lie was embraced by both liberal and conservative voices, concealing the brutal reality that the country's structures of white supremacy were still profoundly intact.

For Black Americans, this "postracial" lie was not just misleading—it was dangerous. Black women continued to earn just 64 cents for every dollar a white man earned. Black people were dying from preventable diseases at higher rates and were four times more likely to die in police custody than white Americans. The myth of two Americas was not a myth but a lived reality.

This reality was violently confirmed on August 9, 2014, when Darren Wilson, a white Ferguson police officer, murdered eighteen-year-old Michael Brown in broad daylight. His lifeless body was left on the street for over four hours. This public lynching ignited an uprising as the people of Ferguson rose up, refusing to submit to a system that perpetuates and normalizes anti-Black violence. The lie of "postracial America" crumbled as the police met the people with tanks, tear gas, and a militarized crackdown designed to break their resistance. But Ferguson fought back.

On that day, the people of Ferguson instinctively took to the streets in a collective act of defiance and grief. They gathered, cried, mourned, and fought back, refusing to allow Michael Brown's death to be swept under the rug. The protests lasted for over 120 days, laying bare the state's violent defense of white supremacy. Ferguson's rapid and instinctual uprising fits into the

BlackOUT Collective's Rapid Response Action Framework, defined as an immediate and visceral reaction to injustice—when communities come together without hesitation to resist violence and oppression in real time.

Within days, activists, organizers, and revolutionaries from across the country descended on Ferguson, ready to stand in solidarity with the people on the ground. What began as a local outcry became a national flashpoint, as cries of "Hands up, don't shoot" and "Black Lives Matter" reverberated through the streets. "Black Lives Matter" quickly became the name the media used to describe this swelling movement, which called attention not only to Michael Brown's murder but also to the systemic, racist violence that continues to kill Black people across the United States. From New York to Oakland to London, solidarity actions erupted across the globe. The rebellion that started in Ferguson was not an isolated incident—it was a continuation of the centuries-long Black liberation movement, reigniting the radical call for freedom and self-determination.

Direct action is not just a tactic—it is an urgent and radical intervention designed to stop business as usual and force a moral crisis. The BlackOUT Collective defines direct action as a transformative force aimed at disrupting

Demonstrators march through the streets while protesting the shooting death of eighteen-year-old Michael Brown on November 23, 2014, in St. Louis, Missouri. Tensions in Ferguson remained high in anticipation of the grand jury decision to determine whether police officer Darren Wilson should be charged in the shooting death of Brown. Sebastiano Tomada/Getty Images News via Getty Images

systems of power, confronting the state, corporations, and elites, and radically shifting the relationships of power in society. Direct action serves to challenge the status quo, creating crises that demand immediate reckoning and change. The practitioners of direct action themselves are transformed in the process as they reclaim agency in the face of violent oppression.

The BlackOUT Collective was born of the flames of resistance in the aftermath of the Ferguson uprising. A national call was made for Black direct-action trainers to come to Ferguson and support the uprising. Upon arrival, they found a critical need for Black leadership in direct action. Residents, activists, and community members were facing off against an overwhelmingly militarized police force, and they needed the tools and strategies not just to survive but to fight back with power and precision.

The BlackOUT Collective coordinated a "Moral Monday" action deeply rooted in the long legacy of civil disobedience within Black radical movements. This was not just an action; it was a reclamation of space, an assertion of power in the face of white supremacy. The action not only brought attention to the militarization of the police but also highlighted the ongoing state-sanctioned violence against Black bodies. Ferguson was a battleground, and the people were ready for the fight.

The Ferguson uprising was not just a moment in history—it was the beginning of a radical shift in the fight for Black liberation in the twenty-first century. The bold declaration of "Black Lives Matter" struck at the heart of the racist American consciousness and began to challenge the deeply embedded systems of anti-Black violence. By 2017, Pew Research found that 54 percent of white Americans had begun to see police killings of civilians as indicative of systemic problems[3]—a slight, yet significant shift that speaks to the transformative power of sustained, radical direct action.

The BlackOUT Collective emerged from this rebellion, rooted in the belief that direct action can transform the material conditions of Black communities. We trained Black communities across the country in the art of disruption, protest, and defiance, equipping newly politicized Black people with the tools to challenge systems of oppression directly. The Ferguson uprising, which began as a visceral response to the murder of Michael Brown, continued to ripple outward, sparking rebellions and solidarity actions across the globe, from the United States to Brazil, Palestine, and beyond.

The uprising in Ferguson catalyzed a renewed Black liberation movement that continues today. In the summer of 2020, after the murders of George Floyd and Breonna Taylor, millions took to the streets, chanting "Defund the Police," calling for the abolition of police and prisons and an investment in alternatives that protect Black lives rather than extinguishing them. Once again, direct action became the tool through which Black communities asserted their right to exist and resist. This movement is not about reform but about the radical reimagination of society itself—one where Black people are no longer the targets of state violence but are the architects of a future rooted in justice, liberation, and collective power.

Ferguson was a flashpoint, and the movement continues to organize. The BlackOUT Collective and the uprising it was born out of represent a radical force for justice rooted in direct action, resistance, and the transformative power of collective struggle. What happened in Ferguson was not just an uprising; it was a declaration that Black people would no longer live under the boot of white supremacy. As practiced by the BlackOUT Collective, direct action remains a radical tool for liberation, pushing the boundaries of what is possible and demanding nothing short of total freedom.

We Are the 99 Percent: A Global Uprising Against Corporate Greed

In 2008, the United States faced its most severe economic collapse since the Great Depression. The Great Recession, caused by the reckless greed of predatory subprime lending and the complete lack of oversight on financial markets, resulted in untold suffering. Between 2007 and 2010, nearly 10 million families were forcibly evicted from their homes, while the same big banks responsible for this destruction raked in massive profits. Wall Street's greed didn't just hurt homeowners—it cannibalized itself. Financial institutions crumbled, dragging the country to the brink of another Great Depression.

Rather than holding the scammers accountable, the U.S. government bailed them out with over $700 billion through the Troubled Asset Relief Program (TARP), declaring that these financial giants were "too big to fail." But of the massive bailout, less than 8 percent went to help the millions of families whose homes were being taken from them by the big banks. While Wall

Street raked in billions, the people on Main Street were abandoned. The government claimed it would help 3 to 4 million homeowners, yet when the program ended in 2015, fewer than 1 million families had received assistance, and more than 6 million had lost everything.

As corporate greed skyrocketed, so did inequality. By 2010, the wealthiest 1 percent of Americans controlled 40 percent of the nation's wealth, while the media remained shamefully silent on the topic of economic injustice. The country was a powder keg waiting to explode.

On September 17, 2011, the people decided enough was enough. Approximately 1,000 activists gathered to Occupy Wall Street in Zuccotti Park, a privately owned park in the heart of the New York City's Wall Street district. This direct action aimed to confront the monstrous greed of the financial elites and the devastating impact of unbridled capitalism. Wall Street, the epitome of capitalist excess, was the chosen battleground. The plan: to occupy the space and refuse to leave until the world acknowledged that the system was rigged and did something about it.

What began with 1,000 protesters soon swelled to 15,000. By mid-October, Occupy Wall Street had captured the imagination of millions. The movement spread like wildfire, inspiring solidarity actions in over twenty-eight cities worldwide, from New York to Paris, São Paulo, and beyond. The occupations didn't just challenge Wall Street—they ignited a global uprising against a broken system. These were not just protests; they were acts of rebellion against the corporate state that prioritized profits over people.

Occupy Wall Street wasn't about raising awareness but about radical transformation. Under BlackOUT's direct action framework, these occupations were resilience-based actions designed to meet community needs while disrupting the status quo. Occupiers weren't just protesting—they were building a new world within the shell of the old. Zuccotti Park became a microcosm of what society could be: a space for mutual aid, horizontal decision making, and collective care. Participants embodied the future they wanted to see, rejecting the hierarchical structures of capitalism and creating prefigurative politics—where the means of protest directly reflected the world they envisioned.

Occupy Wall Street may not have had a clear list of demands, but it didn't need one. Its power was in its message: "We are the 99 percent." This rallying cry didn't just solidify the movement; it exposed the ugly truth of American capitalism. It named the villains—the 1 percent, the financial elites who hoarded wealth and exploited the working class for their gain. The 99 percent represented everyone else—the vast majority of people who faced poverty, wage stagnation, and the crushing reality of systemic injustice.

As Alex Snowden wrote in *Counterfire*, "Speaking of the 1% versus the 99% focuses attention on the central issue of inequality, alerts us to the hollowness of capitalist democracy . . . and reminds us that we, 99% of us, have a shared material interest, which is more important than anything that may divide us."[4]

This slogan wasn't just a rhetorical device—it was a radical call to mobilize, drawing a clear line between the oppressed majority and the oppressors. It shattered the myth of meritocracy and called out the entire system as a tool of exploitation. The media could no longer ignore the conversation. By mid-November 2011, Occupy Wall Street dominated 13 percent of the total news coverage in the United States, forcing the issue of economic inequality to the forefront of national discourse.[5]

Though the occupations eventually ended, the legacy of Occupy Wall Street remains. This was not a movement that sought incremental reform—it sought a revolutionary transformation of our economic systems. It brought the idea of class struggle back into the national conversation, sparking a renewed commitment to radical politics. As sociologist Jonathan Matthew Smucker notes, "Practically overnight, the nascent movement broke into the national news cycle and articulated a popular, albeit ambiguous, critique of economic inequality and a political system rigged to serve 'the one percent.'"[6]

Occupy Wall Street set the stage for the resurgence of socialist ideas in mainstream American politics. Before the movement, socialism was barely mentioned. By 2019, however, 40 percent of Americans under fifty reported having a favorable view of socialism. Occupy organizers went on to work for Bernie Sanders's presidential campaigns, pushing the Democratic Party to embrace more progressive, even socialist, ideas.[7]

Occupy's most significant victory was its ability to radically shift the narrative. It chipped at the façade of American capitalism and exposed the system's core injustice. It demonstrated that when done strategically and with a radical vision, direct action could change the conversation, even if the movement didn't result in immediate policy wins.

But Occupy was not without its contradictions. The very spaces meant to represent solidarity and justice also became sites of violence, particularly for women who were subjected to sexual assaults within the camps. These realities revealed the complexities and tensions within movements that seek to challenge oppressive systems while internally grappling with the same dynamics.

As author L.A. Kauffman argues, "Occupy Wall Street is a great example of a movement that often gets described as having just failed. And I see it as having succeeded in a lot of crucial ways in shifting conversations and putting issues on the agenda and creating new senses of possibility."[8]

Occupy Wall Street was a battle cry for the oppressed. It was a radical experiment in collective action and direct resistance against a rigged system. Though the physical occupations are long gone, the impact of Occupy's rhetoric and its challenge to capitalism continues reverberating through today's progressive and left movements. It was a movement that did not ask for permission to exist or seek the elite's approval. It was a movement that dared to imagine a different world—one where the 99 percent were no longer exploited, and the system no longer served the interests of the few but the many.

Occupy showed us that direct action can spark a revolution in consciousness, shifting the narrative and forcing a confrontation with the brutal realities of capitalist exploitation. The movement may not have passed legislation, but it broke through the walls of silence and gave voice to the struggle against economic oppression. The revolution is ongoing.

Conclusion

Direct action has proven itself as a potent narrative force, not only disrupting systems of oppression but also transforming the practitioners and communities that wield it. The acts of defiance in Ferguson, on the San Francisco–Oakland Bay Bridge, and the global ripple effects of movements like Occupy Wall Street demonstrate the power of using our bodies and collective action as resistance. These movements and interventions do more than just challenge injustice; they expose the systemic violence of capitalism and white suprem-acy while offering a vision of radical possibility.

From demanding self-determination of Black lives to calling out wealth hoarding and economic disenfranchisement, direct action reframes the public discourse, forcing a moral reckoning that can no longer be ignored. As seen through the work of the BlackOUT Collective and the broader Movement for Black Lives, these interventions remind us that real change demands a radical reimagining of society. Through bold and unyielding resistance, these movements and interventions push the boundaries of what is possible, laying the foundation for a future rooted in justice, liberation, and collective power.

The Messenger Matters: Influencer Partnerships as a Tool for Narrative Change

By Olivia Blocker and Jessica Jewell

Our contemporary understanding of an influencer is inextricably tied to social media. Still, social movements have always had a role for those with robust, engaged audiences who can harness their relational power to effect action and social change. With the rise of social media, everyday people now have access to a level of influence that, historically, often only celebrities—those with wealth and fame—could wield. This chapter analyzes how social movements have leveraged influencers across time and technology, and how organizers today can use these strategies to build narrative power.

The Legacy of Celebrity in Social Movements

Individuals with wealth, status, and fame have often served as barometers for the palatability of social movements and the strength of their narrative power. Just as barometers measure changes in atmospheric pressure to predict weather shifts, a celebrity's support can signal a shift in public opinion or bring attention to emerging social issues.

In 1987, Princess Diana was invited to open Middlesex Hospital's first dedicated ward for AIDS and HIV-related diseases. She was famously photographed and interviewed while visiting an HIV-positive patient in his hospital bed, propelling her into the role of celebrity advocate for those suffering from the AIDS epidemic. In 1991, she spoke at the Children and AIDS Conference, stating: "HIV does not make people dangerous to know . . . you can shake their hand and give them a hug, heaven knows they need it. What's more, you can share their homes, their workplaces, and their playgrounds and toys."[1] Her actions were widely considered to have significantly shifted the narrative around the communicability of HIV/AIDS, encouraging compassion and respect at a time when dominant government and media narratives encouraged stigma, discrimination, and homophobia.

Princess Diana used her considerable influence to bring necessary attention to a highly stigmatized and deliberately disregarded issue. But her activism was made possible only because the communities most impacted by HIV/AIDS nurtured a movement that countered homophobic, victim-blaming narratives and laid the groundwork for celebrities to feel safe enough to become advocates. By 1987, queer and trans communities had spent years developing mutual-aid networks and community resources and lobbying to have HIV and AIDS research funded. Activists like Bobbi Campbell and Larry Kramer staged protests, formed organizations like AIDS Coalition to Unleash Power (ACT UP), started movements like the People with AIDS Self-Empowerment Movement, and wrote editorials and pamphlets on safer sex practices.

There is a moment, a cultural tipping point at which the risky becomes reasonable, the radical becomes respectable, or the socially precarious becomes courageous, cool, or even coveted. Six weeks after Princess Diana's initial interview in 1991—and six years after the beginning of the AIDS epidemic—President Ronald Reagan gave his first public speech about AIDS and, soon after, signed an executive order creating the first Presidential Commission on AIDS.[2] This is not to suggest that Princess Diana's actions inspired President Reagan, but rather that her actions—while brave and impactful—were less the radical ignition of a cultural revolution and more a reflection of an already-shifting tone around HIV/AIDS made possible by years of queer-led grassroots organizing.

Celebrities do not fuel social movements—that power lies with people. Celebrity influence is a strategic tool that movements can leverage, but it also exalts the power of the wealthy and reinforces an entrenched culture of bootstraps individualism, in which success is often seen as a result of individual effort and failure as a lack of it.

Celebrities are not the only ones who have held the power of influence. Even within our movements, the balance of charismatic leadership and collective power sharing has always been a struggle. Civil rights leader and lifelong organizer Ella Baker famously critiqued the celebrity leadership styles of primarily male civil rights leaders: "To be very honest, the movement made Martin [Luther King Jr.] rather than Martin making the movement. This is not a discredit to him. This is, to me, as it should be."[3]

Through much of social-movement history, the opportunity for an individual to build the power of influence without the benefit of wealth was rare. Over the last decade, however, social media has acted as a democratizing force, allowing almost anyone—regardless of economic and social status—access to influence.

Organizing in the New Epoch of Social Influence

In the early 2000s, when MySpace and Facebook became our new virtual town squares, we saw a seismic shift in sharing information, building community, and relating to one another. Though initially intended for staying in touch with family and friends, social media widened our spheres of connection to more diverse communities across neighborhoods, state lines, and national borders.

Any teenager with access to their parents' dial-up desktop computer could suddenly reach hundreds or thousands of people across the globe. Today, we all carry tiny supercomputers in our back pockets, and people can build an audience of millions. Celebrities used to hold exclusive access to this social power, but social media's democratization of influence allows organizers to shift away from using celebrity influencers and toward finding impactful, resonant, and influential movement messengers.

Case Study No. 1: Fridays for Future Campaign

In 2018, a young high-school student began a solo student strike: skipping school to sit outside the Riksdag (Swedish parliament) and demanding stronger action on climate change from her government. A then-fifteen-year-old, Greta Thunberg posted a picture of herself striking on her Instagram and Twitter—images that were quickly reposted and shared by high-profile Twitter accounts, one of which had upwards of 200,000 followers. By her fourth day of striking, Greta was joined by an additional thirty-five people outside the Riksdag in what would become an ongoing weekly protest: the global Fridays for Future student strike.[4]

As a youth-led movement, Fridays for Future undermined the dominant narrative that climate policy and global politics are too complex for young people to understand, and that adults are more informed and better suited to create effective policy. World leaders openly mocked the student strikes. In February 2019, then–UK prime minister Theresa May said that youth-led climate protesting "wastes lesson time."[5] In October of the same year, Vladimir Putin implied that Greta Thunberg was being manipulated and did not understand complex global affairs.[6]

Fridays for Future was massively successful. In March 2019, six months after Thunberg's first solo protest, a global strike gathered more than one million people across 125 countries.[7] Subsequent strikes over the following months garnered millions more. While the actions did not create specific policy changes or keep the global temperature rise below 1.5°C,[8] the global movement and, arguably, Thunberg's rise to fame worked to undermine the paternalistic, adultist narrative that youth cannot understand the complexities of international climate policy. This narrative shift asserted that climate change is, first and foremost, a youth issue and that young people have the power to effect change.

Of course, Thunberg was not the only reason the climate strikes were successful. She was building on the momentum of years of youth-led campaigns like #NoDAPL (protesting the Dakota Access Pipeline) and March for Our Lives. The #NoDAPL campaign stands as one of the most recognizable social-media campaigns of the last twenty years in no small part due to young people from the Standing Rock Reservation taking to social media to use the #NoDAPL hashtag.[9] Thunberg has also explicitly stated how she was inspired to action by youth activists out of Parkland, Florida, who organized the March for Our Lives rally for greater gun control.[10] In addition to the political context of her activism, Thunberg's protest came after the hottest summer Sweden had seen in more than 250 years, making her message particularly resonant.[11] Thunberg alone did not make the Fridays for Future strikes possible. However, as an influencer in the climate movement, she plays a unique role—not only as a mobilizer but also as a discrete example of youth voice and organizing power that works to undermine dominant adult narratives.

Case Study No. 2: The #StopLine3 Campaign

From #NoDAPL to Fridays for Future and throughout the 2010s, X (formerly Twitter) served as one of the leading social-media platforms where organizers and movement workers could grow their audiences and influence. Post-2020, short-form video content engaged a new generation of audiences and, once again, redefined our cultural understanding of influencers.

The Stop Line 3 campaign began in 2019, but it wasn't until 2021 that resistance to Enbridge's Line 3 oil pipeline catapulted onto the social-media center stage. Years after the initial campaign launch, influencers with a dedicated following took to social media to get #StopLine3 trending. Creators from across the country jumped on the #StopLine3 hashtag, growing awareness about how this multibillion dollar project would transport 760,000 barrels of crude oil over 200 bodies of water through treaty territory between Canada and the United States. Enbridge's Line 3 would endanger the water of millions and spew the equivalent of forty-five new coal-fired plants of climate-accelerating emissions into the atmosphere.[12]

The #StopLine3 campaign worked to subvert dominant narratives about the necessity of oil pipelines and fossil-fuel use. One of the dominant narratives reinforced by Enbridge's Line 3 construction was the idea that the oil industry creates jobs and economic opportunities for Indigenous people. Enbridge boasts of $378 million in economic opportunities for Tribal nations, Tribal members, and Native American–owned businesses, and more than $41 million in wages to Tribal members who worked on the pipeline.[13]

However, not all jobs are good jobs, and the fossil-fuel industry is one of many sectors that hides environmental or social harms behind a narrative of economic benefits. Winona LaDuke, an Ojibwe leader and Indigenous rights organizer, countered this narrative in an interview with Slate by advocating for alternative clean-energy economies: "We need [a just transition] in northern Minnesota, and we need it now. Or else we're gonna spend the rest of our lives fighting over pipes and mines and for a fifth of the world's water. What we need is to build a just transition of local food, local energy, energy efficiency, renewable energy."[14]

Advocates of the pipeline also deployed a xenophobic narrative around energy independence and national security. By asserting that pipelines are necessary infrastructure to reduce our dependence on foreign oil that keeps us at the mercy of unstable geopolitics,[15] Enbridge and its advocates were able to distract public discourse from Line 3's $7.3 billion price tag.[16]

To counter these dominant narratives, the campaign used the #WaterIsLife hashtag—popularized in 2016 by the #NoDAPL campaign—and the #StopLine3 campaign slogan. The narrative that water is a human right resonated across the political spectrum, with 9 in 10 voters agreeing that safe access is fundamental,[17] and served as a central message to move audiences to action. Messaging about Line 3's threat to drinking water drove thousands of signatures to the Biden administration.[18] In addition to reaffirming the counternarrative that water rights are human rights, #WaterIsLife exposed the patterns of exploitation of Indigenous water and land, reengaged supporters of #NoDAPL, and otherwise kept the organizing momentum of #NoDAPL going.

The campaign also worked to reframe the pipeline construction in the larger context of ongoing, U.S.-sponsored genocidal policies and the exploitation of extractive, privatized industries on Indigenous land. Organizers and influencers of #StopLine3 directly referenced the fact that the pipeline would cross the 1855, 1854, and 1842 treaty areas, and that Enbridge was required to have a permit from the sovereign Ojibwe nation to build.[19] Messaging around Line 3's violation of treaty-protected traditional foods for the Ojibwe people also reinforced counternarratives of the fossil-fuel industry infringing upon Indigenous land and food sovereignty.[20] Stories about how pipeline worksites were vehicles for human trafficking helped shine a light on the increase of missing and murdered Indigenous women.[21]

To amplify coalition counternarratives, organizers of the Stop Line 3 campaign partnered with the Water Hub, a nonprofit communications organization, to engage with influencers. Two such influencers were ClimateDiva—also known as Summer Dean—a Black climate educator and advocate for sustainability in fashion, and—zentouro—also known as Miriam Nielsen—a YouTuber, climate researcher, and PhD candidate in earth and environmental sciences at Columbia University. Zentouro visited the front lines in person to do original reporting, and ClimateDiva shared top lines of the impacts on water, land, and people in her TikTok and Instagram reels. Through storytelling, they reached new people and raised awareness about the fight for climate justice. The sentiments in the comment section were positive—many people had never heard about Line 3—which speaks to the value of reaching different audiences through influencer strategies.

By intentionally partnering with influencers to engage with their audiences, Stop Line 3 organizers had more tools to incorporate messaging into the public discourse, a strategy #NoDAPL organizers didn't have access to in 2016. With short-form social video taking off, this moment created opportunities for people left out of mainstream media to grow an online presence and spur hundreds of thousands into action. Young water protectors, like Giiwedin, who were devoted to the front line, shared stories about how Line 3 threatened water, people, and climate. Influencer video content on Instagram and TikTok offered more personal and accessible storytelling and helped elevate the conversation in digital spaces, alerting younger audiences online of the campaign and organizing efforts, and resulting in thousands of petition signatures.

Unfortunately, the Stop Line 3 campaign was unsuccessful. Today, hundreds of thousands of barrels of tar sands crude oil flow through the Line 3 pipeline, also known as Line 93, threatening the safety of lakes and streams, violating treaties, and further entrenching our energy investments in fossil fuel infrastructure. Despite being unable to stop its construction, #StopLine3 played a critical role in amplifying the counternarratives that water rights are an extension of human rights and that the fossil fuel industry's exploitation of resources is merely a continuation of the genocidal policies upon which the United States was built.

Conclusion

As our technology and our understanding of audience and narrative power have changed, so has our understanding of who wields influence. Regardless of how it may shift in the future, it is important to understand the role of social and political influence, and how to develop digital strategies that benefit our social movements. Integrating influencers into our campaign strategies can help build an ecosystem of storytellers that can broaden and diversify our audiences, decentralize messaging away from a single campaign voice, break messaging out of digital echo chambers, and even disrupt online algorithms that dictate what content we see and from whom.

Whether it's a water protector fighting the construction of a pipeline or teenagers organizing a climate strike at their school, progressive movements can lean in to the future of digital-campaign strategy and partner with influencers who are impacted by the issues they campaign around. Building narrative power requires understanding influence in both offline and digital spaces, and to help push our movements forward, organizers need to harness the relational power of socially engaged influencers.

Tips for Working with Influencers

1. Do your research: Identifying influencers to partner with on your campaigns takes time and a lot of scrolling through feeds. Are you hoping to work with someone from the Gulf South? Or perhaps you're looking for an influencer with intersecting passions such as labor rights. Finding the right person is essential, so give yourself time and space to do it right.

2. Watch out for co-optation: Before reaching out, look at people's feeds carefully. After looking more closely, you might be surprised to find that this person might be doing brand partnerships with corporations that are out of alignment with your values.

3. Give creative freedom: Influencers have the trust of their audiences because they are real people with their own voices. Provide some guidelines but encourage (and trust) them to deliver the message in their own words for the best results.

4. Build authentic relationships: Don't be transactional and reach out only when you have a request! Comment on people's content or email "congrats" when you see them succeed.

5. Be a resource: Influencers don't have the same access to information or capacity as traditional journalists. We've heard feedback that sometimes even getting a new fact sheet or an invite to a media briefing helps people who've been gatekept. Showing up in a spirit of reciprocity goes far.

GLOBAL PERSPECTIVES

The Narrative Influence of #EndSARS: How Young Nigerians' Advocacy Against Police Brutality Went from Twitter to the Streets

By Oluseyi Adegbola, Adeola Abdulateef Elega, and Habibah Ayinke Taiwo

On September 19, 2020, members of the Nigerian Special Anti-Robbery Squad (SARS) shot and killed Daniel Chibuike, a promising twenty-year-old recording artist fondly called "Sleek." Media reports suggest that Daniel and his friends were accosted by members of a SARS squad patrolling the area but ran away, fearing for their lives due to previous reports of extrajudicial killings by SARS. The officers gave chase, raised an alarm referring to the young men as thieves, and eventually shot Daniel—even rejecting pleas to get him medical treatment until he bled out and died in the police vehicle.

Angry Nigerian youth flooded the streets: first in Lagos, the economic capital of the nation, before spreading to other cities. They protested under the #EndSARS banner and called for the scrapping of the police squad. Thus began a series of protests to disband and dismantle the SARS police unit, which had earned a reputation for arresting, torturing, and killing Nigerian youth with impunity. The protests continued for weeks, garnering local and international attention and support, and forcing concessions from the government, including the dissolution of SARS.

In this chapter, we will outline the sociopolitical context within which the events leading to the #EndSARS movement occurred and situate the #EndSARS movement within the broader quest for human rights, justice, and accountability in Nigeria. Further, we will discuss key attributes of the movement and consider the roles of social media and alternative news platforms, as well as population characteristics that contributed to the diffusion and success of the protests. Last, we share lessons from the movement and future trends.

Protests on October 20, 2020, at the Christian Missionary Society junction in Lagos, Nigeria, hours before the Lekki Massacre that left at least twelve protesters dead at the hands of the Nigerian Army. Photo by Emeka Mbaebie

The costs of collective action tend to be notably high in less democratic regimes like Nigeria, where dissent is not tolerated. However, a wide-ranging coalition of diverse activist groups led by Nigeria's youth played a crucial role in expanding the reach and success of the #EndSARS movement. They achieved this by courageously speaking truth to power, challenging the established order, and constructing a narrative that emphasized how the people's discontent and suffering outweighed the potential consequences of state repression.

Repression and Democracy in Nigeria

The move toward democratization in Nigeria has witnessed numerous ups and downs. Shortly after the country gained its independence from the United Kingdom in 1960, it witnessed the first military coup, followed by a civil war from 1967 to 1970. From 1970 to 1999, Nigeria experienced a series of oppressive military dictatorships, with the exception of a brief period from 1979 to

1983, when there was a democratic government. The third democratic republic, which emerged during this time, was unfortunately cut short by a military coup. This period of military rule was characterized by an utter disregard for human rights, including the imprisonment, torture, and assassination of multiple private citizens, journalists, and human-rights activists.

The year 1999 marked a watershed moment with the handover of power from a military to a democratically elected government in Nigeria. Further, in 2015, the country witnessed the first time an incumbent president would be defeated in a competitive election. This development contributed to a growing sense of hope about Nigeria's trajectory toward increased democratization. Despite these milestones, Nigeria ranks poorly on most indices of democratization. It is categorized as a *hybrid regime* (implying that it retains several attributes of authoritarian rule and is yet to fully embrace democratic norms, such as free and fair elections, accountable government institutions, respect for the rule of law, and political pluralism).

Nigeria is also a *gerontocracy,* a system of government characterized by the rule of significantly older members of the population, especially old and wealthy men. For instance, since its return to democratic rule, Nigeria has been governed primarily by old men, including individuals who had formerly ruled as military dictators at the state and national levels. This is so despite the fact that youths aged eighteen and below account for more than half the country's population, while more than 70 percent are under thirty.[1,2,3] While recent advocacy for greater youth empowerment and political involvement has drawn attention to the issue,[4,5] whether or not these efforts are effective remains to be seen.

Despite prior concerns about youth disengagement from politics in Nigeria, the #EndSARS movement was powered by young, disenfranchised, and economically vulnerable Nigerians, especially those between eighteen and thirty-five years of age who had borne the brunt of SARS' brutality.[6,7] Further, women played a crucial role in mobilizing the #EndSARS movement,[8] continuing a long-standing pattern of women's involvement in collective action in Nigeria despite being less involved in conventional politics.[9] Social movements dating back to pre-independence Nigeria, such as the 1929 Aba Women Riot, as well as recent events such as the #bringbackourgirls campaign, have further shown that despite how sudden, informal, and temporary protest coalitions are created, Nigerian women play pivotal roles.

#EndSARS: From Crime Fighting to Rogue Unit

SARS was established in 1992 to address armed robberies and other major crimes. The Criminal Investigation Department (CID) had primary responsibility for fighting armed robbery; however, as the scale and sophistication of weapons used in armed robbery and banditry increased in southern Nigeria, it became necessary to establish a unit that would focus solely on this growing challenge.[10] Despite an obvious lack of confidence in law enforcement's competence or capacity to protect citizens and a resulting growth of vigilante groups and unregulated militias in various communities,[11,12] no public input was requested or considered in the creation of SARS.

The government narrative positioned SARS as a unit that would operate outside of the constraints that typically limit conventional law enforcement. The goal was straightforward: Create a special unit with the training, tactics, and weapons to take on violent, organized crime as well as criminal groups that were increasingly better armed than members of the general police force. Moreover, the SARS unit was granted broader powers than other units of the police force to arrest and investigate suspected criminals.[13]

Using these powers, SARS officers began to extort money and valuable items from citizens, arbitrarily setting up roadblocks to stop, accuse, search, and demand bribes from motorists. An investigative report concluded that SARS and other police-force units collected 9.35 billion naira, equivalent to about $60 million at the time, by extorting Nigerians.[14] SARS officers also extensively used profiling, frequently arresting young people who possessed luxury items, such as jewelry or expensive gadgets. SARS officers detained and accused them of being criminals, and tortured them until they were forced to pay a ransom.[15]

Most important, a catalog of cases involving extrajudicial killing by SARS may have been the final straw. These killings often followed unfounded accusations or unwarranted arrests by SARS officers or were explained away as occurring due to mistaken identity, as was the case in 2010 when SARS officers shot and killed a fifteen-year-old boy at his school and claimed they mistook him for a criminal.[16] Ultimately, the lack of justice for victims of SARS in Nigeria's broken judicial system, prior promises yet failure to dismantle

SARS, and despair over the possibility of reforming the police unit contributed to calls for sustained protests.

#EndSARS: From Twitter to the Streets

Although the most recent iteration of protests against the SARS unit has garnered much attention, calls to end police cruelty and abuses of human rights by police units such as SARS predate the 2020 movement. From popular music calling out the activities of the SARS unit[17,18] to legal action taken against the Nigerian police (specifically SARS), calls to put an end to SARS' brutal activities had grown over the last decade. However, in 2017, following the release of footage said to show SARS brutally killing Segun Awosanya, a young Nigerian activist and businessman, a petition and social-media advocacy campaign to scrap the police unit was launched. The campaign, which used the #EndSARS hashtag, soon gained momentum and was picked up by prominent local and foreign media outlets, including the BBC News and Al Jazeera.

The initial campaign to #EndSARS was accompanied by the sharing on social media of personal experiences with SARS officers, renewed media interest, coverage of previously unreported atrocities committed by SARS, and calls to scrap the police unit by some elites, including members of the Nigerian Senate and House of Representatives.[19] Efforts by the Nigerian police to discredit the movement through their public relations unit, including by characterizing participants as miscreants, were unsuccessful. This was possibly due to a history of distrust between Nigerians and the police[20] and the fact that the #EndSARS movement was rooted in and reflected the lived experiences of many Nigerians. Despite gaining traction on social-media platforms, focusing attention on the issue, and generating debate about whether and how to reform SARS, the movement never translated to offline action.

An important trend to note is the ebb and flow of public opinion and support for disbanding SARS. These shifts in public opinion were often tied to heavily publicized stories of SARS brutality, resulting in widespread outrage on one hand or announcements about the arrest of feared criminals by SARS, which was then used to enhance its image. One instance of the latter involves the 2017 capture of a notorious kidnapper and robber popularly known as Evans, who was apprehended by the unit after years of pursuit. Such events were routinely used to highlight the need for SARS, draw on a "law and order" narrative, and, more subtly, frame SARS' excesses as fundamental to its goals. Regardless, the #EndSARS movement was able to connect the diverse individual stories and experiences of police brutality into a collective, coherent narrative.

The killing of Daniel Chibuike by SARS operatives in 2020 revived calls to disband SARS. But, unlike the initial campaign of 2017, which was limited to online activity, the 2020 #EndSARS campaign gave rise to offline protests. Over the next couple of days after the killing of Daniel, new reports and candid videos, often captured using smartphones, began to emerge about the SARS squad's extrajudicial killings of Nigerian youth. These reports, including graphic images and gory video scenes of SARS' victims, were shared widely on social-media platforms, including WhatsApp, Facebook, and Instagram, as well as on alternative-news websites.

Prominent individuals, including activists, celebrities, popular musicians in Nigeria, and opposition party politicians, renewed calls for the reformation or dissolution of SARS, but now with more urgency than before. Using the #EndSARS hashtag, Nigerians began to express anger at police brutality and specifically at SARS. This was accompanied by weeks of offline protests calling for the disbanding of the squad and more accountability on the part of law enforcement.

While we can only speculate regarding the different trajectories and outcomes of the 2017 and 2020 efforts to disband SARS, some seemingly small yet noteworthy trends may have helped translate widespread anger into action in 2020. First, the ongoing expansion of and access to internet-connected mobile phones in Nigeria and other countries in sub-Saharan Africa has undeniably contributed to the enhanced ability to share information and mobilize for collective action. Second, the economic downturn in Nigeria, accompanied by high levels of youth unemployment, suffering, and disenchantment with the political system between 2015 and 2020, may have helped position protest as a costly yet necessary option for citizens, given the use of violence to quash previous protests. Finally, the transnational effect of the Black Lives

Matter movement as a catalyst for resistance and collective action against police brutality in other countries must be noted.

While the 2020 popular movement to #EndSARS was not the first time there had been such demands, it was inarguably the most sustained, consequential, and far-reaching in its appeal. As #EndSARS protests rocked major cities in Nigeria, Nigerians in the diaspora—from New York to Washington, DC, to London—held protests to demonstrate solidarity with the movement. Given the Nigerian government's track record of making concessions and backtracking, neither its promises to disband SARS nor its imposition of curfews could deter protesters. On October 20, 2020, the Nigerian army opened fire on nonviolent protesters, killing twelve individuals and injuring several others, according to an Amnesty International report. Despite finding the Nigerian army culpable in the killing of more than a hundred protesters during the series of protests, little has been done to hold the security forces responsible.

Why #EndSARS Was Successful in Cultivating Narrative Influence

Whether the #EndSARS movement was successful depends on who is describing it and by what metrics it is evaluated. While many may have described it as a success, others have reservations. For example, Allwell Uwazuruike, a human-rights advocate and on the faculty at Georgetown University, described it as a partial success because police brutality, which was the primary motivator for the protests, is still commonplace in Nigeria.[21] While this is an understandable position, our metric for tagging it as a success includes: (1) speaking truth to power, (2) challenging the status quo, and (3) building a narrative voice. Based on these three positions, we believe it was an outright success.

First, the majority of the #EndSARS protests in major cities around Nigeria were organized and powered by large but decentralized groups of young Nigerians. As noted earlier, young people, especially young men, constitute the primary victims of police brutality and extrajudicial killings by SARS. However, beyond the core of young protesters was a coalition of diverse activist groups and influential voices in opposition politics, the media, and the entertainment industry who helped broaden the movement's appeal and amplify its voice in a manner unlike other protests. Further, while previous protests in Nigeria have been violently repressed, often by military forces, the decentralized nature of the #EndSARS protests may have presented unique challenges to the government. Decentralized protests often defy repressive action, due to the lack of formal hierarchy or identifiable leaders who would otherwise be arrested to weaken the movement.

Apart from the efforts to combat police brutality, the youth-driven protest has a subtext and can be interpreted as the awakening of youthful populations that may have been typically taken for granted.[22] This has also been seen in other countries where young people rise against repressive governments.[23,24] This challenge to the status quo in Nigeria by an otherwise taken-for-granted group, coupled with the power of a clear and concise value-based slogan, was also highly instrumental in the protest's success. More important, it helped the movement build and maintain a voice. A popular protest slogan—*Soro soke*—is a Yoruba term that means "Speak up" and came about as a rebuttal to the culture of silence, thought to be pervasive among members of the older generation. Youth declared themselves through the slogan as the generation who would speak up against impunity and citizenry sabotage. This not only helped build unity among protesters, but it also helped young people to positively self-represent, reject injustice, clarify their mission and vision, and challenge the status quo.[25]

Furthermore, the absence of religious sentiments, political polarity, and other issues historically used as a tool to "divide and rule" helped propel the movement. This is significant because, historically, power-rich incumbents in Nigeria have weaponized religion, Tribal loyalties, and political affiliation to undermine dissident activities and sow discord among protesters. The #EndSARS protests were unique in this sense. It was not out of place to hear protesters singing Christian hymns and songs while marching, or Christian protesters forming human barricades to enable their Muslim co-protesters to finish their prayers.

In addition, the affordances of the democratized nature of social media, especially Twitter, played a major part in the protests' success. The Nigerian Twitter/X space has empowered young opinion leaders, community organizers, and human-rights advocates whose collective voice played a major part in the protest in many ways. Specifically, Twitter was used in three distinct ways to advance the protests. First, it was used to organize protesters through mobilizing information, sharing live updates that potential participants used to weigh the potential for success and decide whether to participate, and securing resources to help sustain the protests. Second, Twitter was used to garner attention and sympathy for the #EndSARS cause beyond the boundaries of Nigeria. In a semi-authoritarian system characterized by state ownership or control of much of the media apparatus, Twitter proved crucial for bypassing state-imposed media blackouts.

Finally, and in the same vein, Twitter was used to speak truth to power and challenge the state's narrative, in part by expanding the voices of dissent to include Nigerians in the diaspora and foreign actors—including the United States and other Western nations, nongovernmental organizations such as Human Rights Watch and Amnesty International, as well as prominent celebrities and activists who expressed their support for the #EndSARS protesters.[26] While the narrative of Nigerian law-enforcement agencies exploiting citizens for personal gain is not a new one and is heavily reflected in the local music and popular culture, the linkage of this narrative into a larger, more coherent transnational narrative of resistance to oppression and misuse of power was likely central to the success of #EndSARS.

Future Trends

What does speaking truth to power, challenging the status quo, building a narrative voice, and the overall success of the #EndSARS protest mean to Nigerian youth? It seems evident that the protest awakened a new consciousness and stimulated increased youth engagement and participation in politics. This interest carried on from 2020 to the 2023 general election in Nigeria, which featured unrivaled youth engagement through turnout as well as young people running for public office.

The participation of young people also powered a formidable third-party effort in what is typically a keenly contested election between the two major parties, the People's Democratic Party (PDP) and the All Progressives Congress (APC). Yet the 2023 election witnessed the resurgence of a competitive

Labour Party and its presidential candidate, Peter Obi, bolstered by heavy youth support. In an environment characterized by youth disengagement and distrust of the political system, Obi and his Labour Party mobilized a base of young activist supporters and drew on the momentum and radical vision of the #EndSARS movement.

Beyond the scrapping of the SARS unit and the spillover effect on the 2023 elections, we can only speculate about the long-term implications of the movement. Regardless, we believe the #EndSARS movement represents a small but significant step toward enduring, positive, people-powered change and a promise of subsequent resistance to other forms of political repression. The short-term benefit of youth political involvement, as seen in the 2023 election, could translate to more enduring youth engagement. In a political context in which activist forms of political action can be particularly costly, the #EndSARS movement could also have the effect of lowering the threshold for subsequent youth activism for social change.

The #EndSARS movement is no longer active, but it may set the stage for subsequent collective action. Given its relative success in terms of the attention drawn to the issue, the coalitions built, and the concessions from the state, it offers a blueprint for subsequent efforts by groups seeking to use protest or activism as a strategy. In many societies, protest is often used as a last resort, only when the potential cost of state repression outweighs discontent and suffering. Yet instances of effective collective action, such as #EndSARS, could normalize the expression of dissent as a viable strategy for social change. Moreover, the structure, strategy, and coalitions utilized by the movement to disband SARS could be applied to existing movements for women's rights, good governance, and election integrity, among other causes.

Black Bixas Blooming Self-Love and Affection

By Diego Cotta and Renata Saavedra

In the last decade in Brazil, there has been a growing movement of effeminate young Black gay men, or, as they prefer to be called, *Black bixas* (*bixas Pretas*), who are producing audiovisual content, especially through YouTube and other social media. In Brazil, *bixa* (or *bicha*) is a way of referring to effeminate gays, with grimaces and "feminine" gestures. It is a term with a class connotation: It points out an "exaggerated" queerness commonly linked to poor and peripheral gays, outsiders to a contained and normative aesthetic.

Black bixas are disseminating content centered on Afro and LGBTQI (lesbian, gay, bisexual, transgender, queer, intersex) folks, as well as discussing and promoting self-esteem, representation, self-care, and healing spaces. Their material is consumed by thousands of young Black gay men who will lead future generations. This digital Afro-gay scene is expanding antiracist and anti-cis-heteronormative narratives and life possibilities. It is a diverse and decentralized scene, united by collectivity, visibility, and affection.

Being Black Bixa/*Bixa Preta*

I as a Black gay, you as a Black gay, we have to love each other. . . . You are not alone! Chat with other Black gays, exchange your experiences. Understand that you are not a problem. . . . By changing behaviors, exposing this reality, we will make the world more comfortable and less oppressive for the next Black gays to come. So, value the Black bixa, value the effeminate gay, and love them![1]

These words are from Spartakus Santiago, a twenty-nine-year-old

YouTuber and advertiser from the interior of Bahia, in the northeast region of Brazil. He was born in the city of Itabuna, and his name was inspired by the Stanley Kubrick film *Spartacus* (1960). He was raised by his grandmother, Dona Lourdes. In childhood and youth, he had a difficult relationship with his father, who did not deal well with his homosexuality.

In late adolescence, he moved to Rio de Janeiro to study advertising at a federal university. He became famous after publishing a YouTube video about cultural appropriation by Brazilian companies, garnering more than four million views.[2]

Spartakus began posting videos on his YouTube channel in 2007, using the space to talk about his experiences, discussing the daily life and problems of Black gays across racism and LGBTQI-phobia, including interracial relationships, loneliness, masculinities, and cultural appropriation.

By October 2022, Spartakus reached more than 236,000 subscribers on YouTube and 411,000 followers on Instagram. He is one of the top twenty innovative Black creators in Brazil[3] and has a platform in the mainstream media.[4]

By identifying himself as Black bixa, Spartakus highlights an increasingly strong and visible community of Black bixas who are disseminating Afro and LGBTQI-centered content. In Brazil, the term *gay* is associated with normalized homosexuality—ideally white, middle or upper class, virile, and "top."[5] Gays frequently affirm themselves by denying bixas and "faggots," who are considered an affront to hegemonic masculinity and are ridiculed and even persecuted.

Effeminate gays suffer discrimination even among the LGBTQI community: In some spaces being gay is acceptable, unless you are "too gay," bicha, bicha *bichérrima*, or *viado* (the latter two being pejorative terms referring to "overly effeminate," exaggerated "faggots"). Faced with structural racism, Black bixas are radically dissident and are targets of even more mockery and disgust. Black men are commonly hypersexualized, facing a larger social expectation around masculinity and heterosexuality.

There is an old narrative rooted in racism, classism, and misogyny that normalizes ideas that Black bixas are unattractive, undesirable, powerless, and should be rejected. It shows that the advancement of the LGBTQI agenda in Brazilian culture largely guaranteed the normalization of mainstream gay culture (white, masculine, middle-class) but did not include those who fall outside of those tightly confined categories.

However, the expression has been given new meaning by the Black bixas themselves, who subvert the pejorative connotation and use it politically to assert their own existence and question exclusionary and colonial patterns. As Linn da Quebrada, multimedia artist and activist, sings in one of the hymns about Black bixas:

Strange, crazy, Black bixa from the favela,
when she's[6] passing by, everyone laughs at her face.
But pay attention, male, sit and watch your destruction.
Bouncing I'll pass and no one else will laugh.
If you're smart, you can see right away
that I'm not kidding anymore.
I will fuck it all.
Black bixa: bang-bang-bang![7]

Together, Black bixas share experiences of neglect, rejection, and hypersexualization of their bodies, changing the lens through which they see the world and themselves. These groups are creating space so that other Black gay men can build their own identities out of rejection and scarcity frames. They are creating new stories, and recovering ancestral knowledge, that demonstrate that Black bixas are desirable, creative, and potent, and should enjoy being themselves. They offer new perceptions and perspectives for young Black gays, weaving a language with which Black bixas can do more than struggle to survive: They can imagine and live futures of prosperity and beauty. They show that healing follows the path of mutual love among Black bixas. By telling these stories, they are building narrative power for a new way of being and existing, and for living with self-determination and daring to be oneself when your country does not accept you and your life is at constant risk.

Since 2010, a diverse and powerful scene of Black gay creators, YouTubers, and digital influencers has blossomed—showing thousands of effeminate young Black gays that they can be who they are and enjoy it, contrary to messaging from the dominant culture.

In this text, we present three of them: Spartakus Santiago (whom we've already discussed), Murilo Araújo, and Diego Mesquita. Murilo Araújo introduces himself as a Black and Christian bixa. He is a journalist, researcher, and creator of the YouTube channel *Muro Pequeno*, where he discusses issues connected to the daily lives of LGBTQI and Black people in Brazil. Diego Mesquita presents himself as a fat Black bixa from the suburbs of Rio de Janeiro, writer, photographer, and creator of the Instagram profile @pretasbixas. Altogether, they are three Black bixa content creators whose stories are subversive and counter to the status quo. They are painting new life possibilities for Black gay men in Brazil.

Resisting in a Racist, LGBTQI-Phobic, and Classist Country

Brazil is the Blackest country outside of Africa. It has the second-largest Black population in the world after Nigeria.[8] Black Brazil would be the world's eleventh largest country by population and the seventeenth largest economy in terms of consumption.[9] Yet, if you come to the country and look at television programming, news, magazines, the government, and the most affluent neighborhoods, universities, and companies, you would think that Brazil is white. This is a country with continental dimensions, and it's among the ten most unequal countries in the world. In the first year of the COVID-19 pandemic, 55.2 percent of Brazilian households, or the equivalent of 116.8 million people, lived with some food insecurity. Nine percent of them, or 19 million people, experienced hunger,[10] which disproportionately falls on households headed by women, Black people, or those situated in the Northeast.[11] In the same period, ten Brazilians became billionaires.[12]

Racism structures inequality in Brazil. Sueli Carneiro teaches us that the perversity of Brazilian racism resides in "the pathological denial of the racial dimension of social inequalities."[13]

The colonization of Brazil, which started in 1500, was based on the enslavement of kidnapped Africans and the genocide of the indigenous population. The country had more time under the slavery regime than without it. It has been only 133 years since the abolition of slavery, which lasted more than

300 years and ended without policies to integrate formerly enslaved people into society. On the contrary, the dehumanization of Black people has been perpetuated through the legal and medical systems, culture, and the media. All systems of power continue to oppress and criminalize Black lives. "Every police wagon has a bit of a slave ship."[14]

Yet we deal with the myth of racial democracy deeply rooted in Brazilian culture; this is the idea that racism does not exist. The concept of racial democracy originates in the books of Gilberto Freyre (1900–1987), an influential and pioneering Brazilian author. The concept continued to be reproduced in various social and political spheres, anchored in the belief that all people are equal and have access to the same opportunities, depending only on their own merit and hard work. It is also anchored in the idea that Brazil is a peaceful country, open to differences, and welcome to all people—even during colonization, when Indigenous people, Blacks, and whites lived in harmony. The strong racial mixing that characterizes the country would prove this harmonious coexistence.

The myth of racial democracy is a dominant narrative even today, deployed to argue against affirmative policies and actions. Many people still deny that racism exists in Brazil. And even among the people who recognize that racism is a reality, few recognize themselves as racist. This denial hinders broader national debate about structural racism.

Additionally, Brazil lives with the genocide of its Black youth: Seventy-seven percent of young people murdered in Brazil are Black. Every twenty-three minutes, a young Black man is murdered.[15] We also have the worst rates of violence against women and LGBTQI people; we are the fifth country in the global ranking of femicides and the world record holder in murders of transgender people. The dominant representations of the poor, savage Black and of the promiscuous, sick, caricatured gay replicate narratives of racism and LGBTQI-phobia that shape social imaginaries and materialize in daily death practices. Racism, LGBTQI-phobia, and classism intersect to limit Black bixas' lives in Brazil. They pave the way for the devaluation and degradation of Black bixas. The oppression and exclusion experienced by Black bixas frequently result in low self-esteem, leading to high rates of depression and suicide. The suicide rate among Black youth is 45 percent higher than that of white youth.[16] When looking specifically at young men, the rate goes up to 50 percent.

Many times, Black bixas cannot access the new stories that are being told about their power, beauty, and creativity due to poverty and limited access to education and the internet. Of the 13.5 million Brazilians living in extreme poverty, 75 percent are Black.[17] Blacks are also the majority (71 percent) of those who cannot access the internet daily. A 2022 study showed that 33.9 million people are offline, and another 86.6 million are unable to connect every day in Brazil.[18] Nevertheless, the gradual expansion of access to the internet and digital media in the last fifteen years was a milestone for the diversification of voices in the public arena.

Within this context, Black bixas resist and confront dominant narratives. They are affirming that racism exists and that we need to, and can, transform society and our parameters of humanity, masculinity, Blackness, beauty, and power. They do this by taking advantage of the explosion of the internet and diverse narratives in pop culture to organize online communities and promote visibility, representation, and resistance.

Stories of Collectivity and Affection

Young Black Brazilian gay effeminate men who have the courage to talk about themselves, their desires, and their projects on the internet are up against deep layers of racial hatred, misogyny, and colonialism. They challenge this not necessarily by discussing hate and racism but by talking about music, pop culture, and humor. Spartakus, for example, talks about pop music on his channel. In an interview with Jup do Bairro and Linn da Quebrada, they discussed expression possibilities for Black bixas.[19]

Jup do Barro says, "Our intention is precisely to get us out of this place where we have always been placed, in a limiting and exhausting way, which is always talking about suffering. I was going to say it's about Blackness, gender, and sexuality, but it's actually about suffering, anyway. We can also talk about our victories, cooking, sports, psychoanalysis, etc."

Says Spartakus, "When we Black bixas have a voice, we always have to discuss the same topics. People dehumanize us; they think that we only live to talk about activism, that we don't have dreams, that we don't talk nonsense, that we don't laugh."

The aforementioned quotes show how the voices of Black bixas act as subversive forces and creators of new possibilities of expression and life. From invisible and voiceless people, who are often the target of jokes and mockery when they appear, Black bixas emerge, affirming their existence and the strength and diversity of their voices. With their proud presence and visibility, they reframe their Blackness, gender identity, and sexual orientation as a source of victory, not just suffering. And they go further, highlighting that their humanization implies their recognition as full and complex people who think, create, and feel beyond the markers of race, gender, and sexuality. Dreams, joy, and art are also part of their new stories. In the same video, talking about her song "Bixa Preta," Linn da Quebrada explains that the song was a way for her to name herself and "to create bridges with others that had identities, lives, and trajectories similar to mine, so that I could build achievements and healing processes. It's a dispute for power, it's a dispute for language, and it's a dispute for political and affective territory." Linn brings an important connection woven by the stories told by Black bixa creators. The political and the affective come together in the collective experience that Black bixas promote.

Murilo Araújo produces a playlist of music videos where he shares "songs to heal the soul." In October 2018, on the eve of the election of Jair Bolsonaro,[20] a homophobic, fascist, anti-Black authoritarian, Murilo Araújo left a musical message for his audience. "What am I going to say to the people at the *Muro Pequeno* [his channel] if Bolsonaro is elected?" he asked himself, wondering if he could bring any message of optimism and hope.

> It's time for us to get together, for us to build bonds of affection, for us to get closer to each other and make the message very clear: that we are going to continue here, and we are going to continue living. In a culture of death, living is civil disobedience. In a hate-promoting culture, loving is civil disobedience. And those are things we know how to do.

Then, with his boyfriend, Murilo plays and sings the song "Alegria, Alegria" ("Joy, Joy") by Caetano Veloso, which ends with: "I want to go on living, love. And I'm going. Why not, why not?"[21]

Murilo's message takes up the idea of joy and love, emphasizing that constructing these new narratives is necessarily collective. Proud presence and visibility cannot be achieved alone; it's something that happens in community, something that Black bixas "know how to do."

Diego Mesquita talks about the importance of this kind of content: Black bixas' love stories: "How in the midst of the chaos of several acts of violence are we going to be able to live affection among us Black bixas? Seeing Black bixas loving each other and living this affection will always be an act of resistance for me."[22]

Black feminists and Black women's struggles are important references for Black bixas. Conceição Evaristo, Djamila Ribeiro, and bell hooks, for example, are cited and recommended at @pretasbixas:

> To resist, we need to love each other; we need to be loved. We need affection. As much as the text "Living to love" by bell hooks is addressed mainly to Black women, it is impossible not to identify with their words. . . . I quickly remember the conversations I had with other Black bixas about loneliness and neglect. I remember that in addition to all the obstacles blocking our affections, we also deal with the white-centric romantic vision. We need to break with whiteness' control over our subjectivities. We need to love each other, we need affection between us.[23]

Self-love is built through a sense of belonging and group solidarity. This group solidarity generates a shared responsibility: As bixas committed to valuing and loving the community, each becomes responsible for the well-being of the others. In this sense, the digital spaces of Black bixas are also spaces of denunciation and visibility that protect them. These collective stories about love and affection retrieve ancestral knowledge and help preserve the memory of Black leaders, activists, and artists who came before and paved the way for Black bixas. They also drive new cultural and political initiatives led by Black bixas.

Black Bixas' Ancestral and Flourishing Pluriverse

The stories told by Black bixas question the colonial system as a universal project or the only one that is possible. And Black bixas' networks go beyond a campaign or an isolated initiative: They comprise a decentralized movement with gender, race, sexuality, age, territory markers, and statements. That is why we call Black bixa communities a pluriverse.

Defining *pluriverse*, the Colombian American anthropologist Arturo Escobar uses the explanation by Ejército Zapatista de Liberación Nacional: "A world where many worlds fit."[24] Escobar studies how Indigenous peoples and Afro-descendants (or Amefricans, as Lélia Gonzalez says) see and create the world from nondualist perspectives, presenting viable alternatives to the discourse and practices of the uniform world of colonialism and neoliberal globalization.[25]

These networks of Black bixas—effeminate, nonbinary, queer people—are being moved by radical communicators from different regions of Brazil who stand on the shoulders of pioneering bixas and *travestis* (men who dress in feminine attire), such as Madame Satã and Jorge Lafond.

Madame Satã was João Francisco dos Santos (1900–76), a drag queen, actor, and dancer who became one of the most representative characters of the outsider nightlife of Lapa in Rio de Janeiro in the first half of the twentieth century. He confused society by being both a feared *malandro* (trickster) and an assumed bixa, mixing characteristics considered feminine and masculine.

Jorge Lafond was Jorge Luiz Souza Lima (1952–2003), an actor, comedian, dancer, and drag queen whose main character was Vera Verão, the first Black bixa to stand out on Brazilian television. As Jurema Werneck and Black feminists teach us, "Nossos passos vêm de longe" ("our steps come from far away").

On @pretasbixas, Diego Mesquita highlights the legacy of Jorge Lafond:

> Jorge Lafond said that he was the target of prejudice for three reasons: being gay, being Black, and being an artist. Even so, he claimed that he did not care about the offenses he heard throughout his life and that he soon "put his hand in the face" of whoever

said something to him. At the height of the success, the name Vera Verão [Vera Summer] was often used in a pejorative way to offend gays, especially Black and effeminate ones. So keeping his memory alive is important to celebrate his life and remind us of the LGBTQI figures who paved the way for so many people.[26]

Mesquita also reveres other pioneers on his Instagram, such as Marsha P. Johnson[27] and the Brazilian funk artist Lacraia [Centipedes].[28]

Diego Mesquita, Murilo Araújo, and Spartakus Santiago are part of a broader and growing pluriverse of Black bixas, expressing themselves through YouTube videos, performances, writing, film, music production, collectives and online platforms. This pluriverse is stimulated by initiatives such as the Latinidades Pretas,[29] an online platform launched in 2020 to gather content, generate income, and support Black and Indigenous culture entrepreneurs. Latinidades Pretas was created by Instituto Afrolatinas and Feira Preta (Black women entrepreneurs' organizations). Its 2021 edition was entirely aimed at Black and Indigenous LGBTQIAP+ (lesbian, gay, bisexual, transgender, queer, intersex, asexual, pansexual, etc.) creators. One of them is the photographer from Bahia, Andre Medina,[30] whose photos from the essay "O Afeto Afeta" appear in this text.

They go beyond the internet and the digital world and create face-to-face social spaces like parties, such as Batekoo[31] and Baphos Periféricos;[32] and collectives like Afrobapho (Bahia), Amo Bixa Preta (Rio de Janeiro), AfroBixas (Distrito Federal), and Afronte (Goiás).

"You understand yourself as a Black bixa in the collective experience," says Vitor Hugo, age twenty-three, in the short film *Afronte*. Written and directed by Bruno Victor and Marcus Vinicius Mesquita, *Afronte* was conceived to show the multiple factors that interfere in the lives of Black gay people living in Brasília through different characters, mixing fiction and reality. Vitor, one of the interviewees, highlights the importance of being together as a way of self-knowledge and empowerment in the face of everyday oppression, citing the relevance of the Afrobixas collective in his process. Surviving a system based on structural racism depends on group solidarity. He says, "Are we Black or are we bixas? Are we both? Where can we be both in peace? Sometimes it's on the lap of a boy or a Black friend. Affection is transformative!"

Black Bixas Building Livable Spaces and Futures of Prosperity and Beauty

We echo Black bixas' community and creators: Healing follows the path of mutual love. Such stories and images embody the sorts of digital uprisings that take advantage of the wide reach provided by streaming platforms to affect hearts and minds and crack exclusionary visibility regimes. The mostly young audience that follows the stories produced by Black bixas have access to other forms of self-building. They promote a sense of belonging and pride. We believe that the cathartic narratives of the daily lives of Black bixas on YouTube can be understood as emotional communions.[33] They are spaces for Black bixas to talk about themselves and experience vulnerability, affection, self-care, and self-knowledge. They are also healing spaces. As bell hooks said, only love can heal the wounds of the past, and healing is an act of communion.

Black bixas show us, among other lessons, that the way to build narrative power is collective. According to the Narrative Initiative, "aspiring for narrative and cultural changes demands unprecedented levels of alignment, coordination, and creativity."[34] Transforming comprehensive and systemic narratives that define our personal and collective identities, inform our values and popular culture, and influence our policies requires collective and networked efforts. Kauan Almeida speaks of intuition and imagination as ways of accessing a new world, awakening "a creative force that exceeds the violence of identity, disrupting the representation and the capture of the racialized body within colonial prerogatives."[35] He is in a creative community with other Black bixas like Diogo Sousa, who claims that the story of Black gay resistance is formed in "first-person narratives that are collectivized from the recognition of other Black LGBTQI people." He says, "We pursue alternatives and narrative disputes that enable the radicality of Black life," assuming that "Black LGBTQI life carries important forms of destruction and construction for the formation of the world that breaks with cisheteronormative white centrism and assimilates other conditions of life."[36]

Gradually, Black bixas collect stories that create new images and shape beliefs. Theirs is a path that includes seeing and recognizing others, looking back at oneself, understanding oneself in the world, and building self-esteem and self-awareness in community. And so, they trigger behavioral changes and empower other Black bixas, expanding their alliances. Step by step, they conquer an indispensable field for any social change: the symbolic.

Models Ruan da Cruz and Ramiro Henrique pose for photographer André Medina's photo essay, "O Afeto Afeta" (Affection Affects), about Black gay love as a form of power:. The essay was made for the 2021 project Latinidades Pretas that featured and curated works from Black and Indigenous Brazilian artists. Photo by André Medina

Countering Fascism: Narrative Power, Social Movements, and the Fight for Justice in the UK and Poland

By Marzena Zukowska and Chantelle Lunt

February 2023 marked a turning point in the Liverpool City Region in the United Kingdom, when the fragile bubble of antiracist and antifascist solidarity burst. A city once infamous for its colonial past, Liverpool had seemingly redeemed itself in modern times. In the 1980s, Scousers (those born in Liverpool) united in opposition to Prime Minister Margaret Thatcher's policies of managed economic decline and the scapegoating of ninety-seven football fans who tragically died in the Hillsborough Stadium disaster.[1] Liverpool fans were falsely blamed and smeared by the police, media, and politicians.

The city's history of marginalization fueled its resistance to elite institutions, racism, and nationalism—an identity that solidified even more post-Brexit. Liverpool defied the national trend to leave the European Union with a 58 percent remain[2] vote during the Brexit referendum (10.1 percent higher than the UK average), and in 2018, Scousers famously drove out a "White Man March," forcing fascists to retreat to Lime Street train station's lost luggage section.[3] Yet this bolstered a sense of Scouse exceptionalism that ultimately harmed local leftist organizing. The discourse that Liverpool was an impenetrable left-wing haven misdirected many from the looming threat of fascism. So, when news broke in 2023 of a far-right riot outside a "Liverpool hotel"[4] housing people seeking asylum, many were shocked.

Initial reports were wrong; this didn't occur in Liverpool but in Knowsley, a borough that forms part of the Liverpool City Region. Knowsley, a borough with a 51.6 percent leave[5] vote, often ranks among the UK's most economically deprived regions and fits the profile of places regularly targeted by the far right. In 2019, far-right influencer Tommy Robinson targeted Liverpool City Region's perceived soft spots: Wirral, Sefton, Bootle, and Knowsley. While

Sefton and Bootle resisted, Knowsley saw crowds waving St. George's flags, associated with the far right, to welcome Robinson to Huyton, a ward in Knowsley. This was especially alarming given that the 2005 racist murder of Anthony Walker[6] took place in Huyton, revealing that too little had changed in the years since.

This visible resurgence of far-right organizing in Liverpool City Region was neither new nor unique to the UK. A year before the Brexit referendum sent shock waves across left movements, Poland had already signaled this shift in Europe's political zeitgeist. In October 2015, the right-wing Law and Justice Party won the majority of seats in the Polish Parliament. In their eight-year reign, they eroded the independence of the judiciary, fomented homophobic hate by warning of the dangers of an LGBT ideology, and effectively banned abortion.

The success of far-right politics in achieving mainstream appeal and even popular support during elections has been part of a broader global trend in the twenty-first century. Dominant narratives that play on existing racist, xenophobic, homophobic, and transphobic tropes while using divide-and-conquer tactics and fervent nationalism to pit communities against each other have been central to building power for the far right. The populist uptake of these politics is a direct result of narrative strategies rooted in fascist ideology.

Throughout this chapter, we use the terms *fascism* and *far right* interchangeably, as we believe they are cut from the same ideological cloth. There has been, however, a hesitancy among mainstream liberals and media to use the term *fascism*, instead opting for softer language, like *far-right* extremists and *populist right*. This is the result of skillful narrative strategies deployed by far-right groups to camouflage themselves as inherently antiestablishment freedom movements, "invok[ing] democratic values and claim[ing] to be the voice of the great mass oppressed by a powerful minority 'elite.'"[7] This echoes the words of philosopher Umberto Eco, who argued that it is enough for one characteristic of fascism to be present in order for the whole ideology to "coagulate around it."[8]

Poland and the UK tell a much larger global story of fascist resurgence in the twenty-first century—one that highlights the scale of the threat in Europe and the strategies for resisting it. In this chapter, we examine how fascist ideology today operates through a narrative lens, and how far-right groups across Europe have used these narratives to become increasingly organized and coordinated. We delve into the lesser-known history of fascist organizing in the twentieth century, showing how it laid the foundation for a global revival decades later. Finally, we present case studies on the abortion rights movement in Poland and the Black Lives Matter (BLM) uprisings in the UK. We demonstrate how these movements have built narrative power to counter fascism, reshape the political battleground for leftist movements, and safeguard progressive gains.

The History of Fascism: From Roots to Resurgence

Twentieth-Century Fascism Emerges

The race problem in which I was interested cut across lines of color and physique and belief and status and was a matter of cultural patterns, perverted teaching and human hate and prejudice, which reached all sorts of people and caused endless evil to all men.[9]

—W.E.B. Du Bois, 1949

In 1949, after visiting a Warsaw ghetto, W.E.B. Du Bois observed that hatred transcends physical attributes, targeting not only race but cultural differences. These patterns of prejudice have persisted throughout history, reverberating across Europe and the world today. To combat modern fascism, it's crucial to recognize these repeating patterns.

Fascism gained prominence in twentieth-century Europe, with Mussolini's Fascists rising to power in Italy in 1922 and Hitler's Nazis in Germany by 1933. Both movements exploited post–World War I economic instability, redirecting workers' anger toward socialists, immigrants, and Jews. Meanwhile, in the UK, a lesser-known chapter of fascism was led by Rotha Lintorn-Orman, who founded Britain's first fascist party, the British Fascisti, in 1923.[10] Her movement attracted former suffragettes and queer women but was soon overshadowed by Oswald Mosley's British Union of Fascists (BUF).

Mosley's BUF gained support from Mussolini and Hitler, pushing nationalist, isolationist, and anti-Semitic narratives.[11] Despite initial growth, the BUF's influence declined after antifascists triumphed at the 1936 Battle of Cable Street, and Mosley's movement was banned in 1940.

Post–World War II, fascism resurfaced, most notably in the UK during the 1948 riots against Black former soldiers and immigrants from the Windrush Generation—who had been invited over from Britain's colonies to either fight for or rebuild the UK.[12] The 1950s saw the rise of anti-immigrant sentiment that could easily rival United States segregation laws. Signs reading "No Blacks, No Dogs, No Irish" were commonplace in the windows of businesses. A.K. Chesterton founded the League of Empire Loyalists (LEL) in 1954, advocating for "white rule over Africa" and pushing a white supremacist agenda alongside anti-immigrant, antisemitic, and anticommunist sentiments. Despite promoting racial hierarchy, Chesterton allowed Jewish and nonwhite individuals to join the LEL, creating a façade of inclusivity that attracted support from mainstream right-wing politicians. Anti-immigrant rhetoric, like that promoted by the LEL, helped incite the 1958 Notting Hill race riots, a violent clash fueled by growing hostility toward Black immigrants. By 1964, this hateful discourse had permeated mainstream politics. Conservative MP Peter Griffiths famously used the slogan, "If you want a n***** for a neighbor, vote Labour," to win a general election. This slogan was a precursor to the deeply divisive and xenophobic political rhetoric that would follow, further embedding racism in British political discourse.

Shadow defense secretary Enoch Powell's infamous 1968 "Rivers of Blood" speech fueled racist fears, citing a constituent who claimed "the black man will have the whip hand over the white man" and spinning anecdotes about white Britons terrorized by Commonwealth migrants. Powell's rhetoric, devoid of evidence, played on racial anxieties, legitimizing fringe far-right ideologies.[13] His speech was divisive enough to trigger his resignation from the Conservative Party. Yet, it bolstered support for neofascist groups like the National Front (NF), which capitalized on the fear of immigration, gaining middle-class Conservative backing with its "Britain First" message.

In parallel, mainland Europe saw a surge in neofascist violence, with Italy's National Vanguard and Germany's National Democratic Party leading deadly attacks, while France's GUP targeted migrants. The NF became the

UK's most prominent far-right party in the 1970s but faced organized resistance from migrant communities and antifascists, notably during the Red Lion Square riot (1974), the Battle of Lewisham (1977), and the Southall riots (1979), where activists Kevin Gately and Blair Peach were killed. Despite this, far-right violence persisted, culminating in the rise of the British National Party (BNP) and the 1999 London nail bombings targeting minority and LGBTQ+ communities.

Post-9/11, the far-right shifted focus, reframing Muslims as the new threat to British culture, echoing the hateful, fear-based narratives that have long underpinned fascist movements in the country. As Du Bois warned decades earlier, hate continues to transcend color, finding new targets in each era.

Twenty-First Century: Resurgence of Fascism

I don't want my daughters to be hidden behind a burqa. I don't want to be forced to eat Halal. I don't want Sharia to replace the laws of the French Republic.

—Marine Le Pen, former far-right French presidential candidate[14]

In 2012, Marine Le Pen garnered 18 percent of the French vote in the presidential elections, placing the far-right Front National in third place on the ballot. Running on an anti-immigration and anti–European Union platform, Le Pen crafted the perfect symbol of a new enemy to scapegoat: Muslims. By playing on existing racist and Islamophobic tropes she was able to construct Muslims as the "foreign other" in contradiction with a country that prides itself on "secularism." The messaging Le Pen deployed relied on the narrative infrastructure of the War on Terror—built a decade earlier by the Bush administration in the United States—which has "continued to position Muslims as a threat to the global world order."[15]

Le Pen's promising yet unsuccessful run for president was a foreshadowing of what was to come. In 2020, political scientist Cas Mudde wrote that in the decade from 2010 to 2019, center-left parties were decimated in Europe, while three of the largest "democracies" in the world—Brazil, India, and the United States—saw far-right politicians seize governing power.[16] At the time of the writing of this chapter, in September 2024, Italy is led by the far-right, antimigration, and anti-LGBTQ+ Brothers of Italy party; their prime minister, Giorgia Meloni, denies that the party is neofascist despite its use of the same three-colored flame logo as do neofascist movements across the country. The far-right Alternative for Germany won its first state parliamentary victory since World War II in Germany. In the UK, the far-right Reform Party, led by Nigel Farage, became the first far-right party to gain parliamentary seats.

Many factors have contributed to this normalization of fascism. In the early 2010s, many European countries were reeling from the 2007–2009 Great Recession, which had caused unemployment to skyrocket and inequality to become further entrenched. Rather than challenging the root causes of the crisis—privatization and deregulation of corporations under neoliberal capitalism—many European countries responded by introducing "austerity" measures to effectively divest from public services like health care, social housing, and welfare.[17] While at this time, various antiglobalization social movements began to transform public perception of this inequality—15-M in Spain, Occupy Wall Street in the United States, the Arab Spring—blaming the 1 percent of people for hoarding the majority of the world's wealth,[18] far-right parties too exploited the political and social unrest with their narrative. Studies have shown that economic precarity is a big factor in explaining electoral support for the far-right.[19] Unemployment and feelings of economic insecurity are capitalized on to drum up hate against immigrants, as well as "globalism," which carries economic consequences such as the globalized import economy and social factors like increased migratory flows and multiculturalism."[20]

Economic precarity and anti-immigrant sentiments alone, however, do not explain the resurgence of the far right. Philosopher Lorenzo Marsili, author of *Planetary Politics*, argues that Europe's decline in global influence and perceived sense of privilege—a far cry from its empire-building past—has become the perfect breeding ground for a nationalist identity for the far right to coalesce around.[21] The nation-state provides a sense of social cohesion at a moment when the perceived gains by marginalized people are deemed threatening to a world that was constructed as white, cisgender, and heterosexual.

The construction of far-right social identity has required a revision of history. In Western Europe, this has manifested itself as colonial nostalgia—

both sanitizing and glorifying a violent colonial past.[22] In the UK, a 2014 YouGov poll found that 59 percent of the British public saw the British empire as something to be proud of, while 49 percent felt that colonized countries were better off because of it.[23] In Eastern European countries without the same imperialist past, we see a narrative of perpetual victimhood that has persisted throughout history. In Poland, the far-right Law and Justice Party (PiS) pushed a narrative of a "Poland in ruins"[24] that "remains constantly under attack—from the European Union, from its stronger neighbor Germany, from domestic minorities, refugees, and even the billionaire financier George Soros."[25] By invoking both a sense of "national greatness" and "national innocence," PiS has built a strong sense of right-wing populist nostalgia to serve its political agenda.[26] This revisionist history conveniently ignores the exploitation, oppression, and violence that were central to both colonialism and authoritarian rule, distorting the reality of these nations' roles in global power dynamics and erasing the lasting harms inflicted on colonized and marginalized communities.

As far-right parties continue to surge in Europe, their broad appeal, especially among working-class communities, extends far beyond the racist or antiestablishment rhetoric used by politicians who exploit crises and economic instability. Beneath the surface of "populist" far-right leaders—many of whom come from elite backgrounds and serve elite interests—are intricate networks, affinity groups, and strategic campaigns designed to mainstream fascism. Understanding the far right as social movement actors, deeply rooted in fascist ideology, dominant narratives, and organizing tools, is essential to building left power and to counter their influence effectively. The following case studies explore these dynamics further.

Case Study: Polish Abortion Rights Movement

In 2020, at the height of the COVID-19 pandemic, Poland's abortion rights movement reached a critical turning point, reshaping the social justice landscape both domestically and across the diaspora. With decentralized leadership, a focus on cross-issue solidarity, and powerful counternarratives, the movement successfully challenged the far-right Law and Justice Party (PiS) since 2016. It normalized the experiences of marginalized groups and redefined the political battleground, laying the groundwork for potential shifts in government.

Central to PiS's political strategy is religious nationalism, exemplified by the motto "God, Honor, Fatherland" (*Bóg, Honor, Ojczyzna*), which links Polish identity to Catholicism. This deep-rooted narrative has long shaped Polish politics, with the Catholic Church playing a key role in resisting Soviet occupation during the 1980s and collaborating with the Solidarity movement. By the early 1990s, after the fall of the Berlin Wall, abortion rights were sacrificed in a political compromise that rewarded the Church for its support against communism.[27]

In parallel, Poland has also grappled with its entanglement in global systems of white supremacy despite not holding colonies. Sociologist Bolaji Balogun explains that colonial economies influenced noncolonial European countries like Poland.[28] Though many Poles deny the existence of racism, citing the country's lack of colonial history, white supremacy is present in nationalist rhetoric and far-right gatherings, such as Poland's Independence March. Chants like "Not Islamic or secular but Catholic Poland" and "No to abortion" push for racial and cultural purity, demonstrating how religious nationalism and white supremacy converge to support a broader far-right agenda.[29]

Dominant Narratives

Dominant ideologies have paved the way for the fascist dominant narratives utilized by PiS. These dominant narratives not only magnify each other but have been deployed by an interconnected web for far-right politicians, local governments, Catholic Church leaders, think tanks, and state co-opted radio stations and media. Collaborating for their survival, these institutions built mutually assured alliances to reinforce each other's messaging and build a narrative infrastructure to uphold a fascist worldview.

The demonization of Black and Brown immigrants: The demonization of Black and Brown immigrants in Poland creates a clear "us vs. them" narrative, portraying Muslims and migrants of color as "backward," "dangerous," and "unclean." At the same time, white Polish people are seen as pure, Catholic, and patriotic. Though Muslims make up only 0.1 percent of the population,[30] this rhetoric frames them as a threat to Polish culture and national security. In the 2015 elections, PiS leader Jarosław Kaczyński used fear mongering about refugees to secure electoral victory. This anti-immigrant narrative has fueled far-right marches and contributed to the illegal pushback of refugees at the Polish-Belarus border, contrasting sharply with Poland's welcoming stance toward Ukrainian refugees.[31]

Far-right groups have extended this narrative of cultural purity to oppose abortion, portraying it as a threat to Poland's Catholic and traditional values. In their view, antiabortion policies are part of safeguarding the nation's moral and demographic integrity against progressive influences, aligning with their vision of a "pure" Poland.

Gender is an ideology: Poland has seen a rise of its own antigender movement, which has proclaimed that "gender ideology"—disguised as feminism and liberal politics from the West—is an attempt to dismantle traditional family values, such as Christian civilization, heteronormative gender roles, and nationalism. Initially, this narrative was used against reproductive rights, sex education, and the Istanbul Convention against gender-based violence. Proponents were labeled "murderers of the unborn" and "sexual degenerates" in parliamentary debates, right-wing media articles, and Catholic Church statements.[32]

By the 2019 parliamentary elections, the discourse shifted toward dehumanizing queer and trans people as an "LGBT ideology." Later that year, a well-known archbishop gave a sermon warning about the "rainbow plague," drawing links between LGBTQ+ communities and the communist "red plague," and echoing the anti-immigrant rhetoric of 2015.[33]

Counternarratives

"Could You Please Fuck Off," read a banner slogan at an October 2020 protest for abortion rights in Poland. Among others were *"Wypierdalać"* ("Fuck Off") and *"Jebać PiS"* ("Fuck PiS"), accompanied by similar call and response chants.[34] The vulgarity of the protest signs signaled a marked shift in activist discourse in Poland: Moving away from asking PiS to respect reproductive freedoms toward making clear that after four years of far-right onslaughts to control women's bodies, respectability politics were over.

Between 2020 and 2021, protests took place across hundreds of cities and towns in Poland and globally in response to a Constitutional Tribunal ruling that would ban and criminalize abortion in a country that already had some of the most stringent abortion laws in Europe. Behind many of the militant abortion rights protests was the Polish Women's Strike (*Ogólnopolski Strajk Kobiet—OSK*), a decentralized organizing network established in 2016 that grew out of waves of decentralized mobilizations. Between 2016 and 2020, the iconic black umbrella–wielding movement, alongside many other independent and local groups,[35] organized some of the largest and most creative protests the country had ever seen in response to countless legislative and constitutional attempts to ban abortion.[36]

By 2020, as the COVID-19 pandemic ravaged the country and dominated national headlines, anger had boiled over. PiS had already been in power for five years, and a constitutional abortion ban was the final straw. Marta Lempart, one of the leaders of OSK, summarized the national mood:

> Almost one million people were left out cold at the end of March, 15,000 businesses folded, people are dying, all of Poland is sewing masks, and yet our leaders concern themselves with banning abortion, sex education . . . instead of helping people, businesses, and the health care system. . . .[37]

To build a movement that could capture international media attention and maintain public momentum over two election cycles, the abortion rights movement had to develop counternarratives that satisfy the four functions of narrative power—agenda-setting, salience, persistence, and permanence.[38]

Agenda Setting: Abortion Rights Is a Global Issue

One of the great successes of far-right groups and parties in Poland has been their ability to set the agenda of political discourse, often leaving the political opposition to remain reactive. By accepting the terms of debate and not offering counternarratives rooted in progressive values, centrist, center-right, and liberal political parties and mainstream media have allowed fascist ideology to become legitimized, shifting public debate further to the right.[39]

When the first legislative attempt to ban abortion came down in September 2015, disguised as a citizen's initiative, it echoed the fears that many activists in Poland had for years. Abortion was already legal under only three circumstances, and the center-right Civic Platform—the ruling party and main opposition to PiS—had opposed the legalization of abortion during the entirety of their tenure from 2007 to 2015. With left and progressive political parties having lost significant seats in the Sejm, abortion rights activists looked beyond political avenues to "put [the] issue on the political agenda despite opposition from political elites."[40]

By April 2016, a legislative ban on abortion was introduced in the PiS-controlled Sejm, leading to protests across the country. As the bill came up for parliamentary debate, human rights groups and abortion rights activists, including members of the left political party Razem, began to mobilize in even greater numbers. The following two months saw a wave of large-scale grassroots demonstrations called *Czarny Protest* (Black Protest) and *Czarny Poniedziałek* (Black Monday), which drew crowds of more than 150,000 across 150 cities and villages. Donning all black and carrying black umbrellas, a sea of protesters took over public space, went on strike from work, and used their clothing to signal a national day of mourning. The protests utilized historical symbolism from the nineteenth-century Polish women's anti-Russian demonstrations and the 1975 Icelandic women's strike. The spectacles drew national and international headlines and went viral on social media under the hashtag #BlackMonday.

The newly formed OSK was able to solidify abortion rights as a national issue by framing it in the context of global women's rights. In 2017, they collaborated with women's rights activists from Argentina, including Ni Una Menos, which organized against femicide and violence against women, to launch an International Women's Strike. People mobilized and coordinated across twenty-eight other countries. Even today, abortion rights activists in Poland continue to wear the green bandanna in solidarity—a symbol of Argentina's abortion rights movement.[41]

Salience: We Have a Common Enemy

The movement was able to make abortion rights an issue relevant to and resonant with the broader public. First, they united the country in opposition to PiS by creating a mandate broader than abortion rights and building a common enemy. The movement spoke out in support of the independence of the judiciary, a free press, support for workers during the COVID-19 pandemic, and LGBTQ+ rights. Rainbow flags were frequently flown at protests, while

Marta Lempart, the co-founder of OSK, spoke about the intersections of her identities as a lesbian woman.

Grassroots groups that were part of the movement used and adapted religious iconography and nationalist symbols that had been co-opted by PiS, such as the *Solidarność* (Solidarity) movement logo or the rainbow-haloed Virgin Mary.[42] The movement's use of these symbols signifies their values and draws the curtain back on the far-right apparatus.

Persistence: Decentralized Organizing

From the outset, the Polish abortion rights movement was able to ground its messaging in diverse experiences across age, gender, sexuality, geography, and economic status. OSK successfully built a decentralized network that did not play into respectability politics or police the choice of messaging and direct actions done by grassroots groups. While the national group often led with slogans and imagery—"*Piekło Kobiet*" ("Women's Hell"), "*Ani Jedna Więcej*" ("Not One More"), or the iconic red lightning bolt—and distributed graphic materials and designs, local groups were able to tailor the messaging to their local needs. The embedding of new stories from the grass roots allowed abortion rights to stay on the agenda long-term. OSK had a Facebook Group where members would regularly upvote the most resonated messaging. At its peak, the organization mobilized tens of thousands of people into the streets in a matter of days.

The same was true for international solidarity. The Polish Women's Strike would do frequent callouts to local Polish feminist groups in other countries to stage direct actions in front of the Polish embassy; in the UK, a regular coalition of movement actors formed, centering on feminist politics and LGBTQ+ rights. Poland's abortion rights movement—and their decentralized organizing approach—further inspired the tactics of organizations like POMOC, which formed in 2020, in order to build solidarity between Polish and Eastern European immigrants and other marginalized communities in the UK, explicitly centering on intersectionality and antiracist principles.

Permanence: Shifting the Ground of Social Justice

By 2023, polls showed that 75 percent of people would vote in favor of legalizing abortion in Poland if a referendum were held,[43] illustrating how the abortion rights movement in Poland shifted voters' views on abortion. The

On October 24, 2020, more than 2,000 people rallied at the Polish Embassy in London in response to Poland's ban on abortion. The protest became one of the largest solidarity mobilizations among the UK's Polish diaspora. Photo by Angela Christofilou

far-right onslaught did not begin or end with abortion, and many groups formed over the years to challenge everything from borders regimes (Grupa Granica), racism and anti-Blackness (Alliance for Black Justice in Poland), and homophobia and transphobia (Grupa Stonewall). These movement actors built strong coalitions to challenge dominant narratives about Polish society enough to shift electoral outcomes. During the 2023 parliamentary elections, a coalition of left, centrist, and center-right political parties banded together to oust PiS from power, ending their eight-year reign. While threats remain—the new ruling government has been reluctant to propose legislation to legal-ize abortion, while the antiestablishment far-right Konfederacja won more seats in parliament than anticipated—the organizing engine of Polish social justice activism will likely not be deterred in the face of fascism.

Case Study: The Legacy of BLM 2020 in the UK

The racial trauma that triggered Black Lives Matter uprisings in the wake of George Floyd's murder was felt around the world as communities rallied against institutional and systemic racism. In the UK, campaigners worked to delegitimize narratives of police racism as solely an American problem, using social media to illustrate how the UK police forces, while less armed than their American counterparts, were just as capable of taking Black lives.

Since 1990, 189 people of color have died in England and Wales as a result of being in police custody or following police contact.[44] In 2016, former footballer Dalian Atkinson was tasered to death, while in 2018, Kevin Clarke said, "I Can't Breathe" while being restrained by nine officers before he died; both were suffering mental health crises at the time of their deaths. But it wasn't until the aftermath of 2020—and the organizing work of movements, groups, and formations like the BLM UK, Operation Withdraw Consent, Merseyside BLM, Inquest, and #KillTheBill—that the legitimacy and function of policing came under national scrutiny.

Despite the narrative power built by BLM and adjacent movements in the UK to challenge the legitimacy of policing, the movements missed an opportunity to contend with the resurgence of the far right. In 2023, the same year a groundbreaking report by Inquest revealed that Black people are seven times more likely to die than white people following restraint by police,[45] the far-right mobilized in the Liverpool City Region, fueled by propaganda about threats to white women and children. To delegitimize both institutions, we must understand their underlying narratives and ideologies.

No More Bad Apples

The 2020 UK BLM movement significantly shifted the conversation around policing by leveraging social media to bypass mainstream narratives and counter the police's "bad apple" theory. Antiracists used real-time footage to show that the problem was not a few individuals but the entire system—portraying the whole "orchard" as rotten. This strategy built public distrust in policing, forcing media and politicians to adjust their language. At an institutional level, it laid the foundation for an independent review by Baroness Louise Casey, conducted after the abduction, rape, and murder of Sarah Everard by a serving officer. The review found London's Metropolitan Police to be institutionally racist, misogynistic, and homophobic.[46] By 2023, identifying the police as a racist institution had become part of mainstream discourse in the UK.

The movement also sparked a national reckoning with colonialism. Calls

Black Lives Matter protest in London on June 3, 2020. Photo by Angela Christofilou

to #decolonisethecurriculum gained traction as BLM highlighted the colonial legacy embedded in the UK education system. A pivotal moment occurred on July 7, 2020, when demonstrators in Bristol toppled the statue of slave trader Edward Colston, tossing it into the harbor. This act symbolized a reclaiming of public space in a country that had long avoided confronting its colonial past. The event exposed the lingering relics of slavery that still occupy places of pride across the UK. Similar actions occurred nationwide, including the defacement of statues like that of Prime Minister Winston Churchill in London.

In response, the far right seized the moment to reinforce a narrative of patriotism, framing the removal of racist statues as an attack on British history. Figures like far-right activist Tommy Robinson rebranded themselves as patriots and used their social media platforms to mobilize supporters for a rally in London to "protect" monuments from antiracist demonstrators. In and around Parliament Square, hundreds of people—many wearing football shirts—gathered, chanting "England, England" and "Winston Churchill, he's one of our own." Ironically, protesters attacked the police, journalists, and the public while giving Nazi salutes outside the Cenotaph war memorial, oblivious to the contradictions of their actions.

Media Reaction: Missed Opportunities

Left-wing media outlets were quick to identify the 2020 protests as organized by far-right groups, while right-wing outlets resisted using such terms, instead labeling the participants as "thugs" or "yobs." This linguistic divide extended to social media, where antiracists highlighted the rise of fascism while right-wing commentators framed the actions as patriotic. Many defenders of these protests fixated on the narrative that participants were protecting Winston Churchill's statue due to his opposition to Hitler, conveniently overlooking Churchill's racist views and his role in the Bengal famine, which killed over 3 million people.[47]

Mainstream media, meanwhile, steered away from addressing fascism directly, focusing instead on the so-called "culture wars," debating road names and statues. While these discussions elevated the profiles of Black historians and decolonial movements, they masked the growing threat of fascism. Antiracists saw BLM 2020 as a fleeting opportunity to spotlight modern-day racism. However, as the media centered on debates over tarnished statues—often ignored for years—the broader discussion of neofascism faded into the background, allowing the far right's narrative of defending British culture to take hold.

In a country steeped in imperial nostalgia, it was unsurprising that nationalism surged under the guise of patriotism. The 2020 COVID lockdown revealed the far right's diverse organizing tactics, with groups like QAnon rallying in Liverpool under the "Save our Children" banner. As antiracist discourse in the city focused on confronting colonial relics, conspiracy theorists promoting the "great reset"—a false narrative linking vaccines to economic collapse—gained traction. This narrative drew in antivaxxers, antilockdown activists, conspiracy theorists, wellness advocates, and far-right supporters, who united on platforms like Telegram, leveraging misinformation to mobilize their base.

Mixed Messages

Mainstream politicians distanced themselves from QAnon and "Save Our Children" groups, yet leaders like President Trump and UK prime minister Boris Johnson amplified and sanitized their messages by parroting conspiracies circulated by these movements. The far right capitalized on growing distrust in a government that had failed to follow its own lockdown rules, blending the "great reset" conspiracy with the "great replacement" theory. This far-right notion posits that elites and governments are attempting to replace white populations with migrants due to low birth rates and cultural erosion. Efforts to roll back women's reproductive rights, driven by far-right fears of the "great replacement," coincided with the growing influence of evangelical Christian groups. Preachers became regular fixtures in city centers and Speakers' Corners across the UK. Despite the clear threat these movements pose to women's freedoms, women remain a core demographic supporting them, much as they did with Trump.

As history shows, women and minority groups do not always support movements that align with their best interests. Today, figures like MP Suella Braverman, herself a daughter of South Asian immigrants, speak of "invaders" coming to Britain's shores, pushing policies on deportation that would make Enoch Powell blush. The aesthetics may have changed, but the message remains the same: migrants and Muslims have become the new top targets of the far right. Their slogans about stopping "boats full of fighting-age men" and "Londonistan" echo the same xenophobic fears of the past. The far right's overlap with free thinkers isn't new either. Hitler's Nazis were fans of astrology, paganism, and alternative medicine. Similarly, the fascists of the 1970s embraced anarcho-primitivism and deep ecology. What's concerning is the sheer volume of fringe movements the far right can now draw from, and how social media has accelerated both their speed and reach.

When antivaxxers proudly declared themselves "pure bloods," antiracists should have taken notice—but many were too busy debating statues.

Developing Counternarratives

While BLM UK may have missed an opportunity to contend with the latest iteration of far-right propaganda, it expanded antiracist networks and developed language to address contemporary racism. This meant that when the far right came to Knowsley in 2023, the Merseyside BLM Alliance swiftly mobilized to expose disinformation portraying asylum seekers as threats to women and children—propaganda spread by the neo-Nazi group Patriotic Alternative through Facebook, Telegram, and leaflets.

In response, the traditional "meet them on the street" approach evolved into a broader strategy, combining social media and street canvassing across the Liverpool City Region to fact-check fascist propaganda. Activists emphasized that the Liverpool City Region is "built from migration" and debunked myths about the strain on public services. To combat this new wave of fascism, campaigners now need a multipronged approach—one that not only challenges grassroots propaganda but also holds MPs and media outlets accountable for perpetuating these narratives. The success of BLM 2020 in reshaping conversations around policing, colonization, and immigration provides a blueprint for how antifascists can challenge far-right ideologies using a combination of grassroots activism, digital platforms, and media accountability to expose and dismantle harmful narratives.

Conclusion

Fascism can feel akin to an indomitable monster—each time antiracist and antifascist forces push it back, it reappears with a new face, continuing to advance its destructive agenda. Campaigners fighting against this latest resurgence of fascism can take solace in knowing that this iteration of hate can be driven back, just as it has been in the past. However, once this is achieved, the understandable reluctance to revisit such dark periods in history does not serve the broader goal of eliminating fascist ideologies and far-right organizing. We must remain vigilant to the dangers and recognize the patterns of "othering" specific communities while manipulating others into hating them. Those aware of such trends often see them coming long in the distance.

Above all, antifascist movements must form broad coalitions of marginalized groups and their allies, united by class consciousness and a shared determination to confront the elites who fund hate to pit workers against workers, all while holding both down in poverty. For what these elites truly fear is not migration or the religion of another but the threat of a unified proletariat, finally ready to claim what is rightfully theirs.

Acknowledgments

We embarked on this narrative and storytelling journey to create a resource for movement communicators built by movement communicators. By collaborating with radical thinkers and visionaries, we sought to craft a collective tool for making meaning in today's complex world. This anthology has been shaped by the brilliance and creativity of many minds, and we are deeply grateful to the movement workers of today who rigorously challenge systems of oppression. We honor those from the past whose efforts laid the groundwork for our narrative organizing to thrive, and we look to future generations who will continue to build narrative power, pushing us ever closer to a genuinely liberatory world.

We offer huge thanks to the following individuals:

- *RadComms Leadership Team:* Zaineb Mohammed, Diana Huynh, Virali Modi Parekh, Beulah Osueke, Bia Jackson, Phuong Pham, Erin Malone, Dr. Annie Neimand, Meredith Fenton, Apyphanie Dawn
- *RadComms Staff:* Ariana Busby
- *Advisory Council:* Dr. Deva Woodly, Ann Elizabeth Christiano, Dr. Siobhán McGuirk, Anna Tellez, Dr. Annie Neimand
- *Designers:* Milli Agency, Matt Mackenzie
- *Copy Editor:* Nirmala Nataraj
- *Intern:* Cassandra Torsiello
- *Photo Researcher:* Olivia Blocker
- *Funders:* Rockefeller Brothers Fund, the Robert Wood Johnson Foundation, the California Endowment, Kataly Foundation, Borealis Philanthropy and Inatai Foundation

Shanelle Matthews would additionally like to thank her:

- grandparents and great-grandparents—Odessa, Trudie, and Charles —whose journeys and courage shaped the possibilities of her life.

- parents and Godparents—Janice, Charles, Kim, Donna, and Seger—whose love and lessons fortified her to grapple with life's most pressing challenges.
- siblings—Sasha, K.C., and Jayden—who keep her close, honest, and laughing.
- friends and comrades, whose deep abiding love, grace, and camaraderie are a reminder of the spiritual power of platonic love.
- mentors—Sujatha Jesudason, Deva Woodly, Annie Neimand, and Malkia Devich-Cyril—whose inspiration, confidence, and coaching have provided fertile ground for her movement and scholarly pursuits.
- political home—the Movement for Black Lives—for embracing narrative power as a discipline in the liberatory canon of Black liberation in the twenty-first century.

Marzena Zukowska would additionally like to give thanks to their:

- mother, Lucyna Zukowska—whose witty sense of humor, wisdom, storytelling prowess, and hard work awakened their sense of social justice and political activism.
- older brother, Lukasz Gruda—who has always been the caretaker, steadfast in his love and support.
- partner, Olivia Blocker—who has offered more abundant love and camaraderie than words can capture.
- colleague and friend Magda Fabianczyk—who created the space for them to dream, reimagine, and build through organizing work at POMOC.
- "mapa" June Barrett—who taught them about the power that exists at the intersections of our identities.
- political homes—including the domestic workers movement, the fight for immigrant justice, queer and trans liberation, and Polish feminist activism.
- so many friends, colleagues, and comrades—who shared guidance, mentorship, and care over the years.

Notes

Foreword: Left Narrative Power: An Antidote to Authoritarianism

1. Powell, J.A., Cutting, H., and Themba, M. *From Talking the Walk: A Communications Guide for Racial Justice.*

2. Fromm, E. *Escape from Freedom*, 5.

3. Christakis, NA, Fowler, JH (2009). *Connected: The surprising power of our social networks and how they shape our lives.* New York: Little, Brown.

Introduction

1. Boggs, G.L. (2010). *The Next American Revolution: Sustainable Activism for the Twenty-First Century.* Berkeley, CA: University of California Press.

2. *The New York Times* (last modified April 21, 2021). "The Death of George Floyd: What We Know." www.nytimes.com/article/george-floyd.html.

3. @darnella_frazier03 (May 28, 2021). Instagram, www.instagram.com/p/CPT5_oIBlie.

4. Jackson, S.J., Bailey, M., and Foucault Welles, B. (2020). *Hashtag Activism: Networks of Race and Gender Justice.* Cambridge, MA: MIT Press.

5. Free Press (2020). "Media 2070: An Invitation to Dream Up Media Reparations." mediareparations.org.

6. Dixon, T.L. (2008). "Crime News and Racialized Beliefs: Understanding the Relationship Between Local News Viewing and Perceptions of African Americans and Crime." *Journal of Communication*, 58(1): 106–25.

7. Levenson, E. (April 2020). "How Minneapolis Police First Described the Murder of George Floyd, and What We Know Now." CNN. www.cnn.com/2021/04/21.

8. Denning, M. (January 2023). "What Antonio Gramsci Offers Today's Organizers." *Jacobin*. jacobin.com/2023/01.

9. Critical Resistance (August 2021). "Abolitionist Steps Against Expansion." criticalresistance.org/wp-content/uploads/2021/08.

10. Woodly, D.R. (2015). *The Politics of Common Sense: How Social Movements Use Public Discourse to Change Politics and Win Acceptance.* Oxford, UK: Oxford University Press.

11. *Throughline* (July 1, 2021). "Capitalism: What Makes Us Free?" Podcast transcript, https://www.npr.org/transcripts/1011062075.

12. Fry, W., Yee, E., and Jetha, R. (Updated June 19, 2024). "California Is the First State to Tackle Reparations for Black Residents. What That Really Means." *CalMatters.* calmatters.org/explainers/reparations-california.

13. Press, B., and Carothers, T. (December 21, 2020). "Worldwide Protests in 2020: A Year in Review." Carnegie Endowment for International Peace. carnegieendowment .org/posts/2020/12.

14. Weidinger, R. (June 15, 2023). "Weaving the Opposite of Fascism: Narrative Organizing to Build Narrative Power." Narrative Initiative. narrativeinitiative.org.

15. Resnikoff, J. (August 31, 2023). "How Bill Clinton Became a Neoliberal." *Jacobin.* jacobin.com/2023/08/a-fabulous-failure-review.

16. Reilly, K. (February 25, 2016). "Hillary Clinton Apologizes for 'Superpredator' Remark." *Time.* time.com/4238230/hillary-clinton-black-lives-matter-superpredator.

17. Semuels, A. (April 1, 2016). "The End of Welfare as We Know It." *The Atlantic.* www.theatlantic.com/business/archive/2016/04.

18. *LGBTQ History* (n.d.). The Trevor Project. www.thetrevorproject.org/wp-content /uploads/2022/02/LGBTQ-History.

19. McDonnell, P.J., and Lopez, R.J. (October 17, 1994). "L.A. March Against Prop. 187 Draws 70,000;" "Immigration: Protesters Condemn Wilson for Backing Initiative That They Say Promotes 'Racism, Scapegoating.'" *Los Angeles Times.* www .latimes.com/archives.

20. Gibson, D. (June 5, 2024). "The Legacy of the 'Battle of Seattle.'" *Jacobin.* jacobin .com/2024/06.

21. Geismer, L. (December 13, 2022). "How the Third Way Made Neoliberal Politics Seem Inevitable." *The Nation.* www.thenation.com/article/politics/third-way-dlc-bill -clinton-tony-blair-1990s-politics.

22. Bush, G.W. (September 20, 2001). "Text: President Bush Addresses the Nation." *The Washington Post.* www.washingtonpost.com/wp-srv/nation/specials/attacked /transcripts/bushaddress_092001.

23. Matthews, S., and Zukowska, M. (eds.) (2025). *Liberation Stories: Building Narrative Power for Twenty-First Century Social Movements* (1st ed.). New York: The New Press.

24. The Rising Majority (2023). 2050 Vision. www.2050vision.us.

25. Ibid.

ANTI-IMPERIALISM

Weaponizing Rhetoric: Legitimations of State Violence in the War on Terror

1. Biden, J. (August 31, 2021). Remarks by President Biden on the End of the War in Afghanistan. White House. www.whitehouse.gov/briefing-room/speeches-remarks /2021/08/31.

2. Bush, G.W. (September 20, 2001). Address to a Joint Session of Congress and the American People. White House. georgewbush-whitehouse.archives.gov/news/releases/2001/09.

3. Ibid.

4. Jackson, R. (2005). "Security, Democracy, and the Rhetoric of Counter-Terrorism," *Democracy and Security* 1(2): 147–71. https://www.jstor.org/stable/48602563.

5. Bush (September 20, 2001). Address to a Joint Session of Congress and the American People.

6. Lifton, R.J. (June 2005). "Americans as Survivors." *New England Journal of Medicine* 352(2): 2263–265. doi.org/10.1056.

7. Gordon, R. (August 15, 2017). "No, We Don't Need a 'War' on Domestic Issues." *The Nation*. www.thenation.com/article/archive.

8. U.S. Congress (2021). USA PATRIOT Act of 2001, Pub. L, No. 107-56, 116 Stat., Title IV, Subtitle B, Sec. 412. www.congress.gov/107/plaws/publ56/PLAW-107publ56.

9. Bush (September 20, 2001). Address to a Joint Session of Congress and the American People.

10. Jackson, R. (2005). "Security, Democracy, and the Rhetoric of Counter-Terrorism." 147–71.

11. Biden (August 31, 2021). Remarks by President Biden on the End of the War in Afghanistan.

12. Bruggeman, L., Dwyer, D., and Ebbs, S. (April 28, 2022). "Climate activist's fight against 'terrorism' sentence could impact the future of protests," ABC News. abcnews.go.com.

13. Aldinger, C. (December 10, 2001). "US bombs al Qaeda cave with 'daisy cutter.'" CBS News. www.cbsnews.com/news.

14. Lane, J. (2003). "The Mass Graves at Dasht-e Leili: Assessing U.S. Liability for Human Rights Violations During the War in Afghanistan." *California Western International Law Journal* 34(1): 145–70. scholarlycommons.law.cwsl.edu/cwilj/vol34/iss1/7.

15. Goddard, S.E., and Krebs, R.R. (2015). "Rhetoric, Legitimation, and Grand Strategy," *Security Studies* 24(1): 5–26. doi.org.

16. Barnett, M. (2016). *American Exceptionalism and the Construction of the War on Terror: An Analysis of Counterterrorism Policies under Clinton, Bush, and Obama.* Syracuse University Institute for National Security and Counterterrorism: Working Paper Series. securitypolicylaw.syr.edu/wp-content/uploads/2016/11.

17. Rubin, G. (2020). *Presidential Rhetoric on Terrorism Under Bush, Obama, and Trump: Inflating and Calibrating the Threat After 9/11.* Berlin, Germany: Springer, 53.

18. Obama, B. (May 23, 2013). Remarks by the President at the National Defense University. White House. obamawhitehouse.archives.

19. Department of Homeland Security (August 2011). "Empowering Local Partners to Prevent Violent Extremism in the United States." www.dhs.gov/sites/default/files/publications.

20. Krebs, R. (2015). *Narrative and the Making of US National Security.* Cambridge, UK: Cambridge University Press, 3.

21. Crawford, N. (March 15, 2023). *Blood and Treasure: United States Budgetary Costs and Human Costs of Twenty Years of War in Iraq and Syria, 2003–2023.* Costs of War Project, Watson Institute at Brown University. watson.brown.edu/costsofwar/files/cow/imce/papers/2023.

22. Seymour, I.S. (2022). "The Oilfields of Mesopotamia: Resource Conflict, Oil Extraction and Heritage Destruction in Iraq." *Human Geography* 15(3): 259–72. doi.org.

23. Mears, D.P., Mancini, C., Beaver, K.M., and Gertz, G. (2013). "Housing for the 'Worst of the Worst' Inmates: Public Support for Supermax Prisons." *Crime & Delinquency* 59(4): 587–615. doi.org.

24. Radil, S.M., Dezzani, R.J., and McAden, L.D. (2016). "Geographies of U.S. Police Militarization and the Role of the 1033 Program," *The Professional Geographer* 69(2): 203–13. doi.org.

25. Walia, H. (2021). *Border and Rule: Global Migration, Capitalism, and the Rise of Racist Nationalism.* Chicago, IL: Haymarket Books.

26. Movement for Black Lives (2021). "Struggle for Power: The Ongoing Persecution of Black Movement by the U.S. Government." m4bl.org/wp-content/uploads/2021/08.

27. Reprieve US (2022). "Guantánamo: Shut It Down." reprieve.org/uk/campaign/guantanamo/faq.

28. Lederer, E.M. (July 6, 2023). "Guantanamo Detainees Tell First Independent Visitor About Scars from Torture and Hopes to Leave." AP News. apnews.com/article.

29. Associated Press (June 1, 2009). "Cheney: Gitmo Holds 'Worst of the Worst.'" NBC News. www.nbcnews.com.

30. Durbin, D. (June 1, 2023). "Ahead of Debt Limit Vote, Durbin Continues to Call for Closure of Guantanamo Bay," 9:19. YouTube. www.youtube.com.

31. Hebron, L. (May 4, 2022). "The High Cost of Guantanamo's 'Forever Prisoners.'" Human Rights Watch. www.hrw.org/news/2022/05/04.

32. Reprieve US (2022). "Guantánamo: Shut It Down."

33. Shabad, R. (December 7, 2015). "Donald Trump Calls for 'Total and Complete Shutdown' of Muslims Entering U.S." CBS News. www.cbsnews.com/news.

34. Abdalla, J. (February 4, 2022). "'Empty Promises': The US's 'Muslim Ban' Still Reverberates." *Al Jazeera.* www.aljazeera.com/news/2022/2/4.

35. Beauchamp, Z. (June 26, 2017). "There Is No Rational Justification for Trump's Travel Ban." *Vox.* www.vox.com/world.

36. Roundhouse (June 20, 2017). The Last Word Festival 2017—Poetry Slam Final: Suhaiymah Manzoor-Khan. YouTube. www.youtube.com.

37. Ibid.

Echoes of the Nakba: The Battle for Narrative Power in the Palestinian Liberation Struggle

1. This question was inspired by Stephano Mendelek, the director of development at AFLAMUNA, which is a cultural nonprofit based in Beirut working to harness the power of independent Arab cinema to elevate the most pressing social, political, and cultural movements of our time.

BLACK LIBERATION AND INDIGENOUS RESISTANCE

The Movement for Black Lives, Narrative Power, and the Black Radical Tradition

1. Taylor, K-Y (2016). *From #BlackLivesMatter to Black Liberation.* Chicago, IL: Haymarket Books.

2. National Center for Institutional Diversity (2019). *The Black Radical Tradition of Resistance: A Series on Black Social Movements.* University of Michigan. medium.com /national-center-for-institutional-diversity.

3. Lipsitz, G. (2017). "What Is This Black in the Black Radical Tradition?" In Johnson, G. and Lubin, A. (eds.), *Futures of Black Radicalism.* New York: Verso.

4. Women's Resource and Leadership Center (n.d.). "State-Sanctioned Violence Against Black Women." University of Illinois, Chicago. wrlc.uic.edu.

5. Movement for Black Lives (2016). Vision for Black Lives Policy Platform. m4bl .org/policy-platforms.

6. Adams, M. (2020). "The Future of the Movement for Black Lives. *In These Times.* inthesetimes.com/article/organizing-movements-mobilizing-rebellion-resist.

7. PBS (n.d.). "Quakers: From Slave Traders to Early Abolitionists." web.tricolib .brynmawr.edu/speccoll/quakersandslavery.

8. Equal Justice Initiative (n.d.). *The Transatlantic Slave Trade.* eji.org/report /transatlantic-slave-trade/new-england/#laws-limiting-freedom.

9. Alexander, M. (2010). *The New Jim Crow: Mass Incarceration in the Age of Color-blindness.* New York: The New Press.

10. Austin, C. J. (2006). *Up Against the Wall: Violence in the Making and Unmaking of the Black Panther Party.* Fayetteville, AR: University of Arkansas Press.

11. Reinsborough, P., and Canning, D. (2017). *Re:Imagining Change: How to Use Story-Based Strategy to Win Campaigns, Build Movements, and Change the World.* Oakland, CA: PM Press.

12. Lindsey, T.B. (2022). *America, Goddam: Violence, Black Women, and the Struggle for Justice.* Oakland, CA: University of California Press.

13. Bowers, J.W., Ochs, D.J., Jensen, R.J., and Schulz, D.P. (2009). *The Rhetoric of Agitation and Control.* 3rd ed. Long Grove, IL: Waveland Press.

14. Ibid.

15. Panetta, G. (December 3, 2020). "Obama Said 'Defund the Police' Is a Bad Slogan. This Shouldn't Come as a Surprise." *Vox.* www.vox.com/2020/12/3/22150452.

16. Movement for Black Lives and CUNY CLEAR (2022). "Struggle for Power: The Ongoing Persecution of Black Movement by the U.S. Federal Government," https://m4bl.org/struggle-for-power.

17. Cohen, Dr. C.J. (March 17–April 3, 2023). "Perspectives on Community Safety from Black America." University of Chicago; GenForward for M4BL.

18. Lenvi, S. (2021, March 11). "These US cities defunded police: 'we're transferring money to the community.'" *The Guardian.* https://www.theguardian.com/us-news/2021/mar/07/us-cities-defund-police-transferring-money-community

Reframing Environmental Justice in the 21st Century: Movement Convergence in the Wake of the 2020 Uprisings

1. Griswold, E. (September 21, 2012). "How *Silent Spring* Ignited the Environmental Movement." *The New York Times.* www.nytimes.com/2012/09/23/magazine.

2. Tompkins, L. (July 22, 2020). "Sierra Club Says It Must Confront the Racism of John Muir." *The New York Times.* www.nytimes.com/2020/07/22/us.

3. Perpuli, F. (July 21, 2023). "Is Teddy Roosevelt's US National Parks Campaign Controversial?" *The Collector.* www.thecollector.com.

4. Howells, R.F. (August 27, 2020). "Revisiting the Complex Legacy of North Dakota's Theodore Roosevelt National Park." *National Geographic.* www.nationalgeographic.com/travel/article.

5. Oglesby, C. (February 1, 2023). "Fighting for Warrenton: The Birth of the Environmental Justice Movement with Rev. Dr. Benjamin Chavis." *Earth in Color.* earthincolor.co/unearthed.

6. United Church of Christ Commission for Racial Justice (1987). *Toxic Wastes and Race in the United States: A National Report on the Racial and Socio-Economic Characteristics of Communities with Hazardous Waste Sites.* www.nrc.gov/docs/ML1310/ML13109A339.

7. First National People of Color Environmental Leadership Summit (1991). "Principles of Environmental Justice." www.ejnet.org/ej/principles.

8. Rubiano, M.P. (November 1, 2021). "The Event That Changed the Environmental Justice Movement Forever." *Grist.* grist.org/equity.

9. Oglesby, C. (July 6, 2024). "Episode 3: Carol Browner—Reshaping Federal Policy with a Clinton-Era Environmental Justice Champion." Environmental Justice Oral History Project. ejohp.com/2024/07.

10. Erickson, J. (April 23, 2019). "Five Years Later: Flint Water Crisis Most Egregious Example of Environmental Injustice, U-M Researcher Says." *University of Michigan News*. news.umich.edu.

11. Madi, M., Izundu, C.C., and Bailey, C. (September 3, 2022). "Jackson water crisis: A legacy of environmental racism?" BBC News. www.bbc.com/news/world-us-canada-62783900.

12. Oglesby, C. (February 17, 2023). "Flooding Is Pummeling the Southeast U.S. These Organizers Are Fighting Back." Yale Climate Connections. yaleclimateconnections.org/2023/02.

13. Oglesby, C. (January 30, 2024). "Organizers Aim to Improve the South's Climate Resilience." Yale Climate Connections. yaleclimateconnections.org/2024/01.

14. Austin, A., and Goubert, A. (February 2, 2022). "The Historic Opportunities for Racial Equity in the Infrastructure Investment and Jobs Act." Center for Economic and Policy Research. www.cepr.

15. Reynolds, M.E. (September 20, 2021). "The Psychological Toll of George Floyd's Murder." *Stanford Report*. news.stanford.edu/stories/2021/09.

16. Simpkins, K. (May 24, 2021). "One Year Later: How George Floyd's Death Changed Us." *CU Boulder Today*. www.colorado.edu/today/2021/05/24.

17. Bellafante, G. (May 29, 2020). "Why Amy Cooper's Use of 'African-American' Stung." *The New York Times*. www.nytimes.com/2020/05/29/nyregion.

18. Nir, S.M. (June 14, 2020). "How 2 Lives Collided in Central Park, Rattling the Nation." *The New York Times*. www.nytimes.com/2020/06/14/nyregion.

19. Oglesby, C. (October 3, 2022). "The Ecology of the Forest: Bringing Black People into the Woods." *Earth in Color*. earthincolor.co/earth-curiosity/the-ecology-of-the-forest-bringing-black-people-into-the-woods.

20. Oglesby, C. (June 21, 2022). "How Black Beaches Were Developed to Combat Jim Crow Segregation." *Earth in Color*. earthincolor.co/earth-curiosity.

21. www.nytimes.com/2021/02/16/opinion/ezra-klein-podcast-heather-mcghee.

22. Murphy, A. (2024). "The Racist Legacy of Urban Green Spaces." *American Scientist* 112(3), 142. doi.org/10.1511/2024.112.3.142.

23. Fausset, R. (August 8, 2022). "What We Know About the Shooting Death of Ahmaud Arbery." *The New York Times*. www.nytimes.com/article.

24. Bragg, K. (August 5, 2020). "Replanting Roots in a Southern Food Desert." *Southerly Magazine*. southerlymag.org/2020/08/05.

25. Bruggers, J., Lavelle, M., Fahys, J., Nieves, E., and Cohen, I. (June 3, 2020). "As Protests Rage over George Floyd's Death, Climate Activists Embrace Racial Justice." *Inside Climate News*. insideclimatenews.org/news/03062020.

26. Melley, B. (July 22, 2020). "Sierra Club calls out founder John Muir for racist views." PBS. www.pbs.org/newshour/nation.

27. Oglesby, C. (April 6, 2021). "Green Groups Promised a Racial Reckoning in 2020. Is It Happening?" *Grist*. grist.org/justice.

28. Oglesby, C. (January 17, 2024). "Nourishing Roots in the Birthplace of Environmental Justice." *Atmos.* atmos.earth.

29. Oglesby, C. (October 20, 2023). "Food Justice Advocates Didn't Set Out to Save the Climate. Their Solutions Are Doing It Anyway." *Grist.* grist.org/equity/ny-urban-gardening.

30. Oglesby, C. (February 10, 2021). "The Generational Rift over 'Intersectional Environmentalism.'" *Grist.* grist.org/justice.

31. Dennis, B., and Grandoni, D. (July 31, 2020). "How Joe Biden's Surprisingly Ambitious Climate Plan Came Together." *The Washington Post.* www.washingtonpost.com/climate-environment.

32. The American Presidency Project (July 14, 2020). "The Biden Plan to Secure Environmental Justice and Equitable Economic Opportunity in a Clean Energy Future." Biden Campaign Press Release. www.presidency.ucsb.edu/documents.

33. White House (2024). "Justice40: A Whole-of-Government Initiative." www.whitehouse.gov/environmentaljustice/justice40.

34. Pruitt-Bonner, C. (December 29, 2021). "U.S. National Infrastructure Funding Could Ease Decades of Neglect in Majority Black Regions." *The Plug.* tpinsights.com.

35. Norwood, C. (April 23, 2021). "How infrastructure has historically promoted inequality." PBS News. www.pbs.org/newshour/politics.

36. Calma, J. (November 29, 2023). "Tens of Billions of Dollars of IRA Funding Will Now Be Earmarked for Environmental Justice." *The Verge.* www.theverge.com/2023/11/29/23981137/biden-ira-inflation-reduction-act-programs-justice40-initiative-exclusive.

37. Oglesby, C. (June 2, 2023). "Report Card: Biden's Accomplishments on Climate Justice." Yale Climate Connections. yaleclimateconnections.org/2023/06.

More Than a Check: Building Narrative Power for Black Reparations

1. *Democracy Now!* (January 10, 2014). "Amiri Baraka (1934–2014): Poet-Playwright-Activist Who Shaped Revolutionary Politics, Black Culture." www.democracynow.org/2014/1/10.

2. United Nations (December 15, 2005). "Basic Principles and Guidelines on the Right to a Remedy and Reparation for Victims of Gross Violations of International Human Rights Law and Serious Violations of International Humanitarian Law." General Assembly Resolution 60/147. www.ohchr.org/en/instruments-mechanisms/instruments.

3. Kelly, R.D.G. (2022). *Freedom Dreams: The Black Radical Imagination.* Boston, MA: Beacon Press.

4. Jenkins, D., and LeRoy, J. (2021). *Histories of Racial Capitalism.* New York, NY: Columbia University Press, 25.

5. California Department of Justice (2023). California Reparations Report. oag.ca .gov/ab3121/report.

6. Hesse, B. (October 2011). "Marked Unmarked: Black Politics and the Western Political." *South Atlantic Quarterly* 110 (4): 974–984; Robinson, C. (2020). *Black Marxism: The Making of the Black Radical Tradition.* Chapel Hill, NC: University of North Carolina Press.

7. Hesse, B. (June 2007). "Racialized Modernity: An Analytics of White Mythologies." *Ethnic and Racial Studies* 30(4): 642–63.

8. Harris, A. (2021). "Racial Capitalism and Law." In Leroy, J. and Jenkins, D. (eds.). *Histories of Racial Capitalism.* New York, NY: Columbia University Press. 8.

9. Beckert, S. (2015). *Empire of Cotton: A Global History.* New York, NY: Penguin Random House.

10. Gilmore, R.W. (2007). *Golden Gulag: Prisons, Surplus Crisis, and Opposition in Globalizing California.* Berkeley, CA: University of California Press.

11. Baptiste, E.E. (2016). *The Half Has Never Been Told: Slavery and the Making of American Capitalism.* New York, NY: Basic Books; Beckert, S. (2015). *Empire of Cotton: A Global History;* Hudson, P.J. *Bankers and Empire: How Wall Street Colonized the Caribbean.* Chicago, IL: University of Chicago Press; Nesbitt, N. (2022). *The Price of Slavery: Capitalism and Revolution in the Caribbean.* Charlottesville, VA: University of Virginia Press.; Williams, E.R. (2021). *Capitalism and Slavery.* Chapel Hill, NC: University of North Carolina Press.

12. Logan, R. (1977). *The Betrayal of the Negro: From Rutherford B. Hayes to Woodrow Wilson.* Cambridge, MA: Da Capo Press.

13. Berry, M.F. *My Face Is Black Is True: Callie House and the Struggle for Ex-Slave Reparations.* New York, NY: Vintage.

14. Ibid.

15. Booker Perry, M. (September 2010). "No Pensions for Ex-Slaves: How Federal Agencies Suppressed Movement to Aid Freedpeople." *Prologue* 42(2). National Archives. www.archives.gov/publications/prologue/2010/summer.

16. Dixon, V. (August 21, 2017). "Hand Back to Us 'Our Own Civilisation.'" Institute of the Black World. ibw21.org/editors-choice.

17. Lil Dee. (January 18, 2016). "We're Coming to Get Our Check." YouTube. www .youtube.com.

18. Berger, D. (April 10, 2018). "'Free the Land!': Fifty Years of the Republic of New Afrika." *Black Perspectives.* www.aaihs.org.

19. The Riverside Church (n.d.). "55th Anniversary of the Black Manifesto. The Black Manifesto at the Riverside Church." www.trcnyc.org/blackmanifesto.

20. Winbush, R. (2000). *Should America Pay? Slavery and the Raging Debate on Reparations.* New York, NY: HarperCollins.

21. Episcopal Archives (n.d.). "The Black Manifesto, The Church Awakens: African American Struggles for Justice." www.episcopalarchives.org/church-awakens.

22. Kelly, R.D.G. (2002). *Freedom Dreams: The Black Radical Imagination.* Boston, MA: Beacon Press.

23. The Riverside Church (n.d.). "55th Anniversary of the Black Manifesto. The Black Manifesto at the Riverside Church."

24. Berry, M.F. (2005). *My Face Is Black Is True: Callie House and the Struggle for Ex-Slave Reparations.*

25. *Tampa Tribune* (May 7, 1969). "Both Races to Blame for U.S. Disorders," 16.

26. Smith, T., and Ragland, D. (August 28, 2023). "Movements of Hope: Abolition and Reparations in These Times." *Prism.* prismreports.org/2023/08/28.

27. Equity and Transformation (EAT). "The Big Payback." www.eatchicago.org/big -payback.

28. Taylor, K.Y. (2020). *Race for Profit: How Banks and the Real Estate Industry Undermined Homeownership.* Chapel Hill, NC: University of North Carolina Press.

Liberation Is Coming: The Fight for Indigenous Sovereignty

1. *Reservation Dogs* (August 9, 2023). "Deer Lady." (TV Show, Season 3, Episode 3.) Hulu.

2. Native American Rights Fund (June 9, 2021). "Tribes Respond to KXL Pipeline Termination." narf.org/keystone-xl.

3. National Indian Law Library (n.d.). *A Practical Guide to the Indian Child Welfare Act.* www.narf.org/nill/documents/icwa.

GENDER JUSTICE AND VIOLENCE PREVENTION

Narratives of Resilience and Resistance: The Evolution of me too. and Survivor Justice

1. Britzky, H. (October 13, 2018). "#MeToo Hashtag Used Over 19 million Times on Twitter." *Axios.* www.axios.com/2018/10/13.

2. Boyd, A., and McEwan, B. (June 13, 2022). "Viral Paradox: The Intersection of 'me too' and #MeToo." *New Media & Society*, 26(6). doi.org.

3. Patriarchal violence is an interconnected system of institutions, practices, policies, beliefs, and behaviors that harm, undervalue, and terrorize girls, women, femme, intersex, gender-nonconforming, LGBTQ, and other gender-oppressed people in Black communities. Patriarchal violence is a widespread, normalized epidemic based on the domination, control, and colonizing of bodies, genders, and sexuality and is happening in every community globally. Patriarchal violence is a global power structure that mani-

fests itself on the systemic, institutional, interpersonal, internalized level. It is rooted in interlocking systems of oppression.

4. Burke, T. (2021). *Unbound: My Story of Liberation and the Birth of the Me Too Movement.* Chicago, IL: Flatiron Books.

5. Burke, T. (n.d.) "The Inception." Just Be Inc. justbeinc.wixsite.com/justbeinc/the -me-too-movement.

6. Ibid.

7. Kochar, R., and Fry, R. (December 12, 2014). "Wealth Inequality Has Widened Along Racial, Ethnic Lines Since End of Great Recession." Pew Research Center. www .pewresearch.org/short-reads/2014/12/12.

8. Protest and Assembly Rights Project (2013). "Suppressing Protest: Human Rights Violations in the U.S. Response to Occupy Wall Street." *The Atlantic.* cdn.theatlantic .com/media/mt/politics.

9. Peabody: Stories That Matter (2015). *Fatal Force:* The Washington Post *Police Shootings Database.* peabodyawards.com/fatalforce.

10. Godfrey, H., Rich, S., Tran, A.B., Amro, D., Lobo, D., Mahatole, S., Rayaprolu, M., and Sherer, M. (May 30, 2015). *Police Shootings Database 2015–2024. The Washington Post.* www.washingtonpost.com/graphics/investigations.

11. Green, M.H. (June 27, 2016). "A Tough Choice for Feminist Black Lives Matter Activists." *YES!* www.yesmagazine.org/opinion/2016/06/27.

12. National Public Radio (February 28, 2011). "Hidden pattern of rape helped stir civil rights movement." *Tell Me More* (Radio Show). www.npr.org/templates/story.

13. Rogers, L.L. (February 24, 2020). "National African American History Month: Remembering Rosa Parks' Work to Address Sexual Assault." U.S. Department of Justice, Office of Violence Against Women. www.justice.gov/archives/ovw/blog.

14. Jamieson, A., Jeffery, S., and Puglise, N. (October 27, 2016). "A timeline of Donald Trump's alleged sexual misconduct: Who, when, and what." *The Guardian.* www .theguardian.com/us-news/2016/oct/13.

15. Milano, A. [@Alyssa_Milano] (October 15, 2017). "If you've been sexually harassed or assaulted write 'me too' as a reply to this tweet." Twitter. x.com /Alyssa_Milano/status/919659438700670976.

16. Whittaker, N. (October 18, 2022). "Elite Capture." *The Point* 28, Politics. thepoint mag.com/politics.

17. Matthews, S. (June 29, 2022). "To Build a Public Safety That Protects Black Women and Girls, Money Isn't the Only Resource We Need." *Nonprofit Quarterly.* nonprof-itquarterly.org.

18. Intentionally lowercase.

19. Ibid.

20. Team Blackbird. www.teamblackbird.org.

21. The Survivors' Agenda. survivorsagenda.org/agenda.

22. Lipsitz, G. (June 24, 2020). "What Is This Black in the Black Radical Tradition?" Verso Books (Website). www.versobooks.com/blogs/news/4766.

Root Causes and Radical Change: Reimagining Gun Violence Prevention in America

1. Bump, P. (February 15, 2023). "Analysis: It's Time to Formalize 'Gen Z' as the 'Lockdown Generation.'" *The Washington Post.* www.washingtonpost.com/politics /2023/02/15/mass-shootings-gen-z-lockdowns.

2. Everytown Research and Policy (Updated May 7, 2024). "Report: Gun Violence in America." everytownresearch.org/report.

3. Ordway, D.M. (August 6, 2019). "How Journalists Cover Mass Shootings: Research to Consider." *The Journalist's Resource.* journalistsresource.org/race-and-gender.

4. Metzl, J.M., Piemonte, J., and McKay, T. (January/February 2021). "Mental Illness, Mass Shootings, and the Future of Psychiatric Research into American Gun Violence." *Harvard Review of Psychiatry* 29(1): 81–89. www.ncbi.nlm.nih.gov/pmc /articles/PMC7803479.

5. Ragland, W. (July 20, 2022). "Media Coverage Often Ignores Guns as the Main Driver of the Recent Rise in Violent Crime." Center for American Progress. www .americanprogress.org/article.

6. Hampton, F. (May 19, 1969). "We Have to Protect Our Leaders" (Speech transcript). The Marxist Internet Archive. www.marxists.org/archive.

7. Serrato, J., Sier, P., and Runes, C. (n.d.). "Mapping Chicago's Racial Segregation." WTTW, *South Side Weekly.* interactive.wttw.com/firsthand/segregation.

8. Poulson, M., Neufeld, M.Y., Dechert, T., Allee, L., and Kenzik, K.M. (November 2021). "Historic redlining, structural racism, and firearm violence: A structural equation modeling approach." *Lancet Regional Health—Americas* 3. www.ncbi.nlm.nih.gov /pmc/articles/PMC8654098.

9. Brady (n.d.). "The Disproportionate Impact of Gun Violence on Black Americans." www.bradyunited.org/resources/research.

10. Nguyen, A. and Drane, K. (August 15, 2024). "Gun Violence in Black Communities." Giffords Law Center. giffords.org/lawcenter/report/gun-violence-in-black -communities/#footnote_18_67066.

11. Johns Hopkins Bloomberg School of Public Health (2022). *Gun Violence in the United States 2022: Examining the Burden Among Children and Teens.* Johns Hopkins Center for Gun Violence Solutions. publichealth.jhu.edu/center-for-gun-violence -solutions/research-reports.

12. Violence Policy Center (April 2011). *Blood Money: How the Gun Industry Bankrolls the NRA.* www.vpc.org/studies.

13. Joint Economic Committee Democrats (n.d.). "Gun Companies Are Making Millions at the Expense of American Lives." www.jec.senate.gov/public/_cache/files.

14. Mascia, J., and Brownlee, C. (March 6, 2023). "How Many Guns Are Circulating in the U.S.?" *The Trace.* www.thetrace.org/2023/03/guns-america-data-atf-total.

15. Violence Policy Center. *Blood Money: How the Gun Industry Bankrolls the NRA.*

16. Miller, M., Zhang, W., and Azrael, D. (December 21, 2021). "Firearm Purchasing During the COVID-19 Pandemic: Results from the 2021 National Firearm Survey." *Annals of Internal Medicine.* www.ncbi.nlm.nih.gov/pmc/articles.

17. Hicks, B.M., et al. (August 29, 2023). "Who Bought a Gun During the COVID-19 Pandemic in the United States? Associations with QAnon Beliefs, Right-Wing Political Attitudes, Intimate Partner Violence, Antisocial Behavior, Suicidality, and Mental Health and Substance Use Problems." PLOS ONE 18(8). www.ncbi.nlm.nih.gov/pmc/articles.

18. NSSF: The Firearm Industry Trade Association (September 9, 2021). "NSSF Retail Surveys Show 3.2 Million Estimated First-Time Gun Buyers in First Half of 2021." www.nssf.org/articles.

19. Detrow, S., Wise, A., and Montanaro, D. (July 18, 2022). "Black People Are the Fastest-Growing Group of Gun Owners in the U.S." NPR Politics Podcast. www.npr.org/2022/07/18/1112095634.

20. Bunn, C. (June 14, 2022). "Why more Black people are looking for safety in gun ownership." NBC News. www.nbcnews.com/news/nbcblk.

21. Fonseca, R. (January 31, 2023). "For Some Asian Americans, Fear Is Driving a Spike in Gun Sales." *Los Angeles Times.* www.latimes.com/california/newsletter/2023-01-31.

22. Nasheed, J. (July 28, 2020). "'Black-on-Black Crime' Is a Dangerous Myth." *Teen Vogue.* www.teenvogue.com/story.

23. Everytown Research & Policy (n.d.). "Gun Laws in Illinois." everytownresearch.org/rankings/state/illinois.

24. World Population Review (n.d.). "Cities with Most Murders, 2024." worldpopulationreview.com/us-city-rankings.

25. Goudie, C., Markoff, B., Tressel, C., and Weidner, R. (June 7, 2022). "Less than half the guns used in Illinois crime come from Illinois, data analysis shows." ABC 7 Eyewitness News. abc7chicago.com/chicago-crime-shooting-guns-illinois-gun-laws.

26. Tucker, E., and Krishnakumar, P. (Updated May 27, 2022). "States with weaker gun laws have higher rates of firearm related homicides and suicides, study finds." CNN. www.cnn.com/2022/01/20/us.

27. Murdock, K., and Kessler, J. (February 28, 2024). "The 21st Century Red State Murder Crisis." Third Way. www.thirdway.org/report.

28. Nasheed, J. "'Black-on-Black Crime' Is a Dangerous Myth."

29. Gun Violence Archive (n.d.). "General Methodology." www.gunviolencearchive.org/methodology.

30. Barton, C. (March 25, 2021). "The Way We Think About Mass Shootings Ignores Many Black Victims." *The Trace*. www.thetrace.org/2021/03/mass-shootings-atlanta-boulder-gun-violence-data.

31. McPhillips, D. (May 9, 2022). "Rise in gun violence during pandemic adds strain to overburdened hospitals." CNN. www.cnn.com/2022/05/09/health.

32. White, K., Stuart, F., and Morrissey, L. (September 17, 2020). "Whose Lives Matter? Race, Space, and the Devaluation of Homicide Victims in Minority Communities." *Sociology of Race and Ethnicity* 7(3). journals.sagepub.com/doi.

33. Arkin, D., and Popken, B. (February 21, 2018). "How the internet's conspiracy theorists turned Parkland students into 'crisis actors.'" NBC News. www.nbcnews.com/news/us-news.

34. Brady (n.d.). Brady Campaign Statistics. www.bradyunited.org/resources/statistics.

The Best Defense Is a Good Offense: What the 2016 Campaign Against the North Carolina Bathroom Bill Can Teach Us About Today's Narrative Battles for Trans Liberation

1. Trans Legislation (n.d.). "2024 Anti-Trans Bill Tracker." translegislation.com.

2. Grant, M.G. (February 10, 2022). "Republicans Are Already Trying to Pass as Many Anti-Trans Bills as Possible in 2022." *The New Republic*. newrepublic.com/article/165334/republicans-anti-trans-bathroom-sports-bills-north-dakota-kristi-noem.

3. @GBBranstetter (June 14, 2022). X, formerly Twitter. x.com/gbbranstetter/status/1536710084478255104.

4. Associated Press (June 12, 2022). "Patriot Front Leader Among Those Arrested Near Idaho Pride." *Politico*. www.politico.com/news/2022/06/12.

5. Reed, E. (n.d.). "Trans Athletes: A Narrative Analysis— ReFrame." This Is Signals. www.thisissignals.com.

6. Thatcher, G., and Thatcher, T. (March 19, 2022). "Swim Parents: 'Inclusion' for Lia Thomas Tramples Inclusion for Our Daughters." *The Federalist*. thefederalist.com/2022/03/19.

7. Grant, M.G. (March 17, 2022). "'Grooming' Is Republicans' Cruel New Buzzword for Targeting Trans Kids." *The New Republic*. newrepublic.com/article/165761/republican-governors-grooming-crt-trans-rights.

8. Ballotpedia (May 18, 2012). "Election Results: North Carolina Amendment 1." ballotpedia.org.

9. FOX8 Digital Desk (March 23, 2016). "Gov. Pat McCrory signs bill blocking transgender ordinance." FOX8.

10. Krieg, G. (May 11, 2016). "North Carolina Gov. Pat McCrory blames Democrats for 'bathroom bill.'" CNN. www.cnn.com/2016/05/11.

11. Bonner, L. (April 25, 2016). "Hundreds Rally Near NC Legislative Building in Raleigh to Support HB2." *Charlotte Observer.* www.charlotteobserver.com/news /politics-government.

12. Jarvis, C. (May 25, 2016). "Black Pastors Rally Support for HB2, Saying LGBT Rights Are Not Civil Rights." *The News & Observer.* www.newsobserver.com/news /politics-government/politics-columns-blogs/under-the-dome.

13. Jarvis, C. (June 14, 2016). "Hispanic Pastors Urge Lawmakers to Stand Firm on HB2." *Charlotte Observer.* www.charlotteobserver.com/news/politics-government.

14. Southerners on New Ground (Website). southernersonnewground.org.

15. Wikipedia (July 30, 2024). "Moral Mondays." en.wikipedia.org/wiki/Moral_ Mondays.

16. @NC Raise Up. X, formerly Twitter. x.com/RaiseUpfor15.

17. Human Rights Campaign (Website). www.hrc.org.

18. National LGBTQ Task Force (Website). www.thetaskforce.org.

IMMIGRANT JUSTICE

Beyond Borders: Building Power and Counternarratives in the Black LGBTQIA+ Migrant Community

1. Kaoma, K.J. (2014). *American Culture Warriors in Africa: A Guide to the Exporters of Homophobia and Sexism.* Somerville, MA: Political Research Associates.

2. Neumann, C.E. (1993). "The Good Immigrant: Naturalization Policy and the Shaping of the Model Immigrant in the United States." *Journal of American Ethnic History* 13(1): 30–52.

Asserting Humanity: Lessons from the Drop the I-Word Campaign

1. *Colorlines* started in 1998 as a quarterly print journal about race and organizing with a subscriber base of 1,200; in 2008, it stopped printing, went online, and started publishing daily. Readership grew exponentially, and by the fall of 2010, colorlines.com had more than 100,000 visitors each month.

2. Hollar, J. (January 28, 2010). "Dropping Dobbs: A Victory for Media Activism, and the Challenge Ahead." NACLA. nacla.org/news.

3. Southern Poverty Law Center (November 30, 2008). "Anti-Latino Hate Crime Up for 4th Year." Intelligence Report. www.splcenter.org/fighting-hate/intelligence-report /2008/hate-crimes.

4. Luntz, Maslansky Strategic Research (October 2005). "Respect for the Law & Economic Fairness: Illegal Immigration Prevention." images.dailykos.com/images /user/3/Luntz_frames_immigration.

5. Passel, J.S., and Cohn, D. (February 1, 2011). "Unauthorized Immigrant Population: National and State Trends, 2010." Pew Research Center. www.pewresearch.org/race -and-ethnicity/2011/02/01.

6. Cavanaugh, K. (January 2019). "Immigrant Rights Protests in Washington State, Spring 2006." Seattle Labor Rights and Oral History Project, University of Washington. depts.washington.edu/civilr/2006_immigrant_rights.

7. Zimmer, B. (October 23, 2009). "Explaining the Origins of Ms." *The New York Times.* www.nytimes.com/2009/10/25/magazine/25FOB-onlanguage.

8. Special Olympics (n.d.). "Why the R-Word Is the R-Slur." www.specialolympics .org/stories/impact.

9. NAHJ (January 20, 2021). "NAHJ Applauds Biden Administration's Focus on Language." nahj.org/2021/01/21.

10. Timeline of Alianza Americas history, 2009, from www.alianzaamericas.org /about/mision-vision.

11. Treviño, M. (December 18, 2009). "Undocumented Students Challenge *USA TODAY*'s Usage of 'Illegal Students,'" *Latina Lista.*

12. Evans, M. (September 21, 2012). "Vargas: Diversity Is Destiny." ONA Student Newsroom, Online News Association. newsroom.journalists.org/2012/09/21.

13. Amlen, D. (February 20, 2012). "The Official Word on Illegal." Wordplay, the *New York Times* Crossword Puzzle Blog. archive.nytimes.com/wordplay.blogs.nytimes.com /2012/02/20/special-post-illegal.

14. Llenas, B. (August 7, 2011). "Giants manager calls radio host's 'illegal alien' comment racist," Fox News. www.foxnews.com/sports.

15. National Hispanic Media Coalition (September 2012). "Latino Decisions: The Impact of Negative Stereotypes on Opinions and Attitudes About Latinos." www.nhmc .org/wp-content/uploads/2012/09/LD_NHMC_Poll_Results_Sept.2012.

16. Kowalski, D.M. (October 20, 2012). "Associated Press on Use of Phrase 'Illegal Immigrant'—and DMK Commentary." Lexis Nexis. www.lexisnexis.com/community /insights/legal/immigration/b/outsidenews/posts.

17. Colford, P. (April 2, 2013). "Illegal Immigrant No More." Associated Press blog. www.apstylebook.com/blog_posts/1.

18. Estes, A.C. (May 1, 2013). "LA Times Ban on Illegal Immigrant Puts Everybody Else on the Spot." *The Atlantic.*

19. Byers, D. (April 11, 2013). "USA Today Revises 'Illegal Immigrant' Use." *Politico.* www.politico.com/blogs/media/2013/04.

20. Zorn, E. (May 5, 2013). "Putting an End to 'Illegal Immigrant.'" *Chicago Tribune* www.chicagotribune.com/2013/05/05.

21. Race Forward—Drop the I-Word Campaign (September 2014). "Moving the Race Conversation Forward, Part 2." act.colorlines.com/acton/attachment.

Relief for All of Us or Relief for None of Us

1. The term *undocumented immigrant* refers to "anyone residing in any given country without legal documentation. It includes people who entered the United States without inspection and proper permission from the government, and those who entered with a legal visa that is no longer valid." See: Immigrants Rising (August 2023). "Defining Undocumented." immigrantsrising.org/resource. More than 11 million undocumented people reside in the United States and immigrate for many reasons, ranging from work to family reunification to safety. See Artiga, S. and Diaz, M. (July 2019). "Health Coverage and Care of Undocumented Immigrants." Kaiser Family Foundation. files.kff.org /attachment.

2. Capps, R. and Fix, M. (2022). *Changing the Playbook: Immigrants and the COVID-19 Response in Two U.S. Communities.* Washington, DC: Migration Policy Institute.

3. Feng, J., Pérez, A., Quiñonez Figueroa, P., Yoshizumi, A., Murguia, D., Reza, L., and Coven, D. (2021). "Community Provides: Undocumented Communities in Washington State During the COVID-19 Pandemic." Washington Dream Coalition. www.washingtondreamcoalition.org/community-provides. After the "Stay at Home, Stay Healthy" proclamation was announced by Governor Jay Inslee on Monday, March 23, 2020, Daniela Murguia, Guillermo Mogollan, Alejandra Pérez, Larissa Reza, Paúl Quiñonez Figueroa, and other WDC organizers started to see their own parents and family members lose hours at work or get laid off. Knowing that the COVID-19 pandemic was going to leave their community—their parents, siblings, relatives, and loved ones—in precarious working environments and without access to jobs or health care, they launched the Washington COVID-19 Immigrant Relief Fund coalition alongside other partner organizations.

4. Ibid.

5. Ibid.

6. Ibid. Among the 94,000 undocumented applications, 96 percent of them lost wages, 92 percent were low income, 87 percent were renters, 77 percent were single parents or the primary income earner in their household, 72 percent did not speak English, and 49 percent were at high risk from COVID-19.

7. Peitzman, L. (June 28, 2017). "The Story Behind the 'Immigrants (We Get the Job Done)' Video from the Hamilton Mixtape." BuzzFeed News. www.buzzfeednews.com /article.

8. Perez de la Rosa, E. (May 21, 2020). "Are their apples worth more than our lives? Yakima Valley Fruit Workers strike for protections." NW News Network. www .nwnewsnetwork.org/economy-business-finance-and-labor/2020-05-21.

9. Canning, D., and Reinsborough, P. (2010). *Re:Imagining Change: How to Use Story-Based Strategy to Win Campaigns, Build Movements, and Change the World.* Binghamton, NY: PM Press.

10. Tuck, E. (2009). "Suspending Damage: A Letter to Communities." *Harvard Educational Review* 79(3): 409–27. doi.org.

11. Feng, J., et al. "Community Provides: Undocumented Communities in Washington State During the COVID-19 Pandemic."

12. Martin, G.E. (2017). "Those Closest to the Problem Are Closest to the Solution." The Appeal.

13. Governor Jay Inslee (August 10, 2020). Press Release. "Inslee announces relief funds to help immigrants and agricultural workers." governor.wa.gov/news/2020.

HEALTH AND DIGNITY

"They Don't Care About Us, But We Care": The Narrative Power of Community Love, Grief, and Resistance from HIV to Long COVID

1. Lowenstein, F., and Davis, H. (March 17, 2021). "Long COVID Is Not Rare. It's a Health Crisis." *The New York Times.* www.nytimes.com/2021/03/17/opinion.

2. *Long COVID* is a term first coined by Elisa Perego in Lombardy, Italy, in May 2020. Long COVID is a patient-created term that describes a spectrum of long-term or permanent symptoms and conditions that appear or continue after the acute phase of a COVID-19 infection has passed, affecting even those who initially had mild cases of the disease.

3. As noted by the U.S. Caucus of People Living with HIV, "In June of 1983, at the Fifth Annual National Lesbian and Gay Health Conference in Denver, Colorado, a group of about a dozen gay men with AIDS from around the U.S. gathered to share their experiences combating stigma and advocating on behalf of people with AIDS. . . . They wrote out a manifesto, now known as The Denver Principles, outlining a series of rights and responsibilities for health care professionals, people with AIDS, and all who are concerned about the epidemic. It was the first time in the history of humanity that people who shared a disease organized to assert their right to a political voice in the decision making that would so profoundly affect their lives." See U.S. People Living with HIV Caucus (n.d.). *The Denver Principles* (1983). www.hivcaucus.org/resource -links.

4. Notably, on the second annual International Long COVID Awareness Day in 2024, ACT UP NY took to Instagram to pledge support for Long-COVID justice struggles, recognizing that Long COVID is two to four times more likely to affect people living with HIV. At their next (hybrid) meeting, ACT UP NY activated the narrative with a presentation from people living with Long COVID and COVID-19 prevention advocates, followed by a vote to require masking at their meetings and protest actions for the foreseeable future. (JD Davids works for Long COVID Justice, which collaborated on the post. As a voting ACT UP NY member and part of their newly formed COVID working group, JD spoke at the meeting in favor of sustained masking.)

5. For more on political funerals, see ACT UP Oral History Project (n.d.). "Political Funerals." www.actuporalhistory.org/actions.

6. Fiona Lowenstein: "I wore my Yale sweatshirt to the ER because I was like, I know this is going to be totally crowded and wild and this is the only sense of power I feel like I have. I don't have wealthy connected parents, but maybe if I wear this, someone will think I'm important. I was playing the game, which is a horrible game." See Romm, A. (March 29, 2023). "On What We All Need to Know About Long COVID." *On Health*, Episode 205 (Podcast). avivaromm.com/long-covid.

7. In response, the Gran Fury collective, which was associated with ACT UP NY and created the well-known pink triangle "Silence = Death" image, released the "All People with AIDS Are Innocent" poster as a part of "Spring AIDS Action 1988: Nine days of nationwide AIDS-related actions and protests." See Gran Fury (1988). "All People with AIDS Are Innocent" (Poster). digitalcollections.nypl.org.

8. Nisheda, A. (2022). *Just Care: Messy Entanglements of Disability, Dependency and Desire*. Philadelphia, PA: Temple University Press, 9. Recognition of the complexities of care is central in the work of multiple disability-focused advocates, artists, and academics—often Black and Brown women/femmes and/or LGTBQ+ people associated with disability-justice or healing-justice movements, including Patty Berne, Johanna Hedva, Leroy F. Moore Jr., Cara Page, and Sami Schalk.

9. Our use of the term *narrative care* intersects with the concept as used in narrative medicine, as defined by: Kenyon, G., and Randall, W. (August 2015). "Introduction." *Journal of Aging Studies* 34: 143–45. www.sciencedirect.com/science/article; quoted as "interventions which, in their implementation, focus on the person and his or her unique life narrative," in Villar, F., and Westerhof, G.J. (March 2023). "A Conversational, Small-Story Approach to Narrative Care for People with Dementia Living in Care Institutions: Strategies and Challenges." *Journal of Aging Studies* 64: 101–05. www .sciencedirect.com/science/article.

10. Butler, J. (2009). *Frames of War: When Is Life Grievable?* London, UK, and Brooklyn, NY: Verso Books.

11. SLAW me (May 23, 2016). "ACT UP Fight Back: Ending an Epidemic." YouTube. youtube/gXyUy-4c9yI?feature=shared.

12. In the era of first-generation HIV advocacy, Schalk documents the early, groundbreaking inclusion of HIV in the work of the National Black Women's Health Project on HIV as a part of their disability-inclusive work, but notes how a relevant article in their newsletter reveals an "avoidance of disability identity language in favor of disability medical language and passive voice . . . largely shaped by the author's focus on disability benefits rather than disability justice, community or identity." See Schalk, S. (2022). *Black Disability Politics*. Durham, NC: Duke University Press. p. 130. doi.org.

13. One of many examples of this narrative damage and neglect is an extreme of permissible fascism in mainstream press, William F. Buckley's AIDS op-ed, which reads in part: "But if the time has not come, and may never come, for public identification, what then of private identification? Everyone detected with AIDS should be tattooed in the upper forearm, to protect common needle users, and on the buttocks, to prevent the

victimization of other homosexuals." See: Buckley Jr., W.F. (March 18, 1986). "Crucial Steps in Combating the Aids Epidemic; Identify All the Carriers." *The New York Times.* archive.nytimes.com/www.nytimes.com/books/00/07/16/specials/buckley-aids.

14. Gawthorp, G. (October 19, 2023). "The Color of Coronavirus: COVID-19 Deaths by Race and Ethnicity in the US." APM Research Lab. www.apmresearchlab.org.

15. Turcotte, M., Sherman, R., Griesbach, R., and Klein, A.H. (Updated August 30, 2021). "The Real Toll from Prison COVID Cases May Be Higher Than Reported." *The New York Times.* www.nytimes.com/2021/07/07/us.

16. Like most reporting on COVID-19, stories on the impact of the pandemic on the incarcerated rarely mention chronic impacts or Long COVID.

17. Caruth, C., and Keenan, T. (Winter 1991). "'The AIDS Crisis Is Not Over': A Conversation with Gregg Bordowitz, Douglas Crimp, and Laura Pinsky." *American Imago* (Johns Hopkins University Press) 48(4): 539–56. www.jstor.org/stable/26303927. In the conversation, Bordowitz says: "The general public is a market, a fictional market. Advertisements are posed to it, and the intention is to get people to identify as a group that would want to buy specific products for specific reasons. . . . As Douglas has clearly articulated, that is a false dichotomy, an opposition which does not exist. *The general public does not exist.*"

18. Farhi, P. (January 12, 2022). "A Rochelle Walensky Interview Sparked Outrage. But the CDC Says ABC Omitted Crucial Context. *The Washington Post.* www .washingtonpost.com/lifestyle/media/walensky-abc-interview/2022/01/12.

19. Autistic Self Advocacy Network (January 13, 2022). "Letter from the Disability Community to CDC Director Rochelle Walensky." autisticadvocacy.org/2022/01.

20. Rao, S., et al. (March 2024). "Postacute Sequelae of SARS-CoV-2 in Children." *Pediatrics* 153(3). publications.aap.org/pediatrics/article.

21. U.S. Centers for Disease Control and Prevention (n.d.). "Long COVID Household Pulse Study." National Center for Health Statistics. www.cdc.gov/nchs/covid19/pulse /long-covid.

22. CDC Foundation (Summer 2023). *Infection-Associated Chronic Conditions: Opportunities for Action. Summer 2023 Workshop Series Summary and Key Takeaways.* solvecfs.org/wp-content/uploads/2024/02/ICUEPublicReport.

23. "DC: I would think that it could be very shocking, since it is not a habit of television—at least not for any group that is reported about, but never directly spoken to (this would be true of an address to queers)—to treat those people not as an ethnographic subject but as the very subject to whom you are speaking. I think that that would be shocking, there would be a kind of shock of recognition. GB: When it first occurred to me that you could address people with AIDS or HIV in television interviews directly and try to engender them as an audience, the secondary effect was that people who were not HIV positive would realize that there were HIV positive people in the audience." From Caruth and Keenan, T. "'The AIDS Crisis Is Not Over': A Conversation with Gregg Bordowitz, Douglas Crimp, and Laura Pinsky."

24. Wright, K., and Ratner, L. (February 1, 2024). *Blindspot* Podcast. The HISTORY® Channel and WNYC Studios, in collaboration with *The Nation*. podcasts.apple.com/us /podcast/blindspot.

25. National Library of Medicine (Fall 1988). "ACT UP Philadelphia: HIV/AIDS Adult Standard of Care." Critical Path AIDS Project 33: 18–22. pubmed.ncbi.nlm.nih .gov/11366364.

26. Additional examples from this era of AIDS activism abound: Self-help groups for Black women with HIV/AIDS sponsored by the National Black Women's Health Project (detailed in Schalk's *Black Disability Politics*), prevention pamphlets for gay San Franciscans distributed by the Sisters of Perpetual Indulgence that pre-dated mass-media AIDS reporting, and community-based educational efforts conducted by the South Carolina AIDS Education Network out of co-founder DiAna DiAna's hair salon, depicted in the short documentary *DiAna's Hair Ego*; see Spiro, E. (1990). *DiAna's Hair Ego: AIDS Info Up Front* (Film).

27. Strikingly, Long COVID has been notably absent from coverage about the COVID-19 pandemic itself. A Strategies for High Impact analysis of COVID-19 stories in the *Washington Post* from March to June 2023 showed only 10 percent of news articles and 15 percent of opinion pieces about COVID-19 even mentioned Long COVID. (Analysis is unpublished.)

28. The national webinar was distributed via two different podcasts as "Coronavirus: Wisdom from a Social Justice Lens"; see Brown, A. and brown, a.m. (March 12, 2020). "Coronavirus: Wisdom from a Social Justice Lens." *How to Survive the End of the World* (Podcast). podcasts.apple.com/us.

29. Patient-Led Research Collective (May 11, 2020). *Report: What Does COVID-19 Recovery Actually Look Like? An Analysis of the Prolonged COVID-19 Symptoms Survey by Patient-Led Research Team*. patientresearchcovid19.com/research/report.

30. In 2024, the National Academies on Science, Engineering, and Medicine affirmed and further delineated a broad definition of Long COVID, in keeping with the original interim definition. See National Academies of Sciences, Engineering, and Medicine (n.d.). "A Long COVID Definition." nap.nationalacademies.org.

31. Millington, M. (April 26, 2024). "Documentary to Spotlight a Black Woman's Journey with Long COVID." *Caribbean Life*. www.caribbeanlife.com.

32. Hedva, J. (2016, 2020). "Sick Woman Theory." The Anarchist Library. theanar chistlibrary.org.

33. This includes Long COVID Justice, Patient Led Research Collaborative, and Body Politic.

34. @crutches_and_spice. Instagram. www.instagram.com.

35. By May 2020, an estimated half of accounts on Twitter talking about COVID were bots. Social media can increase the potential of movement damage since algorithms reward conflict, whether propagated by false actors, lack of information, or misunderstanding. See D'Ambrosio, A. (Updated November 12, 2021). "New Institute Has

Ties to the Great Barrington Declaration." *MedPage Today*. www.medpagetoday.com /special-reports/exclusives.

36. Notably, the victories of HIV/AIDS activism, including securing federal resources, altered the relationship to care and contributed to demobilization of the movement itself. Scholar Jeff Maskovsky describes this dynamic as the "clientization" of people living with HIV, as "their roles in these organizations became increasingly passive as clients receiving care from professional service providers." See Maskovsky, J. (July 2019). "The Allure of Community: The Ethical Journey of People Living with HIV Disease in Philadelphia." In Page-Reeves, J.M. (ed). *Well-Being as a Multidimensional Concept: Understanding Connections Among Culture, Community and Health*. Lanham, MD: Lexington Press, 125–43.

37. Ongoing practices that entwine narratives of grief, grievability, and community care will enable us to move closer to the dreams of HIV movement leaders to address larger systemic causes of the governmental and public health failure that allowed so many to die and that perpetuates what HIV activist Sean Strub first called the "viral underclass," a phrase amplified by journalist Steven Thrasher to describe the dynamics of high rates of chronic illness, disability, and premature death in the United States—particularly among disabled and chronically ill people, racialized communities, and queer and trans people. See Thrasher, S.W. (2022). *The Viral Underclass: The Human Toll When Inequality and Disease Collide*. New York, NY: Celadon Books.

38. Meriquez Vázquez, A. (December 2, 2023). "Still on the Margins: Long COVID Patients of Color." Disability Visibility Project. disabilityvisibilityproject.com/2023/12 /02.

From "Safe, Legal, and Rare" to "Everyone Loves Someone Who Had an Abortion": How We Shifted the Abortion Conversation

1. A phrase coined by Renee Bracey Sherman in 2015.

2. *Saturday Night Live* (November 6, 2022). "Weekend Update: Tammy the Trucker on Gas Prices and Definitely Not Abortion." 4:11. YouTube. youtube/7vO7UQ9DxW U?si=pHkOaocOBi95tdd5.

3. Brenan, M. (June 9, 2021). "Record-High 47% in U.S. Think Abortion Is Morally Acceptable." *Gallup News*. news.gallup.com/poll.

4. North, A. (October 18, 2019). "How the Abortion Debate Moved Away from 'Safe, Legal, and Rare.'" *Vox*. www.vox.com/2019/10/18.

5. Tracy, A. (September 15, 2022). "'Should This Decision Be Made by Dr. Oz?': Abortion-Rights Fight Is Taking Center Stage in Pennsylvania Senate Race." *Vanity Fair*. www.vanityfair.com/news/2022/09.

6. Political messages are persuasive bodies of information that shape how we understand important ideas. To delegitimize harmful or ineffective messages that hurt our communities, we must first recognize what values, assumptions, and political framing are at the core of the issue.

7. Advocates for Youth (n.d.). "Abortion Out Loud." www.advocatesforyouth.org /abortion-out-loud.

8. Sherman, R.B. and Weitz, T. (September 20, 2021). "The Fall of 'Roe' Was Driven by Our Country's Original Sin: Anti-Blackness." *Rewire News Group*. rewirenews group.com/2021/09/20.

9. Sister Song (n.d.). "Reproductive Justice—Sister Song." www.sistersong.net /reproductive-justice.

10. American College of Obstetricians and Gynecologists (December 2020). "Increasing Access to Abortion. Committee Opinion Number 815." www.acog.org/clinical /clinical-guidance/committee-opinion/articles/2020/12

11. Hosie, R. (January 14, 2017). "Five women reveal the heartbreaking reasons they had abortions." *The Independent*. www.independent.co.uk/life-style/health-and -families.

12. Harris, J. (August 15, 2014). "Stop Calling Abortion a 'Difficult Decision.'" *The Washington Post*. www.washingtonpost.com/opinions.

13. Justia U.S. Supreme Court Center (2007). *Gonzales v. Carhart, 550 U.S. 124*. supreme.justia.com/cases/federal/us/550/124/#tab-opinion-1962402.

14. Goodwin, M. (2020). *Policing the Womb: Invisible Women and the Criminalization of Motherhood*. Cambridge, UK: Cambridge University Press, 2020, 32.

15. Gandy, I. (February 8, 2021). "Purvi Patel and the Case of the Self-Managed Abortion." *Rewire News Group*. rewirenewsgroup.com/2021/02/08.

16. Dasgupta, S. (April 26, 2015). "Pregnant Women Are Now Targets: The Tragedy of Purvi Patel." *Salon*. www.salon.com/2015/04/26/a_terrifying_floodgate _for_prosecuting_women_why_purvi_patel_is_not_a_terrorist_partner.

17. Aaronson, B. (June 26, 2013). "Led by Davis, Democrats Defeat Abortion Legislation." *The Texas Tribune*. www.texastribune.org/2013/06/26.

18. Assefa, C. (January 7, 2016). "'All Lives Matter Act' Is a Blatant Attack on Black Female Bodies in Missouri." *The Feminist Wire*. thefeministwire.com/2016/01.

19. HIT Strategies (January 2023). "Criminal Justice Reform Focus Groups." drive .google.com/file/d/1JBkJolVkn_1gzHbVB9LCeZ8SIBo79M40/view.

20. McClain, L.C. (July 1, 2022). "What Would It Mean for the United States to Codify Roe v. Wade?" *YES!* www.yesmagazine.org/democracy/2022/07/01.

21. Guttmacher Institute (May 2021). "The Hyde Amendment: A Discriminatory Ban on Insurance Coverage of Abortion." Guttmacher Institute Fact Sheet. www.guttmacher .org/fact-sheet/hyde-amendment.

22. American Civil Liberties Union (February 28, 2011). "The Facts About 'The No Taxpayer Funding For Abortion Act.'" www.aclu.org/documents.

23. National Network of Abortion Funds (n.d.). "Abortion Funds Renew Call for Taxes to Fund Abortion Care." abortionfunds.org/campaign.

24. Kheyfets, A., et al. (December 5, 2023). "The Impact of Hostile Abortion Legislation on the United States Maternal Mortality Crisis: A Call for Increased Abortion

Education." *Frontiers in Public Health* 11. www.frontiersin.org/journals/public-health /articles.

25. Sister Song (n.d.). "Reproductive Justice—Sister Song." www.sistersong.net /reproductive-justice.

Building People Power: How to Shift the Health Care Narrative in the United States

1. Palmquist, B., and Jacquez, M. (March 17, 2021). "Uninsurance." Partners for Dignity & Rights. dignityandrights.org/resources.

2. Vermont Workers' Center (n.d.). "The Human Right to Healthcare." workerscenter .org/wp-content/uploads/2022/10/human_rights_principles_and_healthcare.

3. For more background on the history and rationale of the campaign, and its intersection with worker organizing, see Kissam, J. (June 24, 2012). "Dollars & Sense Article: 'The Vermont Workers' Center Leads Breakthrough on Healthcare'" (Personal Website). jonathankissam.wordpress.com/2012/06/24.

4. Vermont Workers' Center (December 10, 2008). "Voices of Vermont's Healthcare Crisis: The Human Right to Healthcare." workerscenter.org/wp-content/uploads/2022 /11.

5. Marchenkova, D., and Sheehan, M. (n.d.). "The People's Media Project, Media and Communications in the Movement." healthcareisahumanright.org/wp-content /uploads/2015/06/Final-PMP-article; Center for Story-Based Strategy (Website). www .storybasedstrategy.org.

6. Haslam, J. (October 27, 2011). "Lessons from the Single-Payer State: How to Spread Vermont's Human-Rights Victory Throughout the Country." *In These Times*. inthesetimes.com/article/help-wanted-lessons-from-the-single-payer-state.

7. Partners for Dignity & Rights (n.d.). "The Vermont Breakthrough! How a Human Rights Movement Is Winning a Healthcare System That Puts People First" (Video). vimeo.com/42839142.

8. Healthcare Is a Human Right (n.d.). "The People's Recipe." healthcareisahuman-right.org/wp-content/uploads/2015/04/58.

9. Layson, T. (March 11, 2015). "Vermont Healthcare Justice." *Against the Current*. againstthecurrent.org.

10. Farr, M., and Rudiger, A. (July 2020, revised edition). "Equitable Financing Plan for Vermont's Universal Healthcare System." Partners for Dignity & Rights, Vermont Workers' Center. workerscenter.org/wp-content/uploads/2022/10.

11. Rudiger, A. (December 5, 2016). "Human Rights and the Political Economy of Universal Health Care: Designing Equitable Financing." *Health and Human Rights Journal*. www.hhrjournal.org/2016/12.

12. Rudiger, A. (May 4, 2012). "Toward a People's Budget: Vermont Adopts New Vision for State Spending and Revenue Policies." *HuffPost*. www.huffpost.com/entry /vermont-state-spending_b_1477641.

13. Fuse Brown, E.C. and McCuskey, E.Y. (June 6, 2019). "Federalism, ERISA, and State Single-Payer Healthcare." *University of Pennsylvania Law Review* 168; forthcoming Georgia State University College of Law, Legal Studies Research Paper No. 2019-16. papers.ssrn.com/sol3/papers.cfm?abstract_id=3395462.

Building a Fat-Positive Future: Strategies for Advocacy and Change

1. NYC.gov (May 26, 2023). "Mayor Adams Signs Legislation to Prohibit Height or Weight Discrimination in Employment, Housing, and Public Accommodations." www .nyc.gov/office-of-the-mayor/news/364-23.

2. National Association to Advance Fat Acceptance (n.d.). "Campaign for Size Freedom." naafa.org/sizefreedom.

3. NAAFA Official (August 6, 2020*).* "August 6, 2020 Webinar: Adding 'Weight' to the Anti-Discrimination Law in Your Area." YouTube. www.youtube.com/watch?v=X _QZoAvw0ZU&t=13s.

4. Taylor, S.R. (2018). *The Body Is Not an Apology.* Oakland, CA: Berrett-Koehler Publishers.

5. NAAFA Official (December 10, 2020). "Webinar: Fearing the Black Body: The Racial Origins of Fat Phobia with Dr. Sabrina Strings." YouTube. www.youtube.com /watch?v=wPiK8dIcSSM&t=897s.

6. Rupp, K., and McCoy, S.M. (July 2019). "Bullying Perpetration and Victimization Among Adolescents with Overweight and Obesity in a Nationally Representative Sample." *Childhood Obesity* 15(5): 323–30. doi: 10.1089/chi.2018.0233. Epub 2019 May 7. PMID: 31062988; PMCID: PMC7364321.

7. *Carceral systems* refer to the institutions and practices related to incarceration and the control of people through imprisonment, policing, and surveillance.

8. Mejia, P. (n.d.). "The Size of It: Fat Bias in the News." National Association to Advance Fat Acceptance. naafa.org/mediastudy.

9. Dove (November 2, 2023). "The Real Cost of Beauty Ideals: The Stats." www.dove .com/us/en/stories/campaigns.

10. Krais, R. and Green, H.H. (March 28, 2024). "The Bias We Don't Talk About." *This Is Uncomfortable*, Season 9. (Podcast). www.marketplace.org/shows.

11. New York City Council (Enacted May 26, 2023). "A Local Law to amend the administrative code of the city of New York, in relation to prohibiting discrimination on the basis of a person's height or weight in employment, housing, and public accommodations." legistar.council.nyc.gov/LegislationDetail.

12. Jimenez, N. (May 11, 2023). "New York City passes law barring weight discrimination." BBC. www.bbc.com/news/business-65562288.

13. Tejada, J. (March 1, 2023). "New NYC bill could prohibit weight discrimination." News 12 New Jersey. newjersey.news12.com.

14. New York City Council (April 28, 2022). "A Local Law to amend the administrative code of the city of New York, in relation to prohibiting discrimination on the basis of a person's height or weight in employment, housing, and public accommodations." Committee on Civil and Human Rights. legistar.council.nyc.gov/LegislationDetail.

15. NAAFA in the News (n.d.). NAAFA. naafa.org/news-nyc2023.

16. Fitzsimmons, E.G. (May 11, 2023). "New York City Is Set to Ban Weight Discrimination." *The New York Times*. nytimes.com/2023/05/11/nyregion.

17. Dorfman, L., and Wallack, L. (2013). "Putting Policy into Health Communications." In *Public Communication Campaigns* (4th ed.). Thousand Oaks, CA: Sage, 335–348.

18. Fox, J.C. (Updated May 20, 2023). "New Hope for Bill to Ban Size Discrimination in Massachusetts, After Three Decades of Trying." *The Boston Globe*. www.bostonglobe.com/2023/05/20/metro.

19. Pierre, J. (April 18, 2023). "Fat Acceptance as a Civil Rights Issue." *The Takeaway* (Podcast). WNYC Studios. www.wnycstudios.org/podcasts/takeaway/segments/fat-bias-civil-rights.

20. Hobbs, M., and Gordon, G. (December 29, 2023). "December Bonus: The 2023 Grifties!" *Maintenance Phase* (Podcast). podcasts.apple.com/us/podcast.

21. BMSG researchers used LexisNexis, a news-media database, to search for and quantify articles about the fat-liberation movement (including terms related to the NYC Height and Weight Bill, and stigma, bias, or discrimination related to weight or body size) and "weight loss" from February through July of 2022 and 2023 in U.S. newspapers. These quantitative results may underrepresent the volume of news, given that LexisNexis only provides newspaper articles and search terms were certainly not exhaustive.

ECONOMIC EQUALITY AND WORKERS' RIGHTS

The Power to Win: Occupy Wall Street, the Fight for $15, and Multidimensional Power

1. See Naomi Klein's work, including: Klein, N. (2014). *This Changes Everything: Capitalism vs the Climate*. New York, NY: Simon & Schuster, 72–73; Also on the fourth pillar, see Brown, W. (2019). *In the Ruins of Neoliberalism: The Rise of Antidemocratic Politics in the West*. New York, NY: Columbia University Press.

2. See Darrick Hamilton's work on stratification economics, including: Darity Jr., W.A., Hamilton, D., and Stewart, J.B. (2015). "A Tour de Force in Understanding Inter-

group Inequality: An Introduction to Stratification Economics." *Review of Black Political Economy* 42: 1–6. socialequity.duke.edu/wp-content/uploads/2019/10.

3. See Wendy Brown's work, including: Brown, W. (2019). *In the Ruins of Neoliberalism: The Rise of Antidemocratic Politics in the West.* New York, NY: Columbia University Press.

4. See: Warren, D. (Summer 2019). "Growing the Grassroots." *Democracy Journal.* democracyjournal.org/magazine/53.

5. See Benner, C., and Pastor, M. (2021). *Solidarity Economics: Why Mutuality and Movements Matter.* Cambridge, UK: Polity.

6. See, for example: Democracy Journal (Summer 2019). "Symposium: Beyond Neoliberalism." *Democracy Journal* 53. democracyjournal.org/magazine/53; (Spring 2022). "Symposium: Beyond Neoliberalism Part II." *Democracy Journal* 64. democracy journal.org/magazine/64.

7. Movement power combines three forms of power: (a) organized people who build solidarity to achieve common purpose; (b) visionary ideas that reshape what is possible and break through the noise; and (c) political muscle to elect and unelect leaders who advance and enact the people's agenda.

8. See Lathrop, Y., Wilson, M.D., and Lester, T.W. (November 29, 2022). "Ten-Year Legacy of the Fight for $15 and a Union Movement." National Employment Law Project. www.nelp.org/insights-research.

9. Shenker-Osorio, A. (August 2017). "Messaging This Moment: A Handbook for Progressive Communicators." Community Change. communitychange.org/wp-content /uploads/2017/08.

10. Reinsborough, P., and Canning, D. (2017). *Re:Imagining Change: How to Use Story-Based Strategy to Win Campaigns, Build Movements, and Change the World,* 2nd Edition. Binghamton, NY: PM Press.

11. Kiel, P. (April 10, 2012). "The Great American Foreclosure Story: The Struggle for Justice and a Place to Call Home." *ProPublica.* www.propublica.org/article; Bennett, J. and Kochhar, R. (December 13, 2019). "Two Recessions, Two Recoveries." Pew Research Center. www.pewresearch.org/social-trends/2019/12/13.

12. BBC News (January 10, 2014). "Half of US Congressional politicians are millionaires." www.bbc.com/news/world-us-canada-25691066.

13. On the other side of the spectrum, the Tea Party Movement advanced a purportedly populist economic narrative. However, its message of "outrage over the debt and deficit had another purpose: giving cover and a voice to those who wanted to attack the first black president—people who in some cases showed up at rallies waving signs with racist caricatures and references." Peters, J.W. (August 28, 2019). "The Tea Party Didn't Get What It Wanted, but It Did Unleash the Politics of Anger." *The New York Times.* www.nytimes.com/2019/08/28/us/politics.

14. Miller, Z. (October 16, 2011). "White House Draws Closer to Occupy Wall Street, Says Obama Is Fighting for the Interests of the 99%." *Business Insider.* www .businessinsider.com.

15. See Brown, W. (2011). "Occupy Wall Street." *Adbusters America* 19(97), 50–51. Brown's poster in *Adbusters* and the broader iconography of Occupy Wall Street deserves a deeper analysis as part of a long tradition of art as a form of protest, as Milton Glaser and Mirko Ilic detail in their book: Glaser, M. and Ilic, M. (2005). *The Design of Dissent.* Gloucester, MA: Rockport Publishers.

16. Goldstein, J. (July 2012). "Occuprint: Archiving the Future." *Socialism and Democracy* 26(2). sdonline.org/issue/59.

17. Blitt, B. (October 24, 2011). "Fighting Back." *The New Yorker.* www.newyorker.com/magazine/2011/10/24.

18. DiMaggio, A., and Street, P. (November 19, 2011). "Occupy Wall Street, Mass Media and Progressive Change in the Tea Party Era." *Economic and Political Weekly* 46(47): 10–14. www.jstor.org/stable.

19. Zerbisias, A. (September 20, 2011). "Protests dwindle in attempt to Occupy Wall Street." *Toronto Star.* www.thestar.com/news/world/2011/09/20.

20. Mackinac Center for Public Policy (n.d.). "The Overton Window." www.mackinac.org.

21. Gabbatt, A. (September 17, 2015). "Former Occupy Wall Street protestors rally around Bernie Sanders campaign." *The Guardian.* www.theguardian.com/us-news/2015/sep/17/occupy-wall-street-protesters-bernie-sanders.

22. Shephard, A. (September 14, 2016). "What Occupy Wall Street Got Wrong." *The New Republic.* newrepublic.com/article.

23. Robinson, R. (April 18, 2018). "Changing Our Narrative About Narrative: The Infrastructure Required for Building Narrative Power." Othering and Belonging Institute. belonging.berkeley.edu.

24. Ad Council Research Institute (2022). "The 2022 Trusted Messenger Study: The Annual Study of Who Americans Trust on Social and Societal Issues." ad-council.brightspotcdn.com.

25. McCluskey, M. (January 21, 2021). "People Have Turned Bernie Sanders' Inauguration Fashion into So Much More Than Your Standard Meme." *Time.* time.com/5932101/bernie-memes-mittens.

26. Maher, K. (Updated February 11, 2011). "Big Union to Step Up Recruiting." *The Wall Street Journal.* www.wsj.com/articles.

27. Rosenblum, J. (2017). "Fight for $15: Good Wins but Where Did the Focus on Organizing Go?" *Labor Studies Journal* 42(4): 387–93. jonathanrosenblum.org/lib/img/Labor-studies-journal-December-2017.

28. DeSilver, D. (February 20, 2014). "American Unions Membership Declines as Public Support Fluctuates." Pew Research Center. www.pewresearch.org/fact-tank/2014/02/20.

29. Johnson, S. (February 11, 2021). "A Decade after Act 10, it's a different world for Wisconsin unions." Wisconsin Public Radio. www.wpr.org.

Reframing the Retail Apocalypse: Narrative Strategies for the Future of Worker Organizing

1. Cappetta, M. (March 14, 2018). "The collapse of Toys R Us could mean the loss of around 33,000 jobs." NBC News. www.nbcnews.com/business/consumer/game-over -bankrupt-toys-r-us-files-liquidation; D'Innocenzio, A. (September 17, 2017). "Toys R Us Joins Bankruptcy List as Amazon Exerts Influence." AP News. apnews.com/article /north-america-us-news-ap-top-news-toys-international-news; Varney, S. (September 19, 2017). "Toys R Us bankruptcy is sign of 'Retail Ice Age.'" Fox News. video .foxnews.com.

2. Bhardwaj, P. (May 29, 2018). "Online Sales Still Account for Less Than 10% of All Retail Sales." *Business Insider.* www.businessinsider.com/ecommerce-percent-retail -sales-charts-2018-5.

3. Baker, J., and Vitulli, E. (July 2019). "Pirate Equity: How Wall Street Firms Are Pillaging American Retail." The Center for Popular Democracy, Americans for Financial Reform, Strong Economy for All Coalition, United for Respect, Hedge Clippers, Private Equity Stakeholder Project. united4respect.org/wp-content/uploads/2019/08.

4. Ibid.

5. Requarth, T. (April 30, 2019). "How Private Equity Is Turning Public Prisons Into Big Profits." *The Nation.* www.thenation.com/article/archive; Scheffler, R.M., Alexander, L.M., and Godwin, J.R. (May 18, 2021). "Soaring Private Equity Investment in the Healthcare Sector: Consolidation Accelerated, Competition Undermined, and Patients at Risk." American Antitrust Institute, Petris Center. publichealth.berkeley.edu/wp -content/uploads; Vogell, H. (February 7, 2022). "When Private Equity Becomes Your Landlord." *ProPublica.* www.propublica.org/article.

6. United for Respect (June 27, 2019). "Days Before the Anniversary of Toys 'R' Us' Shutting Down, Judge Approves Severance Settlement for Its Employees" (Press Release). united4respect.org/press-release/people-who-work-at-walmart-sears-amazon -formerly-toys-r-us-more-join-forces-together-as-united-for-respect.

7. Golden, L. (December 5, 2016). "Still Falling Short on Hours and Pay: Part-Time Work Becoming New Normal." Economic Policy Institute. www.epi.org/publication.

8. Unglesbee, B. (November 9, 2018). "Retail's Largest Private Equity Buyouts and How They've Panned Out." *Retail Dive.* www.retaildive.com/news.

9. La, M. and Paul, R. (October 16, 2018). "Hedge funds have killed Sears and many other retailers." CNN. www.cnn.com/2018/10/16/investing.

10. Baker and Vitulli. "Pirate Equity."

11. Bollier, J. (October 15, 2020). "Shopko Severance: Bankruptcy Judge Approves $3 Million in Severance Pay for 4,000 Workers." *Green Bay Press Gazette.* www.green baypressgazette.com/story/money/2020/10/15; Ronalds-Hannon, E. and Coleman-Lochner, L. (June 27, 2019). "Toys R Us Workers Win $2-Million Settlement on Severance." *Los Angeles Times.* www.latimes.com/business.

12. Baker and Vitulli. "Pirate Equity."

13. Rozhon, T. and Sorkin, A. R. (March 17, 2005). "Three Firms Are Said to Buy Toys 'R' Us for $6 Billion." *The New York Times.* www.nytimes.com/2005/03/17/business.

14. Baker and Vitulli. "Pirate Equity."

15. U.S. Department of Labor (May 2023). "Occupational Employment and Wage Statistics: Retail Salespersons." Bureau of Labor Statistics. www.bls.gov/oes/current.

16. Hamilton, G.G., Petrovic, M., and Senauer, B. (eds.) (2011). *Market Makers: How Retailers Are Reshaping the Global Economy.* Oxford, UK: Oxford University Press.

17. Siegel, R. (February 4, 2019). "Toys R Us Workers Are Training Sears Workers to Fight for Severance." *The Washington Post.* www.washingtonpost.com/business/2019 /02/04.

18. United for Respect @forrespect. (June 26, 2019). "Our Member Trina Organizing an Action with Her Coworkers at the Shopko in Dubuque, Illinois. She Says, 'I'm Sad for All of Our Shopko Family, Near and Far, but Now We Have to Fight for What We Believe. I Sure Hope We Can Pull This Off. We Deserve It.'" X, formerly Twitter. twitter.com/forrespect/status.

19. Celarier, M. (December 4, 2021). "Is Private Equity Overrated?" *The New York Times.* www.nytimes.com/2021/12/04/business.

20. Baker and Vitulli. "Pirate Equity."

21. Warren, E. (October 20, 2021). "Private Equity Activity Has Exploded and Continued to Grow During the Pandemic, Exploiting Workers, Consumers, and Communities; Comprehensive Bill Would Hold Wall Street Accountable, Empower Workers, Safeguard the Financial System, and Protect Investors" (Press Release). www.warren.senate .gov/newsroom/press-releases/warren-baldwin-brown-pocan-jayapal-colleagues -reintroduce-bold-legislation-to-fundamentally-reform-the-private-equity-industry.

22. MacArthur, H., Burack, R., De Vusser, C., and Yang, K. (March 7, 2022). "The Private Equity Market in 2021: The Allure of Growth." Bain & Company. www.bain .com/insights/private-equity-market-in-2021-global-private-equity-report-2022; Valdes-Viera, O., Woodall, P., Szakonyi, D., Li, M., Lincoln, T., and Tanglis, M. (September 2021). "Public Money for Private Equity: Pandemic Relief Went to Companies Backed by Private Equity Titans." Americans for Financial Reform Education Fund, Anti-Corruption Data Collective, Public Citizen. ourfinancialsecurity.org/2021/09 /report-public-money-for-private-equity-cares-act.

23. Farrell, M. (March 14, 2022). "Private Equity Is the New Financial Supermarket." *The New York Times.* www.nytimes.com/2022/03/10/business.

24. Bollier, J. "Bankruptcy Judge Approves $3 Million for 4,000 Former Shopko Workers Promised Severance"; Romo, V. (January 22, 2020). "New Jersey mandates severance pay for workers facing mass layoffs." NPR. www.npr.org/2020/01/22; Ronalds-Hannon, E., and Coleman-Lochner, L. (June 30, 2021). "Michigan Democrat Seeks Labor Law Inspired by Art Van Demise." Bloomberg. www.bloomberg.com /news/articles/2021-06-30.

The Past, Present, and Future Narratives of Philanthropy

1. Crowder, C., and Flannery, H. (July 17, 2024). "The True Cost of Billionaire Philanthropy: How the Taxpayer Subsidizes Stockpiled Wealth." Institute for Policy Studies. ips-dc.org.

2. Carnegie, A. (1889). *The Gospel of Wealth*. New York, NY: Carnegie Corporation of New York.

3. Ibid.

4. FoundationMark (n.d.). "Assets and Grantmaking Trends." foundationmark.com /#/grants.

5. Herschander, S. (January 31, 2024). "Foundations Gave $97.5 Billion Last Year as Assets Hit Record Highs." *The Chronicle of Philanthropy*. www.philanthropy.com /article.

6. NPTrust (August 7, 2024). "The 2023 DAF [Donor Advised Fund] Report." National Philanthropic Trust. www.nptrust.org/reports/daf-report.

7. Francis, M.M. (2019). "The Price of Civil Rights: Black Lives, White Funding, and Movement Capture." *Law & Society Review* 53(1): 275–309. www.cambridge.org/core /journals/law-and-society-review/article/abs.

8. The term *nonprofit industrial complex* was coined in this book.

9. INCITE! Women of Color Against Violence (2017). *INCITE! The Revolution Will Not Be Funded: Beyond the Non-Profit Industrial Complex*. Durham, NC: Duke University Press.

DEMOCRACY FOR ALL

Refusing the Status Quo: How Narrative Power Can Shape Policy Change

1. Kaiser Family Foundation (May 2, 2013). "Timeline: History of Health Reform in the U.S." www.kff.org/wp-content/uploads/2011/03/5-02-13-history-of-health-reform.

2. Medicare is the public insurance program that guarantees health care coverage for older Americans. It differentiates itself from Medicaid in that it is available to all U.S. citizens or long-term permanent residents above the age of sixty-five. In contrast, Medicaid is a means-tested health insurance program, and is only available to low-income people who meet a certain income threshold.

3. U.S. Department of Health and Human Services (December 20, 2023). "HealthCare .gov Enrollment Exceeds 15 Million, Surpassing Previous Years' Milestones." www .hhs.gov/about/news/2023/12/20.

4. Harker, L., and Sharer, B. (June 14, 2024). "Medicaid Expansion: Frequently Asked Questions." Center on Budget and Policy Priorities. www.cbpp.org/research/health.

5. U.S. Department of Health and Human Services (June 7, 2024). "Biden-Harris Administration Releases Data Showing Historic Gains in Health Care Coverage in Minority Communities." www.hhs.gov/about/news/2024/06/07.

6. Tolbert, J., Drake, P., and Damico, A. (December 18, 2023). "Key Facts About the Uninsured Population." Kaiser Family Foundation. www.kff.org/uninsured/issue-brief.

Understanding and Combating Online Racialized Disinformation in the 21st Century

1. Disinfo Defense League (Website). www.disinfodefenseleague.org.

2. U.S. Senate (n.d.). *Report of the Select Committee on Intelligence, United States Senate, on Russian Active Measures Campaigns and Interference in the 2016 U.S. Election. Volume 2: Russia's Use of Social Media with Additional News.* www.intelligence .senate.gov/sites/default/files/documents/Report_Volume2.

3. Hampton, R. (April 23, 2019). "The Black Feminists Who Saw the Alt-Right Threat Coming." *Slate.* slate.com/technology/2019/04.

4. Goertzel, T. (December 1994). "Belief in Conspiracy Theories." *Political Psychology*15(4): 731–42. www.jstor.org/stable/3791630.

5. Thorburn, S. and Bogart, L.M. (August 2005). "Conspiracy Theories About Birth Control: Barriers to Pregnancy Prevention Among African Americans of Reproductive Age." *Health Education & Behavior* 32(4). journals.sagepub.com/doi/abs.

6. Kaiser Family Foundation (September 15, 2023). "Large Shares of Black Adults, Hispanic Adults, and Rural Residents Are Unsure Whether to Believe Many False Health Claims" (Press Release). www.kff.org/coronavirus-covid-19.

7. Equis Research (June 21, 2021). "On Latinos, Misinformation and Uncertainty: New Polling Insights." *Medium.* equisresearch.medium.com.

8. Chong, M., and Froehlich, T.J. (October 13, 2021). "Racial Attacks During the COVID-19 Pandemic: Politicizing an Epidemic Crisis on Long-Standing Racism and Misinformation, Disinformation, and Misconception" (Panel). Proceedings of the Association for Information Science and Technology. *ASIS&T* 58(1): 573–76. asistdl .onlinelibrary.wiley.com/doi/abs.

9. Pew Research Center (November 15, 2023). "News Platform Fact Sheet." www .pewresearch.org/journalism.

10. Free Press (n.d.). "Media 2070: An Invitation to Dream Up Media Reparations." www.freepress.net/issues/future-journalism/media-reparations.

11. Altay, S., Berriche, M., and Acerbi, A. (2022). "Misinformation on Misinformation: Conceptual and Methodological Challenges." Sciences Po. sciencespo.hal.science/hal-03700770.

12. Jungherr, A., and Rauchfleisch, A. (January 12, 2024). "Negative Downstream Effects of Alarmist Disinformation Discourse: Evidence from the United States." *Political Behavior.* doi.org/10.1007/s11109-024-09911-3.

13. Guess, A., Nagler, J., and Tucker, J. (January 9, 2019). "Less Than You Think: Prevalence and Predictors of Fake News Dissemination on Facebook." *Science Advances* 5(1). www.science.org/doi/10.1126/sciadv.aau4586.

14. Allen, J., Howland, B., Mobius, M., Rothschild, D., and Watts, D.J. (April 3, 2020). "Evaluating the Fake News Problem at the Scale of the Information Ecosystem." *Science Advances* 6(14). www.science.org/doi/10.1126/sciadv.aay3539.

15. Longoria, J. (December 9, 2020). "As Online Communities Mobilize Offline, Misinformation Manifests a Physical Threat." First Draft. firstdraftnews.org/articles/online-mobilizes-offline.

16. Stray, J., Thorburn, L., and Bengani, P. (April 28, 2023). "Making Amplification Measurable." *Tech Policy Press*. www.techpolicy.press.

17. Stray, J., Thorburn, L., and Bengani, P. (May 19, 2022). "What Will 'Amplification' Mean in Court?" *Tech Policy Press*. www.techpolicy.press.

18. Disinfo Defense League (December 2021). "Disinfo Defense League Policy Platform." www.disinfodefenseleague.org.

Data for Liberation: The Role of Surveys in Social Movement Infrastructure

1. Cohen, C.J. (2020). "Death and Democracy." In *Democracy and Civic Life: What Is the Long Game for Philanthropy?* Knight Foundation. knightfoundation.org.

2. Cathy J. Cohen founded and directs GenForward, Kumar Ramanathan is a post-doctoral researcher in charge of surveys, and Matthew D. Nelsen directs the academic-publication arm of GenForward.

3. Morris, A.D. (1986). *The Origins of the Civil Rights Movement: Black Communities Organizing for Change.* New York, NY: Free Press, xii.

4. Ransby, B. (2018). *Making All Black Lives Matter: Reimagining Freedom in the 21st Century.* Berkeley, CA: University of California Press, 5.

5. Ibid, 6–8.

6. Our approach shares three of the principles of Participatory Action Research. First, we view organizers as key collaborators. Second, rather than designing survey questions that ask *about* movements, we center the knowledge of those working *within* movement spaces to inform the survey design. Third, these collaborations are grounded in an understanding that the information gleaned from our data collections can inform future organizing work. For more on Participatory Action Research, see Duncan-Andrade, J.M. and Morrell, E. (2008). "Youth Participatory Action Research as Critical Pedagogy." *Counterpoints* 285: 105–31. www.jstor.org/stable/42979872.

7. For more on GenForward's work, see www.genforwardsurvey.com.

8. However, surveys and polls that seek to be nationally representative can make incorrect inferences about some groups, due to the process of weighting. Weighting is a method of adjusting data such that some responses count more than others, in order to match the characteristics of the survey responses with the characteristics of the overall population. When surveys include a very small number of respondents from one group,

weighting can inflate any unusual responses from that small number. For example, a 2016 poll infamously weighted responses from one nineteen-year-old Black man thirty times more than the average respondent, skewing the overall results of the poll. See Cohn, N. (October 12, 2016). "How One 19-Year-Old Illinois Man Is Distorting National Polling Averages." *The New York Times.* www.nytimes.com/2016/10/13/upshot.

9. When we make statements about any group—whether the national population or some subgroup—we use weighting to ensure that we are accurately estimating that group's preferences.

10. For more on this point, see chapter 2 of Cohen, C.J. (2010). *Democracy Remixed: Black Youth and the Future of American Politics.* Oxford, UK: Oxford University Press.

11. The weaponization of the *defund* frame was especially prominent in Republican campaign messaging in elections during 2020–22. See Gambino, L., and Greve, J.E. (October 28, 2022). "Democrats try to flip narrative amid barrage of 'soft on crime' attack ads." *The Guardian.* www.theguardian.com/us-news/2022/oct/27/republicans -crime-midterm-election.

12. McGhee White, K. (August 6, 2020). "Black Americans Do Not Want to Defund the Police." *Washington Examiner.* www.washingtonexaminer.com/opinion; Gillespie, N. (August 6, 2020). "81 Percent of Black Americans Want the Same Level, or More, of Police Presence: Gallup." *Reason.* reason.com/2020/08/06.

13. Lahut, J. (October 26, 2021). "Support for Defunding the Police Collapsed in 2021, with Steep Drops Among Black Adults and Democrats, New Poll Shows." *Insider.* www .businessinsider.com; Saletan, W. (October 17, 2021). "Americans Don't Want to Defund the Police. Here's What They Do Want." *Slate.* slate.com/news-and-politics/2021/10 /police-reform-polls-white-black-crime; Elbeshbishi, S., and Quarshie, M. (March 7, 2021). "Fewer Than 1 in 5 Support 'Defund the Police' Movement, USA TODAY/Ipsos Poll Finds." *USA Today.* www.usatoday.com/story/news/politics/2021/03/07.

14. By "carceral practices and institutions," we refer to the formal and informal mechanisms of the state-run system of punishment and imprisonment.

15. The Treatment Not Trauma campaign in Chicago seeks to develop "teams of social workers, paramedics, and peer-support workers (instead of police) who will respond to crises within the community and connect people to ongoing support through [public health] clinics to address social and mental health needs." See Collaborative for Community Wellness (n.d.). "The Treatment Not Trauma Campaign." www .collaborativeforcommunitywellness.org.

VISUALS AND TACTICS

Cultural Engineering: The Use of Design and Creative Strategy in Revolutionary Movements

1. Bambara, T.C. (2012). An Interview with Toni Cade Bambara: Kay Bonetti. In T. Lewis (ed.), *Conversations with Toni Cade Bambara.* Jackson, MS: University Press of Mississippi, 35.

2. Baldwin, J. (1989). The Black Scholar Interviews—James Baldwin. In L.H. Pratt and F.R. Standley (eds.). *Conversations with James Baldwin*. Jackson, MD. University Press of Mississippi, 41.

3. Swann Auction Galleries (n.d.). "A Brief History of AfriCOBRA." www.swanngalleries.com/news/african-american-art/2020/04/africobra.

4. Bowers, J.W., Ochs, D.J., Jensen, R.J., and Schulz, D.P. (2009). *The Rhetoric of Agitation and Control*. Third Edition. Long Grove, IL: Waveland Press.

5. Davis, A. (1990). "On Education and Culture." In *Women, Culture & Politics*. New York: Vintage Books, 200.

Disrupting the Status Quo: Direct Action as a Narrative Force in Uprisings

1. Canning, D., and Reinsborough, P. (2010). *Re:Imagining Change: How to Use Story-Based Strategy to Win Campaigns, Build Movements, and Change the World*. Binghamton, NY: PM Press.

2. Letter from a Birmingham Jail.

3. Pew Research Center (2017). "Behind the Badge." www.pewresearch.org/social-trends/2017/01/11.

4. Snowden, A. (2011). "We are the 99%: The slogan of the Occupy movement." Counterfire. www.counterfire.org.

5. Pew Research Center (2011). News coverage of Occupy Wall Street. www.pewresearch.org.

6. Smucker, J.M. (2017). *Hegemony How-To: A Roadmap for Radicals*. Chico, CA: AK Press.

7. Stewart, E. (September 17, 2019). "We Are (Still) the 99 Percent." *Vox* Media. www.vox.com/the-highlight/2019/4/23/18284303/occupy-wall-street-bernie-sanders-dsa-socialism.

8. Hayes, K. (2020). "Should We All Be in the Streets? Let's Talk About Protest." *Truthout*. https://truthout.org/audio/should-we-all-be-in-the-streets-lets-talk-about-pro test.

The Messenger Matters: Influencer Partnerships as a Tool for Narrative Change

1. Hayes, K. "Should We All Be in the Streets?"

2. The Royal Family Channel (February 1991). Princess Diana Speech at Children and AIDS Conference. YouTube. www.youtube.com/watch?v=EhWlApyMILs.

3. HIV.gov (n.d.). "Timeline of the HIV and AIDS Epidemic." www.hiv.gov/hiv-basics/overview/history/hiv-and-aids-timeline.

4. Baker, E. (June 19, 1968.). Tape-recorded interview conducted by John H. Britton with the Civil Rights Documentation Project (Transcript). www.crmvet.org/nars/baker68.htm.

5. Tait, A. (June 6, 2019). "Greta Thunberg: How One Teenager Became the Voice of the Planet." *Wired*. www.wired.com/story/greta-thunberg-climate-crisis.

6. McGuinness, A. (February 15, 2019). "Theresa May criticises pupils missing school to protest over climate change." Sky News. news.sky.com.

7. Snuggs, T. (October 3, 2019). "Putin: I'm not excited by 'poorly informed' Greta Thunberg." Sky News. news.sky.com.

8. Carrington, D. (March 19, 2019). "School climate strikes: 1.4 million people took part, say campaigners." *The Guardian*. www.theguardian.com/environment/2019/mar/19.

9. Fridays for Future (n.d.). "Our Demands." fridaysforfuture.org/what-we-do/our-demands.

10. Revesz, R. (May 11, 2016). "13-year-old Native American is standing up to a big oil company." *The Independent*. www.independent.co.uk/news/world/americas.

11. CNN (December 23, 2018). "Teen Activist on Climate Change: 'If We Don't Do Anything Right Now, We're Screwed.'" YouTube. www.youtube.com/watch?v=rGmBkIUwYkA.

12. Crouch, D. (September 1, 2018). "The Swedish 15-year-old who's cutting class to fight the Climate Crisis." *The Guardian*. www.theguardian.com/science/2018/sep/01.

13. Nace, A., and Hassanzadeh, E. (May 3, 2023). "Line 3 oil pipeline: A look at what's happened since the pipeline started operating in Northern Minnesota." CBS News. www.cbsnews.com/minnesota/news/line-3-oil-pipeline.

14. Enbridge Inc. (n.d.). Line 3 Newsroom. www.enbridge.com/line3.

15. Andrade, S. (July 28, 2021). "An Indigenous Leader on Why She Still Needs to Protest Pipelines, Even Under Biden." *Slate*. slate.com/news-and-politics/2021/07/line-3-protest-pipeline-biden.

16. Roth, E. (October 11, 2017). "Why We Need to Replace Enbridge Line 3." *Twin Cities*. www.twincities.com/2017/10/12.

17. Kolpack, D. (June 8, 2021). "Oil Pipeline Foes Protest Enbridge's Line 3 in Minnesota." *AP News*. apnews.com/article/mn-state-wire-minnesota-government-and-politics-arts-and-entertainment-environment-and-nature.

18. Lampe, N. (June 2022). "National Voter Poll on Water." The Water Hub. waterhub.org/wp-content/uploads/2022/09/Water-Hub-June-2022-national-poll-report.

19. Jessica Jewell Lanier (personal communication; June 24, 2024) organized the e-action and was responsible for tracking digital engagement.

20. Tad @legwrestle (July 26, 2021). "please take action #stopline3 #line3pipeline #waterprotectors." TikTok. www.tiktok.com/@legwrestle/video/6989406999351921926.

21. LaDuke, W. (February 18, 2019). "Why the White Earth Band of Ojibwe Legally Recognized Wild Rice's Rights." *Civil Eats*. civileats.com/2019/02/08.

22. Beaumont, H. (June 4, 2021). "Sexual violence along pipeline route follows indigenous women's warnings." *The Guardian.* www.theguardian.com/us-news/2021/jun/04.

GLOBAL PERSPECTIVES

The Narrative Influence of #EndSARS: How Young Nigerians' Advocacy Against Police Brutality Went from Twitter to the Streets

1. Ford Foundation (September 13, 2021). "Nigeria Youth Futures Fund Will Equip a New Cadre of Youth Leaders in the Region." www.fordfoundation.org/news-and-stories/news-and-press/news.

2. Institute for Security Studies (April 4, 2023). "Nigeria's youth take center stage in the 2023 polls." issafrica.org/iss-today.

3. UNICEF (2023). "How Many Children Live in Nigeria." data.unicef.org.

4. Krook, M.L., and Nugent, M.K. (2018). "Not too young to run? Age requirements and young people in elected office." *Intergenerational Justice Review* 4(2): 60–67. doi.org/10.24357/igjr.4.2.702.

5. Uwalaka, T. (2020). "Clicktivism and political engagement in Nigeria." *The Nigerian Journal of Communication* 17(1): 1–22.

6. Abimbade, O., Olayoku, P., and Herro, D. (2022). "Millennial activism within Nigerian Twitterscape: From mobilization to social action of #ENDSARS protest." *Social Sciences & Humanities Open* 6(1): 100222. doi.org/10.1016/j.ssaho.2021.100222.

7. Ojedokun, U.A., Ogunleye, Y.O., and Aderinto, A.A. (2021). "Mass mobilization for police accountability: The case of Nigeria's #EndSARS protest." *Policing: A Journal of Policy and Practice* 15(3): 1894–1903. doi.org/10.1093/police/paab001.

8. Haynes, S. (October 21, 2020). "'We Are Able to Get Things Done.' Women Are at the Forefront of Nigeria's Police Brutality Protests." *Time.* time.com/5902123/nigeria-women-endsars-protest-movement.

9. Nwakanma, A.P. (2022). "From Black Lives Matter to EndSARS: Women's Socio-Political Power and the Transnational Movement for Black Lives." *Perspectives on Politics* 20(4): 1246–1259. doi:10.1017/S1537592722000019.

10. Malumfashi, S. (October 22, 2020). "Nigeria's SARS: A Brief History of the Special Anti-Robbery Squad." *Al Jazeera.* www.aljazeera.com/features/2020/10/22.

11. Felbab-Brown, V. (September 3, 2021). "Vigilante Groups and Militias in Southern Nigeria." Brookings Institute. www.brookings.edu/articles.

12. Ogbozor, B. (September 2016). "Understanding the Informal Security Sector in Nigeria." United States Institute of Peace. www.usip.org/sites/default/files.

13. Malumfashi, S. "Nigeria's SARS."

14. Sahara Reporters (July 27, 2010). "How police personnel raked in 9.35 billion naira from roadblocks in Southeast-Nigeria in 18 months."

15. Raji, A.A. (2020). "The Nigeria EndSARS Protest Gain or Loss." ResearchGate. www.researchgate.net.

16. Usman, C. and Oghuvbu, E.A. (2021). "The impact of the media on the #EndSARS protests in Nigeria." Zenodo (CERN European Organization for Nuclear Research). Retrieved September 8, 2024, from: doi.org/10.5281/zenodo.5973151.

17. Akpan, W. (2006). "And the beat goes on? Message music, political repression and the power of hip-hop in Nigeria." In Drewett, M. and Cloonan, M. (eds.). *Popular Music Censorship in Africa.* London, UK: Routledge, 91–106.

18. Onyebadi, U. (2018). "Political Messages in African Music: Assessing Fela Anikulapo-Kuti, Lucky Dube and Alpha Blondy." *Humanities* 7(4): 129. doi.org/10.3390/h7040129.

19. Oloyede, F., and Elega, A.A. (June 2019). "Exploring Hashtag Activism in Nigeria: A Case of #EndSARS campaign." In Conference Proceedings: Fifth International Conference in Communication and Media Studies (CRPC 2018).

20. Akinlabi, O.M. (2017). "Do the Police Really Protect and Serve the Public? Police Deviance and Public Cynicism Toward the Law in Nigeria." *Criminology & Criminal Justice* 17(2):158–74.

21. Uwazuruike, A. (December 13, 2021). "#EndSARS: An Evaluation of Successes and Failures One Year Later." *Georgetown Journal of International Affairs.* gjia.georgetown.edu/2021/12/13.

22. Fayehun, F. (October 25, 2020). "#EndSARS: How Nigeria Can Tap into Its Youthful Population." *The Conversation.* theconversation.com.

23. Amnesty International (January 30, 2020). "New generation of young activists lead fight against worsening repression in Asia." www.amnesty.org/en/latest/news/2020/01.

24. Esveld, B.V., and Sajadi, E. (October 12, 2022). "In Iran, School Girls Leading Protests for Freedom." Human Rights Watch. www.hrw.org/news/2022/10/12.

25. Tade, O. (October 23, 2020). "#EndSARS: Between Sòròsóke and 'Off-the-Mic' generations." *Vanguard.* Originally available at: https://www.vanguardngr.com/2020/10.

26. Obia, V. (2020). "#EndSARS, a unique Twittersphere and social media regulation in Nigeria." Media@LSE. blogs.lse.ac.uk/medialse/2020/11/11.

Black Bixas Blooming Self-Love and Affection

1. Spartakus. (July 15, 2018). "A solidão do gay negro: Desabafo e mensagem pras bichas pretas." YouTube. www.youtube.com/watch?v=-AsqVkC_yuk.

2. Spartakus. (August 20, 2019). "What Is Cultural Appropriation?" YouTube. www .youtube.com/watch?v=QdNRuLC1l3w.

3. Mari, A., and Arbex, G. (September 4, 2020). "Especial inovadores negros: 20 creators que têm muito a dizer." *Forbes.* forbes.com.br/forbes-tech.

4. He participates in TV programs on Rede Globo de Televisão, the country's largest broadcaster. He also writes articles for print media and online. In November 2017, he was one of the guests at the inauguration of YouTube Space in Rio de Janeiro, as one of its poster boys on the company's official page.

5. In the gay community, when it comes to sexual relations, the top is the one who penetrates, and the bottom is the one who is penetrated. This division commonly carries a binary and hierarchical view that associates the person who is penetrated with femininity, and therefore with less power.

6. In the song, "she" represents Black bixas, who often use feminine pronouns.

7. MC Linn da Quebrada (February 23, 2017). "Bixa Preta." YouTube. www.youtube .com/watch?v=VyrQPjG0bbY.

8. Phillips, T. (November 17, 2011). "Brazil census shows African-Brazilians in the majority for the first time." *The Guardian.* www.theguardian.com/world/2011/nov/17.

9. Freelon, K. (March 8, 2018). "The self-sufficiency of Black Panther's Wakanda is inspiring Afro-Brazilians to look to their own." *Quartz Africa.* qz.com/africa/1224485 /black-panther-shook-up-brazils-black-afro-brazil.

10. Rede Brasileira de Pesquisa em Soberania e Segurança Alimentar (Rede PENSSAN) (March 2021). "National Survey of Food Insecurity in the Context of the COVID-19 Pandemic in Brazil." olheparaafome.com.br/VIGISAN _AF_National_Survey_of_Food_Insecurity.

11. According to the 2020 data, in 11.1 percent of households headed by women, the inhabitants were starving, compared with 7.7 percent when the household was headed by men. Of the homes inhabited by Black people, hunger was at 10.7 percent. Among white people, this percentage was 7.5 percent. The Northeast region had the largest absolute number of people in a situation of severe food insecurity, almost 7.7 million. In the Northeast region, which is home to only 7.5 percent of Brazil's inhabitants, 14.9 percent of all hungry people in the country lived here during 2020.

12. Calais, B. (April 10, 2021). "Brasil tem 10 novos bilionários no ranking de 2021" ("Brazil has ten new billionaires in the 2021 ranking"). *Forbes.* forbes.com.br/forbes -money/2021/04.

13. Carneiro, S. (2019). "Ideologia Tortuosa." In *Escritos de Uma Vida.* São Paulo, Brazil: Pólen Livros/Editora Jandaíra, 148.

14. O Rappa (March 29, 2012). "Todo camburão tem um pouco de navio negreiro." YouTube. www.youtube.com/watch?v=x_Tq34rysAc.

15. Barretto Briso, C., and Phillips, T. (February 4, 2022). " 'A George Floyd every 23 minutes': Fury at refugee's brutal murder at Rio beach." *The Guardian.* www .theguardian.com/world/2022/feb/04/brazil-congolese-refugee-murder-racism; United

Nations Office on Drugs and Crime (n.d.) "Black Lives Campaign: Ending Violence Against Black Youth in Brazil." www.unodc.org/lpo-brazil/en/frontpage/2017/12.

16. Brasil, Ministério da Saúde (2018). "Óbitos por suicídio entre adolescentes e jovens negros—2012 a 2016." bvsms.saude.gov.br/bvs/publicacoes.

17. *Valor Economico* (November 13, 2019). "IBGE: Dos 13.5 milhões vivendo em extrema pobreza, 75% são pretos ou pardos." valor.globo.com/brasil/noticia/2019/11/13.

18. *g1.* (March 21, 2022). "Mais de 33 milhões de brasileiros não têm acesso à internet, diz pesquisa." g1.globo.com/tecnologia/noticia/2022/03/21.

19. Canal Brasil (June 10, 2019). "Entrevista: Linn Da Quebrada & Jup Do Bairro—Aquecimento TRANSmissão." YouTube. youtube/t0hjZOd8qR0.

20. Jair Messias Bolsonaro is a retired army captain, politician, and former president of Brazil. He was federal deputy for seven terms between 1991 and 2018. Of the 172 bills that he presented in 26 years of parliamentary life, only two were approved. Three of his sons are also politicians: Carlos Bolsonaro, Flávio Bolsonaro, and Eduardo Bolsonaro. Jair Bolsonaro maintains a fascist and openly anti-Black, anti-LGBTQI, and antiwomen posture, encouraging the dismantling of public policies that serve these populations.

21. Araújo, M. (October 27, 2018). "Eu quero seguir vivendo, amor!" YouTube. youtube/GGNlVOPDICI.

22. @pretasbixas. Instagram. www.instagram.com/p/CUssBPjJjwa.

23. Ibid.

24. "All people's worlds must coexist in dignity and peace, without depreciation, exploitation, or misery. A pluriversal world overcomes patriarchal attitudes, racism, casteism and other forms of discrimination." In Kothari, A., Salleh, A., Escobar, A., Demaria, F., Acosta, A., and Eleonora, I.V. (2021). *Pluriverso: Um dicionário do pós-desenvolvimento* (Pluriverse: A dictionary of postdevelopment). São Paulo, Brazil: Elefante, 46; Escobar, E. (2018). *Designs for the Pluriverse: Radical Interdependence, Autonomy, and the Making of Worlds.* Durham, NC, and London, UK: Duke University Press.

25. Gonzalez, L. (2020). "A categoria político-cultural de amefricanidade." In *Por um feminismo afro-latino-americano.* Rio de Janeiro, Brazil: Zahar. See also Saavedra, R. (2022). "American Alliances for Shifting Powers." In *Stories of Feminist Mobilisation: How to Advance Feminist Movement Worldwide.* Berlin, Germany: Heinrich-Böll-Stiftung. Available at: www.boell.de/en/2022/12/12.

26. @pretasbixas. Instagram. www.instagram.com/p/CUssBPjJjwa.

27. Ibid.

28. Ibid.

29. Latinidades Pretas (Website). www.latinidadespretas.com.

30. @and_medinluiz. Instagram. www.instagram.com.

31. @batekoo. Instagram. www.instagram.com.

32. @baphosperifericos. Instagram. www.instagram.com.

33. Maffesoli, M. (2014). *Homo Eroticus: Comunhões emocionais.* Rio de Janeiro, Brazil: Forense.

34. The Narrative Initiative (June 2017). *Toward a New Gravity: Charting a Course for the Narrative Initiative.* narrativeinitiative.org/wp-content/uploads/2019/08.

35. Almeida, K. "Bichas pretas, pássaros-músicos e outras vertigens curriculares— Para além da comunidade do mesmo." In Camilo, V., and Melgaço da Silva Jr., P. (eds.) (2022). *Masculinidades negras: Novos debates ganhando formas.* São Paulo, Brazil: Ciclo Contínuo Editorial, 87.

36. Sousa, D. (2022). "Constrangendo pela raça: Homens Negros gays nas tramas do genocídio e das masculinidades." In Camilo, V., and Melgaço da Silva Jr., P. *Masculinidades negras: Novos debates ganhando formas.* São Paulo, Brazil: Ciclo Contínuo Editorial, 72.

Countering Fascism: Narrative Power, Social Movements, and the Fight for Justice in the UK and Poland

1. BBC News (April 8, 2022). "Hillsborough: Timeline of the 1989 stadium disaster." www.bbc.com/news/uk-england-merseyside-47697569, 1.tation.

2. BBC News. "EU Referendum local results—K." www.bbc.co.uk/news/politics /eu_referendum/results/local/k.

3. *The Guardian* (November 3, 2018). "Liverpool makes a stand and runs far-right marchers out of town." www.theguardian.com/uk-news/2018/nov/03.

4. Sky News (March 16, 2023). "Knowsley: Asylum seekers attacked outside Merseyside Hotel where anti-migrant protests erupted." news.sky.com.

5. BBC News. "EU Referendum local results."

6. *The Guardian* (November 30, 2005). "Timeline: Anthony Walker Murder." www .theguardian.com/uk/2005/nov/30/ukcrime.race1.

7. Misik, R. (January 9, 2023). "Today's far right and the echoes from history." *IPS Journal.* www.ips-journal.eu/topics/democracy-and-society.

8. Eco, U. (1995). *Ur-Fascism.* The Anarchist Library. theanarchistlibrary.org /library.

9. Goodfellow, M. (November 18, 2019). "Keeping Britain White." *Tribune.* tribune mag.co.uk/2019/11.

10. White, E. (December 2, 2016). "How Rotha Lintorn-Orman Founded British Fascism." *The Paris Review.* www.theparisreview.org/blog/2016/12/02/conservatism-with -knobs-on.

11. wdc.contentdm.oclc.org/digital/collection/tav/id/5210.

12. BBC (n.d.). "Campaigns for racial equality in Britain after 1945—KS3 History." www.bbc.co.uk/bitesize/articles.

13. Earle, S. (April 20, 2018). "Enoch Powell's 'Rivers of Blood' Speech at 50." *The Atlantic.* www.theatlantic.com/international/archive/2018/04.

14. Al Jazeera (2017). "Far right gains a foothold while the Eurozone goes into crisis: The making and breaking of Europe." interactive.aljazeera.com/aje/2017/the-making -and-breaking-of-europe/2000s.

15. Matthews, S., and Zukowska, M. (eds.) (2025). *Liberation Stories: Building Narrative Power for 21st-Century Social Movements* (1st ed.). New York: The New Press.

16. Mudde, C. (January 6, 2020). "The 2010s' grim legacy? The decade of the far right." *The Guardian.* www.theguardian.com/commentisfree/2020/jan/06.

17. New Economics Foundation (November 4, 2022). "Austerity policies have made European citizens €3000 a year worse-off." neweconomics.org/2022/11.

18. Galloway, H. (May 14, 2021). "15-M: How Spain's 'outraged' movement spawned political change." *EL PAÍS English.* english.elpais.com/society/2022-05-02.

19. Georgiadou, V., Rori, L., and Roumanias, C. (2018). "Mapping the European far right in the 21st century: A meso-level analysis." *Electoral Studies* 54, 103–115. doi.org /10.1016/j.electstud.2018.05.004.

20. Kazazis, I. (February 6, 2024). "The creeping ascent of the far-right in mainstream European politics and how to stop it." LSE Blogs. blogs.lse.ac.uk/lseupr/2024/02/06.

21. Marsili, L. (July 13, 2024). "Austerity and immigration no longer explain the far right's rise in Europe." *Al Jazeera.* www.aljazeera.com/opinions/2024/7/13.

22. Andrews, K. (August 24, 2016). "Colonial nostalgia is back in fashion, blinding us to the horrors of empire." *The Guardian.* www.theguardian.com/commentisfree/2016 /aug/24.

23. YouGov (July 26, 2014). "The British Empire is 'something to be proud of.'" you gov.co.uk/politics/articles/9954-britain-proud-its-empire.

24. Owczarek, D. (April 2017). "The roots of populism in Poland: Unsustainable growth and cultural backlash." CIDOB. www.cidob.org/en/publication.

25. Liévano, W. (December 31, 2019). "Democracy Undone: Poland's Law and Justice Party Mixes Victimhood and Strength in Its Messaging." The GroundTruth Project. thegroundtruthproject.org.

26. Kotwas, M. and Kubik, J. (2022). "Beyond 'Making Poland Great Again.' Nostalgia in Polish Populist and Non-Populist Discourses." *Sociological Forum* 37(S1), 1360–1386. doi.org/10.1111/socf.12842.

27. Snitow, A., Detwiler, K., Pinkham, S., and Fincher, L.H. (Fall 2016). "Gender Trouble in Poland." *Dissent.* www.dissentmagazine.org/article/gender-trouble-poland -pis-abortion-ban.

28. Balogun, B. (2022). "Eastern Europe: The 'other' geographies in the colonial global economy." *Area* 54, 460–467. doi.org/10.1111/area.12792.

29. Pikulicka-Wilczewska, A. (November 11, 2019). "'Great Poland': Thousands attend Independence March in Warsaw." *Al Jazeera*, Religion News. www.aljazeera .com/news/2019/11/11.

30. Brady, C. (September 30, 2021). "The Muslim community in Poland today." Culture.pl. (Artykul). culture.pl/en/article.

31. Smith, A.D. (October 25, 2015). "Poland lurches to right with election of Law and Justice Party." *The Guardian.* www.theguardian.com/world/2015/oct/25.

32. Żuk, P., and Żuk, P. (2019). "'Murderers of the unborn' and 'sexual degenerates': analysis of the 'anti-gender' discourse of the Catholic Church and the nationalist right in Poland." In *Critical Discourse Studies* (vol. 17, issue 5, 566–588). Informa UK Limited. doi.org/10.1080/17405904.2019.1676808.

33. Szulc, L. (September 26, 2019). "How LGBT rights became a key battleground in Poland's election." LSE Blogs. blogs.lse.ac.uk/europpblog/2019/09/26.

34. OKO Press (October 30, 2020). "Mowa kobiecej rewolucji, czyli niepohamowana wolność [120 haseł w 16 kategoriach]." *OKO.press.* oko.press/mowa-kobiecej-rewolu cji-120-hasel-w-16-kategoriach.

35. Tait, R. (September 18, 2016). "Thousands protest against proposed stricter abortion law in Poland." *The Guardian.* amp.theguardian.com/world/2016/sep/18.

36. Neumeyer, J., and Wilczek, M. (November 8, 2021). "Poland's Abortion Ban—and the Women's Strike—One Year On." *Foreign Policy.* foreignpolicy.com/2021/11/08.

37. Kim, R. (April 8, 2020). "Protest przeciwko zakazowi aborcji. Sejm pracuje nad ustawą antyaborcyjną napisaną pod dyktando Ordo Iuris." *Newsweek.pl.* www .newsweek.pl/polska/spoleczenstwo.

38. Matthews and Zukowska (eds.). *Liberation Stories.*

39. Downes, J. (September 24, 2020). "How the far right took over the mainstream." openDemocracy. www.opendemocracy.net/en/countering-radical-right.

40. Matthews and Zukowska (eds.). *Liberation Stories.*

41. Miller, L. (June 30, 2022). "Argentina's Green Bandana Makes Its Way to the United States." *Los Angeles Times.* www.latimes.com/world-nation/story/2022-06-30.

42. Amnesty International (November 9, 2021). "Poland: Case against women who stuck up Virgin Mary rainbow halo posters must be quashed." www.amnesty.org/en /latest/news/2021/11.

43. OKO Press (March 30, 2023). "Większość Polek i Polaków poszłaby na referendum. I zdecydowanie wybrała prawo do aborcji [SONDAŻ]." oko.press/wiekszosc-pol ek-i-polakow-wzielaby-udzial-referendum-i-wybrala-legalna-aborcje-sondaz.

44. INQUEST. "BAME Deaths in Police Custody," www.inquest.org.uk.

45. Dodd, V. (February 19, 2023). "Black people seven times more likely to die after police restraint in Britain, figures show." *The Guardian.* www.theguardian.com/uk -news/2023/feb/19.

46. Metropolitan Police Service (March 7, 2023). *Baroness Casey Review Final Report.* www.met.police.uk/SysSiteAssets/media/downloads/met/about-us/baroness-casey-review/update-march-2023.

47. Safi, M. (March 29, 2019). "India: Churchill's policies contributed to 1943 Bengal famine (study)." *The Guardian.* www.theguardian.com/world/2019/mar/29.

About the Authors

Co-editors

Shanelle Matthews collaborates with social justice activists, organizations, and campaigns to inspire action and build narrative power for social justice and liberation. She is the former communications director for the Movement for Black Lives and the Black Lives Matter Global Network. Shanelle founded the Radical Communicators Network, a global community of practice for social movement communications workers. She is also a former Activist-in-Residence and faculty member of Freedom Scholars at The New School. Today, she teaches full-time as a distinguished lecturer at the City College of New York in the Department of Anthropology and Interdisciplinary Studies. Her courses include Narrative Power in the Black Radical Tradition, Rhetoric of Liberation: The Role of Narrative Power in Contemporary Movements, and Black Women's Resistance: Narratives of Safety and Survival. She lives in Brooklyn.

Marzena Zukowska is an organizer, communications strategist, and the co-founder and co-director of the UK-based immigrant rights organization POMOC. For a decade, Marzena has developed narrative and organizing strategies for leading social and political movements in the United States, the UK, and Europe. They are the former media director at the National Domestic Workers Alliance, and a former leadership team member at the Radical Communicators Network. Their work has been published in two anthologies—*Queer Activism After Marriage Equality* (Routledge) and *Asylum for Sale: Profit and Protest in the Migration Industry* (PM Press)—and they co-authored *New Brave World*, a report on the field of pop culture for social change in the UK. Marzena is a queer, nonbinary Polish immigrant who was born in Białystok, Poland, and grew up undocumented in Chicago, United States.

The Radical Communicators Network (RadComms) is a community of practice for emerging and experienced movement and communications workers. They build narrative power for a just and liberatory future.

Authors

Adeola Abdulateef Elega is a communication and media studies scholar with specific interest in journalism, emerging media, and political communication. He is an alumnus of Kogi State University and Eastern Mediterranean University. His research outputs have been published widely in journals with global impact. Dr. Elega is presently a senior lecturer at the Department of Mass Communication, Nile University of Nigeria.

Alejandra Pérez is an educator and a community organizer with the Washington Dream Coalition. She serves as the director of education strategy at Scholar Fund and is pursuing her PhD in culturally sustaining education at the University of Washington. Born and raised in Guatemala, Alejandra emigrated at the age of twelve and resides in Duwamish and Coast Salish lands (South King County, WA).

Aliya Sabharwal is an organizer, strategic campaigner, and coalition builder. She has won national worker-led campaigns, supported the implementation of state reforms for low-wage industries, and fought against the impacts of corporate and Wall Street greed on Black and brown communities since 2018. She is a senior campaign manager at Americans for Financial Reform and was a member of the 2023 Changemaker Authors Cohort, a yearlong intensive coaching program from Narrative Initiative and Unicorn Authors Club supporting organizers and social justice practitioners to develop book projects.

Amanda Cooper is senior partner at LightBox Collaborative, a communications and strategy firm that helps do-gooders do better. She has more than twenty-five years of experience developing messaging and media for labor, civil rights, voter engagement, and gender equity campaigns, among others. She is a board member of the National Association to Advance Fat Acceptance.

Dr. Anja Rudiger is a political theorist and strategist working to advance equity, justice, and human rights. She is currently based in New Mexico, where she campaigns with Indigenous advocates for equity in education. Anja also works with Race Forward on creating frameworks for equitable governance and strategies for countering authoritarianism. Previously, she served as director of programs at Partners for Dignity & Rights, where she partnered with the Vermont Workers' Center on their Healthcare Is a Human Right campaign.

Asha DuMonthier is an organizer from the Bay Area. She has worked on campaigns to decriminalize houselessness, advance racial and gender justice in health care, and to build worker power across the country.

Ben Palmquist does research, strategy and capacity building with community power-building organizations to reshape governance to advance justice, human rights, and bottom-up governing power. Since 2011, he has worked with Partners for Dignity & Rights to support movement organizations across the United States. He previously worked in the United States, Indonesia, and Ecuador on health justice, community development, labor research, and youth development, and holds a masters in Urban and Regional Planning.

Dr. Benjamin F. Chavis Jr. is an African American civil rights movement veteran leader and icon. He is an author, chemist, United Church of Christ–ordained minister, and PBS TV executive producer of *The Chavis Chronicles*. He is currently president and CEO of the National Newspaper Publishers Association. He also chairs the National Association for Equal Opportunity in Higher Education, the Thurgood Marshall Center Trust, We Are Digital, and the Energy Action Alliance.

Cameron Oglesby is an internationally awarded environmental justice organizer, oral historian, journalist, and aspiring land steward. She is the founder and project lead for the Environmental Justice Oral History Project, a storytelling hub and repository that combines a diverse set of storytelling modalities to provide a comprehensive view of environmental justice in the U.S. South. Her journalism has appeared in *The Nation*,

The Margin, The Assembly, Atmos magazine, *Grist, Southerly, Scalawag,* Yale Climate Connections, and Earth in Color.

Cathy J. Cohen is the chair of the Department of Race, Diaspora, and Indigeneity and the D. Gale Johnson Distinguished Service Professor at the University of Chicago. She formerly served in numerous administrative positions, including chair of the Department of Political Science, director of the Center for the Study of Race, Politics, and Culture, and deputy provost for graduate education at the University of Chicago. Cohen is the author of two books, *The Boundaries of Blackness: AIDS and the Breakdown of Black Politics* (University of Chicago Press) and *Democracy Remixed: Black Youth and the Future of American Politics* (Oxford University Press), and is a longtime activist whose political affiliations include Kitchen Table Women of Color Press, the Audre Lorde Project, and Scholars for Social Justice.

Celeste Faison is an organizer, former National Domestic Workers' Alliance campaigns director, chief strategy officer at me too. International, and co-founder of the BlackOUT Collective.

Chantelle Lunt is a writer, lecturer, PhD researcher, and activist with a rich professional background in public services, including roles in policing and children's social care. As the chair of the Merseyside Alliance for Racial Equality CIC (MARE), a leading nonprofit organization, Chantelle is dedicated to advancing racial equality across Merseyside through innovative, grassroots community-led education initiatives. In addition to her activism and academic pursuits, Chantelle serves as a Labour Borough Councillor for St. Gabriel's Ward in the UK, where she has made history as the first Black woman to be elected to this position. She also serves as deputy mayor of the Halewood Town Council.

Chelsea Fuller is the managing partner and senior strategist at Black Alder, a radical communications and movement capacity-building firm. Known for her work within the Movement for Black Lives, the me too. movement and other formations working to end systemic violence, Chelsea has led countless successful campaigns and messaging strategies, effectively shifting national and international narratives around central issues like race, white supremacy, patriarchal violence, and community safety.

Chinyere Tutashinda is a Black organizer, educator, trainer, and direct action strategist, who was born in Oakland with southern roots. She is a founding member of the BlackOUT Collective and current Executive Director of the Center for Third World Organizing Hub. She is dedicated to the liberation of Black people and all oppressed people and it is her deep love of people that grounds her work and her approach to life. On any day of the week, you can find her sitting with a cup of hot tea and listening to the wonders of a Spotify playlist while plotting for collective freedom.

Denise Beek is a writer, performer, and narrative strategist who has worked with arts, culture, and social-justice organizations for over a decade. She currently serves as vice president of original storytelling for Represent Justice and board co-chair of BlackStar Projects.

Diego Cotta has a PhD in media and everyday life and is a journalist who has been working on building narrative power in third-sector organizations in Brazil for over fifteen years. He is a researcher at the Center for Audiovisual and Multimedia Studies and Experimentations at Fluminense Federal University and researches language and production of meaning in audiovisual and digital media, focusing on LGBTI+, racism, and human rights. In addition, he carries out a postdoctoral internship in communication at the State University of Rio de Janeiro with a focus on diversity, equity, and inclusion.

Dorian T. Warren is co-president of Community Change and Community Change Action and co-founder of the Economic Security Project. A progressive scholar, organizer, and media personality, Dorian has worked to advance racial, economic, and social justice for more than two decades. He previously taught at the University of Chicago and Columbia University and is the co-author of *The Hidden Rules of Race* and co-editor of *Race and American Political Development*.

Eesha Pandit is co-founder of the Center for Advancing Innovative Policy (CAIP). She has worked in national and international movements for racial justice, human rights, reproductive justice, and ending gender-based violence. She is a member of the Crunk Feminist Collective and a founder of South Asian Youth in Houston Unite (SAYHU).

Fresco Steez is a young, Black feminist, queer, and an abolitionist freedom fighter from the South Side of Chicago. A grassroots community organizer for the past fourteen years, Fresco's work ranges from housing disparities in Black communities, to juvenile justice, to racial justice, to the disruption of the police state. Fresco's proudest work has been co-creating BYP100 with comrades, coining the phrase "Unapologetically Black," and anchoring the term and political framework for a Black queer feminist lens. As the minister of culture for BYP100, Fresco's focus has been on training and politically educating radical Black leadership as organizers contributing to the legacy of the Black radical tradition. Fresco is proud to currently work as one-half of the strategic communications and creative design firm Culture Society.

Habibah Ayinke Taiwo is a master's student at Nile University of Nigeria.

hermelinda cortés uses organizing, narrative, and strategic communications to build power, fortify lasting connections between communities, dismantle systems of domination, and build the liberated world we and future generations deserve. The child of Mexicans and West Virginians, country folks, farmers, factory workers, and trailer parks, she has dedicated her life to the journey of liberation and to the work of social movements for the last fifteen years. She is the executive director of ReFrame and has had the great fortune of serving the visions of the Radical Communicators Network, Southerners on New Ground, and Country Queers.

Jacquelyn Mason is the interim executive director at the Media Democracy Fund, where she spearheads initiatives to create positive change in the digital landscape. Previously, as director of programs, she grew the Disinfo Defense League into a powerful coalition of over 600 members across 225 organizations, dedicated to combating racialized disinformation in communities of color. With a diverse background that includes roles at First Draft, NYU, and TED conferences, and a solid foundation in art and digital media, Jacquelyn is passionate about tackling technological challenges with innovative, equity-focused solutions.

Jaime Longoria is the manager of research and training for the Disinfo Defense League at Media Democracy Fund. Previously, he was a senior researcher and project manager at First Draft, where he focused on political and health disinformation in Spanish-language and Latinx communities. He also worked as a researcher at NBC News Investigations and served as a data editor at Type Investigations. Jaime holds a BA in international relations from Boston University and attended the Craig Newmark Graduate School of Journalism at CUNY.

JD Davids, a disabled and chronically ill strategist and writer who served on the inaugural leadership team for Radical Communicators Network, is in the biography and memoir program at CUNY Graduate Center. He's dedicated to building the power of chronically ill and disabled people, with a long history in HIV activism, queer and trans liberation, and digital communications. A longtime member of ACT UP Philadelphia, he later served as director of strategic communications for TheBody.com, co-founded Long COVID Justice, and writes *The Cranky Queer Guide to Chronic Illness.*

Jean-Pierre Brutus is an attorney and scholar interested in Black politics, critical race theory, reparations, and postcolonial studies. He is a reparations advocate committed to Black liberation, racial and social justice, and multiracial egalitarian democracy. He obtained his JD and PhD in Black studies from Northwestern University and his BA in sociology from Georgetown University.

Jen Soriano is a Filipinx American writer, independent scholar, and performer who has long worked at the intersection of grassroots organizing, narrative strategy, and art-driven social change. They are the author of the chapbook *Making the Tongue Dry* and the lyric essay collection *Nervous*, as well as the co-editor of the anthology *Closer to Liberation: Pina/xy Activism in Theory and Practice*. Jen helped build the organization that became MediaJustice, and they are currently the co-founder and board chair of the narrative power-building institution ReFrame. As principal of Lionswrite Communications, Jen has strengthened the narrative capacity and impact of social justice groups working from local to international scales. Originally from a landlocked part of the Chicago area, Jen now lives with their family in Seattle, near the Duwamish River and the Salish Sea.

Jennifer Johnson Avril is a communications worker whose focus on narrative change to address health care disparities, poverty, and queer rights has included a role in advocacy communications at the NYC nonprofit Housing Works. She is also a former floor member of ACT UP NY and was an original member of the NYC COVID-19 Working Group. Jennifer's writing has been published in TheBody.com and *Advocate*, and she is a proud graduate of the master's program in media studies for social change at Queens College/CUNY.

Jess St. Louis is a lesbian white trans woman who lives and loves in Greensboro, North Carolina, and who works as a narrative strategist and somatic practitioner. She spends her spare time writing about grief, embodiment, and principled struggle. Her leadership emerges from LGBTQ liberation, racial justice, and abolitionist movements in the U.S. South. She most recently served as a coordinator at ReFrame creating, supporting, and coordinating programming that builds narrative power to win.

Jessica Jewell is a multichannel communications and digital strategist passionate about creating change through arts and culture to tell human stories about the right to clean and affordable drinking water and the fight for environmental justice. Accustomed to existing in liminal spaces as a multiracial Colombiana and daughter of an immigrant mother,

Jessica invites us all to imagine radical futures while centering care and compassion in her storytelling. She's currently the digital director at the Water Hub, a pro bono communications shop serving the water justice movement.

Joseph Torres is the senior advisor for reparative policy and programs at Free Press, a media and tech advocacy organization. As co-creator of Media 2070, a media reparations project, Joseph writes on media and internet issues and co-authored the *New York Times*'s bestseller *News for All the People: The Epic Story of Race and the American Media* with Juan González. Joseph received the 2015 Everett C. Parker Award for his work in the public interest. Before joining Free Press, he served as deputy director of the National Association of Hispanic Journalists.

Julie Feng is a communications strategist and cultural studies scholar. Currently, she serves as communications director at Scholar Fund and is a doctoral candidate at the University of Washington. Julie is an immigrant from Taiwan who is now based on Duwamish land (Seattle, WA).

Katherine Ollenburger is a writer, connector, and strategist who helps social justice organizations tell their stories. For more than fifteen years, she has worked with nonprofits and movement groups to create communications strategies that build brands and bring abundance to the infrastructure for social change, including as the director of brand strategy and chief writer at Community Change.

Khury Petersen-Smith is the Michael Ratner Middle East Fellow and the co-director of the New Internationalism Project at Institute for Policy Studies. He researches the U.S. empire, borders, and migration, and strategizes with activists against U.S. militarism. Khury graduated from the Clark University Graduate School of Geography in Massachusetts after completing a dissertation that focused on militarization and sovereignty. He is one of the co-authors and organizers of the 2023 Black Voices for Ceasefire Statement, which more than six thousand Black activists, artists, and scholars signed.

Kumar Ramanathan is a Bridge-to-Faculty postdoctoral scholar in the Department of Political Science at the University of Illinois Chicago. He was previously a GenForward postdoctoral scholar at the University of Chicago and a doctoral fellow at the American Bar Foundation. His research explores how the politics of law and public policy shape inequalities in the United States, and has been published in numerous journals.

Dr. Maha Hilal is a Muslim Arab American expert on institutionalized Islamophobia, the War on Terror, and counternarrative work, and the author of the book *Innocent Until Proven Muslim: Islamophobia, the War on Terror, and the Muslim Experience Since 9/11*. Her writings have appeared in *Vox*, *Al Jazeera*, *Middle East Eye*, *Newsweek*, *Business Insider*, *The Daily Beast*, and *The Nation* among others. Dr. Hilal is also the founding executive director of Muslim Counterpublics Lab, an organization that works to disrupt and subvert dehumanizing narratives that are designed and deployed to justify state violence against Muslims.

Malkia Devich-Cyril is an activist, writer, and public speaker on issues of digital rights, narrative power, Black liberation, and collective grief. Devich-Cyril is also the founding and former executive director of MediaJustice—a national hub boldly advancing racial justice, rights, and dignity in a digital age. After twenty years of leadership, Devich-Cyril now serves as co-director of the Healing, Sustainability and Culture Strategy at the Movement Innovation Collaborative; founder of the Radical Loss Initiative—a Black-led change lab transforming how modern freedom movements face loss; and is a contributing writer to various publications, including *The Atlantic*, *Wired Magazine*, *Convergence Magazine*, *The Nation*, *Yes Magazine,* and *Truthout*, among others.

Mandy Van Deven is the founder of Both/And Solutions, a global consulting collective that provides strategic advice to individual wealth holders and philanthropic institutions, and the co-lead of Elemental, a community of practice for funders that cultivates the conditions to resource narrative power.

Matthew Nelsen is an assistant professor in the Department of Political Science at the University of Miami. His work explores the possibilities and challenges of forging a vibrant, multiracial democracy. This includes projects on political socialization in public schools and the role of geography in shaping political attitudes and preferences. His book, *The Color of Civics: Civic Education for a Multiracial Democracy*, is published by Oxford University Press.

Miski Noor is the publisher of *The Forge*, a movement publication that elevates the strategy and practice of organizing by sharing ideas, methods, history, and inspiration. Miski is the former communications strategist at the BLM Global Network and the former co-director of Black Visions, a power and base-building force for Black queer and trans people in Minneapolis, Minnesota.

Olivia Blocker is a communications strategist, researcher and movement worker with over a decade of experience. As a former senior program director at Resource Media, she developed narrative and communications strategies for clean energy and climate justice campaigns across the United States. Prior to her work at Resource Media, she co-created and managed the Final Five campaign to close youth prisons in Illinois and stayed connected to abolitionist organizing over the last few years through her work as a steering committee member at Liberation Library. Olivia is now studying strategic communications at the University of Liverpool in the UK.

Oluseyi Adegbola is an assistant professor of public relations at the University of Tennessee, Knoxville. His research explores news and communication influences on public opinion and political behavior, especially in emerging democracies. Oluseyi also examines public relations and strategic communication within the context of politics and government.

Pamela Mejia is the associate program director and director of research at the Berkeley Media Studies Group, a nonprofit dedicated to narrative change and strategic communication. She has more than fourteen years of experience researching media portrayals of public health and social justice issues, including how those portrayals can influence organizing and advocacy efforts.

Rachel Jacoby is a Highland Park resident and currently works in a local office of Gun Violence Prevention in Illinois. As a former organizer with March For Our Lives, Rachel has led organizing efforts across Illinois, Massachusetts, and Washington, DC, in support of gun violence prevention legislation. Most significantly, she helped lead the grassroots organizing effort in support of the Protect Illinois Communities Act, which made Illinois the ninth state in the country to ban assault weapons, high-capacity magazines, and switches. Today, Rachel serves on the Board for March for Our Lives and is the President of the Illinois Alliance to Prevent Gun Violence.

Renata Saavedra is a Brazilian journalist, researcher, and intersectional feminist working to strengthen grassroots organizations, connecting people for power sharing and shifting. She is a specialist in gender and sexuality, and holds a master's in history and a PhD in communication and culture. She has been working in philanthropy for social justice for ten years.

Regina Mahone is a writer and editor whose work explores the intersections between race, class, and reproductive rights. She currently serves as a senior editor at *The Nation* magazine. She is also the co-author of *Liberating Abortion: Claiming Our History, Sharing Our Stories, and Building the Reproductive Future We Deserve* and co-host of *The A Files: A Secret History of Abortion*, a podcast from The Meteor.

Renee Bracey Sherman is an award-winning abortion activist, writer, and founder and co-executive director of We Testify, an organization dedicated to the leadership and representation of people who have abortions. She is also the co-author of *Liberating Abortion: Claiming*

Our History, Sharing Our Stories, and Building the Reproductive Future We Deserve and co-host of *The A Files: A Secret History of Abortion,* a podcast from The Meteor.

Rinku Sen is a racial justice strategist, organizer, and writer. She is the current executive director of Narrative Initiative, whose mission is to strategize with social movements to make equity and justice foundational to multiracial democracy. She is the former director of Race Forward, where she led the teams that produced the award-winning news site Colorlines.com and the influential Facing Race conference. She is the author of *Stir It Up: Lessons in Organizing and Advocacy*, and *The Accidental American: Immigration and Citizenship in the Age of Globalization*.

Roberto Lovato is a longtime journalist and author writing about numerous issues, including immigration, racial justice, violence, and poverty. He was a co-founder of numerous advocacy organizations like presente .org and Dignidad Literaria, and is currently an assistant professor of English at the University of Nevada, Las Vegas. His book *Unforgetting: A Memoir of Family, Migration, Gangs, and Revolution in the Americas* was called "groundbreaking" by the *New York Times* and was listed in the *Los Angeles Times* best books of 2020. His essays and reports from around the world have appeared in the *New York Times*, *Guernica* magazine, *The Believer*, *The Boston Globe*, the *Los Angeles Times*, and many others.

Shadia Fayne Wood is the executive producer and founder of the Survival Media Agency and is an Arab American film director and photographer. She has been deeply involved in the journey to shape and share the narratives of grassroots communities of color who are innovatively leading the way in organizing and solutions while also being the first and worst impacted by economic and political systems. She is a recipient of the Yoshiyama Award and the Brower Youth Award, has been featured in the 2007 Green Issue of *Vanity Fair*, and is a recipient of *Elle* magazine's

2008 Green Awards. Her photos have been featured in *The New Yorker*, *The Boston Globe*, MSNBC, and the front page of the *Huffington Post*, among many others.

Tigress Osborn is the executive director of the National Association to Advance Fat Acceptance (NAAFA) and a co-founder of the Campaign for Size Freedom. She is a two-time women's college graduate with a BA in Black studies from Smith College and an MFA in creative writing from Mills College.

Trevon Bosley, from Chicago's South Side, grew up witnessing gun violence and poverty. After losing his cousin Vincent Avant, killed near Vincent's home, and brother Terrell Bosley, killed at church, to gun violence, Tre committed his life to violence prevention. Since 2011, he has worked with The B.R.A.V.E. Youth Leaders of St. Sabina, organizing peace marches, mentoring, job fairs, and voter registration. Today, Tre is an electrical engineer, board co-chair for March for Our Lives, a Giffords Courage Fellow alumnus, and a community organizer for the Community Justice Action Fund.

Trevor Smith is the co-founder and executive director of the BLIS (Black Liberation-Indigenous Sovereignty) Collective. He is a writer, poet, researcher, and strategist focused on racial and wealth inequality, reparations, and narrative change. Formerly the director of narrative change at Liberation Ventures, he launched the Reparations Narrative Lab. Trevor has also held roles at the Surdna Foundation, the NYCLU, the Center on Budget and Policy Priorities, and M+R Strategic Services. He received his BA in journalism from American University and his MPA from New York University. He is a son and a brother originally from Maryland, by way of Freetown, Sierra Leone. He currently resides in Lenapehoking, now known as New York City.

Verónica Bayetti Flores is co-founder of CAIP and has led national policy and movement-building work on the intersections of racial justice, immigrants' rights, health care access, young parenthood, police accountability, and LGBTQ liberation. Verónica also moonlights as a music journalist, focusing on sociopolitical meaning in Latin music cultures, with bylines at *Rolling Stone* and *Crack* magazine and as a cofounder and former co-host of the podcast Radio Menea.

Wambui Gichobi has worked with environmental and social justice organizations for over a decade. She and the other Survival Media Agency team members have been engaged in rapid response work in Africa, Europe, the Americas, Asia, and Oceania for global conferences and events. Together, the team has brought grassroots narratives and people to audiences with policy changing and resource diversion power. Powerful stories only bring about collaboration and global changes when known and shared.

Zaineb Mohammed is the communications director at the Kataly Foundation and a member of the Radical Communicators Network Leadership Team.

Publishing in the Public Interest

Thank you for reading this book published by The New Press; we hope you enjoyed it. New Press books and authors play a crucial role in sparking conversations about the key political and social issues of our day.

We hope that you will stay in touch with us. Here are a few ways to keep up to date with our books, events, and the issues we cover:

- Sign up at www.thenewpress.com/subscribe to receive updates on New Press authors and issues and to be notified about local events
- www.facebook.com/newpressbooks
- www.twitter.com/thenewpress
- www.instagram.com/thenewpress

Please consider buying New Press books not only for yourself, but also for friends and family and to donate to schools, libraries, community centers, prison libraries, and other organizations involved with the issues our authors write about.

The New Press is a 501(c)(3) nonprofit organization; if you wish to support our work with a tax-deductible gift, please visit www.thenewpress .com/donate or use the QR code below.